Functional Reactive Programming

Functional Reactive Programming

STEPHEN BLACKHEATH
ANTHONY JONES

MANNING
SHELTER ISLAND

Manning Publications Co.	Development editor: Jennifer Stout
20 Baldwin Road	Technical development editor: Dennis Sellinger
PO Box 761	Review editor: Aleksandar Dragosavljevic
Shelter Island, NY 11964	Project editor: Tiffany Taylor
	Copyeditor: Tiffany Taylor
	Proofreader: Melody Dolab
	Typesetter: Marija Tudor
	Cover designer: Marija Tudor

ISBN: 9781633430105
Printed in the United States of America
1 2 3 4 5 6 7 8 9 10 – EBM – 21 20 19 18 17 16

brief contents

contents

foreword

In 1968, in a presentation that would later become known as the "the mother of all demos," computer scientist Douglas Engelbart and his team started the personal computer revolution by demonstrating a system that featured text editing on a screen, his newly invented mouse, mixing of text and graphics, outline views, hypertext links, screen-sharing, and even videoconferencing. At a time when computers were room-sized machines conceived to outperform humans at computational tasks, he instead proposed that they help the human perform intellectual tasks, "augmenting" human intelligence by becoming interactive assistants in everyone's daily work. The graphical user interface was born.

But in addition to its groundbreaking interactivity, Engelbart's system is also interesting for the way it was built: it was written in several different programming languages that were specifically designed for it and adapted as the system changed. Building a truly innovative system also required building appropriate languages to program it. The next important milestone inspired by Engelbart's vision was the Xerox Alto system in 1973. In addition to introducing the desktop metaphor and other user interface innovations, it also featured the first object-oriented language, Smalltalk.

Today, building graphical user interfaces and using object-oriented languages have become mainstream. Unfortunately, though, programming user interfaces is still surprisingly difficult. Code written in the currently predominant style, event-driven programming and the observer pattern, has an uncanny tendency to quickly evolve into an unmaintainable mess, commonly referred to as *spaghetti code*. Is there a better way?

I think it's time for another step in the evolution of user interfaces and programming languages. In recent years, the ideas of *functional programming* and a (separate) programming style called *functional reactive programming* (FRP) have shown great promise in making it easier to develop any kind of interactive programs.

This text is one of the first comprehensive introductions to functional reactive programming in book form. With great enthusiasm, Stephen Blackheath and Anthony Jones teach you the basic concepts of FRP, explain a large example in detail, and discuss various patterns that commonly occur in practice. To show that FRP does indeed make things simpler, the pair of brothers also presents an illuminating case study where they solve one problem in three different programming styles and compare the results. Of the three approaches—event-based programming, actors, and functional reactive programming—the latter compares most favorably.

Functional reactive programming is a style that is usually supported by a library for a particular programming language. The authors have written an FRP library called Sodium that is available for several languages, including Java, and this book profits from their experience in detail. For the sake of concreteness, they use it in this book as well. Of course, the concepts apply more generally, and the authors also present a short guide to many other FRP libraries.

Not all programming languages are created equal. As the name suggests, functional reactive programming derives much of its expressive power from functional programming. In this book, Stephen and Anthony don't assume any prior knowledge of functional programming; instead, they gently introduce you to the necessary concepts as needed. But this heritage also means that FRP libraries can only exist in languages that support them. Java is a popular example, and the authors have chosen it as the main vehicle for explaining FRP. Still, Java is mainly an imperative language, and I think the mismatch is showing in some places. That is why personally, I prefer the purely functional language Haskell for my FRP work. But I think the authors made an excellent choice by picking a more popular and widely used language for this book and not shying away from the difficulties of dealing with the imperative aspects of Java.

Not all FRP libraries are created equal, either. As already mentioned, this book focuses on the Sodium library. But for the case where your programming environment is limited, the authors also discuss libraries like RxJS, which implement a style called *reactive programming*. This is very similar to functional reactive programming, but the authors rightfully note that it lacks some benefits and guarantees, such as a deterministic merge primitive. I wholeheartedly recommend the Sodium library as designed by the authors.

The field of functional reactive programming is still very young, and you may find that you'll need to think in new ways to express your code in this style. This book gives you the necessary tools and foundation for doing that.

HEINRICH APFELMUS
OPEN SOURCE DEVELOPER
AUTHOR OF THE FRP LIBRARY REACTIVE-BANANA

preface

This book was born of frustration. We were each involved in a large project with a lot of event-based logic. Petty problems regularly turned into long days of debugging.

Anthony joined a team working on a complex configuration GUI full of plumbing that was replicated over and over. He decided to tidy this up by shifting all the logic to a single abstraction called `PublishedScalar`. This was a revolutionary change.

Stephen was working on embedded development for vehicle telematics, and the challenges kept coming. He started fantasizing about a career change to truck driving but instead found new approaches in functional programming.

A lot of leading-edge work goes on quietly in the Haskell programming language community. Stephen found a gem called *functional reactive programming*. He later worked with Ryan Trinkle on a video game projcct; they decided to use FRP but weren't happy with any of the existing implementations. Using FRP is great, but implementing an FRP system turned out to be more challenging than expected.

Stephen's fifth attempt at FRP became the Sodium project, and Ryan went on to develop Reflex. Since that time, Stephen has been using FRP every day on the telematics project, now in its tenth year.

Stephen and Anthony regularly compared notes and strategized about sharing this great discovery with the world. Manning picked up the signal, and this book was born.

acknowledgments

We'd like to thank the following people:

- Our wives and children, for their forbearance.
- The first and second waves: the FRP pioneers and those who are making FRP practical.
- Our many reviewers and critics, for making this book better, and everyone who has raised bugs and asked technical questions, including Danae Aguilar, Jim Andrew, Mark Butler, Alessandro Campeis, Ron Cranston, Rafael Freire, Bruce Hernandez, Unnikrishnan Kumar, Yuri Kushch, Michael Lund, Sergio Martinez, Bhakti Mehta, Orlando Méndez, Wil Moore III, Giovanni Morana, Jean-François Morin, Chris Pearce, Thomas Peklak, Patrick Regan, Paulo Rios, Bruno Sonnino, William E. Wheeler, Henry Widd, and Arthur Zubarev. Thank you!
- Adam Buczynski, for JavaScript assistance.
- The many Manning staff who do an amazing job of taking people who know technical stuff and somehow transmogrifying them into authors: publisher Marjan Bace and everyone on the editorial and production teams, including Michael Stephens, Jennifer Stout, Janet Vail, Tiffany Taylor, Melody Dolab, and many others who worked behind the scenes. There's a reason their books are so good.
- Duncan Hill, for the beautiful illustrations: http://duncanhill.nz/.

about this book

Functional programming (FP) holds real solutions to today's complex software needs, especially the challenges of parallelism. It's catching on, but there are barriers to its adoption. FRP is a subset of FP that doesn't require you to learn a new language. This makes FRP an ideal gateway drug to functional programming. FRP solves a specific problem now, yet it gives you grounding in ideas that have wide application.

Lambda expressions have now been added to every language. The only thing standing in the way of wide adoption of FRP is gone. FRP is essentially an embedded logic language, so code written in it looks basically the same in any language. It turns out that Java has especially clear FRP syntax, and this was why we chose it as the primary vehicle in this book, but the language really doesn't matter.

There's a need for FRP, the languages are ready, and functional programming is in vogue. The time is right for FRP to take over a small corner of the world.

Roadmap

Chapter 1, "Stop listening!" introduces the *what* and *why* of FRP and finishes with a simple example.

Chapter 2, "Core FRP," covers all the basics of FRP and includes a minimal example for each element except the `switch` and `sample` primitives (covered in chapter 7) and operational primitives (chapter 8). In chapter 3, "Some everyday widget stuff," the examples become more practical.

Chapter 4, "Writing a real application," shows the practicalities of writing a real-world example—the logic for a petrol pump—entirely in FRP.

At this point, you may be wondering why we're doing things in this strange way. Chapter 5, "New concepts," covers the theoretical background that justifies FRP's radical departure from the usual way of doing things.

Chapter 6, "FRP on the web," talks about JavaScript FRP systems and can be read any time.

As presented so far, FRP code has a fixed structure. Chapter 7, "Switch," introduces the `switch` primitive that enables the all-important capability of making runtime changes to the logic structure.

Chapter 8, "Operational primitives," deals with interfacing FRP to the rest of your program.

Chapter 9, "Continuous time," describes an amazing capability of FRP: modeling your system with continuously varying values instead of having values change in discrete steps.

FRP is better for some tasks than others. Chapter 10, "Battle of the paradigms," compares the strengths and weaknesses of FRP against classic state machines and the actor model to help you decide which tool to use for which job.

Chapter 11, "Programming in the real world," covers different ways of modeling I/O in FRP programs.

Chapter 12, "Helpers and patterns," presents an assortment of interesting problems that come up and how to solve them with FRP.

Chapter 13, "Refactoring," explains why FRP is so easy to refactor by comparing an example with the equivalent object-oriented code.

Chapter 14, "Adding FRP to existing projects," recommends some practices for step-by-step conversion of non-FRP code to FRP.

Chapter 15, "Future directions," covers areas for potential development of FRP.

Who should read this book

This book is for programmers familiar with object-oriented programming. No prior knowledge of functional programming is needed. A familiarity with graphical user interface (GUI) programming is useful but not required.

Code conventions

This book provides copious examples. Source code in listings and code terms in text are in a `fixed-width font like this` to separate them from ordinary text. In some places, we've added line breaks and reworked indentation to accommodate the available page space in the book. When even this was not enough, listings include line-continuation markers. Additionally, comments in the source code have often been removed from the listings when the code is described in the text. Code annotations accompany some of the source code listings, highlighting important concepts.

Source code downloads

All the examples can be found on the publisher's website at www.manning.com/books/functional-reactive-programming. You can also find them in the book/directory of the Sodium project at https://github.com/SodiumFRP/, where you can download them with this command:

```
git clone https://github.com/SodiumFRP/sodium
```

To run the Java examples, you'll need to install the Java Development Kit (JDK) version 8 or higher and either the `maven` or `ant` build tool. Windows users may find `maven` easier:

- https://maven.apache.org/
- https://ant.apache.org/

About the authors

STEPHEN BLACKHEATH lives near Palmerston North, New Zealand. He has done a lot of event-based commercial programming, got into functional programming around 2007, and is the founder of the open source Sodium FRP system. He likes to play Go.

ANTHONY JONES lives in Auckland, New Zealand. He has spent half a decade refactoring a Java-based configuration GUI to a FRP-based framework and is a contributor to the Sodium project. He likes riding his bicycle.

Author Online

Purchase of *Functional Reactive Programming* includes free access to a private web forum run by Manning Publications where you can make comments about the book, ask technical questions, and receive help from the lead author and from other users. To access the forum and subscribe to it, point your web browser to www.manning.com/books/functional-reactive-programming. This page provides information on how to get on the forum once you are registered, what kind of help is available, and the rules of conduct on the forum.

Manning's commitment to our readers is to provide a venue where a meaningful dialog between individual readers and between readers and the author can take place. It is not a commitment to any specific amount of participation on the part of the author, whose contribution to the Author Online remains voluntary (and unpaid). We suggest you try asking the author some challenging questions lest his interest stray! The Author Online forum and the archives of previous discussions will be accessible from the publisher's website as long as the book is in print.

about the cover

The caption for the illustration on the cover of *Functional Reactive Programming* is "Turban-Bearer to the Grand Signior." The illustration is taken from a collection of costumes of the Ottoman Empire published on January 1, 1802, by William Miller of Old Bond Street, London. The title page is missing from the collection, and we have been unable to track it down to date. The book's table of contents identifies the figures in both English and French, and each illustration bears the names of two artists who worked on it, both of whom would no doubt be surprised to find their art gracing the front cover of a computer programming book...200 years later.

The collection was purchased by a Manning editor at an antiquarian flea market in the "Garage" on West 26th Street in Manhattan. The seller was an American based in Ankara, Turkey, and the transaction took place just as he was packing up his stand for the day. The Manning editor didn't have on his person the substantial amount of cash that was required for the purchase, and a credit card and check were both politely turned down. With the seller flying back to Ankara that evening, the situation was getting hopeless. What was the solution? It turned out to be nothing more than an old-fashioned verbal agreement sealed with a handshake. The seller proposed that the money be transferred to him by wire, and the editor walked out with the bank information on a piece of paper and the portfolio of images under his arm. Needless to say, we transferred the funds the next day, and we remain grateful and impressed by this unknown person's trust in one of us. It recalls something that might have happened a long time ago. We at Manning celebrate the inventiveness, the initiative, and, yes, the fun of the computer business with book covers based on the rich diversity of regional life of two centuries ago, brought back to life by the pictures from this collection.

Stop listening!

This chapter covers

- What FRP is
- What events are, and how they cause trouble
- What FRP is for: the problem we're trying to solve
- The benefits of FRP
- How an FRP system works
- A different way of thinking that underlies FRP

Welcome to our book! We love *functional reactive programming* (FRP). Many people like the idea too, yet they aren't entirely clear what FRP is and what it will do for them. The short answer: it comes in the form of a simple library in a standard programming language, and it replaces listeners (also known as *callbacks*) in the widely used *observer pattern*, making your code cleaner, clearer, more robust, and more maintainable—in a word, *simpler.*

It's more than this: FRP is a very different way of doing things. It will improve your code and transform your thinking for the better. Yet it's surprisingly compatible with the usual ways of writing code, so it's easy to factor into existing projects in stages. This book is about the concepts of FRP as they apply to a range of FRP systems and programming languages.

1

FRP is based on ideas from functional programming, but this book doesn't assume any prior knowledge of functional programming. Chapter 1 will lay down some underlying concepts, and in chapter 2 we'll get into the coding. So stop listening, and start reacting!

1.1   *Project, meet complexity wall*

It seemed to be going so well. The features weren't all there yet, but development was swift. The boss was happy, the customers were impressed, the investors were optimistic. The future was bright.

It came out of nowhere … Software quality crumbled. The speed of development went from treacle to molasses. Before long, there were unhappy customers and late nights. What happened?

Sooner or later, many big projects hit the complexity wall. The complexities in the program that seemed acceptable compound exponentially: At first you hardly notice, and then—BAM! It hits broadside. The project will then typically go one of four ways:

- It's shelved.
- It's rewritten from scratch, and a million dollars later, it hits the same wall again.
- The company staffs up. As the team expands, its productivity shambles off into the realm of the eternal quagmire. (Often the company has been acquired around this time.)
- It undergoes major refactoring, leading eventually to maintainable code.

Refactoring is the only way forward. It's your primary tool to save a project that has hit the wall, but it's best used earlier, as part of a development methodology, to prevent disaster before it happens.

But this book isn't about refactoring. It's about *functional reactive programming* (FRP), a programming style that works well with refactoring because it can prevent or repair out-of-control complexity. FRP isn't a methodology, and—apologies if you bought this book under false pretenses—it won't solve all of your problems. FRP is a specific programming technique to improve your code in an area that just happens to be a common source of complexity (and therefore bugs): event propagation.

Simple things taking too long

I joined a team that was developing a Java-based configuration tool for an embedded system. The software was difficult to modify to the point where a request for adding a check box to one of the screens was estimated as a two-week job.

This was caused by having to plumb the Boolean value through layers of interfaces and abstraction. To solve this, we put together what we'd later discover was a basic FRP system. Adding a check box was reduced to a one-line change.

We learned that every piece of logic, every listener, and every edge case you need to write code for is a potential source of bugs.

1.2 *What is functional reactive programming?*

FRP can be viewed from different angles:

- It's a replacement for the widely used *observer pattern*, also known as *listeners* or *callbacks*.
- It's a composable, modular way to code event-driven logic.
- It's a different way of thinking: the program is expressed as a reaction to its inputs, or as a flow of data.
- It brings order to the management of program state.
- It's something fundamental: we think that anyone who tries to solve the problems in the observer pattern will eventually invent FRP.
- It's normally implemented as a lightweight software library in a standard programming language.
- It can be seen as a complete embedded language for stateful logic.

If you're familiar with the idea of a domain-specific language (DSL), then you can understand FRP as a minimal complete DSL for stateful logic. Aside from the I/O parts, an arbitrarily complex video game (for example) can be written completely in FRP. That's how powerful and expressive it is. Yet it isn't all-or-nothing—FRP can be easily introduced into an existing project to any extent you like.

1.2.1 *A stricter definition*

Conal Elliott is one of the inventors of FRP, and this book is about FRP by his definition. We'll call this *true FRP* as a shorthand. What is and isn't FRP? Here's part of Elliott's reply to a Stack Overflow post, "Specification for a Functional Reactive Programming language" (http://mng.bz/c42s):

> *I'm glad you're starting by asking about a specification rather than implementation first. There are a lot of ideas floating around about what FRP is. For me it's always been two things: (a) denotative and (b) temporally continuous. Many folks drop both of these properties and identify FRP with various* implementation *notions, all of which are beside the point in my perspective.*
>
> *By "denotative," I mean founded on a precise, simple, implementation-independent, compositional semantics that exactly specifies the meaning of each type and building block. The compositional nature of the semantics then determines the meaning of all type-correct combinations of the building blocks.*

A true FRP system has to be specified using denotational semantics.

DEFINITION *Denotational semantics* is a mathematical expression of the formal meaning of a programming language. For an FRP system, it provides both a formal specification of the system and a proof that the important property of *compositionality* holds for all building blocks in all cases.

Compositionality is a mathematically strong form of the concept of composability that is often recommended in software design. We'll describe it in detail in chapter 5.

This book emphasizes the practice of FRP as expressed through FRP systems you can use right away. Some of the systems we'll cover aren't true FRP. As we go, we'll point out what's specifically lacking and why it's so important that an FRP system should be based on denotational semantics. We'll cover continuous time in chapter 9.

1.2.2   Introducing Sodium

The primary vehicle for FRP in this book is the authors' BSD-licensed Sodium library, which you can find at https://github.com/SodiumFRP. It's a system with a denotational semantics that we give in appendix E. It's a practical system that has passed through the crucible of serious commercial use by the authors.

We're using Sodium because it's a practically useful, simple, true FRP system. At the time of writing, there aren't many systems like this available in nonfunctional languages. There's minimal variation between FRP systems, so the lessons learned from Sodium are applicable to all systems. To aid in understanding, we'll use Sodium as a common reference point when discussing other systems. This book is about FRP, and Sodium is the best means to that end available to us.

Like anything, Sodium is the product of design decisions. It isn't perfect, and we don't wish to promote its use over any other system. We intend Sodium to be four things:

- A production-ready library you can use in commercial and non-commercial software across a range of programming languages
- A vehicle to promote the true definition of FRP
- A reference and benchmark for future innovation
- A solid learning platform, due to its minimalist design philosophy

1.3   Where does FRP fit in? The lay of the land

> **NOTE** This book assumes knowledge of general programming, but not *functional programming*. Further, to use FRP, you only need a subset of the concepts from functional programming, and we'll explain what you need to know along the way. FRP gives you many of the benefits of functional programming with a shorter learning curve, and you can use it in your existing language.

It may sound oversimplified, but it turns out that FRP is the intersection of *functional programming* and *reactive programming*—see figure 1.1. Here's what these technologies are:

- *Functional programming*—A style or paradigm of programming based on functions, in the mathematical sense of the word. It deliberately avoids shared mutable state, so it implies the use of immutable data structures, and it emphasizes *compositionality*.

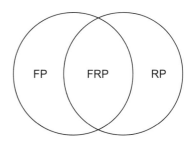

Figure 1.1   FRP is a subset of both functional and reactive programming

Compositionality turns out to be a powerful idea, as we'll explain. It's the reason why FRP can deal with complexity so effectively.

- *Reactive programming*—A broad term meaning that a program is 1) event-based, 2) acts in response to input, and 3) is viewed as a flow of data, instead of the traditional flow of control. It doesn't dictate any specific method of achieving these aims. Reactive programming gives looser coupling between program components, so the code is more modular.
- *Functional reactive programming*—A specific method of reactive programming that enforces the rules of functional programming, particularly the property of compositionality.

Typically, systems described as *reactive programming* emphasize distributed processing, whereas FRP is more fine-grained and starts with strong consistency. Consistency must be relaxed to achieve scalability in a distributed system. (We explain why in section 11.3.) FRP and reactive programming take different approaches to this question. FRP can be useful for distributed processing, but it isn't designed specifically for it.

The *Akka* system is classified as reactive programming. It's designed for distributed processing and is largely based on the *actor model*. (We'll contrast FRP against actors in chapter 10.)

Microsoft's *Reactive Extensions* (Rx) isn't true FRP at the time of writing. It sits somewhere between Akka and FRP. There's a difference in design goals between Rx and FRP. Rx is mostly concerned with chaining event handlers, and it gives you many options for how you do it. FRP controls what you do more tightly and gives you strong guarantees in return. Most of what you'll learn in this book can be applied to Rx. We'll cover the FRP-like parts of Rx in chapter 6.

1.4 Interactive applications: what are events?

Most applications are architected around one of two programming models, or a mix of the two:

- Threads
- Events

They're both aimed at managing state changes in response to input, but they achieve it in different ways. Which one to choose depends mainly on the nature of the problem you're trying to solve:

- *Threads* model state transitions as a control flow. They tend to be a good fit for I/O or for any situation where the state transitions fall into a clearly defined sequence. We put actors and generators in this category, too.
- *Events* are discrete, asynchronous messages that are propagated around the program. They're a suitable model where a sequence is less obvious, especially where the interactions between components are more complex. Typical applications include graphical user interfaces (GUIs) and video games.

People have debated which model is the best over the years. We don't think one is better than the other; rather, we consider each good for its proper purpose. When a thread is best, you should use a thread. But this book is about the second programming model: events. Often they're the best choice, and when they are, this book will teach you how to stay out of trouble.

1.5   *State machines are hard to reason about*

The term *state machine* refers to any system that works in the following way:

1   An input event comes into the system.
2   The program logic makes decisions based on the input event and the current program state.
3   The program logic changes the program state.
4   The program logic may also produce output.

We've drawn this in figure 1.2. The arrows depict the flow of data.

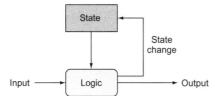

Figure 1.2   The flow of data in a generalized state machine

We normally use the term *state machine* to describe programs or, more commonly, parts of programs, that directly reflect the structure just described. In fact, any program that does anything useful is functionally equivalent to a state machine because it's possible to rewrite any program as a state machine and have it function the same way.

We could say that all programs are fundamentally state machines. But code written in a traditional state-machine style tends to be unreadable and brittle. (Any embedded C programmer will attest to this.) It also tends to be extremely efficient, which is the usual excuse for using this style. The job of the programmer could be seen as finding ways to organize state machines so they're maintainable. Of course, a programmer must express the program so that a computer can run it, but their responsibility doesn't end there. It's not possible to keep all the code in your head at once, unless the code is small or your head is especially large, so a programmer's main task is to structure the code so as to make the program easy to modify. Or, we can say that a programmer's primary focus is managing complexity.

We argue that all programs are state machines, and state machines are inherently difficult to reason about, and this is why programming is difficult. Programmers achieve their task of transforming chaos into order by using a bag of tricks, or a set of abstractions they have learned, which they add to over the years through both study and creativity. Threads and events are two abstractions you'll find rattling about in there. There are many others, and they all have their advantages and disadvantages for different problem domains. This book is about a powerful and very general abstraction you can add to your toolbox that directly addresses the problem of managing the complexity of state machines.

1.6　*Interactive applications without the bugs*

The problems we're trying to solve have inherent difficulties; this is true. In spite of this, most of our problems come from the way we're doing things.

Hikers often say that there's no such thing as bad weather, only bad equipment. We say that there's no such thing as bad code, only bad infrastructure.

A large portion—the majority—of bugs in event-based programs are preventable. That's the message of this book.

1.7　*Listeners are a mainstay of event handling, but …*

Listeners or callbacks—also called the observer pattern—are the dominant way of propagating events in software today. But it wasn't always this way.

In the old days, when the walls were orange, the mice living in them weren't the event sources we know today but were small animals, and list boxes hadn't been invented yet. If you wanted to propagate some value around your program, you got the value and called all the places where that value was going to be used. Back then, the producer had a dependency on its consumers. If you wanted to add a new consumer of your events, then you made the producer call it, too. Programs were monolithic, and if you wanted to reuse some code that produced events (such as a list box), it was a bit of work, because it was wired into the rest of the program.

The idea of a list box as a reusable software component doesn't work well if it has to know in advance what all its consumers are. So the observer pattern was invented: if you want to start observing an event producer, you can come along at any time and register a new consumer (or listener) with it, and from then on, that consumer is called back whenever an event occurs. When you want to stop observing the producer, you deregister the consumer from it, as shown in the following listing.

Listing 1.1　Listeners: the observer pattern

```
public class ListBox {
    public interface Listener {
        void itemSelected(int index);
    }

    private List<Listener> listeners = new ArrayList<>();
    public void addListener(Listener l) {
        listeners.add(l);
    }
    public void removeListener(Listener l) {
        listeners.remove(l);
    }
    protected void notifyItemSelected(int index) {
        for (l : listeners) l.itemSelected(index);
    }
}
```

In this way, listeners invert the natural dependency. The consumer now depends on the producer, not the other way around. This makes the program extensible and gives you modularity through a looser coupling between components.

1.8   *Banishing the six plagues of listeners*

What could possibly go wrong with the wonderful observer pattern? Uh…yeah. We've identified six sources of bugs with listeners; see figure 1.3. FRP banishes all of them. They are as follows:

- *Unpredictable order*—In a complex network of listeners, the order in which events are received can depend on the order in which you registered the listeners, which isn't helpful. FRP makes the order in which events are processed not matter by making it completely nondetectable.
- *Missed first event*—It can be difficult to guarantee that you've registered your listeners before you send the first event. FRP is transactional, so it's possible to provide this guarantee.
- *Messy state*—Callbacks push your code into a traditional state-machine style, which gets messy fast. FRP brings order.
- *Threading issues*—Attempting to make listeners thread-safe can lead to deadlocks, and it can be difficult to guarantee that no more callbacks will be received after deregistering a listener. FRP eliminates these issues.

Figure 1.3   The six plagues of listeners

- *Leaking callbacks*—If you forget to deregister your listener, your program will leak memory. Listeners reverse the natural data dependency but don't reverse the keep-alive dependency as you'd like them to. FRP does this.
- *Accidental recursion*—The order in which you update local state and notify listeners can be critical, and it's easy to make mistakes. FRP eliminates this issue.

You'll find a detailed explanation of these problems with examples in appendix B.

1.9   *Why not just fix listeners?*

We think that if you fix the problems with listeners, you'll invent FRP. In fact, many people in industry have done exactly this, usually for a specific problem domain, and usually without calling it FRP.

We took the research of Conal Elliott, Paul Hudak, and others, and our own experience, and developed a general-purpose, open source (BSD3-licensed) FRP library called Sodium for multiple programming languages with an emphasis on minimalism and practicality. We and Heinrich Apfelmus, the developer of another FRP system called *Reactive Banana*, have compared his system against Sodium, and even though they were developed independently, they turn out to be equivalent apart from naming. We weren't as surprised by this as you might expect.

We believe that FRP isn't so much a clever idea as something fundamental: that when motivated people independently try to fix the observer pattern, after much stumbling, they will eventually converge on similar solutions; and that there are only a few possible variations in that "perfect" design. We'll discuss these. FRP is a discovery, not an invention.

Implementing an FRP system turns out to be surprisingly difficult. We had the work of others to steal from, yet it took more than six person-months of work to understand the issues and develop an FRP system. And the library is only 1,000 lines of code!

We think the reason is that event handling is an inherently hard problem. With listeners, we deal with the frustrations in small doses every day, but to develop an FRP library, you need to deal with them all at once.

We highly recommend that you choose an existing library and not reinvent the wheel. If there isn't one available for your language of choice, we recommend that you consider porting an existing implementation.

1.10   *"Have you tried restarting it?" or why state is problematic*

We've all had the same experience. The software you're using gets into a bad state. *Something* inside the program hasn't been updated properly, and it won't work anymore. That's right, you know what to do, and there are lots of internet memes about it:

- KEEP CALM and REBOOT.
- CTRL ALT DELETE fixes everything.
- If all else fails, RESTART.
- How I fix stuff working on IT: Restart whatever isn't working 88%. Quick Google search 10%. Weird IT voodoo 2%.

- WHAT IF I TOLD YOU A restart will fix your computer.
- [And the best one:] Restart the world!

We think programming needs a reboot. In most languages, you can declare a variable like this

```
int x = 10;
```

and then modify its value, like this:

```
x = x + 1;
```

In FRP, we don't use normal mutable variables because they're sensitive to changes in execution sequence. A common bug is to read the variable before or after it was updated when you intended to do the opposite.

FRP keeps state in containers called *cells*. They solve the sequence problem because they automatically come with update notification and sequence management: the state is always up-to-date. State changes happen at predictable times.

The strange case of program configuration

Have you worked on a program with a complex configuration that affects many parts of the code? What happens in your project when the configuration changes while the program is running?

Each module that uses the configuration has to register a listener to catch the updates, or it won't catch the updates. This complicates the code, and it's easy to make mistakes in propagating the configuration changes to the right places.

And how is it tested? That's right: it isn't. This sort of code is difficult to put into a form suitable for unit testing.

How many software projects have given up entirely and require a program restart to pick up the new configuration? When you change something on your ADSL router, does it take effect immediately, or are you required to reboot?

Why is program configuration, which should be simple, such an intractable problem in practice? Could this be indicative of something fundamental we've gotten wrong in the way we program?

1.11 The benefit of FRP: dealing with complexity

We all know from experience that the complexity of a program can get out of control. This is so common that it's considered normal in industry. When complex parts interact in complex ways, the complexity can compound.

FRP deals with complexity in a specific way. It enforces a mathematical property called *compositionality*. This enables software components to be composed without unexpected side effects. As the program gets larger and more complex, compositionality becomes more and more important. It makes software more scalable in a fundamental

way. The reasons behind this will be easier to explain when you've grasped the funda-
mentals, so we'll cover compositionality in detail in chapter 5.

1.12 How does FRP work?

We'll illustrate how FRP works with a simplified
flight-booking example, shown in figure 1.4.
Here's the specification:

- The user can enter their departure and
  return dates using two date field widgets.

- While the user is using the mouse and keyboard to enter the dates, some business
  logic continuously makes decisions about

**Figure 1.4   Simplified flight-booking
example**

whether the current selection is valid. Whenever the selection is valid, the OK
button is enabled, and when it's not, the button is disabled.

- The business rule we're using is this: *valid if departure date <= return date.*

In the figure, we're trying to depart in September and return in August of the same
year, which is the wrong order. So the business rule returns `false`, and you can see
that the OK button is disabled (grayed out).

A conceptual view of this application is shown in figure 1.5. We're representing the
GUI widgets as clouds to indicate that their internal structure is hidden. In other
words, they're *black boxes.*

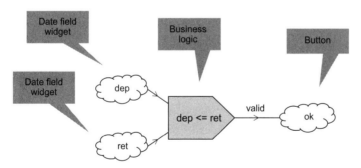

Figure 1.5   Conceptual view of the flight-booking example

A central idea is this: *departure and return dates, as well as the "valid" status from the business logic, all change dynamically in response to user input events.* The lines show a *flow of
data* from the two dates, through some logic, and into the OK button. As the user
changes the dates, the OK button is enabled or disabled dynamically according to the
decision made by the logic.

The next listing gives the code to construct the widgets and the logic, with the Java GUI setup left out. Don't expect to understand every detail right now; we'll return to this code in section 1.16.2.

Listing 1.2   Flight-booking example using FRP

```
SDateField dep = new SDateField();
SDateField ret = new SDateField();
Cell<Boolean> valid = dep.date.lift(ret.date,
            (d, r) -> d.compareTo(r) <= 0);
SButton ok = new SButton("OK", valid);
```

We're using Java and the authors' Sodium FRP library. We'll branch out into other FRP systems and languages later in the book. What we use doesn't matter much for the teaching of FRP. Apart from surface differences, FRP is much the same in any language or FRP system.

FRP uses two fundamental data types:

- *Cells* represent *values that change over time.* Your programming language already has variables that allow you to represent changing values. This book is about the advantages that FRP abstractions give you if you use them, instead.
- *Streams* represent *streams of events.* We'll introduce streams in chapter 2.

The key idea we want you to get is that the code directly reflects the conceptual view in figure 1.5.

We're using a toy library that we wrote with GUI widgets that all start with *S*: SDate-Field and SButton are like normal widgets, except we've added an FRP-based external interface. This allows us to avoid some mechanics we don't want to cover yet.

SDateField exports this public field:

```
Cell<Calendar> date;
```

Calendar is the Java class that represents a date. We said a cell is a value that changes over time, so Cell<Calendar> represents a date that changes over time.

As you can see, Cell takes a type parameter that tells us the type of value the cell contains, and we do this in Java with generics in the same way we do with lists and other data structures. For instance, you might have a list of dates, and that would have the type List<Calendar>. Cell<Calendar> is the same concept, but it represents a single date that can change, instead of a list of dates.

The date field of SDateField gives the date as it appears on the screen at any given time while the user is manipulating the SDateField widget. In the code you can see the two dates being used with a lift() method.

> **NOTE** The expression (d, r) -> d.compareTo(r) <= 0 in listing 1.2 is lambda syntax, which is new in Java 8. If this confuses you, don't worry. We're only talking about concepts at this stage. We'll explain how this all works in chapter 2.

You can check out and run this example with the following commands. You'll need Java 8, which means at least version 1.8 of the Java Development Kit (JDK). We've written scripts for both Maven and Ant, which are two popular build systems in Java, both from the Apache Software Foundation. Windows users might find Maven easiest. The Windows version of Ant is called *WinAnt*. Here are the commands:

```
git clone https://github.com/SodiumFRP/sodium
cd sodium/book/swidgets/java
mvn test -Pairline1    or    ant airline1
```

Look in other directories. You may find that the examples have been translated into other languages.

> **NOTE** Sodium can be found on Maven's Central Repository with a groupId of `nz.sodium`.

1.12.1 Life cycle of an FRP program

Figure 1.6 shows the mechanics of how FRP code is executed. In most FRP systems, this all happens at application runtime. There are two stages:

- *Stage 1: Initialization*—Typically during program startup, FRP code statements are converted into a directed graph in memory.
- *Stage 2: Running*—For the rest of the program execution you feed in values and turn the crank handle, and the FRP engine produces output.

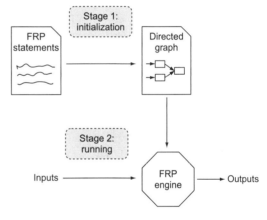

Figure 1.6   The stages of execution of an FRP program

> **NOTE** In practice, the program spends most of its time in the *running* stage with an already-constructed directed graph. But the graph can also be dynamically modified during the running stage. We cover this in chapter 7.

A major task of the FRP engine is to ensure that things are processed in the order specified by the dependencies in the directed graph that's maintained in memory. In spreadsheets, this is referred to as *natural order recalculation*. It could be better described as the "correct order" to distinguish it from any other order, which could give the wrong result.

This separation between *initialization* and *running* stages is similar to the way GUI libraries normally work. You construct all your widgets first (*initialization*), and afterward an event loop handles events from the user (*running*). The Java GUI framework Swing, which we're using here, works this way.

During the initialization stage, the flight-booking example executes this FRP statement:

```
Cell<Boolean> valid = dep.date.lift(ret.date,
        (d, r) -> d.compareTo(r) <= 0);
```

This code expresses a relationship between the widgets, and nothing else.

> **NOTE** *Lifting* is a general functional programming concept. We'll return to it in chapter 2.

Once the initialization is over, we enter the running stage. Java creates a window and processes incoming mouse and keyboard events from the user. The FRP engine's job is to maintain the relationship we expressed, ensuring that the value of valid is always up to date.

We could write a spreadsheet to do this, as shown in figure 1.7. In fact, FRP works the same way a spreadsheet does. Our choice of the class name Cell to represent dynamically change-able values was partially influenced by this.

Can you really write arbitrarily complex application logic in the style of a spreadsheet? Yes, you can. That's exactly what FRP allows you to do. But you'll have to think a bit differently.

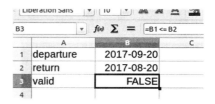

Figure 1.7   We can express the flight-booking example as a spreadsheet.

1.13 *Paradigm shift*

In his 1962 book *The Structure of Scientific Revolutions,* Thomas Kuhn argued that science progresses in leaps, which he called *paradigm shifts,* rather than in a slow, linear progression as people often thought.

> **DEFINITION** A *paradigm* is a way of thinking, a world view, a philosophical framework, or a frame of reference. A paradigm usually applies to a particular area of knowledge. It's based on a set of underlying assumptions.

FRP belongs to a new paradigm. Although you can use FRP to make incremental improvements to an existing code base, there's a different way of thinking underlying it. If you embrace that way of thinking, you'll get the most out of FRP.

1.13.1 *Paradigm*

Everyone's way of thinking is based on a set of assumptions, mostly at the subconscious level, which are taken to be true. They may or may not be true. They underlie everything that person knows. No matter how clever someone is, there are always some assumptions that have gone unquestioned.

Most people share most of their assumptions about the world around them, and these shared assumptions provide a frame of reference that enables us to communicate with each other. When there's a significant difference in the assumptions between two people, communication becomes more difficult. We say that people are operating in different paradigms. A good example is the culture shock you can experience when you visit another country.

In certain areas of knowledge, people's assumptions can be very different indeed. When this happens, the experience can be jarring. A statement made in terms of frame of reference *A* can be nonsensical with respect to frame of reference *B*. Each person may even think the other is insane. Thomas Kuhn described this situation by saying that the two ways of thinking are *incommensurable*.

By way of example, on Christmas, we like to eat ice cream at the beach and then jump into the sea. This may seem like strange behavior, but what else would you do on a hot summer day?

1.13.2 *Paradigm shift*

A person can change their paradigm, either slowly or all at once through an epiphany. You usually need a crisis to bring about an epiphany, so we prefer the first method.

If you're used to object-oriented programming (OOP), then you'll be entering a new paradigm. FRP will appear a bit strange. We can claim all day that FRP is a simple idea, and it is. But *simple* and *easy to understand* aren't the same thing. The reality is that until your thinking slots into place, you will encounter some challenges.

FRP rests on certain notions about what's important in programming that may go against your current understanding. Without these ideas, FRP is just a way of taking something that should be straightforward and doing it in an eccentric, limiting way. The claimed benefits will be remote.

We're talking about standard functional programming ideas. If you've done functional programming, it will be easier to learn FRP. If not, that's no problem. You don't need to know everything about functional programming to use FRP, and we'll teach you what you need to know.

> **NOTE** FRP made it easier for one of the authors to learn functional programming. The other author learned these the other way around.

We're asking you to question some of your assumptions. This can be intriguing, challenging, and liberating. Through this process, you either change your beliefs or strengthen them. Either way, it's beneficial, but it's never easy.

Next we'll start laying the foundation for thinking in FRP. We'll continue throughout the book.

1.14 *Thinking in terms of dependency*

Traditionally, software is expressed as a sequence of steps, written by the programmer and executed by the machine. Each step has a relationship with the steps that came before. Some steps will depend on the previous step, and some may depend on things from much earlier. Consider these steps:

- Comb hair
- Wash face

There is no dependency between these two statements. They can be executed in any order or simultaneously if you have enough hands.

Here's another classic example that functional programmers use:

1 Open silo doors
2 Fire missiles

In this case, the dependency implied by the sequence is critical.

If we weren't using FRP, we'd write the flight-booking example much like in listing 1.3. We assume the existence of a JDateField widget, which doesn't exist in reality. Notice that there are certain places where the order of statements is critical—things will break if it isn't right.

Listing 1.3   Flight-booking example in a traditional non-FRP style

```
public class BookingDialog {
    public BookingDialog() {
        JDateField startField = new JDateField(...);        <—— GUI
        JDateField endField = new JDateField(...);
        this.ok = new JButton("OK");
        ...;
        this.start = startField.getDate();        <—— Logic
        this.end = endField.getDate();
        update();
        startField.addDateFieldListener(new DateFieldListener() {
            public void dateUpdated(Calendar date) {
                BookingDialog.this.start = date;
                BookingDialog.this.update();
            }
        });
        endField.addDateFieldListener(new DateFieldListener() {
            public void dateUpdated(Calendar date) {
                BookingDialog.this.end = date;
                BookingDialog.this.update();
            }
        });
    }
    private JButton ok;
    private Calendar start;
    private Calendar end;
    private void update() {
        boolean valid = start.compareTo(end) <= 0;
        ok.setEnabled(valid);
    }
}
```

(Order is critical — marked beside `this.start = startField.getDate();` block)

(Order is critical — marked beside `BookingDialog.this.start = date;` block)

(Order is critical — marked beside `BookingDialog.this.end = date;` block)

Threads allow you to express sequence; events allow you to express dependency. In different situations, both are needed. A lot of problems come from trying to express dependency with threads, or sequences with events.

Given a conceptual diagram like the one we drew for the flight-booking example, we can extract the dependency relationships easily, as shown in figure 1.8. All we need to do is remove the unnecessary bits and reverse the data-flow arrows to turn them into a "depends on" relationship.

The FRP engine knows all these relationships, so it can automatically determine the dependencies. From that, the correct sequence is guaranteed.

The example we've given is simple, but sequence-dependent code can get complex. The problem with representing dependencies as a sequence comes when you go to change the code. To make something happen earlier or later, you need to make sure you fully

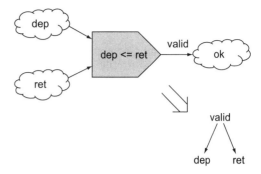

Figure 1.8　Extracting "depends on" relationships from a conceptual diagram: reverse the data-flow arrows.

understand the dependencies implicit in the existing sequence. In FRP, you express dependencies directly, so you can just add or remove the dependencies, and the sequence is automatically updated. It's impossible to make a sequence mistake.

With regular listener-based event handling, you can express dependency, but it's still difficult to maintain a reliable sequence. The order of processing depends on when the code propagates events and also on the order in which listeners were registered. (This is the plague we call *unpredictable order*.) It's easy to change this inadvertently, resulting in unwanted surprises. When this happens in a complex program, it can take some time to unravel.

We naturally think of our problems in terms of dependency. Programming has largely been concerned with translating that into a sequence. You've no doubt become good at this. FRP does away with this aspect of programming so you stay in dependency-land, and you can program in a way that's closer to the problem description.

1.15　Thinking declaratively: what the program is, not what it does

In FRP we talk about working in the *problem space* rather than working in the *machine space*. Decades of software development have made the authors lazy. We don't want to add sequence information to our code if we don't have to. We'll only end up having to debug it.

The sequence can be derived from dependencies, so you can write less code by leaving the sequence out altogether. You end up with a lot more "what" and a lot less "how." This style is referred to as *declarative programming*: you tell the machine what the program is, not what it does. You directly describe *things* and the *relationships between them*.

We wanted to demonstrate that the "what" of programming is easier to combine, reason about, and understand than the "how"—but we didn't want to do it on an empty stomach. So we decided to cook some lasagna. But when we looked up the recipe, we were horrified to see this:

1　Heat the oil in a large pan.
2　Fry the onions until golden.
3　Add ground beef and tomato.

A sequence! We'll spare you any more of this torture.

This recipe is a list of tiny sequence-dependent details with no overview. Imagine if you were asked what lasagna is by someone from Australia, where lasagna is practically unknown. If you gave them the full monologue of the recipe, they'd have a hard time understanding what they were going to get. This is no way to write a cookbook: it's an *operational definition* of lasagna, defined in terms of the steps needed to create it. Declarative programming instead uses a *conceptual definition*—see figure 1.9.

Figure 1.9   A conceptual definition is easier to grasp than a long list of detailed instructions.

This is how our cookbook would be written:

- *Lasagna* is grated cheese on cheese sauce on flat pasta on cheese sauce on Bolognese on flat pasta on cheese sauce on Bolognese on flat pasta on cheese sauce baked for 45 minutes.
- *Bolognese* is onion and oil fried until golden mixed with ground beef mixed with tomato simmered for 20 minutes.
- *Cheese sauce* is milk and cheese added progressively to roux while frying it until the sauce thickens.
- *Roux* is flour and butter fried briefly.

- *Baked* is put in an oven dish in a hot oven.
- *Fried* is put in a pan on high and mixed frequently.
- *Simmered* is put in a pan on low and mixed infrequently.

We're fond of code reuse, so we thought we'd include some further recipes:

- *Spaghetti Bolognese* is Bolognese on boiled and drained spaghetti.
- *Macaroni and cheese* is cheese sauce on boiled and drained macaroni.

We want everyone to enjoy functional cooking, so some may find this alternative useful:

- *Cheese sauce* is tomato paste, tahini, oil, rice flour, red miso, soy sauce, soy milk, and nutritional yeast mixed.

Notice a few things:

- We express dependencies directly. The sequence is derived from them. We don't care whether the cheese sauce is made before or after the Bolognese or simultaneously, and neither should anyone else.
- It's closer to a conceptual view of the food, so it's easy to understand.
- It's short, so our cookbook will need to be padded out with a lot of pictures.
- We can compose the parts into new recipes easily.

As we go through, we'll give concrete examples of what a program *is*, not what it *does*. For now, we'll leave you with this thought that is the basis of the philosophy behind FRP:

- A program is a transformation from inputs to outputs.

1.16 Conceptual vs. operational understanding of FRP

There are two ways to understand how FRP works: *operationally* or *conceptually*, like we did with the lasagna. A large part of the point of FRP is that it's *conceptually* simple.

Most programmers are accustomed to operational thinking, and we want to turn you away from that. With FRP, operational thinking not only is a more complex way to approach it, but also pollutes your mind with unnecessary details. Pay no attention to the man behind the curtain, as it were.

A few sections back, we presented some code for a flight-booking example. Later, we showed how you'd implement this in a traditional style, using listeners or callbacks. It probably won't surprise you to learn that under the covers of most FRP systems, everything is done with listeners.

> **NOTE** Not all FRP systems use listeners internally. Push-based FRP systems typically do, but there are also pull-based systems—where values are calculated on demand—and hybrids of the two. How a system works internally affects performance only. It makes no difference to the meaning of the FRP code you write. Sodium is a push-based system.

You may well ask, "What's really going on when the code runs?" We'll tell you in a moment, but first, we want to emphasize the importance of conceptual thinking.

1.16.1 Opening your mind to FRP

We ask you to clear your mind so it's receptive, like an empty rice bowl. Picture data flowing through a limitless stream of code (see figure 1.10). Are you feeling it?

Figure 1.10   A stream of code

What is the essential nature of the `Cell` class we introduced to you? FRP is said to be *reactive* because in writing the code, you're always responding to input. When working in FRP, we need you to view cells only as sources of information, and as the only sources of information. You never say, "And now, the code will push this value." Banish such thoughts from your mind.

FRP logic is a flow of data. Data flows into your logic through *streams* and *cells*. Data flows out the output side. The bit in the middle is also a flow of data. FRP code is a reaction to its input. Data flows from input to output. FRP is fundamentally *a declarative description of the output in terms of the input.*

In FRP, you're conceptually working at the level of the data flow, not the individual event value. We've found from experience that when you introduce people to FRP, they inevitably ask one question:

"How do you get the value?"

"In the far north," we reply, "a stream of values flows over rocks. Seeking a moment's rest, a value alights on a willow."

When working with FRP, try to stay conceptual in your thinking. Try to stay at the level of the relationships between things, not the mechanics of their interaction.

1.16.2 *What's really going on when the code runs?*

In the flight-booking example we gave earlier, we presented some code. Listing 1.4 gives the same code with more of the ancillary detail, but we've left out some ultra-verbose layout-related tomfoolery. The `nz.sodium.*` import gives the Sodium FRP system including `Cell`.

The `swidgets.*` import gives our "toy library" for GUI widgets. The `SDateField` and `SButton` widgets are like normal widgets, but jazzed up with an FRP interface. We did this because otherwise we would have needed to tell you how to feed data into `Cell` and how to get it out.

Interfacing FRP to the outside world isn't difficult, but we consider it of the highest importance at this early stage to keep you away from operational thinking. Our experience in teaching FRP is that people gravitate toward the things they know. When someone new to FRP sees a listener-like interface, they'll say, "I know how to use this." They then slip back into established habits and ways of thinking. We'll tell you how to interface FRP to the rest of your program later in the book.

> **Listing 1.4　More detail for the flight-booking example**

```
import javax.swing.*;
import java.awt.*;
import java.util.Calendar;
import swidgets.*;
import nz.sodium.*;

public class airline1 {
    public static void main(String[] args) {
        JFrame view = new JFrame("airline1");
        view.setDefaultCloseOperation(JFrame.EXIT_ON_CLOSE);

        SDateField dep = new SDateField();
        SDateField ret = new SDateField();
        Cell<Boolean> valid = dep.date.lift(ret.date,
            (d, r) -> d.compareTo(r) <= 0);
        SButton ok = new SButton("OK", valid);

        GridBagLayout gridbag = new GridBagLayout();
        view.setLayout(gridbag);
        GridBagConstraints c = new GridBagConstraints();
        ...
        view.add(new JLabel("departure"), c);
        view.add(dep, c);
        view.add(new JLabel("return"), c);
        view.add(ok, c);
        view.setSize(380, 140);
        view.setVisible(true);
    }
}
```

What goes on when this code runs? During *initialization*, a push-based FRP system typically constructs a network of listeners like the one we've drawn in figure 1.11. We're showing these in a style more akin to unified modeling language (UML), where each box represents a Java object in memory with a list of listeners that are currently registered. Objects that listen to other objects are called back on their `update(..)` method.

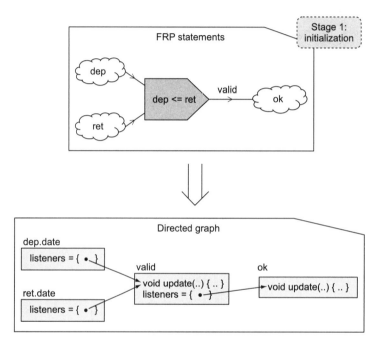

Figure 1.11   Behind the scenes, the FRP system translates FRP statements into a directed graph of listeners.

During the *running* stage, nothing happens until the user changes the departure or return date. Then this sequence of events occurs:

1 `dep.date` or `ret.date` notifies its listeners of the change.
2 The `update(..)` method for `valid` is called, and the logic for the business rule is recalculated with the latest values. `valid` then notifies its listeners.
3 The `update(..)` method for `ok` is called, which causes the button widget to be enabled or disabled.

1.17 *Applying functional programming to event-based code*

A lot of the power of FRP comes from the fact that FRP *cells* and *streams* follow the rules of functional programming in a way that listener/callback code can never hope to do.

It becomes possible to manipulate event-based code using functional programming. FRP allows functional programming to become a *meta-language* for event-based logic.

> **DEFINITION** *Meta-language*—A language used to manipulate the code of a second language

With FRP, functional programming isn't manipulating logic directly—it's manipulating the statements of a logic language. We want to give you a taste of that.

> **NOTE** This final section of chapter 1 will be difficult for people who are completely new to functional programming. It's just to show you what FRP can do, and it isn't necessary for learning the material. If this example gives you a dose of cataplexy, skip it for now. It'll be easy to follow after you've finished chapter 2.

We're going to encapsulate business rules with a class called `Rule` so we can manipulate rules as a concept. We can rewrite the rule from the first example (return can't precede departure) like this:

```
Rule r1 = new Rule((d, r) -> d.compareTo(r) <= 0);
```

Here we're writing the code of the rule using Java 8 lambda syntax and passing that as the argument to `Rule`'s constructor.

In China, the numbers 4, 14, and 24 are considered unlucky. You can define a new business rule that doesn't allow travel on unlucky dates. Given a function

```
private static boolean unlucky(Calendar dt) {
    int day = dt.get(Calendar.DAY_OF_MONTH);
    return day == 4 || day == 14 || day == 24;
}
```

the rule is expressed as

```
Rule r2 = new Rule((d, r) -> !unlucky(d) && !unlucky(r));
```

You also need a way to combine rules, such that this rule

```
Rule r = r1.and(r2);
```

returns `true` if rules `r1` and `r2` are both satisfied.

Listing 1.5 gives the code for the `Rule` class. It's a container class for a function that takes two dates (`Calendar`s) and returns `true` if the rule deems the given dates to be valid. The `Lambda2` class comes from Sodium.

> **DEFINITION** *Reify*—A functional programming term meaning to convert an abstract representation of something into real code

In line with this definition, the `reify()` method "compiles" the abstract rule into real FRP code. You use `Rule` first to manipulate rules as an abstract concept, and then you *reify* the result into executable code. In this example, `reify()` takes the cells representing the departure and return dates and returns a cell representing whether the supplied dates are valid according to that rule.

and() is a method for manipulating existing rules. It combines two rules to give a new rule that is satisfied if both the input rules are satisfied.

Listing 1.5   Encapsulating a business rule

```
class Rule {
    public Rule(Lambda2<Calendar, Calendar, Boolean> f) {
        this.f = f;
    }
    public final Lambda2<Calendar, Calendar, Boolean> f;
    public Cell<Boolean> reify(Cell<Calendar> dep, Cell<Calendar> ret) {
        return dep.lift(ret, f);
    }
    public Rule and(Rule other) {
        return new Rule(
            (d, r) -> this.f.apply(d, r) && other.f.apply(d, r)
        );
    }
}
```

NOTE Old programming text books may frown on nondescriptive variable names like f for *function*, but functional programmers do this because they always want their code to be general unless it absolutely has to be related to a specific problem space. The class name Rule says what it is. The contained function's name doesn't need to add to this.

The following listing is the logic of the main program. It implements the two business rules described using the new Rule class.

Listing 1.6   Manipulating abstract business rules

```
private static boolean unlucky(Calendar dt) {
    int day = dt.get(Calendar.DAY_OF_MONTH);
    return day == 4 || day == 14 || day == 24;
}
...
    SDateField dep = new SDateField();
    SDateField ret = new SDateField();
    Rule r1 = new Rule((d, r) -> d.compareTo(r) <= 0);          ← **Return can't precede departure.**
    Rule r2 = new Rule((d, r) -> !unlucky(d) && !unlucky(r));   ← **Can't travel on unlucky dates**
    Rule r = r1.and(r2);
    Cell<Boolean> valid = r.reify(dep.date, ret.date);
    SButton ok = new SButton("OK", valid);
```

To run this example, check out the code with git if you haven't done so already, and then run it. These are the commands:

```
git clone https://github.com/SodiumFRP/sodium
cd sodium/book/swidgets/java
mvn test -Pairline2     or     ant airline2
```

This is a small example of an approach that becomes powerful as the problem gets more complex. In chapter 12, we'll take this concept further and present an implementation of a GUI system done this way.

1.18   Summary

- *Listeners* or *callbacks* have a set of problems that we call the six plagues.
- FRP replaces state machines and listeners or callbacks.
- FRP deals with complexity through a mathematical property called *compositionality*.
- Thinking in terms of dependency is better than thinking in terms of sequence.
- FRP code has a structure like a *directed graph*, and an FRP engine derives execution order automatically from it.
- FRP uses a *declarative programming* style, meaning you think of the program in terms of what it is, not what it does.
- FRP is something fundamental: it's a discovery, not an invention.
- FRP allows functional programming to be used as a *meta-language* for writing event-based logic.

Core FRP

This chapter covers

- `Stream` and `Cell` types
- `map`, `merge`, `hold`, `snapshot`, `filter`, `lift`, `never`, and `constant` primitives
- Forward references with `StreamLoop` and `CellLoop`
- Making an accumulator with `hold` and `snapshot`

To demonstrate the core principles of FRP, in the first few chapters of this book we'll use our Sodium library in Java. We chose Java because it has static typing (which works well with FRP), and the syntax turns out to be quite nice. We're trying to teach the concepts of FRP, not the implementation details of specific systems. We designed Sodium to embody those basic concepts as minimally and completely as possible. Sodium and Java are just a convenient vehicle for this purpose; we hope you won't see this book as specific to a language or FRP system.

In later chapters, we'll delve into other FRP systems and languages. FRP systems are all the same conceptually, but the design and naming can differ.

2.1   *The Stream type: a stream of events*

FRP is based on two classes or data types. The example in chapter 1 used *cell*, and now we're going to look at its counterpart, *stream*. Recall the following:

- *Cells*—represent a *value that changes over time*
- *Streams*—represent a *stream of events*

Figure 2.1 shows an example: a window with a text field and a button. You can type text into the field, and when you click the button, the text field is cleared.

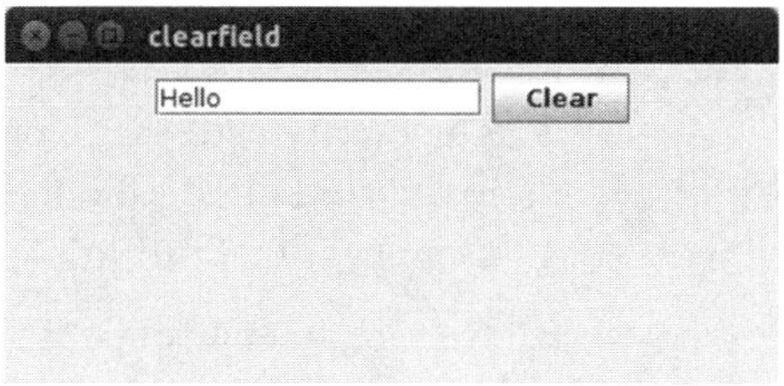

Figure 2.2 gives a conceptual view like the one we gave in chapter 1:

- *Arrows* represent *streams*. They're labeled with variable names.
- *Boxes* represent *transformations* on streams. The label above a box

Figure 2.1   When you click Clear, the text you entered disappears.

gives the name of the FRP operation being used. Arguments can appear in the center of the box.

- Conceptual *modules* or *black boxes* are shown as *clouds* to indicate that their internals have been obscured. They export or import streams or cells.

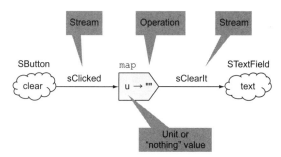

Figure 2.2   Conceptual representation of the clearfield example

Three things happen when the user clicks the button:

1. An event is generated and fed into a stream named sClicked. Because a button click has no associated information other than the fact it happened, the event in sClicked contains a "nothing value" of a predefined type Unit. We'll explain this type shortly.

NOTE   The convention used in this book is to prefix the variable names of streams with s.

2 This event propagates to a map operation that transforms the Unit value into "", an empty string value. This map operation produces a new stream that we have called sClearIt.

NOTE If you've done any sort of functional programming before, you'll have encountered the concept of map, but if not, don't worry—we'll go into more detail shortly. Don't confuse map with the Java data structure Map that stores key/value pairs.

3 The event in sClearIt propagates to the text field and changes its text contents to the contained value, which is "". This is how the text field is cleared when the user clicks the button.

Recall from chapter 1 that Cell has a type parameter that you express with Java generics to indicate the type of values contained in the cell. Stream also has a type parameter, telling you the type of the values propagated through the stream. The type of sClicked is Stream<Unit>, so the type of the values propagated by the stream is Unit.

The Unit data type

Unit is a sort of "nothing value." *Unit* is a term and concept from functional programming. Here's why it's useful.

In OOP programming, an event handler can take any number of arguments as needed. Because a button click has no information associated with it other than the fact that it happened, you'd normally define a handler that takes no arguments, like this:

```
public void buttonClicked() { ... }
```

FRP is a little different. You can think of it as internally using event handlers that always take one argument. If there's no value, you need a nothing value to plug the gap. Sodium defines a type Unit for this:

```
public enum Unit { UNIT };
```

In OOP style, the equivalent would be an imaginary one-argument event handler like this, although you don't do this in FRP:

```
public void buttonClicked(Unit u) { ... }
```

The handler's code would ignore u because it contains no information.

Listing 2.1 gives the code, including all the Java stuff to make it work. Again, we're using FRP-enhanced widgets from the toy SWidgets library.

NOTE If you want to experiment with the SWidgets library in your own code, you can install it into your local maven repository by going into the directory sodium/book/swidgets/java/swidgets and typing mvn install.

SButton is like a Swing JButton, but it exports an FRP stream that fires when the button is clicked, through a public field declared like this:

```
public Stream<Unit> sClicked;
```

STextField is a text field with the following constructor:

```
STextField(Stream<String> sText, String initText)
```

You can pass it a stream in the first argument that can write text into the text field. It's a simple matter to connect one to the other, but the types are different, so you need a map operation as we described to convert the Unit value to the empty string. The example is again using Java 8 lambda syntax here with map(), and we'll go into more detail in a moment. Note how closely the code corresponds to the conceptual diagram.

Listing 2.1 `clearfield`: a text field and a Clear button

```
import javax.swing.*;
import java.awt.FlowLayout;
import swidgets.*;
import nz.sodium.*;

public class clearfield {
    public static void main(String[] args) {
        JFrame frame = new JFrame("clearfield");
        frame.setDefaultCloseOperation(JFrame.EXIT_ON_CLOSE);
        frame.setLayout(new FlowLayout());
        SButton clear = new SButton("Clear");              ← Button with an
        Stream<String> sClearIt = clear.sClicked.map(u -> "");   FRP interface
        STextField text = new STextField(sClearIt, "Hello");   ← Feeds sClearIt into
        frame.add(text);                                         STextField's "write
        frame.add(clear);                                        to text" input
        frame.setSize(400, 160);
        frame.setVisible(true);
    }
}
```

Maps the "button clicked" stream to a stream of empty string events

To run the example, check it out with git if you haven't already done so, and then run it as follows:

```
git clone https://github.com/SodiumFRP/sodium
cd sodium/book/swidgets/java
mvn test -Pclearfield    or    ant clearfield
```

We encourage you to tinker with the examples. If you're using mvn, you can edit pom.xml to add your own build entries; for ant, edit build.xml.

DEFINITION *Event*—The propagation of an asynchronous message from one part of a program to another.

DEFINITION   *Stream*—A stream of discrete *events*. Also known in other FRP systems as an *event* (in which case the things it contains are termed *event occurrences*), an *event stream*, an *observable*, or a *signal*. When an event propagates through a stream, we sometimes say that the stream has *fired*.

Sodium defines a class called `Stream` for an FRP stream. The example uses `Stream` to represent button clicks. Here are some other examples of things it might make sense to model as streams:

- Mouse clicks and touchscreen events
- A monster being created or destroyed in a video game
- A video game character receiving damage from a hit in a fight
- A connection to a server being established or lost
- Bookmarking a website in a browser
- Adding, moving, or deleting a vertex in a polygon editor
- Zeroing a trip-distance meter on a vehicle

When a stream fires, an event or a message is propagated from one part of the program to another. That message consists of a value, often referred to as a *payload*, and the type of that value is specified (in Java) using generics, in the same way you represent the type of elements in a `List` or other container. For example, to represent a stream of keypress positions, you'd want the `Stream` to have a payload of type `Char`, so you'd declare it like this:

```
Stream<Char> sKeyPresses = ...
```

NOTE   The examples in the next few chapters are in Java. We'll give examples in some other languages later in the book. Look online for examples that have been translated to other programming languages.

2.2   *The map primitive: transforming a value*

In the `clearfield` example, you convert a button click to a text value to write into the text field. The button click is represented by this

```
Stream<Unit> sClicked
```

and the change to the text field is represented by

```
Stream<String> sClearIt
```

You use `map` to convert one into the other with this line of code:

```
Stream<String> sClearIt = clear.sClicked.map(u -> "");
```

This uses the Java 8 lambda syntax. If this is unfamiliar, please refer to the sidebar for an explanation.

Java 8 lambda syntax

FRP tends to use a lot of small functions, which you pass as arguments to FRP operations. You could use Java's inner classes for this, but in this book we'll use Java 8's new lambda syntax, because it's awesome.

For example, if you want to define a function that adds 1 to an integer, you can express it as an inner class, like this:

```
new Lambda1<Integer, Integer> {
    public Integer apply(Integer k) {
        return k+1;
    }
}
```

The new lambda syntax in Java 8 lets you write this using much shorter code, with no fewer than six variations of the syntax:

```
(Integer k) -> { return k+1; }
(k) -> { return k+1; }
k -> { return k+1; }
(Integer k) -> k+1
(k) -> k+1
k -> k+1
```

We won't go into detail here because this isn't a book about Java. We're only using a couple of Java 8's new features, so if our brief explanations aren't enough, online resources should suffice. If you want a more complete treatment of Java 8, we recommend *Java 8 in Action* by Raoul-Gabriel Urma, Mario Fusco, and Alan Mycroft (Manning, 2014).

2.2.1 Transforming a stream

map transforms a stream into a new stream of the same type or a different type. It does this using a function you supply it to convert the contained values.

In the example, you convert the button click into a text-field update by passing a function to map that converts a Unit to a String, and map uses it to convert the input Stream<Unit> to the desired Stream<String>. This sets things up so that when the sClicked stream fires with its Unit event value, the sClearIt stream created by map fires at the same time with a value of "". To perform this conversion, map executes the code inside the function you gave it each time sClicked fires.

> **NOTE** It may seem strange that we're saying the new stream fires at the same time as the old one. Clearly this isn't what's actually occurring, but in FRP we don't think operationally. Conceptually, in FRP, we can view these two events as truly simultaneous. A transactional context makes this so. We'll explain soon.

map returns a new stream that fires events at the same time as the original stream, but the payload is transformed by the given function. More generally, map takes a transformation on values (that is, a function) and performs a transformation on streams.

A quick recap: streams and maps

In FRP, the word *stream* refers to a stream of events—for example, a stream of keypresses.

- When a stream *fires*, this means an event of a particular payload value is propagated from one part of the program to another. For example, a stream of type `Stream<String>` might fire with the value "Lucy's Bins".
- `map` takes a stream and creates a new stream that fires (conceptually) at the same time. You supply a function to transform the value. For example, if you `map` a button-click stream with the function `u -> ""`, it will convert each click event into an empty string.

Recall that with Java 8 lambda syntax, `u -> ""` is a short form for

```
new Lambda1<Unit, String> {
    public String apply(Unit u) {
        return "";
    }
}
```

2.3   The components of an FRP system

An FRP system is usually implemented as a lightweight library in a standard programming language. Most FRP systems are based on two *classes* and 10 basic operations called *primitives*, although there are variations on this design.

DEFINITION   *Operation*—A function or other code that converts streams or cells to other streams or cells.

DEFINITION   *Primitive*—A fundamental operation—that is, an operation that can't be expressed in terms of other operations. Primitives are implemented using methods or functions. All FRP operations are made out of a small set of fundamental operations. That's what makes them primitive.

We've already introduced the `Stream` class. We'll get to the other class, `Cell`, shortly.

There are ten primitives: `map`, `merge`, `hold`, `snapshot`, `filter`, `lift`, `never`, `constant`, `sample`, and `switch`. FRP systems also need some other mechanisms that relate to their implementation that are outside the conceptual core of FRP.

NOTE   We have 10 primitives to deal with six plagues, which works out to an average of 1-2/3 primitives per plague.

2.3.1   Combining primitives

At its heart, FRP programming consists of applying primitive operations to values of type `Stream` and `Cell` to produce new values of these types. Primitives can be combined into arbitrarily complex constructions, and this is what you'll find yourself doing when writing FRP code. You use plain old classes and methods to structure these constructions.

Many FRP systems come with useful helper methods and functions, and this can make that system seem complex at first. But it isn't so bad. These helpers are combinations of the 10 primitives. Once you understand the primitives, everything else will be easy to follow. Sodium is minimalist with extra helper functions, but some systems aren't.

The way streams and cells act is clearly defined. The primitives maintain that definition, no matter how they're combined. The *denotational semantics* for an FRP system are the mathematical proof of this. This is how FRP guarantees the property of *compositionality* that gives so many advantages. We'll explain the idea of compositionality in chapter 5.

> **DEFINITION** *Compositionality*—The property that the meaning of an expression is determined by the meanings of its parts and the rules used to combine them.

2.3.2 Separating I/O from logic

Usually you'll keep logic and I/O separated when writing applications with FRP. Actually, doing so is required, but we wanted to butter you up a bit first. This is a good thing: the restrictions that FRP places on you will—paradoxically—free you from drudgery and frustration, and let you focus on what you want your program to do.

In England, breakfast is a yes or no question. Instead of being forced to choose between mediocre breakfasts, you're guaranteed the full spread. Sometimes, being prevented from making a bad choice isn't a bad thing. FRP gives you what you need, not what you think you want. Type safety is another example of this principle.

The logic in a program doesn't have to be—but can be—entirely FRP, whereas the I/O is normally written outside FRP in a standard flow-of-control style. We'll explain how to interface FRP with the rest of your program, but now isn't the time.

2.4 Referential transparency required

For FRP to work properly, the code you pass as a function to map must be *referentially transparent*, also referred to as *pure*. The requirements are as follows:

- You must not perform any I/O.
- You must not throw any exceptions unless they're caught and handled within the function.
- You must not read the value of any external variable if its value can change, but constants are allowed and encouraged.
- You must not modify any externally visible state.
- You must not keep any state between invocations of the function.
- In short, the function must have no external *effects* other than through the returned value, and it must not be affected by any external state.

> **NOTE** We expect you've thrown down the book in disgust by now. But don't panic. The primitives provide all the tools you need to avoid doing any of what we just listed. It's usually pretty simple—it's "just" a matter of changing your habits.

A referentially transparent function is a function in the mathematical sense. One test of referential transparency is that for a given input value, the function must always give the same output value.

The easiest way to think about it is that it shouldn't matter when or where you run the code, or even how many times. The code shouldn't see or change the outside world, and therefore it should always give the same result for a given input. This may seem unnecessarily restrictive at first, but we need this restriction to guarantee compositionality, which is at the core of the benefits of FRP.

> **DEFINITION**   *Cheating*—Using functions that aren't referentially transparent in functional code (such as FRP).

Can you cheat just a little? No, you can't. It may be difficult to grasp this now, but we promise you'll get a lot in return. Experience shows that cheating inevitably leads to introducing otherwise-avoidable bugs.

Having given you that lecture, there's one small exception: diagnostic trace messages are acceptable when you're trying to see what values are passing through your FRP logic to find a bug. These have no logical effect on the rest of the program. Expect the unexpected with execution order, however.

2.5   *The Cell type: a value that changes over time*

You've seen streams that represent a stream of events. Now we'll look at the other type used in FRP—*cell*—representing *a value that changes over time*.

Figure 2.3 shows a trivial example. A GUI label shows the current value of the text in the text field. Change the text, and the label's text will also change.

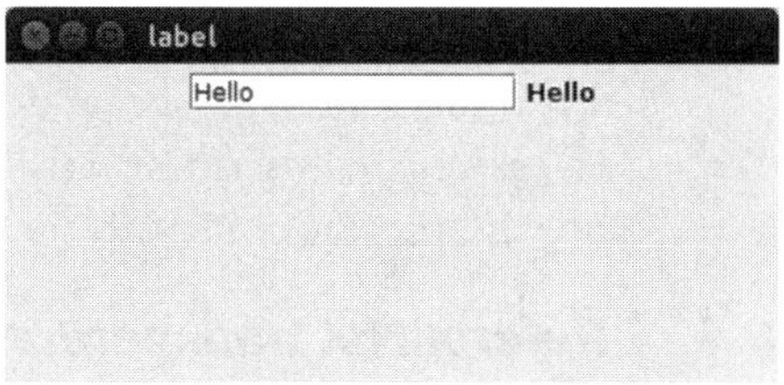

A cell is a nice fit for a GUI label widget. The `SLabel` in `SWidgets` gives a visible representation of a `Cell<String>` so that the screen representation is always kept up to date with the changing cell value. Figure 2.4 shows the conceptual view of plugging the text field's output `text` into the `SLabel`, and listing 2.2 gives the code.

Figure 2.3   A label that always shows the current text of the text field

> **NOTE**   Cells don't initiate state changes like streams do, so we're drawing cells with a small arrow head in the middle of the line. This is to indicate that they're passive, while streams are the active agency in FRP. We think this idea is important.

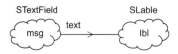

STextField   SLable

msg   —text→   lbl

Figure 2.4   Conceptual view of the label example: `STextField` exports its current text, and `SLabel` imports it.

Listing 2.2 `label` example: a label showing text field's text

```
import javax.swing.*;
import java.awt.FlowLayout;
import swidgets.*;
import nz.sodium.*;

public class label {
    public static void main(String[] args) {
        JFrame frame = new JFrame("label");
        frame.setDefaultCloseOperation(JFrame.EXIT_ON_CLOSE);
        frame.setLayout(new FlowLayout());
        STextField msg = new STextField("Hello");
        SLabel lbl = new SLabel(msg.text);
        frame.add(msg);
        frame.add(lbl);
        frame.setSize(400, 160);
        frame.setVisible(true);
    }
}
```

Check it out with git if you haven't done so already, and run it like this:

```
git clone https://github.com/SodiumFRP/sodium
cd sodium/book/swidgets/java
mvn test -Plabel      or      ant label
```

> **DEFINITION** *Cell*—A container for a value that changes over time. Some FRP systems call it a *behavior*, *property*, or *signal*.

> **NOTE** The term *signal* is mostly used in systems that don't distinguish between *stream* and *cell*.

A stream contains events that fire at discrete times. A stream event only has a value instantaneously when it fires, but a cell always has a value that can be sampled at any time. In FRP, cells model state, while streams model *state changes*.

What? Cell is a mutable variable?!

When you learn functional programming, it's drummed into you that you shouldn't use non-local mutable variables. Mutable variables break *compositionality*, a property that's highly prized in functional programming. We agree completely.

Yet an FRP cell is modified in place, making it technically a non-local mutable variable. What's going on here? This paradox is resolved as follows.

State mutation is evil—in the technical sense of the word, meaning it breaks compositionality. Event handling is inherently stateful, so it's similarly touched by the mark of Cain. FRP can't change this unavoidable fact.

In horror stories, demons can never be killed; they can only be banished. This is a good thing, because it means you can always make more money off a sequel.

(continued)

In a similar way, FRP takes the evil of event handling, divides it into little pieces, and then banishes each piece into an evil-proof box called a *stream* or a *cell*. The evil is then divided so it can't conspire against you, and it's contained, rendering it good on the outside.

By *good* we mean it has been transformed into something that obeys the rules of functional programming. Although the value held inside is mutable, the container itself—Stream or Cell—is an immutable value, so it can be used in referentially transparent functions.

It may take a little while to get your head around this, but it's an important point, so please make sure you understand it. The immutability of the Stream and Cell classes means your FRP code is *compositional*. Now the techniques of functional programming are available to you, and that's where the true benefits of FRP come from.

Note that the evil is contained only as long as Pandora doesn't come along and open the evil-proof box. This is why it's vital that you don't break the rules: the functions you pass to FRP primitives *must* be referentially transparent. We'll say it one more time just to be clear: cheats never prosper.

Here are some things that may make sense modeled as a cell:

- The position of the mouse cursor in an application window
- The position of a spaceship in a video game
- The current state of a polygon you're editing
- Vehicle speed, vehicle odometer, or current GPS position
- Time
- Whether the Wi-Fi network is online or offline
- Signal strength
- Temperature

2.5.1   *Why Stream and Cell?*

The clearfield example changes the contents of an STextField, and the label example changes an SLabel. In both cases, you pass something in to the constructor to cause those changes to occur. Compare these lines:

```
STextField text = new STextField(sClearIt, "Hello");      ◁— clearfield example
SLabel lbl = new SLabel(msg.text);                ◁— label example
```

In the first line, you pass a stream; and in the second, you pass a cell. Why the difference?

- In clearfield, both the user and the program can change the STextField's text. Should the text field follow what the program says, or what the user says? It needs to change according to events from both sources. A stream, representing discrete events, is a better fit, because you want to model the ability to make discrete changes to the text field's current text string.

- In `label`, the label's text is completely controlled by the program, and its display represents a string value that can change. `Cell` fits this better.

2.5.2 *The constant primitive: a cell with a constant value*

Cells usually change over time, but it's also possible to construct them with a constant value:

```
Cell<Integer> dozen = new Cell<>(12);
```

There's no way to modify a cell after it's created, so its value is guaranteed to be constant forever.

2.5.3 *Mapping cells*

We can illustrate `map` on cells by reversing the string in the previous example. See figure 2.5.

Figure 2.6 shows the conceptual view again. (If you're viewing this in color, we'll show operations that output cells in blue.) Listing 2.3 shows the code.

Figure 2.5 **Using `map` to reverse the text in a cell**

Figure 2.6 **The conceptual review of the `reverse` example**

Listing 2.3 Using `map` to reverse the text

```java
import javax.swing.*;
import java.awt.FlowLayout;
import swidgets.*;
import nz.sodium.*;

public class reverse {
    public static void main(String[] args) {
        JFrame frame = new JFrame("reverse");
        frame.setDefaultCloseOperation(JFrame.EXIT_ON_CLOSE);
        frame.setLayout(new FlowLayout());
        STextField msg = new STextField("Hello");
        Cell<String> reversed = msg.text.map(t ->
            new StringBuilder(t).reverse().toString());
        SLabel lbl = new SLabel(reversed);
        frame.add(msg);
        frame.add(lbl);
```

```
        frame.setSize(400, 160);
        frame.setVisible(true);
    }
}
```

Check it out with git if you haven't done so already, and run it like this:

```
git clone https://github.com/SodiumFRP/sodium
cd sodium/book/swidgets/java
mvn test -Preverse    or    ant reverse
```

2.6   *The merge primitive: merging streams*

Let's say you like playing Japanese board games online. The game window has a little chat window next to it. Let's add a couple of buttons for canned messages to make it more convenient to say two commonly used phrases: "Onegai shimasu" to greet your opponent, and "Thank you" at the end of the game. See figure 2.7. This is essentially the same as the clearfield example, but with two buttons instead of one.

Figure 2.7   Buttons for poking canned messages into the text field

In figure 2.8, we have two sources of canned messages, and we use the new merge primitive to merge them together. We'll draw merge as a trapezoid. (It was our childhood wish to one day write a book with the word *trapezoid* in it.)

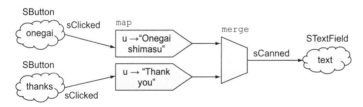

Figure 2.8   Merging two text streams into one

Listing 2.4 gives the code. STextField takes only one stream as input, so you need to merge the two into one. This example uses a Sodium variant of merge called .orElse(). This naming has to do with how it handles simultaneous events, which we'll explain next.

Listing 2.4   Merging two canned message sources into one

```
import javax.swing.*;
import java.awt.FlowLayout;
import swidgets.*;
import nz.sodium.*;
```

```
public class gamechat {
    public static void main(String[] args) {
        JFrame frame = new JFrame("gamechat");
        frame.setDefaultCloseOperation(JFrame.EXIT_ON_CLOSE);
        frame.setLayout(new FlowLayout());
        SButton onegai = new SButton("Onegai shimasu");
        SButton thanks = new SButton("Thank you");
        Stream<String> sOnegai = onegai.sClicked.map(u ->
            "Onegai shimasu");
        Stream<String> sThanks = thanks.sClicked.map(u -> "Thank you");
        Stream<String> sCanned = sOnegai.orElse(sThanks);
        STextField text = new STextField(sCanned, "");
        frame.add(text);
        frame.add(onegai);
        frame.add(thanks);
        frame.setSize(400, 160);
        frame.setVisible(true);
    }
}
```

Check it out with git, if you haven't done so already, and run it like this:

```
git clone https://github.com/SodiumFRP/sodium
cd sodium/book/swidgets/java
mvn test -Pgamechat    or    ant gamechat
```

> **DEFINITION** The merge primitive puts the events from two streams together into a single stream. The name merge for this primitive is universal, but you may encounter the more mathematical terms union and append.

The two input streams and one output stream of the merge operation must all have the same type. In the example, Stream<String> is the type. merge gives you a stream such that if either of the input streams fires, an event will appear on the output stream at the same time.

2.6.1 *Simultaneous events*

We alluded earlier to the fact that FRP processing takes place in a transactional context. This is basically the same idea as the transactions used in databases.

> **How are transactions started in Sodium?**
>
> Sodium automatically starts a transaction whenever an input value is pushed into a stream or cell. Any state changes that occur as a result of that input are performed within the same transaction. Mostly you don't need to do anything, but it's possible to start a transaction explicitly.
>
> For the reasons we've explained, we want to leave the explanation of how to push input values until a later chapter.

sOnegai and sThanks both come from the SButton class. We wrote SButton in such a way that it starts a new transaction for each button click event, so we happen to know that two different button events can't occur in the same transaction. Thus sCanned will never encounter the situation where two events can occur in the same transaction.

> **DEFINITION**   *Simultaneous events*—Two or more stream events that occur in the same transaction. In Sodium, they're truly simultaneous, because their order relative to each other can't be detected.

It's normal practice in FRP for each external event to run in a new transaction, so it's normally OK to assume that no two events from external streams will be simultaneous. This is what we did in SButton. But we can't always assume events aren't simultaneous. Because external streams aren't usually a source of simultaneity, simultaneous events are almost always caused by two streams that are modifications of a single input stream.

EXAMPLE: SIMULTANEOUS EVENTS IN A DRAWING PROGRAM

Let's say you're developing a program for drawing diagrams, in which graphical elements can be selected or deselected. The rules are these:

- If you click an item, it's selected.
- If an item is selected, and you click elsewhere, the item gets deselected.

Figure 2.9 illustrates us performing three steps with the diagram program:

1   At first nothing is selected, and we're ready to click the triangle.
2   When we've clicked the triangle, it's highlighted.
3   We get ready to click the octagon.

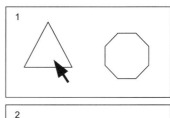

At this point, a single mouse click will cause two simultaneous events to be generated:

- Deselecting the triangle
- Selecting the octagon

You'll almost certainly want to merge these streams at some point in the program. Because these two events originate in the same mouse click event, they're simultaneous. All three events—the mouse click, the deselect, and the select—are conceptually truly simultaneous in FRP, meaning it's impossible to detect any ordering in their occurrence.

In appendix B, we use this example to illustrate the first plague of listeners: *unpredictable order.* You'll find the code there.

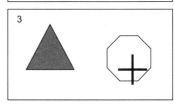

Figure 2.9   Three steps in using the diagram program

DEALING WITH SIMULTANEOUS EVENTS

Each FRP system has its own policy for merging simultaneous events. Sodium's policy is as follows:

- If the input events on the two input streams are simultaneous, `merge` combines them into one. `merge` takes a combining function as a second argument for this purpose. The signature of the combining function is `A combine(A left, A right)`.
- The combining function is not used in the (usually more common) case where the input events are not simultaneous.
- You invoke merge like this: `s1.merge(s2, f)`. If `merge` needs to combine simultaneous events, the event from `s1` is passed as the left argument of the combining function `f`, and the event from `s2` is passed on the right.
- The `s1.orElse(s2)` variant of `merge` doesn't take a combining function. In the simultaneous case, the left `s1` event takes precedence and the right `s2` event is dropped. This is equivalent to `s1.merge(s2, (l, r) -> l)`. The name `orElse()` was chosen to remind you to be careful, because events can be dropped.

This policy has some nice results:

- There can only ever be one event per transaction in a given stream.
- There's no such thing as event-processing order within a transaction. All events that occur in different streams within the same transaction are truly simultaneous in that there's no detectable order between them.

Some formulations of FRP don't force you to combine simultaneous events, so they allow more than one event per stream. But we think Sodium's policy—forcing the decision for every merge—is the right thing to do because we get true event simultaneity. This helps simplify the job of reasoning about logic.

> **NOTE** Heinrich Apfelmus, author of the Reactive Banana FRP system, is also a proponent of forcing the programmer to combine simultaneous events for every merge.

How simultaneous events are handled depends only on things specified locally to `merge`, not on things in distant parts of the program. This guarantees compositional semantics, and compositionality is vital for reducing bugs. We'll go into the reasons for this in chapter 5.

> **NOTE** In some FRP-like systems, there is no concept of simultaneous events, so `merge` can't be guaranteed to act consistently. This breaks compositionality, so these systems technically aren't true FRP systems. At the time of writing, the system known as *Reactive Extensions* (*Rx*) and the many systems inspired by it don't meet this requirement. We hope this will change because the problems that result from it aren't just theoretical.

2.6.2   *Collection variants of merge*

Sodium's `Stream` class also provides the following variants of `merge` that work on collections of streams. Every FRP system has an equivalent:

```
static <A> Stream<A> orElse(java.lang.Iterable<Stream<A>> ss)
static <A> Stream<A> merge(java.lang.Iterable<Stream<A>> ss, Lambda2<A,A,A> f)
```

2.6.3   *How does merge do its job?*

How does `merge` do the job of combining simultaneous events? To answer this question, we're going to descend once again into the fetid world of the operational.

The bottom of figure 2.10 shows the execution of the `merge` example from the previous section operationally in sequence. You see a transaction executing in time.

Conceptually, the order of the events on `sDeselect` and `sSelect` isn't detectable; but here we show them occurring operationally in the opposite of the desired order. The `merge` implementation has to store the events in temporary storage until a time when it knows it won't receive any more input. Then it outputs an event: if it received more than one, it uses the supplied function to combine them; otherwise, it outputs the one event it received.

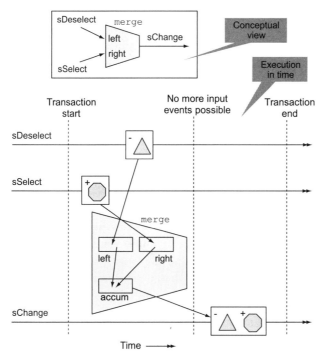

Figure 2.10   The mechanics of how merge deals with simultaneous events

> ## The function must be referentially transparent
>
> As a reminder, all functions passed to FRP primitives must be referentially transparent, or pure. This means they must not perform I/O, modify or read external state, or keep internal state. Cheating always ends in tears. This is important.

2.7   *The hold primitive: keeping state in a cell*

In figure 2.11, the user can click Red or Green. You'll use a new primitive `hold` to hold the result in a cell that you then show in an `SLabel`; the code is shown in listing 2.5.

Figure 2.12 shows the conceptual view. The stream events represent the changes to the state, and the cell holds the state. `SLabel` then shows the current state on the screen. To recap, we're using the following diagram elements:

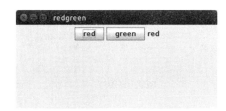

Figure 2.11 Selecting the color red or green, after clicking Red

- *Yellow* boxes for primitives that output *streams* (assuming you're viewing this in color)
- *Arrows* for *streams*
- *Blue* boxes for primitives that output *cells*
- *Lines* with a small arrow head in the middle for *cells*

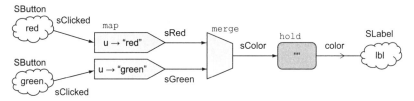

Figure 2.12   Conceptual view of holding red or green event

Listing 2.5   Holding a stream to turn it into a cell

```
import javax.swing.*;
import java.awt.FlowLayout;
import swidgets.*;
import nz.sodium.*;

public class redgreen {
    public static void main(String[] args) {
        JFrame frame = new JFrame("redgreen");
        frame.setDefaultCloseOperation(JFrame.EXIT_ON_CLOSE);
        frame.setLayout(new FlowLayout());
        SButton red = new SButton("red");
```

```
        SButton green = new SButton("green");
        Stream<String> sRed = red.sClicked.map(u -> "red");
        Stream<String> sGreen = green.sClicked.map(u -> "green");
        Stream<String> sColor = sRed.orElse(sGreen);
        Cell<String> color = sColor.hold("");                    ⟵┐  Specifies the initial
        SLabel lbl = new SLabel(color);                           │  value of the cell
        frame.add(red);
        frame.add(green);
        frame.add(lbl);
        frame.setSize(400, 160);
        frame.setVisible(true);
    }
}
```

Check it out with git, if you haven't done so already, and run it like this:

```
git clone https://github.com/SodiumFRP/sodium
cd sodium/book/swidgets/java
mvn test -Predgreen      or     ant redgreen
```

> **DEFINITION**   The hold primitive converts a stream into a cell in such a way that the cell's value is that of the most recent event received. Other names you might encounter are stepper and toProperty.

> **NOTE**   The name stepper comes from FRP systems that emphasize continuous time. With continuous time, you can represent a cell that changes continuously over time. In continuous-time systems, stepper is the primitive for constructing non-continuous cells that change their value at discrete times, so the name reflects this.

Note that cells are how you model state in FRP, and they're the only mechanism for doing so. hold allows you to store a stream event's value so it can be retrieved later.

There's a golden rule for cells: a cell *always* has a value. It can be sampled at any time. To ensure that this invariant is maintained, hold requires you to specify an initial value to use as the cell's value until the first change event is received.

A quick recap: cells and hold

A cell models a value that changes over time.

- A cell always has a value that can be sampled at any time, whereas a stream only has a value instantaneously when it fires. A cell has a memory, although it's probably best to say a cell *is* a memory.
- hold takes a stream and an initial value and creates a cell that starts off with the initial value; then the value changes to the stream event's value whenever that stream fires.
- You can use map on a cell to create a new cell. This is analogous to what we did with streams.

2.8   The snapshot primitive: capturing the value of a cell

In the cell example, the SLabel's text changed as the user typed into the text field. In a real application, this might be a bit distracting for the user. Now we're going to show you a different way of reading the text from a text field using the snapshot primitive: you'll let the user type, and only capture the text when they click a button.

Figure 2.13 shows what happens when the user clicks Translate: you capture the text, translate it into mock Latin,[1] and show the result in an SLabel. Figure 2.14 gives the conceptual view; the code is in listing 2.6. text is sampled when sClicked fires, and the output is the result of the translate function applied to the two input values. The function discards the button's Unit value.

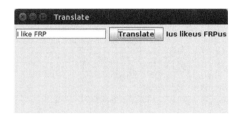

Figure 2.13   Clicking Translate translates the text into mock Latin.

We hope that drawing cell lines without big arrow heads will help show that streams are the active agency in FRP. When performing the snapshot, the stream event "pulls" the value out of the cell.

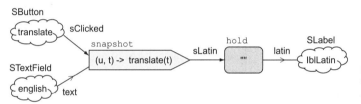

Figure 2.14   Conceptual view of capturing text when the user clicks a button

---

Listing 2.6   Capturing a cell's value when a button event occurs

```java
import javax.swing.*;
import java.awt.*;
import java.awt.event.*;
import swidgets.*;
import nz.sodium.*;

public class translate {
    public static void main(String[] args) {
        JFrame view = new JFrame("Translate");
        view.setDefaultCloseOperation(JFrame.EXIT_ON_CLOSE);
        view.setLayout(new FlowLayout());
        STextField english = new STextField("I like FRP");
        SButton translate = new SButton("Translate");
```

---

[1] To create mock Latin, you add *us* to the end of each word. It's useful in situations where a superficial air of authority is called for, although none immediately come to mind. Note that we've only tested this with English input; it may work in other languages, too.

```
        Stream<String> sLatin =
            translate.sClicked.snapshot(english.text, (u, txt) ->
                txt.trim().replaceAll(" |$", "us ").trim()
            );
        Cell<String> latin = sLatin.hold("");
        SLabel lblLatin = new SLabel(latin);
        view.add(english);
        view.add(translate);
        view.add(lblLatin);
        view.setSize(400, 160);
        view.setVisible(true);
    }
}
```

Check it out with git, if you haven't done so already, and run it like this:

```
git clone https://github.com/SodiumFRP/sodium
cd sodium/book/swidgets/java
mvn test -Ptranslate   or    ant translate
```

> **DEFINITION**   The snapshot primitive captures the value of a cell at the time
> when a stream event fires; it can then combine the stream and cell events
> together with a supplied function. In other FRP systems, it goes by the name
> withLatest, attach, or tag.

Figure 2.15 shows the time sequence of the execution of a snapshot operation. We've
drawn the cell's value stretched across the length of the transaction, to illustrate the
idea that a cell always has a value; this is in contrast to streams, which only have a value
instantaneously when they fire.

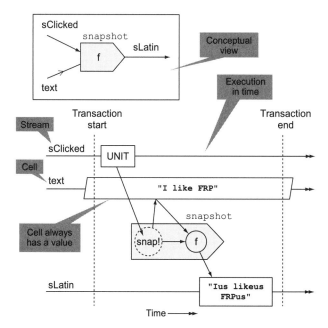

**Figure 2.15   Execution in time
of a snapshot operation**

snapshot also has a variant without the second function argument that ignores the stream value and just captures the cell value. For example, to capture the English without translating it, you could do this:

```
Stream<String> sEnglish = translate.sClicked.snapshot(english);
```

NOTE Most systems including Sodium have variants of snapshot that can take more than one cell as input, up to some sensible limit in the implementation.

2.9 Looping hold and snapshot to create an accumulator

To illustrate how you can accumulate state changes, let's implement a simple spinner—see figure 2.16. The accumulated value is kept in a cell, and you use an SWidgets SLabel to display it.

Figure 2.17 shows the conceptual view. The accumulator is circled.

Figure 2.16 A spinner example: + increments the value, and - decrements it.

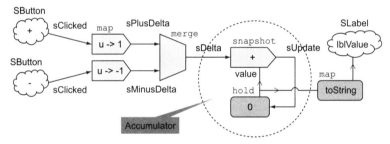

Figure 2.17 Conceptual view of accumulating + and - button clicks, with the accumulator circled

2.9.1 Forward references

Before we give the complete listing, we need to have a little chat about forward references. Are you sitting comfortably? Then we'll begin.

You start by making a stream of deltas of 1 when + is clicked and -1 when - is clicked, like this:

```
Stream<Integer> sPlusDelta = plus.sClicked.map(u -> 1);
Stream<Integer> sMinusDelta = minus.sClicked.map(u -> -1);
Stream<Integer> sDelta = sPlusDelta.orElse(sMinusDelta);
```

All you have to do is accumulate the sDeltas:

```
Stream<Integer> sUpdate = sDelta.snapshot(value,
                (delta, value_) -> delta + value_
            );
Cell<Integer> value = sUpdate.hold(0);
```

Unfortunately, Java won't let you write this, because you're defining `value` in terms of itself. `value` depends on `sUpdate`, and `sUpdate` depends on `value`.

> **DEFINITION**   *Value loop*—In functional programming, a value (in this case, a stream or cell) defined directly or through other variables in terms of itself.

In our youth, we considered it important to make our breakfast before eating it. We recognized long ago that there was a dependency relationship between the two. But only in a Euclidean universe must one be *temporally* before the other, which is to say we prefer to think in terms of dependency rather than sequence.

Java isn't entirely on board with this way of thinking, so in Sodium we use a trick called `CellLoop` to get around it. Here's the Sodium code:

```
CellLoop<Integer> value = new CellLoop<>();
Stream<Integer> sUpdate = sDelta.snapshot(value,
        (delta, value_) -> delta + value_
    );
value.loop(sUpdate.hold(0));
```

`CellLoop` is like an immutable variable that you assign once through its loop() method. But unlike a normal variable, you can reference it *before* it's assigned.

> **NOTE**   For streams, there is a corresponding `StreamLoop`.

`CellLoop` and `StreamLoop` are subclasses of `Cell` and `Stream`. They're equivalent in every way to the `Cell` or `Stream` assigned to them using `loop()`—and the key idea is that you can use them freely before `loop()` is called. The only purpose they serve is to make forward references possible. But we take it one step further and allow cycles in variable references. This may look like black magic, and it is, but we assure you it isn't complex. It only looks that way because your thoughts are cluttered with complexities relating to execution sequence. Banish them from your mind.

> **NOTE**   FRP code exists outside of time. Less poetically, there is no concept of sequence in FRP statements. You could take a blob of FRP code, arrange the lines in a random order, and insert `CellLoops` and `StreamLoops` as needed, and the code would work exactly the same. We call this the "sea sponge in a blender" principle, because it's said that if you put a sea sponge through a blender, it can reassemble itself. We don't really believe this.

2.9.2   *Constructing FRP in an explicit transaction*

The recommended practice with Sodium is to construct the FRP logic for a program under a single big, explicit transaction. In most cases, Sodium will start transactions automatically for you as needed. But `CellLoop` and `StreamLoop` are sensitive petals and require the declaration and the `.loop()` call to be in the same transaction. They will throw an exception if this isn't done.

To wrap some code in an explicit transaction, you can write this (we're using Java 8 lambdas again):

```
Transaction.runVoid(() -> {
    ... your code ...
}
```

If you want to return a value from the transactional block, do this:

```
A a = Transaction.run(() -> {
    ... your code ...
    A a = ...;
    return a;
}
```

> **DEFINITION**   *Loan pattern*—Method where you pass a lambda to some function that opens and closes a resource for you. It's often used with files. This is a good idea because it's impossible to accidentally forget to close the resource. If this isn't making sense, please skip ahead to the more detailed explanation of the loan pattern in section 8.3; that section also covers transactions in more detail.

2.9.3   Accumulator code

The following listing puts together all the elements of the accumulator.

Listing 2.7   Accumulating + and - button clicks

```
import javax.swing.*;
import java.awt.FlowLayout;
import swidgets.*;
import nz.sodium.*;

public class spinner {
    public static void main(String[] args) {
        JFrame view = new JFrame("spinner");
        view.setDefaultCloseOperation(JFrame.EXIT_ON_CLOSE);
        view.setLayout(new FlowLayout());
        Transaction.runVoid((() -> {                          ◁─── Forward
            CellLoop<Integer> value = new CellLoop<>();              reference
            SLabel lblValue = new SLabel(
                        value.map(i -> Integer.toString(i)));
            SButton plus = new SButton("+");
            SButton minus = new SButton("-");
            view.add(lblValue);
            view.add(plus);
            view.add(minus);
            Stream<Integer> sPlusDelta = plus.sClicked.map(u -> 1);
            Stream<Integer> sMinusDelta = minus.sClicked.map(u -> -1);
            Stream<Integer> sDelta = sPlusDelta.orElse(sMinusDelta);
            Stream<Integer> sUpdate = sDelta.snapshot(value,
                    (delta, value_) -> delta + value_
                );
```

Wraps code in an explicit transaction (annotation pointing to `Transaction.runVoid`)

```
              value.loop(sUpdate.hold(0));
          });
          view.setSize(400, 160);
          view.setVisible(true);
      }
}
```

Check it out with git, if you haven't done so already, and run it like this:

```
git clone https://github.com/SodiumFRP/sodium
cd sodium/book/swidgets/java
mvn test -Pspinner     or     ant spinner
```

> **DEFINITION** *Accumulator*—A piece of state that's updated by combining new information with the existing state.

We've shown you how to build an accumulator from three basic elements: hold, snapshot, and *loops* or *forward references.* Sodium and other FRP systems give you a more convenient way to write accumulators through methods with names like accum() and collect(), but they are just helpers based on these three elements.

2.9.4 *Does snapshot see the new value or the old value?*

When an event enters your FRP logic through a stream, it causes a cascade of state changes. As we explained, this happens under a transactional context, so all the state changes that result from a given event are made atomically.

> **DEFINITION** If a set of state changes is made *atomically*, it means to all appearances they're made at the same time. That is, it's impossible to observe a situation where some have been made but not others. The property of *atomicity* can save you from a cosmos of lamentation.

In the last example, we looked at an accumulator, where you read from a cell using snapshot and wrote to it using hold in the same transaction. Does snapshot see the new value or the old value of value? In this case, it would be impossible to update value before reading it because the new value to be written depends on what was read. It would eat its own tail and implode to a singularity.

But what about the more general case, where the same event—implying the same transaction—causes cell A both to be updated through a hold and also to be snapshotted? Does snapshot see cell A before or after the update?

Each FRP system takes a different approach to this problem. Sodium works the same as Conal Elliott's formulation of FRP, saying that snapshot always sees the old value. You can view this in two equivalent ways. Either

- snapshot sees the value as it was at the beginning of the transaction.

or

- hold updates are performed atomically at the end of the transaction. This is how we've shown it in figure 2.18.

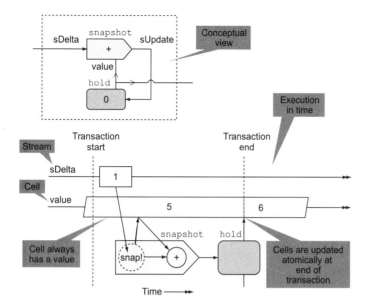

Figure 2.18   The execution sequence of updating an accumulator: value is 5, and the user clicks +.

Figure 2.18 shows the execution sequence of hold committing its updates at the end of the transaction. Here value is 5 and the user clicks +.

Here are some approaches you might see in other FRP systems:

- Some say their snapshot equivalent sees the new value and will behave unpredictably if there's a loop.
- Some normally give the new value but have an explicit delay primitive so you can get the old value. An accumulator is expressed as a loop of hold-delay-snapshot.
- Some don't allow value loops and provide only higher-level accum-style primitives.

So delay can be seen as a separate primitive, but in Sodium it's implicit.

The need for a non-delaying hold

Sodium's hold has an implicit delay. Some people argue that a non-delaying hold is also needed in some circumstances. We've done quite well without it. We aren't convinced that a non-delaying hold is necessary, but we'll leave this for you to contemplate.

> **(continued)**
>
> In Sodium, there are two ways to work around the need for a non-delaying `hold`. The first is to use a combination of a non-core primitive `Operational.updates()` and the `merge` primitive to capture the update of a cell that's being made in the current transaction. The second is to use a non-core primitive called `Operational.defer()` that creates a new transaction. We'll cover all of these in chapter 8; we've found that this sort of thing isn't often needed in practice.

2.10   The filter primitive: propagating an event only sometimes

Let's say you want to modify the previous `spinner` example so that the accumulated number can't be negative. Figure 2.19 gives the conceptual view of how to do this with a primitive called `filter` (circled). We're borrowing the decision box diamond from flowcharts to represent the decision of whether to keep the event.

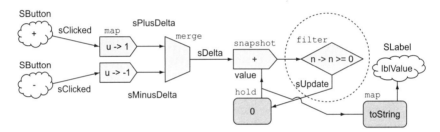

Figure 2.19   Add a filter to prevent the spinner's value from becoming negative.

Instead of a full listing, here's the modified line, with the addition shown in bold:

```
Stream<Integer> sUpdate = sDelta.snapshot(value,
        (delta, value_) -> delta + value_
    ).filter(n -> n >= 0);
```

If the value of `sUpdate` is >= 0, it's let through. If not, it's discarded, and no update is received by `hold`.

Check it out with git, if you haven't done so already, and run it like this:

```
git clone https://github.com/SodiumFRP/sodium
cd sodium/book/swidgets/java
mvn test -Pnonegative     or     ant nonegative
```

> **DEFINITION**   *Filter*—To let stream values through only sometimes. This is a general functional programming concept, and this name is used universally in FRP systems.

We've said it before, and we'll say it again (and again). Like all functions you use with FRP, a `filter` function must be pure or referentially transparent. This means

- It must not cause external effects such as I/O or state changes.
- It must be not be affected by external state.
- For a given input value, it must always give the same output value.

If you need to `filter` based on some state, you need to `snapshot` a cell first and then `filter` the output. Referential transparency is important.

> **NOTE** In Sodium there is a variant of `filter` called `filterOptional` that's more suitable for this case. We'll show some examples of it later.

2.11 The lift primitive: combining cells

The `lift` primitive allows you to combine two or more cells into one using a specified combining function. Let's add two integers together with an `add` function. In figure 2.20, the label shows the sum of the values in the text fields.

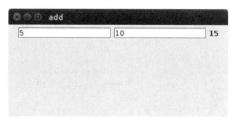

Figure 2.20   Adding two cells together

Figure 2.21 shows the conceptual view. You convert the input text field values to integers, add them with `lift`, and then convert the result back to a string to stick into an `SLabel`.

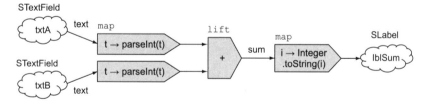

Figure 2.21   Conceptual view of adding two text fields together

The following listing shows the code. The first argument to `lift` is the cell to combine with this one, and the second argument is a function to perform that, in our case, adds two integers together.

> **Listing 2.8   Adding two text fields together**

```
import javax.swing.*;
import java.awt.FlowLayout;
import swidgets.*;
import nz.sodium.*;
```

```java
public class add {
    public static void main(String[] args) {
        JFrame frame = new JFrame("add");
        frame.setDefaultCloseOperation(JFrame.EXIT_ON_CLOSE);
        frame.setLayout(new FlowLayout());
        STextField txtA = new STextField("5");
        STextField txtB = new STextField("10");
        Cell<Integer> a = txtA.text.map(t -> parseInt(t));
        Cell<Integer> b = txtB.text.map(t -> parseInt(t));
        Cell<Integer> sum = a.lift(b, (a_, b_) -> a_ + b_);
        SLabel lblSum = new SLabel(sum.map(i -> Integer.toString(i)));
        frame.add(txtA);
        frame.add(txtB);
        frame.add(lblSum);
        frame.setSize(400, 160);
        frame.setVisible(true);
    }
    private static Integer parseInt(String t) {
        try {
            return Integer.parseInt(t);
        } catch (NumberFormatException e) {
            return 0;
        }
    }
}
```

Check it out with git, if you haven't done so already, and run it like this:

```
git clone https://github.com/SodiumFRP/sodium
cd sodium/book/swidgets/java
mvn test -Padd     or      ant add
```

lift is like the map operation that works with cells, except that it takes two or more cells as input instead of one. lift takes as its last argument a function with the multiple input arguments matching the number and types of the cells.

> **DEFINITION** *Lift*—A functional programming term meaning to make a function that operates on values into a function that operates on some type of container of those values. It's called this because you're "lifting" a function that operates on values into the world of cells. Cell is the container type in the example, but you can lift into any container type such as List or Optional. We won't say more, because it isn't needed for FRP, but you'll find this discussed in any book on functional programming such as *Grokking Functional Programming* by Aslam Khan (Manning, forthcoming).

You can lift any number of cells up to some sensible limit in the FRP library implementation. lift's output cell is automatically kept up to date when the inputs change. You never again need to worry about whether a value is up to date or not.

> **NOTE** map on cells can be seen as a lift of a single cell. Some FRP systems use the term map for both single-cell and multiple cell cases, and some use

lift for both. In Sodium, you `map` a single `Stream` or a `Cell`, and you `lift` when you have two or more `Cells`.

2.12 *The never primitive: a stream that never fires*

There's one more primitive to cover in this chapter, and it's an easy one, because…well…it doesn't do anything.

> **DEFINITION** *Never stream*—A stream that can't ever fire. This name is universal in FRP systems.

In Sodium it doesn't have the name *never*. You get it by constructing a stream with no arguments. For example:

```
Stream<String> sNone = new Stream<String>();
```

A stream constructed this way has no mechanism to cause it to fire, so it's guaranteed never to fire.

> **NOTE** All state changes in FRP are caused by stream events. FRP is *reactive*, and this property requires that all events should originate in I/O from outside the FRP logic. This is an important principle. That's why—apart from external events originating in I/O—the only kind of stream you're allowed to construct directly is one that never fires.

never is primarily used when you don't want a particular feature of some logic you've written. We used it in when implementing `SWidgets`. `STextField` has two constructors:

```
public STextField(String initText)
public STextField(Stream<String> sText, String initText)
```

The second constructor has the extra feature of allowing the text field's text to be changed programmatically. We wrote the first constructor by passing a never stream to the second constructor:

```
this(new Stream<String>(), initText);
```

Incidentally, a constant cell is equivalent to holding a never stream:

```
Cell<Integer> dozen = new Stream<Integer>().hold(12);
```

> **NOTE** Strictly speaking, `constant` isn't a primitive, because it can be written in terms of `hold` and `never`.

2.13 *Referential transparency dos and don'ts*

As we've said, it's important that all functions you pass to FRP primitives be pure, or referentially transparent. Table 2.1 lays this out and gives suggestions on what to do in situations that commonly arise.

Table 2.1   Referential transparency (which is important): some guidance in the face of temptation

Do / Don't	Explanation / Do instead
Don't read state from outside the function.	When dealing with streams: model your state as a cell, and capture its value with `snapshot`. When dealing with cells: model your state as a cell, and capture its value with `lift`. The test: for given input arguments, the function must always produce the same value.

Do read constants from outside the function.	If the function captures a value as a constant from the enclosing scope—that is, it can't change for the life of the function—this isn't state. We encourage constants:
	
	``java
	final double kmPerMile = 1.609344;
	Cell<Double> km = mi.map(mi_ -> mi_ * kmPerMile);
	``

Don't modify state visible outside the function.	When dealing with *streams*: place the value you want to write in a data structure or tuple along with the value you're already returning from the function, and then split the output stream in two using two `map`s. Feed the wanted stream into the `hold` of a cell.
	Example: let's say you have timestamped mouse events, and you want to extract the positions of mouse-down events:
	
	``java
	Stream<Point> sDown = sMouse
	    .filter(m -> m.type == MouseEvent.DOWN)
	    .map(m -> m.pos);
	``
	
	Now you want to record the timestamp of the last mouse down. You're not allowed to write directly to a variable. Here is how to follow our advice directly, although it can be shortened:
	
	``java
	Cell<new Tuple2<Point, Time>> sPair = sMouse
	    .filter(m -> m.type == MouseEvent.DOWN)
	    .map(m -> new Tuple2<Point, Time>(m.pos, m.time));
	Stream<Point> sDown = sPair.map(p -> p.a);
	Cell<Time> sLastTime = sPair.map(p -> p.b).hold(0);
	``
	
	When dealing with *cells*: the idea is the same as with streams. Tuple the values up, and split with two `map`s.
	If you want to output a stream, you can't. You aren't allowed to output a stream from a primitive that works on cells. State changes in cells aren't allowed to be converted to streams directly. If you're trying to do this, you should be using streams instead of cells.

Don't keep state between invocations of the function.	For given input values, the function must always produce the same output value. That means no internal state.
	When dealing with *streams*: keep your state in a cell, and `snapshot` it to read its value. To write back to the cell, tuple the update value up with whatever stream value you're returning from your function, and then split the output stream in two using two `map`s. Feed the update stream into the `hold` of the cell you're using to store the state.
	Example—suppose you're parsing some sort of network packet:
	
	``java
	Stream<Message> sMessage = sPkt.map(p -> parseMsg(p));
	``
	
	What if you want to add a unique ID to each message? You're not allowed to use an external variable directly. Instead, you do this:
	
	``java
	StreamLoop<Integer> sID = new StreamLoop<>();
	Cell<Integer> id = sID.hold(0);
	Stream<Tuple2<Message, Integer>> sPair = sPkt.snapshot(id,
	    (p, i) -> new Tuple2<Message, Integer>(
	        new Message(i, parseMsg(p)),
	        i+1));
	Stream<Message> sMessage = sPair.map(p -> p.a);
	sID.loop(sPair.map(p -> p.b));
	``
	
	When dealing with *cells*: if you need to initiate a state change from a cell primitive, you should be using streams, not cells.

Table 2.1 Referential transparency (which is important): some guidance in the face of temptation

Do / Don't	Explanation / Do instead
Don't do I/O.	To *write* to I/O: do it in a *listener* (to be covered in section 8.1). To *read* from I/O: push the value into a `StreamSink` or `CellSink` (also in section 8.1).
Don't throw exceptions.	Exceptions are OK if they're caught within the function and turned into a returned value, but you mustn't allow them to escape.
Do add debug traces.	Debug traces have no logical effect on the rest of a program, so they're acceptable and can be useful. FRP implementations make no guarantees about when and how often functions will be executed, so you may get some surprises.

We've said that all functions passed to FRP primitives must be referentially transparent, which means no direct contact with the outside world. This is important. FRP as we've presented so far is a closed universe.

Later we'll explain how to interface Sodium with the rest of your program, but we explained why we don't want you to do that too soon: we've presented you with a lot of unfamiliar material. We're concerned that if we show you things you're familiar with too early, you'll gravitate toward them. These are precisely the things we're trying to steer you away from in order to get you to think conceptually instead of operationally. We know you can swim, but you may not, and that's why we've thrown you in far from shore.

2.14 FRP cheat sheet

The 10 core primitives are shown in table 2.2. `map` and `switch` have stream and cell variants, but we're counting them as one each. We'll cover `sample` and `switch` in chapter 7.

Table 2.2 Table of primitives as they appear in the Java version of Sodium

Class	Outputs a stream	Outputs a cell	Outputs a value
Stream	`map()` `merge() / orElse()` `snapshot()` `filter()` `never / new Stream()`	`hold()`	
Cell	`switchS()`	`map()` `lift()` `new Cell(`*constant*`)` `switchC()`	`sample()`

These 10 primitives are made more powerful by helpers, which are built out of the primitives. Sodium provides some common helpers, but the design philosophy is minimalist. A lot of the power in FRP comes from the generalness of the helpers you write yourself. You can watch your code shrink as you introduce into your code more and more helpers specific to your particular problem. FRP facilitates code reuse.

Sodium emphasizes completeness and minimalism with enough practicality to make it suitable as a base infrastructure for large projects. Other FRP systems have different design philosophies. Some emphasize practicality, giving you lots of useful helpers, and some are designed to be used in a style that mixes FRP with standard programming approaches. You can mix it up with Sodium, too, but in order to provide strong guarantees, there's a clear delineation between the two paradigms.

We aren't trying to promote Sodium over any other FRP system. We've written Sodium so that FRP is available with a consistent API in a wide range of languages. Making it minimal and domain-agnostic helps with that goal.

2.15 *Summary*

- A *stream* is a stream of events, each consisting of a payload value. We also say that a *stream* has *fired*. Other names for *stream* include *event, event stream, observable,* and *signal.*

- map is a primitive that gives you a new stream or cell that modifies the contained value according to a specified function.

- Given two streams, merge gives you a stream that combines the events from both input streams.

- Two events are simultaneous if they occur within the same transaction. By default, in the simultaneous case with sLeft.orElse(sRight), the event from the sLeft argument takes precedence, and the sRight event is dropped. If you want to combine simultaneous events some other way, you can use sLeft.merge(sRight, f) with your own combining function f.

- A *cell* contains a value that changes over time. Other names for *cell* include *behavior, property,* and *signal.*

- hold constructs a cell that has an initial value, and changes its value according to the values fired at it by a stream.

- Given a stream and a cell, snapshot captures the cell's value when the stream fires and allows you to combine the two values (from the stream and the cell) using a specified function.

- filter gives you a new stream that lets only some of the events through, decided by a predicate (a function that returns a Boolean value).

- Give lift a function that works on two or more input values, and that number of cells, and it'll give you a cell that combines the input cells using the specified function. It's like map on a cell, but for more than one cell. It's called lift because it *lifts* a function into the world of cells.

- never gives a stream that never fires.

- constant gives a cell with a constant value.

- Functions that you pass to FRP primitives must be *referentially transparent*: they mustn't affect or be affected by the outside world, except through their arguments and return value.
- In Sodium, cell updates aren't visible in the cell until the next transaction. Other FRP systems may have different policies.
- We talked about looping things with `CellLoop` and `StreamLoop`, and how they can be used to implement accumulators. Other FRP systems can take different approaches to this.

Some everyday
widget stuff

3

This chapter covers

- Some simple GUI widget examples

We're using this short chapter to cement the concepts of FRP with two more simple SWidget examples. We're continuing to avoid telling you about StreamSink and CellSink for now so we can achieve a clear separation in your mind between FRP and non-FRP. We've talked about how people tend to gravitate toward familiar concepts—we don't want you saying, "I know how to do this" and mixing sinks into your FRP logic, because this breaks the model. We want you to see what becomes possible when you view streams and cells only as sources.

These examples use the same primitives introduced in chapter 2, so you may need to refer back to it to refresh your memory. Let's get started.

3.1 Spinner as a standalone SWidget

Let's take the spinner concept from the previous chapter and separate it out into a new SWidget. You'll also use a text field instead of a label so it's more useful. Figure 3.1 shows what it looks like after you click + once.

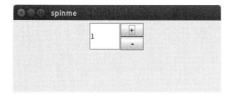

Figure 3.1   The spinner after clicking + once

The next listing shows the separated-out SSpinner class. We've left out the main program. It just constructs an SSpinner and adds it to the view. On the input and output side of the text field, you convert between integer and string using map.

Listing 3.1   SSpinner: your own spinner widget

```
import javax.swing.*;
import java.awt.*;
import swidgets.*;
import nz.sodium.*;

public class SSpinner extends JPanel {
    SSpinner(int initialValue) {
        StreamLoop<Integer> sSetValue = new StreamLoop<>();
        STextField textField = new STextField(
            sSetValue.map(v -> Integer.toString(v)),        ◁──┐ Converts integer to
            Integer.toString(initialValue),                     │ string for setting the
            5                                                   │ textField's text
        );
        this.value = textField.text.map(txt -> {            ◁── Converts textField's current
            try {                                               text to an integer to give
                return Integer.parseInt(txt);                   current spinner value
            }
            catch (NumberFormatException e) {
                return 0;
            }
        });
        SButton plus = new SButton("+");
        SButton minus = new Sbutton("-");

        setLayout(new GridBagLayout());
        add(textField, ...);
        add(plus, ...);                                     ◁──┐ Java layout
        add(minus, ...);                                        │ stuff omitted

        Stream<Integer> sPlusDelta = plus.sClicked.map(u -> 1);
        Stream<Integer> sMinusDelta = minus.sClicked.map(u -> -1);
        Stream<Integer> sDelta = sPlusDelta.orElse(sMinusDelta);
        sSetValue.loop(
            sDelta.snapshot(
                this.value,
                (delta, value) -> delta + value
            ));
    }

    public final Cell<Integer> value;
}
```

Size of text field ⊳ (annotation pointing to `5`)

Adds the delta to the current value ⊳ (annotation pointing to snapshot block)

Check this out with git, if you haven't done so already, and run it like this:

```
git clone https://github.com/SodiumFRP/sodium
cd sodium/book/swidgets/java
mvn test -Pspinme    or    ant spinme
```

3.2   Form validation

This chapter is about mundane, day-to-day widget programming, and widget programming doesn't get much more day-to-day than form validation. Let's expand on the theme of form validation with the flight-booking example from chapter 1. Form validation can be a tedious, bug-prone task, but FRP makes it straightforward.

Figure 3.2 shows the form with these rules:

- Name must be non-blank and contain at least one space.
- The number of email addresses must be in the range of 1–4.
- Only the selected number of email address fields is enabled.
- Emails must contain an @ character.

If a validation error occurs, it's shown in an SLabel to the right of the field with the error. The OK button is enabled only when the form is validated.

Figure 3.2   A form with validation rules

Listing 3.2 gives the form's field construction and validation logic. We've omitted the verbose Java layout.

There's a lot of FRP construction here, and it's all done in an explicit transaction as recommended in chapter 2. First you construct the validation rule for each field, giving a string where "" means it's valid. You can put this validation result into the dialog box using an SLabel.

In a for loop at the end, you map each validation result from a string to a Boolean cell (where true means the field is valid) and build a chain of lift operations to produce an allValid cell that is the logical *AND* of the Boolean valid result of each field. You pass this to the enabled argument of the SButton's constructor. Whenever all fields are valid, the OK button is enabled.

The FRP describes the validation rules, and all the work of keeping everything up-to-date is done for you.

```
Transaction.runVoid(() -> {
    final int maxEmails = 4;

    JLabel[] labels = new JLabel[maxEmails+2];
    JComponent[] fields = new JComponent[maxEmails+2];
    Cell<String>[] valids = (Cell<String>[])Array.newInstance(
        Cell.class, maxEmails+2);
    int row = 0;

    labels[row] = new JLabel("Name");
    STextField name = new STextField("", 30);
    fields[row] = name;
    valids[row] = name.text.map(t ->
        t.trim().equals("")        ? "<-- enter something" :
        t.trim().indexOf(' ') < 0 ? "<-- must contain space" :
                                   "");
    row++;

    labels[row] = new JLabel("No of email addresses");
    SSpinner number = new SSpinner(1);
    fields[row] = number;
    valids[row] = number.value.map(n ->
        n < 1 || n > maxEmails ? "<-- must be 1 to "+maxEmails
                               : "");
    row++;

    STextField[] emails = new STextField[maxEmails];
    for (int i = 0; i < maxEmails; i++, row++) {
        labels[row] = new JLabel("Email #"+(i+1));
        final int ii = i;
        Cell<Boolean> enabled = number.value.map(n -> ii < n);
        STextField email = new STextField("", 30, enabled);
        fields[row] = email;
        valids[row] = email.text.lift(number.value, (e, n) ->
                    ii >= n              ? "" :
                    e.trim().equals("") ? "<-- enter something" :
                    e.indexOf('@') < 0  ? "<-- must contain @" :
                                         "");
    }

    Cell<Boolean> allValid = new Cell<Boolean>(true);
    for (int i = 0; i < row; i++) {
        view.add(labels[i], ...);
        view.add(fields[i], ...);
        SLabel validLabel = new SLabel(valids[i]);
        view.add(validLabel, ...);
        Cell<Boolean> thisValid = valids[i].map(t -> t.equals(""));
        allValid = allValid.lift(thisValid, (a, b) -> a && b);
    }
    SButton ok = new SButton("OK", allValid);
    view.add(ok, ...);
});
```

Constructs the FRP in an explicit transaction

Java's way to construct an array of generic types

Each validation is an error message or " " when valid.

The first n email fields are enabled.

STextField is enabled according to a given Boolean cell.

Disabled fields don't fail validation.

Valid if the validation error is " "

Logical AND of each row's Boolean validity

The button is enabled if allValid is true.

Check this out with git, if you haven't done so already, and run it like this:

```
git clone https://github.com/SodiumFRP/sodium
cd sodium/book/swidgets/java
mvn test -Pformvalidation     or     ant formvalidation
```

3.3   *Summary*

FRP fits nicely into GUI programming, as illustrated with a couple of practical widget examples.

Writing a real application

We've introduced FRP with some contrived examples and shown you some more realistic GUI code. Now we want to show you how to write a real-world FRP application, this time in the industrial space. In this chapter, you'll develop a petrol pump.

It can be difficult to find the right example for FRP. FRP's pretensions to stardom conglomerate around the notion that it deals with complexity, but this doesn't manifest in a small example. If the example is too simple, you'll say, "That was a weird way of doing things for no apparent benefit." If the example is too big, it can be a lot of work for you. We chose the petrol pump idea to strike a balance: the size is about right, it should be easy to follow because it's a familiar real-world application, and the level of complexity is enough for our purpose.

> **NOTE** This chapter is dense, and we think it will repay the effort you spend on it, but you don't have to study it closely right now. If it fits your learning

style, feel free to read parts of it briefly, carry on with the book, and come back here later.

This example uses industry-standard development methodology: you'll add features one by one without much deliberate design. We've left out refactoring; refactoring is simple in FRP, and we'll cover this subject in chapter 13.

4.1 *The petrol pump example*

We understand that some parts of the United States have fancy gasoline pumps. This example uses the common or garden-variety petrol pump seen in more ordinary parts of the world.

Although the logic of a petrol pump may seem straightforward to someone using it, it's difficult enough to cause a few migraines for the programmer once you start stacking on the features. Fuel flows through a petrol pump into your car, but we're going to show you a petrol pump with data flowing through it, too. It's useful to view FRP programs as flows of data, and that's why FRP is sometimes put under the heading of *data flow programming*.

The petrol pump has the following features:

- Three nozzles for three fuels
- Three price displays
- Displays for dollars paid and liters of petrol delivered (we're using metric volume measurements, as do most countries other than the United States)
- A keypad and display for a preset dollar amount
- A beeper
- A means of communication with the point-of-sale system

Figure 4.1 shows the petrol pump's user interface. The user experience is simple: when you lift one of the three nozzles, the nozzle you lifted selects which fuel to deliver. The simulator then pretends to be the mechanical parts of the pump and causes imaginary fuel to begin flowing. This book won't cover the code for the UI graphics and simulated mechanics; we'll only concern ourselves with the application logic. But you can download the source code and look at it if you like.

NOTE The petrol pump's three fuels are strawberry, lime, and kerosene.

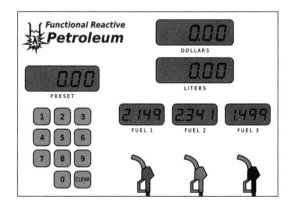

Figure 4.1 Petrol pump user interface

A real petrol pump nozzle has a mechanical trigger so you can make the fuel flow only when you've put the nozzle in the car, but the simulator acts as if this is always on, so the fuel will start flowing as soon as the nozzle is lifted. As the fill progresses, you see a running total of dollars and liters delivered, as shown in figure 4.2.

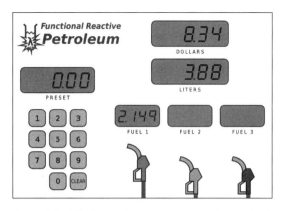

Figure 4.2   Lift the nozzle, and you see running totals of liters of simulated fuel and dollars spent as you fill your imaginary car.

Figure 4.3 shows that when you hang up the nozzle, the fuel flow stops, and a message is sent to the point-of-sale system. This is simulated with a dialog box that pops up. When you click OK, the fill values are cleared, and the pump returns to its initial state.

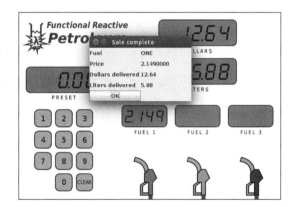

Figure 4.3   When you hang up the nozzle, the sale details are sent to the point-of-sale system.

The pump has one other feature: you can enter a preset value on the keypad, which then appears in the display on the left. When you get near to the preset dollar value, the fuel flow slows down, and when you reach it, the fuel flow stops. See figure 4.4.

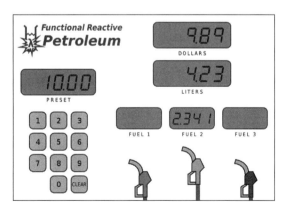

Figure 4.4   The petrol pump's flow slows down when you approach the preset dollar amount.

4.2   *Running the petrol pump example*

To run the petrol pump example, check it out if you haven't done so already, and run it with these commands:

```
git clone https://github.com/SodiumFRP/sodium
cd sodium/book/petrol-pump/java
mvn test    or    ant run
```

At the top of the window, you can select which pump logic you want to run from those given in the book. Please confirm your understanding of how the code works by trying the examples; we encourage you to play with the code.

4.3   *Code, meet outside world*

Each version of the petrol pump logic is an implementation of the interface given in listing 4.1, where Inputs and Outputs are simple container classes with Stream and Cell type fields. Each class that implements Pump creates the machinery that connects the inputs to the outputs; all the logic you'll need can be done in this way. When you run the simulator, you can select which pump logic you want to run in a drop-down box at the top.

Listing 4.1   Interface for the petrol pump logic

```
package pump;

public interface Pump {
    public Outputs create(Inputs inputs);
}
```

Figure 4.5 is a diagrammatic representation of the inputs and outputs of the pump logic encapsulated by Inputs and Outputs, and how they connect to things in the real world.

Listing 4.2 shows Inputs. These are the input streams:

- sNozzle1, sNozzle2, sNozzle3—For each of the three fuels, a stream that fires when the nozzle is lifted (signaling the start of a fill) or hung up.
- sKeypad—A stream representing a press of one of the buttons on the preset keypad, used to enter the fill amount. Key is an enumerated type identifying which button was pressed.
- sFuelPulses—Pulses counted through the fuel-flow meter. The event payload is an integer number of pulses counted since the last event.
- sClearSale—A signal sent from the point of sale once payment is completed, to unlock the pump for the next fill.

The input cells are as follows:

- calibration—The multiplier to turn pulses into liters
- price1, price2, price3—The price of each of the three fuels in dollars per liter

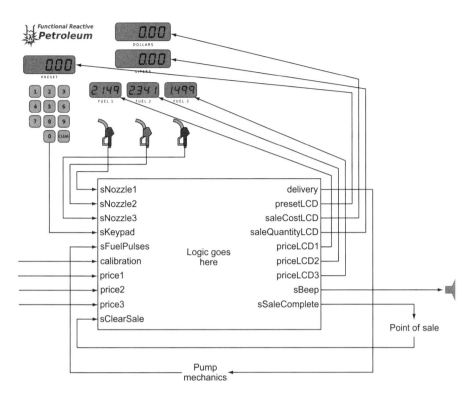

Figure 4.5 The interface between the pump logic and the (simulated) outside world

Java forces you to write a bit of container-class boilerplate here, but we've given the entire code in listing 4.2 to make sure it's clear.

Immutability is extremely important in FRP, so you make all the fields `final`, which means they can only be modified in the constructor. This is a good habit, and you should follow it whenever you can. In your FRP code, you can do this all the time.

Listing 4.2 Inputs to the petrol pump logic

```java
package pump;

import nz.sodium.*;

public class Inputs {
    public Inputs(
            Stream<UpDown> sNozzle1,
            Stream<UpDown> sNozzle2,
            Stream<UpDown> sNozzle3,
            Stream<Key> sKeypad,
            Stream<Integer> sFuelPulses,
            Cell<Double> calibration,
```

```
            Cell<Double> price1,
            Cell<Double> price2,
            Cell<Double> price3,
            Stream<Unit> sClearSale) {
        this.sNozzle1 = sNozzle1;
        this.sNozzle2 = sNozzle2;
        this.sNozzle3 = sNozzle3;
        this.sKeypad = sKeypad;
        this.sFuelPulses = sFuelPulses;
        this.calibration = calibration;
        this.price1 = price1;
        this.price2 = price2;
        this.price3 = price3;
        this.sClearSale = sClearSale;
    }

    public final Stream<UpDown> sNozzle1;
    public final Stream<UpDown> sNozzle2;
    public final Stream<UpDown> sNozzle3;
    public final Stream<Key> sKeypad;
    public final Stream<Integer> sFuelPulses;
    public final Cell<Double> calibration;
    public final Cell<Double> price1;
    public final Cell<Double> price2;
    public final Cell<Double> price3;
    public final Stream<Unit> sClearSale;
}
```

Listing 4.3 shows the outputs. The output streams are as follows:

- sBeep—When this stream fires, the simulator emits a short beep.
- sSaleComplete—A message that's sent to the point-of-sale system giving the details of the sale once it's complete. Recall the input stream sClearSale: the simulated point of sale uses this to convey a response back from the point of sale to clear the sale and unlock the pump for the next fill.

The output cells are as follows:

- delivery—Specifies whether to deliver fuel and, if so, which fuel and at what speed. Values: OFF, SLOW1, FAST1, SLOW2, FAST2, SLOW3, and FAST3.
- presetLCD—The LCD that appears above the keypad in which you can enter a preset dollar amount.
- saleCostLCD—Displays the dollars spent.
- saleQuantityLCD—Displays the liters delivered.
- priceLCD1, priceLCD2, priceLCD3—Displays the price for each fuel.

You're writing the set methods in an unusual way: each method returns a copy of the structure, replacing one field's value (shown in bold). You're doing this to make the data structure immutable, meaning it can't be modified in place. Then you know the values contained in it can't be changed. This makes the code easier to reason about and preserves *compositionality*. This technique also makes the examples easier to read because you only have to specify the fields you care about; the rest can be left as defaults. We don't recommend that you use this pattern all the time, but it can often be useful.

NOTE Copying the entire data structure to modify one field may feel inefficient, but it's not as inefficient as you may think. This pattern isn't absolutely needed, but we recommend it as a way of making sure you do things the right way. When performance considerations drive software design, the result is usually bad. In fact, most assumptions that people make about performance turn out to be incorrect. For this reason, performance decisions should almost always be made on the basis of profiling.

Listing 4.3 Outputs from the petrol pump logic

```java
package pump;

import nz.sodium.*;

public class Outputs {
    private Outputs(
            Cell<Delivery> delivery,
            Cell<String> presetLCD,
            Cell<String> saleCostLCD,
            Cell<String> saleQuantityLCD,
            Cell<String> priceLCD1,
            Cell<String> priceLCD2,
            Cell<String> priceLCD3,
            Stream<Unit> sBeep,
            Stream<Sale> sSaleComplete) {
        this.delivery = delivery;
        this.presetLCD = presetLCD;
        this.saleCostLCD = saleCostLCD;
        this.saleQuantityLCD = saleQuantityLCD;
        this.priceLCD1 = priceLCD1;
        this.priceLCD2 = priceLCD2;
        this.priceLCD3 = priceLCD3;
        this.sBeep = sBeep;
        this.sSaleComplete = sSaleComplete;
    }

    public Outputs() {
        this.delivery = new Cell<Delivery>(Delivery.OFF);
        this.presetLCD = new Cell<String>("");
        this.saleCostLCD = new Cell<String>("");
        this.saleQuantityLCD = new Cell<String>("");
        this.priceLCD1 = new Cell<String>("");
        this.priceLCD2 = new Cell<String>("");
        this.priceLCD3 = new Cell<String>("");
        this.sBeep = new Stream<Unit>();
        this.sSaleComplete = new Stream<Sale>();
    }
```

```java
public final Cell<Delivery> delivery;
public final Cell<String> presetLCD;
public final Cell<String> saleCostLCD;
public final Cell<String> saleQuantityLCD;
public final Cell<String> priceLCD1;
public final Cell<String> priceLCD2;
public final Cell<String> priceLCD3;
public final Stream<Unit> sBeep;
public final Stream<Sale> sSaleComplete;

public Outputs setDelivery(Cell<Delivery> delivery) {
    return new Outputs(delivery, presetLCD, saleCostLCD,
            saleQuantityLCD, priceLCD1, priceLCD2, priceLCD3, sBeep,
            sSaleComplete);
}
public Outputs setPresetLCD(Cell<String> presetLCD) {
    return new Outputs(delivery, presetLCD, saleCostLCD,
            saleQuantityLCD, priceLCD1, priceLCD2, priceLCD3, sBeep,
            sSaleComplete);
}
public Outputs setSaleCostLCD(Cell<String> saleCostLCD) {
    return new Outputs(delivery, presetLCD, saleCostLCD,
            saleQuantityLCD, priceLCD1, priceLCD2, priceLCD3, sBeep,
            sSaleComplete);
}
public Outputs setSaleQuantityLCD(Cell<String> saleQuantityLCD) {
    return new Outputs(delivery, presetLCD, saleCostLCD,
            saleQuantityLCD, priceLCD1, priceLCD2, priceLCD3, sBeep,
            sSaleComplete);
}
public Outputs setPriceLCD1(Cell<String> priceLCD1) {
    return new Outputs(delivery, presetLCD, saleCostLCD,
            saleQuantityLCD, priceLCD1, priceLCD2, priceLCD3, sBeep,
            sSaleComplete);
}
public Outputs setPriceLCD2(Cell<String> priceLCD2) {
    return new Outputs(delivery, presetLCD, saleCostLCD,
            saleQuantityLCD, priceLCD1, priceLCD2, priceLCD3, sBeep,
            sSaleComplete);
}
public Outputs setPriceLCD3(Cell<String> priceLCD3) {
    return new Outputs(delivery, presetLCD, saleCostLCD,
            saleQuantityLCD, priceLCD1, priceLCD2, priceLCD3, sBeep,
            sSaleComplete);
}
public Outputs setBeep(Stream<Unit> sBeep) {
    return new Outputs(delivery, presetLCD, saleCostLCD,
            saleQuantityLCD, priceLCD1, priceLCD2, priceLCD3, sBeep,
            sSaleComplete);
}
public Outputs setSaleComplete(Stream<Sale> sSaleComplete) {
    return new Outputs(delivery, presetLCD, saleCostLCD,
            saleQuantityLCD, priceLCD1, priceLCD2, priceLCD3, sBeep,
            sSaleComplete);
}
}
```

4.4　*The life cycle of a petrol pump fill*

Now you now know about the `map`, `merge`, `hold`, `snapshot`, `filter`, `lift`, `never`, and `constant` primitives. That's all you need to build the petrol pump. There are only two core primitives to go: `sample` and `switch`. You don't need them for this example, so we'll get to them in chapter 7.

The first thing you'll do is translate the nozzle input events into the life cycle of a pump fill, as shown in figure 4.6. The outputs are as follows:

- `sStart`—A stream indicating the start of the fill
- `fillActive`—A cell telling you whether a fill is currently active and, if so, what fuel was selected
- `sEnd`—A stream indicating the end of the fill

Here are the requirements:

- When a nozzle is lifted, you select a fuel depending on the nozzle that was chosen.
- When that nozzle (and only that nozzle) is hung up, the fill ends. The other two nozzles are ignored while the fill is in progress.

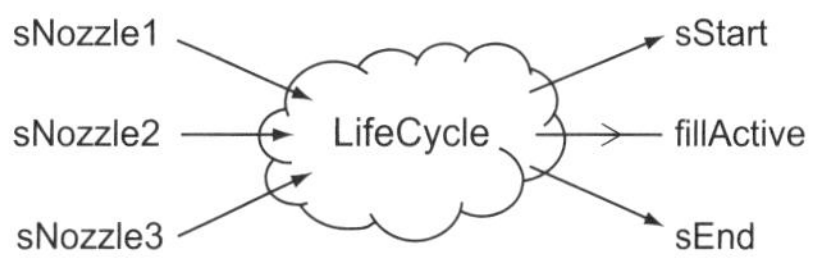

Figure 4.6　Inputs and outputs of a `LifeCycle` class

As we mentioned, `fillActive` is a cell representing whether you're filling or not. Its type is `Cell<Optional<Fuel>>`, using Java 8's `Optional` type (see the following sidebar), and an enum called `Fuel`, identifying which fuel was selected. The possible values of `fillActive` are these:

- `Optional.empty()`—You aren't filling.
- `Optional.of(fuel)`—You're filling, and the selected fuel is `fuel`.

Java 8's Optional type

Java 8 defines a new class called `Optional` under `java.util`. It takes a type parameter. `Optional<A>` represents a nullable value of type `A`; that is, either it contains a value of type `A` or it has a "nothing" value.

It's a replacement for the traditional approach of using a `null` reference. If you consistently use `Optional` instead of `null`, then whether a value is nullable is captured in the type; thus it's much harder to accidentally forget to deal with the `null` case. Forgetting to check for `null` is a common source of bugs. Tony Hoare, who invented the `null` reference in 1965, calls it his "billion dollar mistake."

We won't go into any more detail here. If this doesn't explain things well enough, online resources will probably be all you need. We're not trying to be Java 8 power users, but a couple of Java 8 features turn out to be compelling for our purposes. For a more complete treatment of Java 8, see *Java 8 in Action* by Raoul-Gabriel Urma, Mario Fusco, and Alan Mycroft (Manning, 2014, www.manning.com/books/java-8-in-action).

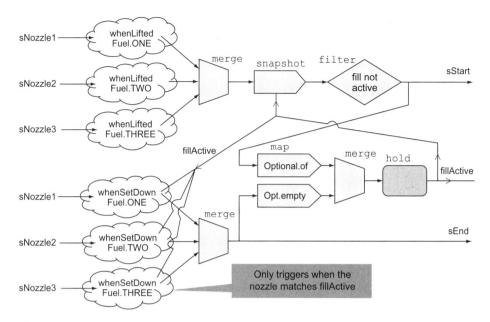

Figure 4.7 Conceptual overview of the logic for `LifeCycle`

Figure 4.7 zooms in on the implementation of `LifeCycle` in the style of one of the familiar conceptual diagrams from chapter 2. You've seen each of the primitives used already, but now more of them are put together.

We've left some of the logic out of this diagram and drawn it as clouds or black boxes. We haven't diagrammed these two, so look at how they're implemented as methods in the code:

- `whenLifted`—Takes a constant value of a fuel number (`ONE`, `TWO`, or `THREE`), and, when that nozzle is lifted, outputs that constant.
- `whenSetDown`—Also takes a constant fuel number. In addition, looks at `fillActive`, the currently selected fuel, and only outputs an event if a fill is active and the nozzle that was set down matches the fuel of the current fill.

Here's the flow of events when nozzle 1 is lifted:

1 The stream returned by `whenLifted(Fuel.ONE)` outputs an event containing the value `Fuel.ONE`.
2 This event causes a snapshot of the current value of `fillActive` and is filtered so that it only outputs the fuel number if there isn't already a fill active. This is exported as the stream `sStart`.
3 `sStart` feeds through a `map` that wraps the event value inside an `Optional` type so the value becomes `Optional.of(Fuel.ONE)`.
4 This is held by `fillActive` so the fill state becomes active with a selected fuel of `Fuel.ONE`.

When nozzle 1 is set back down, this happens:

- whenSetDown(Fuel.ONE) checks that a fill is active on Fuel.ONE, and, if so, it outputs an event. This is exported as the stream sEnd.
- sEnd then feeds through a map that turns it into an Optional value of Optional.empty().
- This is held by fillActive so the fill state becomes inactive.

4.4.1 *Code for LifeCycle*

This section presents two classes. The logic is given in the LifeCycle class in listing 4.4. A bit later, listing 4.5 will give a second class, LifeCyclePump, that connects the logic to the pump inputs and outputs so you can run it.

Whenever you want to get an initial understanding of an FRP-based class or method, we suggest you start by looking at what the inputs and outputs are, with an understanding of the stated intent. Then, slowly examine how the inputs are transformed into outputs.

Fuel is an enum defined like this, used to identify which of the three fuel nozzles was selected:

```
public enum Fuel { ONE, TWO, THREE }
```

If you look at the code, you can see that sStart and sEnd depend on fillActive, which depends back on sStart and sEnd. As we discussed in chapter 2, CellLoop is the magic trick to deal with these cyclic dependencies.

Recall that StreamLoop and CellLoop must be loop()ed in the same transaction as they're constructed. In this example, we've made this issue go away: the petrol pump simulator main program—which we haven't listed in the book—wraps the invocation of create() in a transaction. This is how we always recommend constructing FRP logic, and you should normally assume this for any FRP construction code.

> **NOTE** This code uses a variant of filter that you haven't seen much of yet: filterOptional. It takes a Stream<Optional<A>> and gives a Stream<A>. Java 8's Optional is useful again. Where the value is present, filterOptional unwraps the value and propagates it to the new stream as a value of type A. Events where the value is empty are filtered out (they don't propagate). Because the input stream has an Optional type, Java won't let you declare it as a method of Stream; it's a static method, instead, and hence Stream .filterOptional(..).

Listing 4.4 Life cycle of a petrol pump fill

```
package chapter4.section4;

import pump.*;
import nz.sodium.*;
import java.util.Optional;
```

```
public class LifeCycle {
    public final Stream<Fuel> sStart;
    public final Cell<Optional<Fuel>> fillActive;
    public final Stream<End> sEnd;

    public enum End { END }

    private static Stream<Fuel> whenLifted(Stream<UpDown> sNozzle,
                                           Fuel nozzleFuel) {
        return sNozzle.filter(u -> u == UpDown.UP)
                .map(u -> nozzleFuel);
    }

    private static Stream<End> whenSetDown(Stream<UpDown> sNozzle,
                Fuel nozzleFuel,
                Cell<Optional<Fuel>> fillActive) {
        return Stream.<End>filterOptional(
            sNozzle.snapshot(fillActive,
                (u,f) -> u == UpDown.DOWN &&
                        f.equals(Optional.of(nozzleFuel))
                                    ? Optional.of(End.END)
                                    : Optional.empty()));
    }

    public LifeCycle(Stream<UpDown> sNozzle1,
                     Stream<UpDown> sNozzle2,
                     Stream<UpDown> sNozzle3) {
        Stream<Fuel> sLiftNozzle =
            whenLifted(sNozzle1, Fuel.ONE).orElse(
            whenLifted(sNozzle2, Fuel.TWO).orElse(
            whenLifted(sNozzle3, Fuel.THREE)));
        CellLoop<Optional<Fuel>> fillActive = new CellLoop<>();
        this.fillActive = fillActive;
        this.sStart = Stream.filterOptional(
            sLiftNozzle.snapshot(fillActive, (newFuel, fillActive_) ->
                fillActive_.isPresent() ? Optional.empty()
                                    : Optional.of(newFuel)));
        this.sEnd = whenSetDown(sNozzle1, Fuel.ONE, fillActive).orElse(
                whenSetDown(sNozzle2, Fuel.TWO, fillActive).orElse(
                whenSetDown(sNozzle3, Fuel.THREE, fillActive)));
        fillActive.loop(
            sEnd.map(e -> Optional.<Fuel>empty())
                .orElse(sStart.map(f -> Optional.of(f)))
                .hold(Optional.empty())
        );
    }
}
```

If a fill is active, identifies the selected fuel

Start of the fill stream

End of the fill stream

Only allows "up" to pass through from up/down events

Outputs what fuel this nozzle corresponds to

End instead of Unit for type safety

Only the nozzle matching the current fill can end the fill.

This stream fires when a nozzle is lifted, along with an identifier of which nozzle it was.

Declares a fillActive forward reference

Start of fill can only happen when a fill isn't already in progress.

Checks each nozzle to see if it's ending the fill

Cleared at the end of the fill

fillActive implementation

fillActive is set to the selected fuel at the start of the fill.

The next listing gives a petrol pump logic implementation that tests this out. Try it in the pump simulator, and you'll see that the number 1, 2, or 3 appears on the Liters display to indicate which nozzle has been lifted.

Listing 4.5 Petrol pump implementation that demonstrates `LifeCycle`

```
package chapter4.section4;

import pump.*;
import nz.sodium.*;
import java.util.Optional;

public class LifeCyclePump implements Pump {
    public Outputs create(Inputs inputs) {
        LifeCycle lc = new LifeCycle(inputs.sNozzle1,
                                    inputs.sNozzle2,
                                    inputs.sNozzle3);
        return new Outputs()
            .setDelivery(lc.fillActive.map(
                of ->
                    of.equals(Optional.of(Fuel.ONE))    ? Delivery.FAST1 :
                    of.equals(Optional.of(Fuel.TWO))    ? Delivery.FAST2 :
                    of.equals(Optional.of(Fuel.THREE))  ? Delivery.FAST3 :
                                                          Delivery.OFF))
            .setSaleQuantityLCD(lc.fillActive.map(
                of ->
                    of.equals(Optional.of(Fuel.ONE))    ? "1" :
                    of.equals(Optional.of(Fuel.TWO))    ? "2" :
                    of.equals(Optional.of(Fuel.THREE))  ? "3" : ""));
    }
}
```

Turns on the motor when a fuel is selected ← (annotation pointing to `.setDelivery`)

Displays which fuel was selected → (annotation pointing to `.setSaleQuantityLCD`)

Take this code for a spin. You've probably already checked it out, so you won't need the `git` line, but here's the complete list of commands:

```
git clone https://github.com/SodiumFRP/sodium
cd sodium/book/petrol-pump/java
mvn test    or    ant run
```

4.5   Is this really better?

The way you write code with FRP is different than the normal way of writing it. You're probably wondering why we think this is better. The code isn't shorter; it's a bit verbose, if anything.

We want to say two things at this point: first, remember that we emphasized that FRP provides improvements as a program becomes larger. In a small example, the advantage isn't apparent—there aren't enough edge cases to bite you.

Second, when expressed directly in general programming languages, FRP syntax is a bit clunky. There's a lot of potential for improvement with preprocessors and such things, but FRP is still new and this work hasn't been done. We'll return to the topic of syntax in chapter 15.

4.6   *Counting liters delivered*

Figure 4.8 shows the conceptual view of an `accumulate()` method you'll use to count
liters delivered. `accumulate()` adds the new pulses coming in `sDelta` to the snapshotted existing total and `holds` the result, looping the whole thing with a `CellLoop`.

It also has a bit of logic to clear the value at the start of the fill. To do this, you
merge an extra stream `sClearAccumulator` into the snapshot-hold loop that can set
the value to 0. `accumulate()` finally applies a calibration to convert the pulse count
`total` to a liter count.

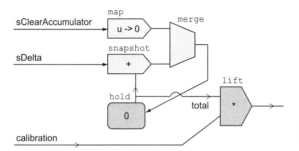

**Figure 4.8   Conceptual view of the
`accumulate()` method**

The `create()` method in the following listing gives a petrol pump implementation
that displays the liters delivered on the LCD. As with all the examples, you can try it by
running the pump simulator.

Listing 4.6   Counting liters delivered

```
package chapter4.section6;

import pump.*;
import chapter4.section4.LifeCycle;
import nz.sodium.*;
import java.util.Optional;

public class AccumulatePulsesPump implements Pump {
    public Outputs create(Inputs inputs) {
        LifeCycle lc = new LifeCycle(inputs.sNozzle1,
                                     inputs.sNozzle2,
                                     inputs.sNozzle3);
        Cell<Double> litersDelivered =
            accumulate(lc.sStart.map(u -> Unit.UNIT),          // Clears total
                       inputs.sFuelPulses,                     // on fill start
                       inputs.calibration);
        return new Outputs()
            .setDelivery(lc.fillActive.map(                    // Delivers the
                of ->                                          // selected fuel
                    of.equals(Optional.of(Fuel.ONE))  ? Delivery.FAST1 :
                    of.equals(Optional.of(Fuel.TWO))  ? Delivery.FAST2 :
```

```
                        of.equals(Optional.of(Fuel.THREE)) ? Delivery.FAST3 :
                                                            Delivery.OFF))
            .setSaleQuantityLCD(litersDelivered.map(
                q -> Formatters.formatSaleQuantity(q)));
    }

    public static Cell<Double> accumulate(
            Stream<Unit> sClearAccumulator,
            Stream<Integer> sPulses,
            Cell<Double> calibration) {
        CellLoop<Integer> total = new CellLoop<>();
        total.loop(sClearAccumulator.map(u -> 0)
            .orElse(
                sPulses.snapshot(total, (pulses_, total_) ->
                    pulses_ + total_)
            )
            .hold(0));
        return total.lift(calibration,
            (total_, calibration_) -> total_ * calibration_);
    }
}
```

Displays liters delivered — (arrow to `.setSaleQuantityLCD` line)

Accumulates pulses — (arrow to `sPulses.snapshot` line)

Zeroes the pulse count on sClearAccumulator — (arrow to `total.loop(sClearAccumulator.map(u -> 0)` line)

Multiplies by calibration to give liters — (arrow to `return total.lift` line)

4.7 Showing dollars of fuel delivered

Now you want to show the number of dollars of fuel delivered along with liters delivered, and you'll factor the logic for this out into a new class called `Fill`. Figure 4.9 shows the conceptual view of `Fill`. Here are the inputs:

- `sClearAccumulator`—The mechanism for clearing the accumulator
- `sFuelPulses`—Pulses from the flow meter
- `calibration`—The conversion from pulse count to liters
- `price1, price2, price3`—The prices for the three fuels
- `sFuelPulses`—An event for the start of the fill, identifying the fuel that was selected

Most of `Fill`'s work is done by `accumulate()`, which we gave in the last section, and `capturePrice()`, which we'll describe next. Finally, you multiply `litersDelivered` by price to give `dollarsDelivered`.

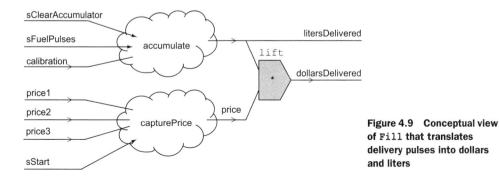

Figure 4.9 Conceptual view of Fill that translates delivery pulses into dollars and liters

Listing 4.7 gives the code for the `Fill` class. When a group of FRP statements corresponds to something at a conceptual level, it's both easy and a good idea to separate them out into a module, which can be implemented as a method or a class. `capturePrice()` is an example of a module implemented as a method. In Java, it's easiest to use a static method if there's one output or a class if more than one. We'll return to the subject of modules shortly.

NOTE Making the parameters distinct types will help you avoid making mistakes. For example, you could create a `Dollars` type instead of using `Double`, although we haven't done this here. In some languages, you can use named parameters. You can also use simple container objects to group things together, as we've done with `Inputs` and `Outputs`.

Listing 4.7   State and logic for the fill

```
package chapter4.section7;

import pump.*;
import chapter4.section6.AccumulatePulsesPump;
import nz.sodium.*;
import java.util.Optional;

public class Fill {
    public final Cell<Double> price;
    public final Cell<Double> dollarsDelivered;
    public final Cell<Double> litersDelivered;

    public Fill(
            Stream<Unit> sClearAccumulator, Stream<Integer> sFuelPulses,
            Cell<Double> calibration, Cell<Double> price1,
            Cell<Double> price2, Cell<Double> price3,
            Stream<Fuel> sStart) {
        price = capturePrice(sStart, price1, price2, price3);
        litersDelivered = AccumulatePulsesPump.accumulate(
                sClearAccumulator, sFuelPulses, calibration);
        dollarsDelivered = litersDelivered.lift(price,
                (liters, price_) -> liters * price_);
    }

    public static Cell<Double> capturePrice(
            Stream<Fuel> sStart,
            Cell<Double> price1, Cell<Double> price2,
            Cell<Double> price3) {
        Stream<Double> sPrice1 = Stream.filterOptional(
            sStart.snapshot(price1,
                (f, p) -> f == Fuel.ONE ? Optional.of(p)
                                        : Optional.empty()));
        Stream<Double> sPrice2 = Stream.filterOptional(
            sStart.snapshot(price2,
                (f, p) -> f == Fuel.TWO ? Optional.of(p)
                                        : Optional.empty()));
```

Price as it was when the fill started

Multiplies liters by price to give dollars

Captures price1 if Fuel.ONE was selected

```
            Stream<Double> sPrice3 = Stream.filterOptional(
                sStart.snapshot(price3,
                    (f, p) -> f == Fuel.THREE ? Optional.of(p)
                                              : Optional.empty()));

        return sPrice1.orElse(sPrice2.orElse(sPrice3))
                      .hold(0.0);
    }
}
```

The first thing you do in `Fill` is call `capturePrice()` to capture the price as it was when the fuel was selected. In `capturePrice()`, you snapshot each price, taking the value only where you match the right fuel selected. You `merge` these together with `orElse()` and then `filterOptional` so you get the `Optional` value only when it has a value. You must maintain state here: you need to know the price throughout the fill, so you `hold` the captured price in a cell.

Finally, as discussed, you calculate and return dollars spent. This is the same idea as in the previous section, where you multiplied pulses by calibration to give liters delivered.

The next listing shows the pump implementation that uses the new `Fill` class.

Listing 4.8 Petrol pump that shows dollars

```
package chapter4.section7;

import pump.*;
import chapter4.section4.LifeCycle;
import nz.sodium.*;
import java.util.Optional;

public class ShowDollarsPump implements Pump {
    public Outputs create(Inputs inputs) {
        LifeCycle lc = new LifeCycle(inputs.sNozzle1,
                                     inputs.sNozzle2,
                                     inputs.sNozzle3);
        Fill fi = new Fill(lc.sStart.map(u -> Unit.UNIT),
                           inputs.sFuelPulses, inputs.calibration,
                           inputs.price1, inputs.price2, inputs.price3,
                           lc.sStart);
        return new Outputs()
            .setDelivery(lc.fillActive.map(
                of ->
                    of.equals(Optional.of(Fuel.ONE))   ? Delivery.FAST1 :
                    of.equals(Optional.of(Fuel.TWO))   ? Delivery.FAST2 :
                    of.equals(Optional.of(Fuel.THREE)) ? Delivery.FAST3 :
                                                         Delivery.OFF))
            .setSaleCostLCD(fi.dollarsDelivered.map(
                q -> Formatters.formatSaleCost(q)))
            .setSaleQuantityLCD(fi.litersDelivered.map(
                q -> Formatters.formatSaleQuantity(q)))
            .setPriceLCD1(priceLCD(lc.fillActive, fi.price, Fuel.ONE,
                inputs))
```

Constructs the new **Fill** class (previous listing)

```
        .setPriceLCD2(priceLCD(lc.fillActive, fi.price, Fuel.TWO,
            inputs))
        .setPriceLCD3(priceLCD(lc.fillActive, fi.price, Fuel.THREE,
            inputs));
}

public static Cell<String> priceLCD(
        Cell<Optional<Fuel>> fillActive,
        Cell<Double> fillPrice,                        ◁──┐ Captured price
        Fuel fuel,                                         │ for the fill
        Inputs inputs) {
    Cell<Double> idlePrice;                            ◁──┐ Price to show
    switch (fuel) {                                        │ when not filling
        case ONE:   idlePrice = inputs.price1; break;
        case TWO:   idlePrice = inputs.price2; break;
        case THREE: idlePrice = inputs.price3; break;
        default:    idlePrice = null;
    }
    return fillActive.lift(fillPrice, idlePrice,
        (oFuelSelected, fillPrice_, idlePrice_) ->
            oFuelSelected.isPresent()
                ? oFuelSelected.get() == fuel               Prices for fuels not
                    ? Formatters.formatPrice(fillPrice_)    selected are blank
                    : ""                               ◁──  during the fill.
                : Formatters.formatPrice(idlePrice_)); ◁──┐
    }                                                      │ When not filling
}
```

Shows captured price when filling → (points to fillPrice_ line)

As always, please try this example out.

4.8   *Communicating with the point-of-sale system*

In this section, you'll communicate asynchronously with a remote point-of-sale system through two streams:

- sSaleComplete—An output stream telling the point-of-sale system that a sale has completed
- sClearSale—An input stream telling the pump that the point-of-sale system has finished processing the sale and the pump is allowed to process a new fill

Between these two events, you lock the pump so it can't fill any more. This complicates the definition of when the fill begins and ends. You now have three state transitions:

- Lifting the nozzle to start a fill
- Hanging up the nozzle to end a fill and notifying the point-of-sale system
- Clearing the sale at the point-of-sale system

Listing 4.9 gives the petrol pump implementation, and listing 4.10 shows the new NotifyPointOfSale. To make the code robust, you use scoping: you ensure that the LifeCycle is passed directly to new NotifyPointOfSale so it isn't hanging around in a variable visible in create(). NotifyPointOfSale can then output a modified view of the fill life cycle, and it's difficult for you to use the original life cycle by mistake. Limiting scope in various ways is an important key to avoiding bugs in FRP code.

If you view the petrol pump conceptually, point-of-sale communications are a concept in that view. Thus it makes sense for you to put the logic that pertains to it into a `NotifyPointOfSale` module (that is, class). FRP code is naturally loosely coupled, so it leaves you free to arrange the order and grouping of FRP statements to fit a conceptual view of the logic.

Listing 4.9 Pump implementation in which you clear the sale

```
package chapter4.section8;

import pump.*;
import chapter4.section4.LifeCycle;
import chapter4.section7.Fill;
import chapter4.section7.ShowDollarsPump;
import nz.sodium.*;
import java.util.Optional;

public class ClearSalePump implements Pump {
    public Outputs create(Inputs inputs) {
        StreamLoop<Fuel> sStart = new StreamLoop<>();
        Fill fi = new Fill(
                        inputs.sClearSale.map(u -> Unit.UNIT),
                        inputs.sFuelPulses, inputs.calibration,
                        inputs.price1, inputs.price2, inputs.price3,
                        sStart);
        NotifyPointOfSale np = new NotifyPointOfSale(
                    new LifeCycle(inputs.sNozzle1,
                                  inputs.sNozzle2,
                                  inputs.sNozzle3),
                    inputs.sClearSale,
                    fi);
        sStart.loop(np.sStart);
        return new Outputs()
            .setDelivery(np.fuelFlowing.map(
                of ->
                    of.equals(Optional.of(Fuel.ONE))   ? Delivery.FAST1 :
                    of.equals(Optional.of(Fuel.TWO))   ? Delivery.FAST2 :
                    of.equals(Optional.of(Fuel.THREE)) ? Delivery.FAST3 :
                                                         Delivery.OFF))
            .setSaleCostLCD(fi.dollarsDelivered.map(
                q -> Formatters.formatSaleCost(q)))
            .setSaleQuantityLCD(fi.litersDelivered.map(
                q -> Formatters.formatSaleQuantity(q)))
            .setPriceLCD1(ShowDollarsPump.priceLCD(np.fillActive, fi.price,
                    Fuel.ONE, inputs))
            .setPriceLCD2(ShowDollarsPump.priceLCD(np.fillActive, fi.price,
                    Fuel.TWO, inputs))
            .setPriceLCD3(ShowDollarsPump.priceLCD(np.fillActive, fi.price,
                    Fuel.THREE, inputs))
            .setBeep(np.sBeep)
            .setSaleComplete(np.sSaleComplete);
    }
}
```

The accumulator is cleared by the point-of-sale system instead of when the nozzle is lifted.

NotifyPointOfSale()'s implementation of sStart

Constructs point-of-sale logic (next listing)

Listing 4.10 shows the `NotifyPointOfSale` class. In a cell called `phase`, you keep track of the three phases of a fill: idle, filling and waiting for the point-of-sale system. We represent these with an enum:

```
private enum Phase { IDLE, FILLING, POS };
```

`gate()` is a method on `Stream` that allows events through only when its cell argument is `true`. It isn't treated as a primitive in this book because it's built from `snapshot` and `filter`. You use `gate()` to ensure that nozzle lift and hang-up are only let through in the right phases:

```
sStart = lc.sStart.gate(phase.map(p -> p == Phase.IDLE));
sEnd   = lc.sEnd.gate(phase.map(p -> p == Phase.FILLING));
```

This protects against things happening at the wrong times. For instance, if a nozzle is lifted while we are waiting for the point-of-sale system, it's ignored.

sSaleComplete is a little fiddly because you get the selected fuel from `fuelFlowing`, which has no value when you aren't filling. You have to deal with this undesirable edge case. You can read the code carefully and reason that it will always have a value when you need it, but it's far better to eliminate these kinds of invalid states. This is the kind of improvement that `switch` will allow you to make when we cover it in chapter 7. The rest is explained in the code annotations.

Listing 4.10   Module to handle notifying the point-of-sale system

```
public class NotifyPointOfSale {
    public final Stream<Fuel> sStart;
    public final Cell<Optional<Fuel>> fillActive;
    public final Cell<Optional<Fuel>> fuelFlowing;
    public final Stream<End> sEnd;
    public final Stream<Unit> sBeep;
    public final Stream<Sale> sSaleComplete;

    private enum Phase { IDLE, FILLING, POS };          // Three phases
                                                        // of a fill

    public NotifyPointOfSale(
            LifeCycle lc,
            Stream<Unit> sClearSale,
            Fill fi) {                                  // Allows fill end only
        CellLoop<Phase> phase = new CellLoop<>();       // when FILLING
        sStart = lc.sStart.gate(phase.map(p -> p == Phase.IDLE));
        sEnd   = lc.sEnd.gate(phase.map(p -> p == Phase.FILLING));  // <--
        phase.loop(
                sStart.map(u -> Phase.FILLING)
                .orElse(sEnd.map(u -> Phase.POS))
                .orElse(sClearSale.map(u -> Phase.IDLE))
                .hold(Phase.IDLE));                     // Cleared when the
        fuelFlowing =                                   // nozzle is set down
                sStart.map(f -> Optional.of(f)).orElse(
                sEnd.map(f -> Optional.empty())).hold(Optional.empty());
```

Annotations:
- Allows fill start only when IDLE
- Changes phase on three different events

Cleared when the
sale is cleared by
the point of sale

Captures the sale
details at nozzle
set-down

Undesirable
edge case

Beeps when the
sale is cleared

```
        fillActive =
            sStart.map(f -> Optional.of(f)).orElse(
            sClearSale.map(f -> Optional.empty())).hold(Optional.empty());
        sBeep = sClearSale;
        sSaleComplete = Stream.filterOptional(sEnd.snapshot(
            fuelFlowing.lift(fi.price, fi.dollarsDelivered,
                                    fi.litersDelivered,
            (oFuel, price_, dollars, liters) ->
                oFuel.isPresent() ? Optional.of(
                        new Sale(oFuel.get(), price_, dollars, liters))
                                : Optional.empty())
        ));
    }
}
```

4.9 *Modularity illustrated: a keypad module*

Listing 4.11 shows a module for a keypad on which you can enter a dollar amount up
to three digits. It beeps when you press a key, but not if the number already has three
digits.

This uses the same pattern you've seen before, where you loop a value with `Cell-`
`Loop` and then use `hold` and `snapshot` to build an accumulator. You've also used
`filterOptional` because you sometimes want to ignore a keypress—for example,
when you already have three digits.

`sBeep` comes from `sUpdate`, and it makes sense that these two streams should fire
at the same time, because `sBeep` is meant to provide feedback to the user that the key
has had an effect. Where the key has no effect (three digits have already been
entered), there should be no beep.

The first constructor takes an extra Boolean cell argument `active`. You want keypresses to be ignored when `active` is `false`, and you do this by blocking them with
`gate()`.

> **NOTE** You may notice that we like to use `: ?` instead of `if ()` / `then` / `else`.
> The reason is that `: ?` forces you to output a value, or the compiler will com-
> plain. You can't omit the `else` case or forget to `return` or assign the value you
> want to output. We like to take any opportunity we can to make the compiler
> help us avoid bugs.

This example shows the basis for how a GUI library can be implemented with FRP. We
think FRP is a better way to write a GUI library than the object-oriented approach that's
universally used. We'll show you an FRP-based GUI implementation in chapter 12.

Listing 4.11 Keypad module

```
package chapter4.section9;

import pump.*;
import nz.sodium.*;
import java.util.Optional;
```

```
public class Keypad {
    public final Cell<Integer> value;
    public final Stream<Unit> sBeep;

    public Keypad(Stream<Key> sKeypad,
                  Stream<Unit> sClear,
                  Cell<Boolean> active) {
        this(sKeypad.gate(active), sClear);
    }

    public Keypad(Stream<Key> sKeypad, Stream<Unit> sClear) {
        CellLoop<Integer> value = new CellLoop<>();
        this.value = value;
        Stream<Integer> sKeyUpdate = Stream.filterOptional(
            sKeypad.snapshot(value,
                (key, value_) -> {
                    if (key == Key.CLEAR)
                        return Optional.of(0);
                    else {
                        int x10 = value_ * 10;
                        return x10 >= 1000
                                ? Optional.empty()
                                : Optional.of(
                                    key == Key.ZERO ? x10 :
                                    key == Key.ONE ? x10 + 1 :
                                    key == Key.TWO ? x10 + 2 :
                                    key == Key.THREE ? x10 + 3 :
                                    key == Key.FOUR ? x10 + 4 :
                                    key == Key.FIVE ? x10 + 5 :
                                    key == Key.SIX ? x10 + 6 :
                                    key == Key.SEVEN ? x10 + 7 :
                                    key == Key.EIGHT ? x10 + 8 :
                                                       x10 + 9
                                );
                    }
                }
            )
        );
        value.loop(sKeyUpdate.orElse(sClear.map(u -> 0))
                            .hold(0));
        sBeep = sKeyUpdate.map(k -> Unit.UNIT);
    }
}
```

Variant that blocks input keys when active is false

No more than three digits are allowed.

External clear command

Beeps when a key caused an update

The following listing shows a pump implementation that only tests the `Keypad` module. You can, of course, try it in the pump simulator.

Listing 4.12   Pump implementation that just tests the keypad module

```
package chapter4.section9;

import pump.*;
import nz.sodium.*;
import java.util.Optional;
```

```
public class KeypadPump implements Pump
{
    public Outputs create(Inputs inputs) {
        Keypad ke = new Keypad(inputs.sKeypad, new Stream<Unit>());
        return new Outputs()
            .setPresetLCD(ke.value.map(v ->
                Formatters.formatSaleCost((double)v)))
            .setBeep(ke.sBeep);
    }
}
```

You don't want to use the sClear feature, so you pass a "never" stream.

4.10 Notes about modularity

Putting things into modules is an important part of FRP programming. Here are a few tips.

4.10.1 The form of a module

We like to torment object-oriented programmers by making all the fields `final`; when we've knocked them off balance, we complete the job by putting all the code in the constructor. When they've recovered somewhat, we use a `static` method instead of a class. Because that's how we roll. (As a last resort, we put a crocodile in their swimming pool.)

In Java, you can use a *static method* or a *class* to implement a module. You may have noticed that whenever we've used a class,

- All fields are declared `public final`.
- The constructor is usually the only method.

We have specific reasons for doing these things:

- *All fields are* `public`. The only purpose of a field is to make a stream or cell available, so it makes no sense to use a `private` field. To make something `private`, you'd instead use a local variable in the constructor.
- *All fields are* `final`. You want the class to be immutable. Changing it after it's constructed can only cause problems, as we've mentioned before.
- *All code is usually in the constructor.* Java allows `final` fields to be assigned only in the constructor.

But there's a madness to our method, or rather, our complete absence of methods: this isn't really OOP. The purpose of OOP is to manage the mutation of state. In FRP, we use streams and cells to do this instead. We use classes only for their ability to group values together and their constructors to limit scope.

If you want to write a module that has only one output, a `static` method is a good approach, as you've seen a few times in the examples. You normally declare them `public` because there usually isn't any reason not to. When everything is immutable, it's not possible to monkey directly with the workings of an interface. But sometimes it's appropriate to use `private` visibility if the static method is only useful locally.

4.10.2 *Tuples vs. classes*

Some languages have convenient syntax for arbitrarily typed n-tuples, so it's trivial to return several values from a method or function. It makes sense to use whichever is idiomatic in the language you're using. It happens that in Java, classes are idiomatic.

4.10.3 *Explicit wiring*

A feature of FRP is that the inputs and outputs of a module are explicit. An FRP module is pure stateful logic, and the caller has full control over wiring that into the rest of the code so it actually does something. This may be more bureaucracy than you're used to, but the key concept is that you're attempting to prove to the compiler that you've written your code correctly. You get a lot of assistance from the compiler in return.

4.10.4 *When inputs and outputs proliferate*

The number of arguments to a module of FRP code can often be large. In most programming situations, when this happens, it's a *code smell* that suggests a need for refactoring. In FRP, this is still true, but less so.

One thing to note is that in FRP code, you can't directly hide the ways in which parts of the program communicate with each other. Often this means there are more explicit input and outputs than you would get in normal programming. It's not that there are more inputs and outputs; it's just that they're more visible. We think this is a good thing because inputs and outputs are a source of complexity. Having them right up in your face pushes you to deal with them earlier.

This doesn't mean you can't abstract them away at all, though. If you extended the keypad concept to implement a full GUI, for example, the number of inputs and outputs for each widget would be large enough to require more sophisticated management.

The basic way to do this is to abstract detail away by hiding things in container classes. It may be surprising at first, but this simple approach is enormously powerful. You'll see a real example of this in an FRP-based GUI library in chapter 12.

4.10.5 *Some bugs are solved, some aren't*

FRP makes a lot of bugs harder to write, but you can still write some:

- You can easily forget to use an input `Stream` or `Cell` in a module, or the caller may forget to use a module's output value. Generally, if you haven't used a value, it's a bug, because if it wasn't needed, it wouldn't be there. Often this manifests as a compiler warning of an unused variable (but not always). Be vigilant for these warnings.

- This isn't always true. Sometimes you deliberately don't want to use a value. For instance, you may be reusing a keypad module but want it to be silent. Then you throw away the returned `sBeep`.

- Forgetting to supply an input value is hard to do accidentally because the compiler will require you to provide *something*, even if it's a *never* stream as in `KeypadPump`.

- Another bug that occurs sometimes in FRP is mixing up values when they accidentally have the same type. FRP code often has a large number of local variables, and this contributes to the problem. A good way to deal with this is to wrap your contained values in custom container classes with only one value in them, so that the meaning of the value is reflected in its type. For unit values—that is, "nothing" values—use an enum with only one element. We did this with the End type in a Stream<End> to signal the end of the fill. We don't know if this helps, but it can't hurt.

DEFINITION   *Newtype pattern*—A common pattern in functional programming is to wrap a value in a class to give it meaning and extra type safety. For example, you might wrap a double in a class called Liters, or a String in a class called ErrorMessage. This powerful technique is named after a keyword in the programming language Haskell.

DEFINITION   *Primitive obsession*—An anti-pattern that's the opposite of the *newtype pattern*, in which you use primitive types for everything.

4.10.6 *Testability*

Another thing you get in return for being forced to make your dependencies explicit is testability. It's easy to write unit tests for modules like these. We haven't shown you how to interface FRP code to the rest of your program yet, so we'll unit test the petrol pump's Keypad class in chapter 11, section 3.

4.11 *Adding a preset dollar amount*

Now that you have a keypad module, you can add the final bit of logic for a complete petrol pump and bring this chapter to a close: the new Preset class/module in listing 4.13 causes the pump to stop pumping at the preset number of dollars.

Here are the inputs:

- *Preset value*
- *Fuel price*
- *Dollars delivered*
- *Liters delivered*
- *Fuel flowing*—Whether the nozzle is lifted, and what fuel is being pumped.
- *Fill active*—Fuel is flowing or has flowed, but the fill hasn't been cleared by the point-of-sale system yet.

Here are the outputs:

- *Delivery*—Which fuel to pump, and whether to go fast or slow
- *Keypad active*—Whether the user can type on the keypad

This is the logic you want:

- 0 means no preset number of dollars.
- You start pumping slowly just before the preset dollar value is reached.

- You stop when the preset dollar value is reached.
- The user can change the preset value any time before pumping slows; then the keypad is locked.

Listing 4.13 Logic for a preset dollar amount

```
package chapter4.section11;

import pump.*;
import chapter4.section7.Fill;
import nz.sodium.*;
import java.util.Optional;

public class Preset {
    public final Cell<Delivery> delivery;
    public final Cell<Boolean> keypadActive;

    public enum Speed { FAST, SLOW, STOPPED };

    public Preset(Cell<Integer> presetDollars,
                  Fill fi,
                  Cell<Optional<Fuel>> fuelFlowing,
                  Cell<Boolean> fillActive) {
        Cell<Speed> speed = presetDollars.lift(
            fi.price, fi.dollarsDelivered, fi.litersDelivered,
          (presetDollars_, price, dollarsDelivered, litersDelivered) -> {
            if (presetDollars_ == 0)
                return Speed.FAST;
            else {
                if (dollarsDelivered >= (double)presetDollars_)
                    return Speed.STOPPED;
                double slowLiters =
                        (double)presetDollars_/price - 0.10;
                if (litersDelivered >= slowLiters)
                    return Speed.SLOW;
                else
                    return Speed.FAST;
            }
        });
        delivery = fuelFlowing.lift(speed,
            (of, speed_) ->
                speed_ == Speed.FAST ? (
                    of.equals(Optional.of(Fuel.ONE))   ? Delivery.FAST1 :
                    of.equals(Optional.of(Fuel.TWO))   ? Delivery.FAST2 :
                    of.equals(Optional.of(Fuel.THREE)) ? Delivery.FAST3 :
                                                         Delivery.OFF
                ) :
                speed_ == Speed.SLOW ? (
                    of.equals(Optional.of(Fuel.ONE))   ? Delivery.SLOW1 :
                    of.equals(Optional.of(Fuel.TWO))   ? Delivery.SLOW2 :
                    of.equals(Optional.of(Fuel.THREE)) ? Delivery.SLOW3 :
                                                         Delivery.OFF
                ) :
                Delivery.OFF);
```

Calculates the pump speed (annotation pointing to `Cell<Speed> speed = presetDollars.lift(`)

Converts the pump speed/fuel to an instruction for the motors (annotation pointing to `delivery = fuelFlowing.lift(speed,`)

If not active, keypad keys are ignored.

```
        keypadActive = fuelFlowing.lift(speed,
            (of, speed_) ->
                !of.isPresent() || speed_ == Speed.FAST);
    }
}
```

All the inputs and outputs to Preset are cells, and the only primitive you use is to combine them in different ways with lift. You first work out what speed to fill by encoding an enum of FAST, SLOW, or STOPPED. You combine that information with the fuelFlowing state to give a Delivery value to the pump's motors. Finally, you decide whether the keypad should be active. You can change the preset amount any time before the motors switch to slow delivery.

The following listing shows the completed petrol pump.

Listing 4.14 Completed petrol pump implementation with preset

```
package chapter4.section11;

import pump.*;
import chapter4.section4.LifeCycle;
import chapter4.section4.LifeCycle.End;
import chapter4.section6.AccumulatePulsesPump;
import chapter4.section7.Fill;
import chapter4.section7.ShowDollarsPump;
import chapter4.section8.NotifyPointOfSale;
import chapter4.section9.Keypad;
import nz.sodium.*;
import java.util.Optional;


public class PresetAmountPump implements Pump {
    public Outputs create(Inputs inputs) {
        StreamLoop<Fuel> sStart = new StreamLoop<>();
        Fill fi = new Fill(inputs.sClearSale.map(u -> Unit.UNIT),
                           inputs.sFuelPulses, inputs.calibration,
                           inputs.price1, inputs.price2, inputs.price3,
                           sStart);
        NotifyPointOfSale np = new NotifyPointOfSale(
                new LifeCycle(inputs.sNozzle1,
                              inputs.sNozzle2,
                              inputs.sNozzle3),
                inputs.sClearSale,
                fi);
        sStart.loop(np.sStart);
        CellLoop<Boolean> keypadActive = new CellLoop<>();
        Keypad ke = new Keypad(inputs.sKeypad,
                               inputs.sClearSale,
                               keypadActive);
        Preset pr = new Preset(ke.value,
                               fi,
                               np.fuelFlowing,
                               np.fillActive.map(o -> o.isPresent()));
        keypadActive.loop(pr.keypadActive);
```

From preset()

Preset value from the keypad

**preset()
determines this.**

```
return new Outputs()
    .setDelivery(pr.delivery)
    .setSaleCostLCD(fi.dollarsDelivered.map(
        q -> Formatters.formatSaleCost(q)))
    .setSaleQuantityLCD(fi.litersDelivered.map(
        q -> Formatters.formatSaleQuantity(q)))
    .setPriceLCD1(ShowDollarsPump.priceLCD(np.fillActive, fi.price,
        Fuel.ONE, inputs))
    .setPriceLCD2(ShowDollarsPump.priceLCD(np.fillActive, fi.price,
        Fuel.TWO, inputs))
    .setPriceLCD3(ShowDollarsPump.priceLCD(np.fillActive, fi.price,
        Fuel.THREE, inputs))
    .setSaleComplete(np.sSaleComplete)
    .setPresetLCD(ke.value.map(v ->
        Formatters.formatSaleCost((double)v)))
    .setBeep(np.sBeep.orElse(ke.sBeep));
    }
}
```

**You now have two
beep sources, so
you merge them.**

You feed `Preset`'s `keypadActive` into the `Keypad` module. Because this is called before you construct `Preset`, you use your old friend `CellLoop` to loop it.

There are now two sources of beeps: `NotifyPointOfSale` beeps when the sale is cleared, and `Keypad` beeps when a key is pressed. You must return the `merge` of these two in `Outputs`.

4.12   *What have you achieved?*

We've shown you some pretty complex code that solves a real-world problem. For this program's size, it has a fair amount of logic, but we've managed to break it into sensible pieces and keep it tidy, although it could still be improved.

You wrote the code in six revisions and added a major feature each time. Notice that the code mainly consists of two things:

- About half of it is the overhead of values being passed around.
- The rest is mostly stateful logic.

The purpose of all this passing things around is keeping things tidy by limiting the scope of variables. From the viewpoint of writing logic, it's overhead, but it's overhead that gives you something.

We hope you're starting to notice what this code *doesn't* contain:

- There's no explicit sequence. The order and grouping of statements is chosen to aid comprehension and for no other reason. FRP leaves you free to arrange things into conceptual groupings.
- Practically no attention is given to the edge conditions of when things are updated. Many of these issues tend to disappear, but not all.
- No state is kept in normal mutable variables: cells are used instead.
- There are no threads or anything resembling a flow of control.
- There's no direct initiation of state changes. Cells and streams are always sources of information. From within the FRP paradigm, it's impossible to

express the concept of a sink in your code: "OK—now I'm going to push a value out." This makes sense when you consider that FRP doesn't allow for the normal concept of a flow of control. Stream events are the only way to cause state changes in FRP, and the only type of stream that can be created directly is a never stream, which can never fire. Therefore, all initiation of state changes has to come from sources outside of FRP land. It's called *reactive* programming precisely because the code can only react to input.

- There's no memory management. This is 100% automatic in FRP.

The code can only react to external input, but we haven't yet shown you how to generate this external input. As we've explained, we've done this deliberately to get you fully immersed in an FRP way of thinking.

If you're new to FRP, we expect that this code is unlike any code you've seen before. You may want to think about how you'd normally write code like this and what kinds of issues you'd run into.

4.13 Summary

- FRP code is typically half pure logic and half management of variable scoping.
- You usually write modules in a class or static method.
- If a module is written as a class, you write all the code in the constructor and the outputs as `public final` fields.
- FRP code is naturally testable because you're forced to make all inputs and outputs explicit.

New concepts

You've seen a practical example done in FRP style. In chapter 1, we said that a new way of thinking will help you get the most out of FRP. In this chapter, we'll continue breaking that down.

5.1 In search of the mythical von Neumann machine

In this section, we'll explain what the von Neumann machine is and why it's the source of some assumptions that not only are unhelpful in programming but also turn out to be largely false. The "stored program" computer architecture (see figure 5.1) has served us well since John von Neumann described it in 1945. It's the basis for the modern computer: the processor reads the program instructions from

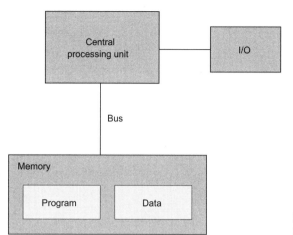

Figure 5.1 von Neumann "stored program" hardware architecture

memory and executes them, giving rise to the manipulation of data in memory. The memory and processor are separate entities, connected by a bus.

Now we're going to demonstrate some performance characteristics of a machine that don't quite fit the von Neumann picture. A singly linked list is a sequence of nodes where each item contains a reference to the next item in the list. Many languages provide linked lists as part of their standard library. We'll give the example in C because it's close to the underlying machine instructions.

You traverse a linked list of a million items 1,000 times (see listing 5.1). The code shuffles the nodes into a random order before linking them, but if you give the `--no-shuffle` option on the command line, it won't do that. You generate the random numbers for the shuffle even when not shuffling, so you can be sure the random-number generation doesn't account for the performance difference. You can find this code under `sodium/book/von-neumann/` in the Sodium project.

Listing 5.1 How long does it take to traverse a linked list?

```
#include <stdlib.h>
#include <assert.h>

typedef struct Node {
    struct Node* next;
    unsigned value;
} Node;

void shuffle(Node** nodes, unsigned n, int doit) {
    unsigned i;
    for (i = 0; i < n; i++) {
        unsigned j = (unsigned)(((long long)random() * n) /    ⟵  Generates random
                    ((long long)RAND_MAX + 1));                     numbers
```

```
        if (i != j && doit) {
            Node* node = nodes[i];
            nodes[i] = nodes[j];
            nodes[j] = node;
        }
    }
}

int main(int argc, char* argv[])
{
    const unsigned n = 1000000;
    const unsigned iterations = 1000;
    Node* head;
    Node* node;
    unsigned iter;
    {
        Node** nodes = malloc(sizeof(Node*) * n);
        unsigned i;
        for (i = 0; i < n; i++) {
            nodes[i] = malloc(sizeof(Node));
            nodes[i]->value = i;
        }
        shuffle(nodes, n,
            argc == 2 && strcmp(argv[1], "--no-shuffle") == 0);
        for (i = 0; i < n; i++)
            nodes[i]->next = (i+1) < n ? nodes[i+1] : NULL;
        head = nodes[0];
        free(nodes);
    }
    for (iter = 0; iter < iterations; iter++) {
        unsigned long long sum = 0;
        for (node = head; node != NULL; node = node->next)
            sum += node->value;
        assert(sum == (unsigned long long)(n - 1) * n / 2);
    }
}
```

◁──┐ **Swaps only if shuffle is
   │ enabled**

Let's link the nodes in the order in which they were allocated and see how long it takes:

```
time ./linked-list --no-shuffle
user 0m3.390s
```

What if you link the nodes in random order?

```
time ./linked-list
user 1m19.563s
```

It takes 23 times as long. Why?

5.1.1   *Why so slow? The cache*

Actually, the second run wasn't slow: the first one was such an amazing feat of engineering that it made the second one look slow by comparison. Today's machines are based on an architecture called *non-uniform memory access (NUMA).*

The code doesn't quite do what the von Neumann picture would suggest. What's going on here? Between the main memory and processor in a modern machine, there's a bit of sorcery known as a *cache* (see figure 5.2). A cache is a bank of memory that keeps a local copy of the most recently accessed parts of the main memory.

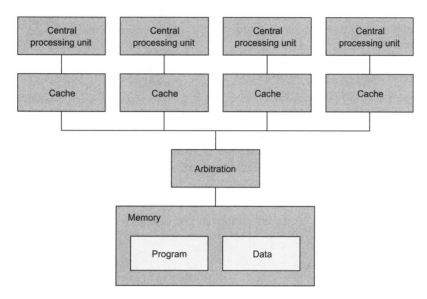

Figure 5.2   Today's non-uniform memory access (NUMA) architecture

When you access data that's already in the cache, it's called a *cache hit*, and when you require a costly read from slower memory, it's a *cache miss*. When it misses, the cache doesn't just fetch the requested data. It fetches a small chunk of data, typically 128 bytes or so, and stores that in the cache. This is done because an assumption of *locality* often holds true in practice: any memory you access is likely to be *near* something accessed recently.

That's why in the example, shuffling the nodes killed the performance. It just happens to be likely in our operating system that each allocated memory block is adjacent to the previous one. The assumption of locality holds true, and when you come to read data, it has often been prefetched. But when you shuffle the nodes, locality is destroyed, so each loop is almost guaranteed to be a cache miss.

A cache miss exposes you to the *latency* of a fetch to main memory. Latency itself isn't bad if you can give the CPU other work to do while it's waiting. The linked-list structure means each loop depends on information from the previous loop. Because of this, the program can't supply the CPU with any work, and the CPU must block. The program falls off a performance cliff.

MULTIPROCESSOR MACHINES

Caches get a lot more complicated with more than one processor. If one processor writes to memory, it must clear the caches of all the other processors. If several write at once, any conflicts must be resolved. *Arbitration* is the term for all the negotiation that takes place. Having processors fight over the same memory causes a lot of arbitration and is known as *cache contention*.

Ultimately, the NUMA architecture is a set of processors with local memory with an elaborate illusion of shared memory between them. Can it scale to 1,000 processors? We don't know.

5.1.2   *The madness of bus optimization*

Often people optimize their code for cache and bus performance. The general rule is that memory accessed temporally nearby should be physically nearby, and each processor should have its own local memory pool. But there are many more rules.

The C programming language gives you almost direct access to a contiguous block of memory. The ability of the compiler to optimize automatically for cache and bus performance is limited. For example, when you have a pointer in C, the compiler is prevented by the design of the language from transparently relocating the allocated block somewhere that might better fit the temporal memory-access patterns of the program.

Q: Why are we in this strange situation?

A: Because modern machines are forced by current languages to pretend to be a machine that hasn't existed since the 1970s.

To get the performance we expect today out of existing software, caches have become extremely complicated. For an application programmer to optimize their code for cache efficiency is generally not a good idea, yet people do exactly this. These are our reasons for saying so:

- Hardware architectures have been made complicated so they can run existing software quickly.
- This complicated architecture means optimization is largely beyond the ability of a programmer to optimize for cache and bus performance by hand. Programming is difficult enough already.
- This optimization should be the job of the language compiler, but most of our languages aren't well designed for this.
- Optimizing an application by hand locks it into today's architecture, but it won't be optimized for tomorrow's. This entrenches the approach, making innovation in hardware more difficult.
- End result: a situation where software and hardware mutually complicate each other.

Getting the best bus performance out of your code

The *Intel 64 and IA-32 Architectures Optimization Reference Manual* is 800 pages long and contains advice like this (section 3.6.12):

> If there is a blend of reads and writes on the bus, changing the code to separate these bus transactions into read phases and write phases can help performance.

> Note, however, that the order of read and write operations on the bus is not the same as it appears in the program.

> Bus latency for fetching a cache line of data can vary as a function of the access stride of data references. In general, bus latency will increase in response to increasing values of the stride of successive cache misses. Independently, bus latency will also increase as a function of increasing bus queue depths (the number of outstanding bus requests of a given transaction type).

Did you get that?

The processor is working with sequential instructions that mutate state in place. When it blocks on a memory read, it must analyze the dependencies in the code to find anything it can execute that doesn't depend on the outstanding data. In chapter 1, we talked about how the programmer's job is typically largely concerned with translating dependencies into a sequence.

The way we write software today, the compiler doesn't have the original dependencies to generate better code. Now the processor has to extract whatever dependency information it can from the sequential instructions to get any performance. Its ability to do this is limited. Large-scale parallelism on a single processor isn't possible with this design.

WHAT ARE WE EVEN DOING THIS FOR?

We've built our practices on some shaky assumptions. The von Neumann machine is a hardware architecture designed around in-place mutation of state, and this worked well in the 1970s. Our programming languages were designed to mutate state on a von Neumann machine, and they haven't changed much. State mutation is assumed to be efficient, but the reality is more complex.

There are mathematical reasons behind the "complexity wall" experienced in commercial software projects: state mutation creates a maze of possible data dependencies such that unraveling them is an intractable problem. This makes programming harder and complicates parallelism and optimization. Object-oriented programming brings order to state mutation, but this just entrenches an approach that doesn't help software or hardware designers.

The von Neumann machine has a design bottleneck that limits its speed, but our languages tie us to it. In order to run existing software fast, modern machines go to great lengths to pretend to be von Neumann machines.

Complex? Now add more processors

When your code is based on mutating program state in place, and you want to parallelize it to run on multiple processors, you have to protect the state with locks. This style of programming is prone to nondeterministic bugs, meaning you can get race conditions or deadlocks that occur only one time out of a million runs at random.

This style doesn't scale with program size. The reason: coarse-grained locks are safe but defeat parallelism. Fine-grained locks require policies for acquiring them in the right order that increase in complexity with program size until they become intractable.

Result: nondeterministic, difficult-to-reproduce bugs that increase with ballooning complexity. If you're an experienced programmer, then this ought to give you the *wehi*—the fear.

In summary, we're programming in a bad way, because it's compatible with a nonexistent, inefficient hardware architecture, forcing us to make complicated hardware emulations of it, so that it's complicated to optimize our software, further entrenching the hardware emulation. See figure 5.3.

Figure 5.3   Maxine is dismayed to discover that the von Neumann machine doesn't exist.

BUT WE CAN BREAK THE CYCLE

To think NUMA—today's optimization of the von Neumann machine—is the only possible architecture is to think in a limited way. There are many ways to build a computer. For example:

- Single processors with local memory connected by fast Ethernet
- Massively parallel array processors, such as graphics processing units (GPUs)
- Field programmable gate arrays (FPGAs), where memory and code are near each other
- Optical computers
- Quantum computers

Perhaps future computers will be seamless hybrids of multiple architectures, where each bit of code runs on the hardware that best suits the underlying problem.

The fundamental mistake we're making is programming away from the problem and toward the machine. In the process, we make the job harder than it needs to be, and we limit the options of the compiler and the processor maker.

5.1.3 How does this relate to FRP?

To future-proof our code and free us for hardware innovation, we need to do one simple thing: program in a way that fits the problem and gives dependency information to the compiler—and, in our specific case, the FRP system—so it can write the best code for whatever machine it's targeting. Functional programming in general does this by tracking data dependencies and removing in-place state mutation. FRP does this in a more specific way for one problem space. Of the architectures just listed, the one that fits FRP the best is the FPGA, although the fit isn't perfect. This relationship would be interesting to research.

When a program runs in parallel, it can achieve the same throughput with considerably less power consumption. This basic fact is the true reason why parallelism is here to stay. Parallelism is the pachyderm in the parlor that will ultimately force us to adopt ways of programming that are focused on the problem, not on the machine.

> **NOTE** FRP is still in its early days, and we're a long way from saying parallelism is a direct selling point of FRP. Current FRP implementations don't do much for parallelism yet. And in general, parallelism isn't an easy problem. But FRP is inherently parallelizable in a way that traditional programming isn't.

5.2 Compositionality

A major claim of FRP is that it tames complexity. It does this in a specific way: by enforcing something called *compositionality*.

5.2.1 When complexity gets out of control

We all know this from experience: the complexity of a program can get out of control. When complex parts interact in complex ways, the complexity can compound, with the result that overall software complexity grows exponentially with program size.

DEFINITION *Exponential growth*—When a quantity's growth rate is proportional to its current value. Compounding bank interest is a common example. The typical experience is that the increase starts off imperceptibly and then suddenly overwhelms you. There are some good videos on YouTube that explain this idea. Any software project whose complexity is growing exponentially will hit a *complexity wall* once it reaches a certain size.

How do we stop ballooning software complexity? Refactoring is a technique to counter-balance it.

We say FRP is compositional because it imposes mathematical rules that force the interaction of program elements to be simple and predictable, without subtleties. Their complexities add instead of multiplying, so overall complexity stays closer to proportional to program size. Put things together, and you don't get any surprises.

We defined the term *denotational semantics* in chapter 1. This is what gives us the mathematical proof of compositionality for an FRP system. It follows that any FRP code, no matter how complex, is guaranteed to be compositional.

5.2.2 *Reductionism and engineering*

Software development is a form of engineering, and engineering is based on the philosophy of reductionism. This methodology is powerful; it has been enormously successful at providing us with technology that has transformed the way we do almost everything.

The reductionist approach to engineering has four steps:

1 Start with a complex problem.
2 Break the problem into simpler parts.
3 Solve the parts.
4 Compose the parts of the solution into a whole.

Step 4 is where we get into trouble. Reductionism has a hidden assumption of compositionality: that the nature of the parts doesn't change when we compose them. When this isn't true, we can fail badly. If we wrongly assume compositionality, then we have committed a logical fallacy called the *fallacy of composition*. What is true of the parts in isolation may not be true when they're combined. For example:

- If someone stands up at a football game, they can see better. Therefore if everyone stands up, everyone can see better.
- Cells are invisible. I am composed of cells. Therefore I am invisible.
- If I ignore my problems for an hour, they go away for an hour. Therefore if I ignore them for two hours, they go away for two hours. Therefore …

Event propagation is a widely used "glue" for composing software components. FRP gives us event propagation with guaranteed compositionality. By imposing compositionality, FRP makes the assumptions of reductionism valid, and in this way, it makes software engineering work the way it should.

Defining compositionality and complexity

The idea of *compositionality* as a mathematical property comes from linguistics and semantics. The formal definition is "The property that the meaning of an expression is determined by the meanings of its parts and the rules used to combine them."

In order to understand this definition, you need to understand the meaning of *meaning* (see the following figure). But how can you understand your understanding if you don't know what "means" means? We were confused, so we went down to the pub for a lime and kerosene.

Contemplating meaning

After much contemplation, we came to realize that in linguistics, *meaning* refers to the informational content that's transmitted through human language. Information has structure, structure implies complexity, and complexity is our chief concern as programmers.

Without compositionality, the consequences of composing program modules are ad hoc. FRP works because it imposes rules on composition, making it fit the previous definition.

Complexity can be tricky to pin down, and there are different approaches for measuring it. We're clearly not measuring what the program does. Two programs may do the same thing, but one may be more complex in structure than the other. We're concerned with the structure of the program now, not the structure it might have after being refactored.

Cyclomatic complexity measures the number of linearly independent paths through a program. Each `if` statement or loop adds to the metric. FRP reduces the number of `if` statements.

The *Kolmogorov complexity* of a string of text (which could be a program) is the length of the shortest description of it or program that can output it. For example, "abcab-cabcabc" could be described as "output 'abc' four times".

These may be helpful, but we prefer a less formal but more practical view of complexity, where we measure the complexity of a program by the time and effort required to understand it. To modify a program safely, we need to understand all the implications of the change. The more complex the structure of the program, the longer it takes someone to understand it, and the greater the probability that they will make a mistake. That's why complexity has such practical negative consequences for programming.

5.2.3   *Compositionality is no longer optional*

The problems we programmers are trying to solve are more and more parallel and distributed in nature, and more complex. Functional programmers know from their own experience that functional programming deals with complexity better, but many can't put their finger on the reason, so they can't explain it to others. Compositionality is the reason. Functional programming works because it enforces compositionality, although it doesn't claim a monopoly on this.

Not all problems can be dealt with in a compositional way. Stateful event-based logic has always been in the non-compositional category, and it has always been a major source of bugs. This situation has now been changed by FRP, and perhaps other problems can be addressed in similar ways.

Compositionality is a missing element in the understanding of most programmers. This idea can lead to great improvements in the way we do things. In time, increasing complexity will force us to embrace it.

5.3   *Lack of compositionality illustrated*

In chapter 2, we used an example of a drawing program to illustrate the merge primitive. As a reminder, you're working on some kind of drawing program, which is an editor for documents that contain drawing elements. You're coding a part of it where the graphical elements can be selected or deselected. These are the rules, with two more added (shown in italics):

- If you click an element, it's selected.
- If an element is selected, and you click elsewhere, the element gets deselected.
- *When nothing is selected, you get a cross-hair cursor.*
- *When any element is selected, the cursor is an arrow.*

Figure 5.4 shows three steps being performed with the drawing program:

1 Nothing is selected, and we're ready to click the triangle.
2 When we've clicked the triangle, it's highlighted, and we get an arrow cursor.
3 We get ready to click the octagon.

At this point, a single mouse click will cause two events to be generated:

- Deselecting the triangle
- Selecting the octagon

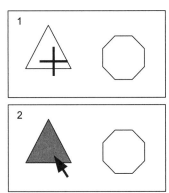
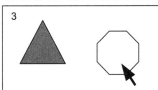

Figure 5.4   Three steps in selecting and deselecting elements in the drawing program

The following listing shows some pseudocode in an object-oriented/observer-pattern style to set the shape of the cursor depending on how many elements are selected.

> **Listing 5.2 Setting the mouse cursor according to the number of elements selected**

```
public interface SelectionListener {
    void selected(Element e);
    void deselected(Element e);
}

public class CursorMonitor implements SelectionListener {
    private HashSet<Element> selectedElts = new HashSet();
    public void selected(Element e) {
        selectedElts.add(e);
        updateCursor();
    }
    public void deselected(Element e) {
        selectedElts.remove(e);
        updateCursor();
    }
    private void updateCursor() {
        if (selectedElts.isEmpty()) crosshairCursor(); else
                                    arrowCursor();
    }
}
```

Now, what if the customer wants the cursor to stay solidly as an arrow in this case, without any brief flicker? To achieve this, you'd either need to guarantee to process the selection before the deselection, or wrap the whole thing in some sort of transaction and update the cursor at the end of it. The first option is difficult because the order of arrival of the events is unpredictable: it depends on the order in which the listeners were registered, and this is out of your control in this part of the code. The second option is possible but could complicate the code significantly.

If you instead code this in FRP, the problem is neatly solved by the fact that merge imposes a predictable order when events are simultaneous. To solve this problem, you can guarantee to process selections first with the following code, assuming an append() operation that combines two actions into one:

```
sSelected.merge(sDeselected, (s, d) -> s.append(d))
```

5.3.1 Why the OO version lacks compositionality

In the object-oriented code given in the previous section, there are two event handlers: selected() and deselected(). Each one is called when an event occurs. Let's look at this code through FRP goggles.

As mentioned, in FRP, you'd model these as two streams: sSelected and sDeselected. We haven't given the code where these events are generated, but let's assume that somewhere there exists something like the following:

```
CursorMonitor cm = new CursorMonitor();
selectionLogic.addListener(cm);
deselectionLogic.addListener(cm);
```

Arranges for cm.selected() to be called later

Arranges for cm.deselected() to be called later

The `updateCursor()` method roughly equates to the conceptual FRP `merge` of `sSelected` and `sDeselected`. Let's give the name `sUpdate` to the result of the conceptual `merge` operation you imagine to be represented by this code.

The semantics of FRP tell us that an FRP `merge` gives a result that is *compositional.* According to the definition of that term, the meaning of `sUpdate` should be determined by "the meanings of the elements [`sSelected` and `sDeselected`] and the rules used to combine them [`merge`]."

But the imaginary `merge` represented by this code adds something else: the propagation order of `sUpdate`—concretely, the order in which the events arrive at `updateCursor()`—depends on the relative order of listener registration somewhere else in the code. We showed some listener registration earlier, but this isn't the place where the order matters. It comes earlier still, where `selectionLogic` and `deselectionLogic` are set up.

This code isn't a true FRP `merge` because it introduces something from a source completely outside the elements and the rules. Something nonlocal is having an effect on the order of event processing at `updateCursor()` and therefore on the meaning of the results of the "merge." And so compositionality is broken.

Subtleties like this are fairly harmless in isolation, but these minor plagues will compound. Soon they will eat all your lamingtons, leaving a trail of desiccated coconut everywhere.

5.4   *Compositionality: eliminating whole classes of bugs*

FRP enforces a lot of discipline on the way we do things. At first this may be difficult to deal with, but we hope you'll bear with us. We know from experience that FRP can express anything. But you'll find that the way you're used to doing things may no longer work.

But you do get something in return: some of the mistakes we colorfully described as the "six plagues" are a lot harder to make, but most of them are impossible to make.

We aren't just eliminating bugs, we're eliminating whole classes of bugs. We can't squash all bugs, but we can fundamentally transform the riskiness of event-handling code. What's left over mostly consists of the following:

- *A few silly mistakes,* such as mixing up two variables of the same type.
- *Logic errors*—and we can't help you much with these. These are the cases where unit testing is helpful.
- Not fully understanding your customer's requirements.

So, try our new FRP bug spray!

Enlightenment

You've reached the point of enlightenment when the predominant source of bugs is not understanding your customer's requirements. This is the point at which you rewrite old parts of the code base to keep yourself busy and start spending more time with your family. Your manager will insist you keep your team at more or less the same size because they will be unable to comprehend how productive you have become.

This really happened to one of the authors.

5.5 *Don't pull out the rug: use immutable values*

Both cells and streams contain values. These are passed through the FRP system and are seen by different parts of your code at different times. It's important that the FRP system can provide the value intact. The values contained in the streams or cells mustn't be changed during this process.

The way to guarantee this is to make all of your data structures immutable. In most languages, you make the fields private and only define getters. In Java, you can mark the fields as `public final`. The field types also need to be immutable. If your team is disciplined enough not to modify them, you can keep things simple with regular public fields.

5.5.1 *Immutable data structures*

Referential transparency or *purity* means functions passed to FRP primitives must not perform I/O, modify or read external state, or keep internal state.

Pop quiz: is referential transparency

    a. Completely unimportant

    b. Somewhat important

    c. Moderately important

    d. Very important

Top marks! It's very important. If we don't make you sick of hearing about it, then we haven't emphasized it enough. This book comes with special reinforcement for when you throw it down in disgust because we've banged on about referential transparency too much.

It's a consequence of referential transparency (which is very important) that you should always use *immutable data structures*. There are tree-based implementations of maps, sets, and other things that can't be modified in place, but they're efficiently "copied" to a new structure when they're modified. Java doesn't have anything like this in its standard library, but there are several projects out there. These are sometimes referred to as *functional data structures* or *persistent data structures*. (This last term, *persistent*, has an unfortunate double meaning: we aren't talking about writing data structures to persistent storage.)

You can achieve the same effect by always copying your mutable data structure and then modifying the copy, but this is inefficient if the structure is large. A true immutable data structure is typically nearly as efficient as a mutable one. We're teaching you to build software that's correct and easy to modify. That is a greater priority than performance in most projects. Right now there are performance costs to this, but they aren't large. They will become smaller in mainstream languages as people use more functional approaches and compilers are optimized accordingly. Functional programming languages have demonstrated that a lot can be done to optimize the handling of immutable data. As parallelism becomes more important, immutable structures may well end up faster.

5.6   *Clarity of intent*

We said at the end of chapter 4 that FRP code consists mainly of two things:

- Pure logic
- Structure that limits scope

FRP has factored out most of the extraneous detail directly, and you have a free hand to limit scope in ways that work for you at a conceptual level.

We'll cover refactoring in detail in chapter 13. Refactoring is easy in FRP. If two aspects of some logic are complicating each other, it's a simple matter to separate them out into different modules:

- Explicit dependencies make the mechanics of separating code out easy. You remove the lines you want to separate out, and pass arguments around as necessary.
- Type safety makes the risk of breakage low, so you can refactor with abandon without the need for unit tests.

When your code has been refactored a few times, it tends toward well-defined, self-contained, conceptually simple layers of abstraction. The compositionality guarantee of FRP is strong in preventing abstractions from being "leaky"—the interface between two bits of code is well defined, and its rules can't be violated. The types of the values passed between them mostly define the semantics of the interface, but not entirely; there may still be some details in the sequencing and meaning of stream events and changes to cell values that aren't captured in the types. Overall, it's a great improvement over traditional programming in this area.

When a complex program has become stratified into layers with a level of abstraction appropriate to the problem, you'll find you have achieved *clarity of intent*. Abstraction has a cost as well as a benefit: the reader of the code first needs to take the time to understand the concepts behind the layer of abstraction they're working at. Once they've done that, it should be possible to read the code and know exactly what it does. That's *clarity of intent*.

Recall that the lasagna example in chapter 1 was easy to understand because we described it in the concepts of human thought, not the minutiae of constructing it. Even though the program is complex on a large scale, it's expressed as simple layers that don't interfere in unpredictable ways. Each layer expresses the "what," not the "how," where "what" corresponds to some concept in the problem description. It's both simple and understandable.

The true test of *clarity of intent* is this: if someone has reported a bug, you should be able to see it just by reading the code. You should be able to understand what the program does without running it.

5.7 The consequences of cheap abstraction

FRP has something in common with all other forms of functional programming: abstraction is cheap, so we tend to use it more. Abstraction is where we hide the details of something so we can interact with it in a simpler way. In FRP, this is mostly achieved in practice by simple techniques that limit scope. Abstraction simplifies our code overall—sometimes dramatically—and makes the intent of the code clearer, but as we said, there's an up-front cost: extra time is required to understand the concept behind a given abstraction.

But the cost is often not so high. *Cheap abstraction* means the usefulness of an abstraction tends to outweigh its cost. Abstractions in FRP are often more general than in "normal" programming, so code reuse is easier. This generality maximizes the usefulness of a given abstraction so the number and variety of abstractions needed is smaller. This keeps down the overall costs of understanding them.

We said that FRP is compositional in that you're composing parts of your program according to well-defined rules, so you don't get surprises. FRP does this at a fine level of granularity. We also said that refactoring is easy in FRP code. Part of the reason for this is that even small fragments of code are compositional. Compositionality permeates the code.

> **NOTE** Aspects of the code that would be too cumbersome to factor out in "normal" programming are often easy to do in FRP. This is what we mean when we say abstraction is cheap. When coding in FRP, we find ourselves refactoring continuously, identifying bits of common logic and factoring them out into reusable functions. We call this "the incredible shrinking code."

One issue with a highly abstracted style of coding is that it can be different than what people are used to. We've encountered pockets of resistance in our efforts to dominate the entire universe. But this is becoming less and less of a problem as functional programming goes mainstream; formerly esoteric concepts are becoming familiar.

Ultimately, cheap abstraction leads to a sort of enlightenment or "superconductor effect," where simplicity compounds instead of complexity, and you find yourself programming at a higher level. We can't get this across to you with words. It has to be experienced, and we hope you'll get a glimpse of it by the end of the book.

5.8 Summary

- Our machines aren't really von Neumann machines. This idea ties us to sequence, making parallelism difficult, making the programmer's job difficult, and limiting hardware innovation.

- You should program to the problem and let the compiler deal with the machine. FRP is a step in the right direction.
- FRP tames complexity by enforcing *compositionality*.
- FRP requires the use of immutable data structures and referential transparency (purity).
- You should aim for clarity of intent in your code. The code should be simple to understand.

FRP on the web

This chapter covers

- Observables in RxJS
- How to manage state in RxJS
- RxJS examples
- A glimpse of Kefir.js and Flapjax
- Glitches/inconsistent handling of simultaneous events

FRP fits some problems better than others. User interfaces and networking are two event-based areas where it fits especially well. Not surprisingly, FRP is excellent for web applications.

RxJS—part of the Reactive Extensions suite—is a system widely used in web applications that has an FRP capability. In this chapter, we show how to use it for FRP by contrasting it against Sodium, which we're treating as a model of true FRP.

> **NOTE** Appendix C contains comparison charts for all the systems discussed here.

6.1   *RxJS*

Reactive Extensions started as a library from Microsoft for the .NET platform, known for short as Rx.NET. It has now been translated into almost every language, and the JavaScript version is called RxJS.

There are many other JavaScript systems inspired by RxJS, including Bacon.js, Kefir.js, and Meteor Tracker. Flapjax is another JavaScript system from the same "classic FRP" lineage that Sodium comes from. We'll compare one example among three systems: RxJS, Kefir.js, and Flapjax.

The goals and design philosophy of Rx are a little different than Sodium's:

- Sodium is intended to put the core concept of "true FRP" into a practical, minimalist form. It takes a restrictive approach with the aim of making certain kinds of bugs either impossible or more difficult.
- Rx is designed to assist with a range of real-world problems. When using Rx, people often combine FRP and non-FRP ways of doing things. We aren't keen on this because you're effectively writing your own primitives. When you do this, it's all too easy to break compositionality. To get the best advantage out of FRP, we recommend a strict delineation between FRP and I/O, so this is the approach we take here.

Rx has many features, but a subset of it is FRP-like and looks a lot like Sodium. Both systems are ultimately wrappers for the observer pattern. Our approach will be to compare Rx to Sodium. We're doing this first so we can look at Rx through an FRP lens, and second to give you a frame of reference because you're now familiar with Sodium.

> **NOTE**   One important thing Rx lacks is *denotative semantics*. This means the building blocks lack compositionality in certain areas. We'll explain those areas in this chapter. Rx isn't "true FRP" for this reason.

This book isn't about how to get the most out of Rx: it's about how to get FRP out of Rx. For a more thorough treatment of the Rx family of systems, look at *Reactive Extensions in Action* by Tamir Dresher (Manning, 2016).

6.2   *Observable*

Rx is based around an interface called `Observable` that corresponds to Sodium's `Stream`. Sodium `Stream` has, in keeping with classic FRP, only one type of event—a value—but Rx `Observable` has three:

- *onNext*—A value
- *onError*—An error
- *onCompleted*—The end of the stream

> **NOTE**   We have a minimalist view of FRP, and we think errors and end-of-stream shouldn't be built into an FRP system. They're domain-specific: for

instance, they would be meaningless in a stream of mouse events. Where these concepts are needed, they can be encoded in the values. Of course, this is just our purist opinion. The way Rx does things make sense for Rx's design goals because its goal is to make common tasks easier.

`Observable` represents a sequence of values. To get the values out, you subscribe to it, and you're called back with each value in turn. For example:

```
var numbers = Rx.Observable.range(1, 3);
console.log("---1");
var subscription = numbers.subscribe(
    function (x) { console.log('onNext: %s', x); },
    function (e) { console.log('onError: %s', e); },
    function ()  { console.log('onCompleted'); });
console.log("---2");
```

This is the output:

```
---1
onNext: 1
onNext: 2
onNext: 3
onCompleted
---2
```

> **NOTE** You can use `subscription.dispose()` to unsubscribe, but Rx is designed for fire-and-forget scenarios, so in most cases it's not needed.

6.2.1 *Hot and cold observables*

In the previous example, all the action took place when `subscribe()` was invoked. This is a *cold* observable. If you were to subscribe to `numbers` again later, the new subscriber would get the same sequence from the beginning.

A cold observable can be seen as equivalent to a list in functional programming. This makes sense if you understand that part of the goal of Rx is to provide infrastructure for general functional programming in nonfunctional languages.

Hot observables correspond to Sodium's `Stream`. The subscriber doesn't receive any callbacks immediately, but only later as "live" events come in. Mouse events are a good example:

```
var sMouseDown = Rx.Observable.fromEvent(document, 'mousedown');
var subscription = sMouseDown.subscribe(
    function (x) { console.log('onNext: %s', x.clientX+','+x.clientY); },
    function (e) { console.log('onError: %s', e); },
    function ()  { console.log('onCompleted'); });
console.log("---");
```

If you click the document twice, you get this output:

```
---
onNext: 100,87
onNext: 84,175
```

6.2.2 How to maintain state

RxJS observables work much the same as streams in Sodium or any other FRP system, but state-keeping is a little different. RxJS employs three methods and one class in the management of state:

- `scan()`
- `withLatestFrom()`
- `combineLatest()`
- `BehaviorSubject`

We'll give illustrations of all of these.

RxJS doesn't have a direct equivalent of a cell type, but you can achieve a similar effect by other means. The difference between the concepts of *stream* and *cell* is an important part of FRP. RxJS doesn't make this distinction with data types, so we'll emphasize it using the same convention as in the Sodium examples where you prefix "stream" variable names with s.

6.2.3 A stateful accumulator with scan()

Figure 6.1 shows a toy application that draws lines between the positions of mouse clicks. The first line is drawn from (0,0) to the first mouse-click position.

The code is shown in listings 6.1 and 6.2. To draw the line, you need to keep the state of the previous mouse-click position. To do this, you use the `scan()` method that keeps a state value from last time it processed an event, giving you a stateful accumulator. On each invocation, the supplied function is passed the state and the new value, and it returns the new state value. That

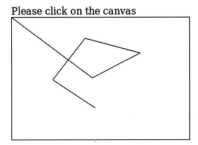

Figure 6.1 A web application that draws lines between mouse-click positions

new state value is then output on the sLines observable. Sodium has an equivalent to `scan()` called `accum()` that's implemented using a hold-snapshot loop.

Listing 6.1 connect-the-dots.html: drawing lines between mouse-click positions

```
<html><head>
    <title>Connect the dots</title></head>
    <style>
      #myCanvas { border-style: solid; border-width: 1px }
    </style>
    <script src="rx.all.min.js"></script>
    <script src="connect-the-dots.js"></script>
</head>
<body onload="init()">
    <div>Please click on the canvas</div>
    <canvas id="myCanvas" width="300" height="200">No canvas!</canvas>
</body>
</html>
```

The actual graphics are done in the subscriber. Note that the HTML5 canvas object keeps the drawn image in its own state, so the lines you drew earlier stay on the screen.

Listing 6.2 connect-the-dots.js

```
function init() {
    var canvas = document.getElementById("myCanvas");
    var sMouseDown = Rx.Observable.fromEvent(canvas, 'mousedown');
    var initial = { x0 : 0, y0 : 0, x1 : 0, y1 : 0 };
    var sLines = sMouseDown.scan(initial, function(last, e) {
        var x = e.pageX - canvas.offsetLeft;
        var y = e.pageY - canvas.offsetTop;
        return { x0 : last.x1, y0 : last.y1,
                 x1 : x,       y1 : y };
    });
    var subscription = sLines.subscribe(function (l) {
        var ctx = canvas.getContext("2d");
        ctx.beginPath();
        ctx.moveTo(l.x0, l.y0);
        ctx.lineTo(l.x1, l.y1);
        console.log('{ x:'+l.x1+', y:'+l.y1+' },');
        ctx.stroke();
    });
}
```

Takes an initial state value ... → (to `var sLines = sMouseDown.scan(initial, function(last, e) {`)

← *... and a function to update the state*

← *We never dispose() this subscription.*

You can check out this code and try it like this:

```
git clone https://github.com/SodiumFRP/sodium
```

Point your browser at sodium/book/web/connect-the-dots.html

You'll notice that the state management and logic are in a `scan()` so they're handled by FRP. You put only what you have to—the I/O—into the `subscribe()`.

6.2.4 *The most recent value of an observable with withLatestFrom()*

Figure 6.2 shows a program that, when you release the mouse button, draws a line from the mouse-down position to the mouse-up position, and a cross at each end. In listing 6.3 you use `withLatestFrom()` to capture the most recent `sMouseDown` position when `sMouseUp` fires. `withLatestFrom()` does the state keeping, so you're treating `sMouseDown` as a cell, but without any explicit conversion to one.

The approximate Sodium equivalent would be this

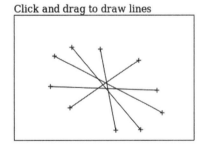

Click and drag to draw lines

Figure 6.2 Drawing a line between the mouse-down and mouse-up positions

```
sMouseUp.snapshot(sMouseDown.hold(null), ...);
```

but with the difference that if `sMouseDown` has never fired before, `withLatestFrom()` won't output anything. Take the HTML as read; it's only trivially different from the previous example.

Listing 6.3   line-stretch.js: Drawing a line from mouse-down to mouse-up position

```
function init() {
    var canvas = document.getElementById("myCanvas");
    var getXY = function(e) { return { x : e.pageX - canvas.offsetLeft,
                                       y : e.pageY - canvas.offsetTop }; };
    var sMouseDown = Rx.Observable.fromEvent(canvas, 'mousedown')
                                  .map(getXY);
    var sMouseUp = Rx.Observable.fromEvent(canvas, 'mouseup')
                                .map(getXY);
    var sLines = sMouseUp.withLatestFrom(sMouseDown,
                         function(up, down) {                      ←──  Captures the most recent
        return { x0 : down.x, y0 : down.y,                              mouseDown position
                 x1 : up.x,   y1 : up.y };                              when mouseUp fires
    });
    var sub1 = sMouseDown.merge(sMouseUp).subscribe(function (d) {  ←──┐
        var ctx = canvas.getContext("2d");
        ctx.beginPath();                                              Draws a cross at the
        ctx.moveTo(d.x-4, d.y);                                         mouseUp and
        ctx.lineTo(d.x+4, d.y);                                     mouseDown positions
        ctx.moveTo(d.x, d.y-4);
        ctx.lineTo(d.x, d.y+4);
        ctx.stroke();
    });
    var sub2 = sLines.subscribe(function (l) {                      ←──  On mouseUp, draws a line
        var ctx = canvas.getContext("2d");                             from the mouseDown to
        ctx.beginPath();                                              the mouseUp position
        ctx.moveTo(l.x0, l.y0);
        ctx.lineTo(l.x1, l.y1);
        ctx.stroke();
    });
}
```

To run this example, point your browser at sodium/book/web/line-stretch.html.

6.3   *Keeping state in RxJS, Kefir.js, and Flapjax*

BehaviorSubject is the thing that truly corresponds to Sodium's Cell, having the concept of a current value. It starts off as a cold observable. When you subscribe, you get called back once immediately with the current value. Then it becomes a hot observable, giving you the updates as they come in.

For instance, figure 6.3 shows a program that allows you to select a dog or cat polygon. When you click OK, an alert pops up, saying "You selected cat" or "You selected dog."

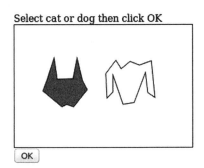

Select cat or dog then click OK

Figure 6.3   The Select application with the cat selected by default

Listings 6.4 and 6.5 show the Sodium `hold` equivalent, where you construct

```
var selected = new Rx.BehaviorSubject("cat");      ⟵── Cell with a default value
sSelected.subscribe(selected);          ⟵┐  Changes it according
                                         │  to sSelected
```

The equivalent in Sodium would be

```
selected = sSelected.hold("cat");
```

The argument says that the cat is selected by default. Using this instead of using `sSelected` directly has two positive effects on the program:

- It draws the scene on page load. Without the `BehaviorSubject`, you'd see nothing, because `sSelected` doesn't fire until the user clicks the canvas.
- If you only click OK, the program captures the default value (`"cat"`) that you passed to the `BehaviorSubject`. If you used `sSelected` directly, then if the user only clicked the OK button, nothing would happen. `withLatestFrom()` wouldn't see any event on `sSelected`, so it would output nothing when it got an event on `sOK`.

Forward references

The `Observable.subscribe(BehaviorSubject)` line can be written much later than the construction of the `Rx.BehaviorSubject`. This allows forward references, equivalent to `CellLoop` in Sodium. You can use this to write a state accumulator with a looped value, as you do in Sodium.

In a similar way, streams can be looped using a class called `Rx.Subject()`, giving an equivalent of Sodium's `StreamLoop`:

```
var s0 = new Rx.Subject();
...
s.subscribe(s0);
```

Listing 6.4 select-rxjs.html: Select application for selecting polygons

```
<html><head>
    <title>Select cat or dog then click OK - Rx.JS</title>
    <style>
      #myCanvas { border-style: solid; border-width: 1px }
    </style>
    <script src="rx.all.min.js"></script>
    <script src="select-rxjs.js"></script>
</head>
<body onload="init()">
    <div>Select cat or dog then click OK - Rx.JS</div>
    <canvas id="myCanvas" width="300" height="200">No canvas!</canvas>
    <div><button id="ok">OK</button></div>
</body>
</html>
```

```
function insidePolygon(pos, poly) {
    var x = pos.x, y = pos.y, coords = poly.coords, inside = false;
    var v = coords[coords.length-1], x1 = v.x, y1 = v.y;
    for( var i = -1; v = coords[++i]; ) {
        var x2 = v.x, y2 = v.y;
        if( ( y1 < y  &&  y2 >= y ) || ( y2 < y  &&  y1 >= y ) )
            if ( x1 + ( y - y1 ) / ( y2 - y1 ) * ( x2 - x1 ) < x )
                inside = ! inside;
        x1 = x2, y1 = y2;
    }
    return inside;
}
var shapes = [
    { id: "cat", coords: [{ x:55, y:90 },{x:67,y:54},{x:72,y:89},
          {x:99,y:88},{x:106,y:54},{x:115,y:91},{x:123,y:106},
          {x:100,y:134},{x:88,y:130},{x:80,y:134},{x:48,y:108}]},
    { id: "dog", coords: [{x:171,y:58},{x:154,y:80},{x:156,y:120},
          {x:166,y:110},{x:166,y:82},{x:183,y:130},{x:202,y:127},
          {x:221,y:78},{x:225,y:111},{x:237,y:119},{x:231,y:59},
          {x:211,y:66},{x:195,y:60},{x:180,y:72}]}
]

function init() {
    var canvas = document.getElementById("myCanvas");
    var getXY = function(e) { return { x : e.pageX - canvas.offsetLeft,
                                       y : e.pageY - canvas.offsetTop }; };
    var sMouseDown = Rx.Observable.fromEvent(canvas, 'mousedown')
                                  .map(getXY);
    var sSelected = sMouseDown.map(function(pos) {
        for (var i = 0; i < shapes.length; i++)
            if (insidePolygon(pos, shapes[i]))
                return shapes[i].id;
        return null;
    });
    var selected = new Rx.BehaviorSubject("cat");
    sSelected.subscribe(selected);
    var okButton = document.getElementById('ok');
    var sOK = Rx.Observable.fromEvent(okButton, 'click');
    sOK.withLatestFrom(selected, function(ok, sel) { return sel; })
        .subscribe(function(sel) {
            alert('You selected '+sel);
        });
    selected.subscribe(function(selected) {
        var ctx = canvas.getContext("2d");
        ctx.clearRect(0, 0, canvas.width, canvas.height);
        for (var i = 0; i < shapes.length; i++) {
            var coords = shapes[i].coords;
            ctx.beginPath();
            ctx.moveTo(coords[0].x, coords[0].y);
            for (var j = 0; j < coords.length; j++)
                ctx.lineTo(coords[j].x, coords[j].y);
            ctx.closePath();
            if (selected == shapes[i].id) {
```

"hold" a stream

```
            ctx.fillStyle = '#ff0000';
            ctx.fill();
        }
        ctx.stroke();
    }
  });
}
```

To run this example, point your browser at sodium/book/web/select-rxjs.html.

6.3.1 startWith() as shorthand for BehaviorSubject

In the previous example, these two lines

```
var selected = new Rx.BehaviorSubject("cat");
sSelected.subscribe(selected);
```

could be written like this:

```
var selected = sSelected.startWith("cat");
```

This will give you an observable that reports "cat" once on any new subscription. In this program, the effect would be the same, but they aren't equivalent.

On a new subscription, BehaviorSubject gives you "cat" if there haven't been any events yet, or the latest value if there have been events. Because it remembers the latest change, it works like an FRP cell. But startWith always gives "cat" as the initial value on a new subscription, no matter how many events have gone before. It doesn't remember the most recent event value like BehaviorSubject does. These two are only equivalent if you only ever subscribe to them during program initialization (before the first event is received) as many programs do.

6.3.2 The same again with Kefir.js

Now let's do it again in Kefir.js (see listing 6.6). Kefir is based on RxJS, but the equivalent of Cell/BehaviorSubject is called Property. It behaves more like a distinct type, as in Sodium. toProperty is exactly equivalent to Sodium's hold, and sampledBy is Sodium's snapshot with the first two arguments reversed.

> **Listing 6.6 select-kefir.js: Select application again in Kefir.js**

```
function init() {
    var canvas = document.getElementById("myCanvas");
    var getXY = function(e) { return { x : e.pageX - canvas.offsetLeft,
                                        y : e.pageY - canvas.offsetTop }; };
    var sMouseDown = Kefir.fromBinder(function(emitter) {
        canvas.addEventListener("mousedown", emitter.emit);
        return function() {
            canvas.removeEventListener("mousedown", emitter.emit);
        }
    }).map(getXY);
    var selected = sMouseDown.map(function(pos) {
```

```
        for (var i = 0; i < shapes.length; i++)
            if (insidePolygon(pos, shapes[i]))
                return shapes[i].id;
        return null;
    }).toProperty("cat");
    var okButton = document.getElementById('ok');
    var sOK = Kefir.fromBinder(function(emitter) {
        okButton.addEventListener("click", emitter.emit)
        return function() {
            okButton.removeEventListener("click", emitter.emit);
        }
    });
    selected.sampledBy(sOK, function(sel, ok) { return sel; })
            .onValue(function(sel) {
                alert('You selected '+sel);
            });
    selected.onValue(function(selected) {
        ...
```

To run this example, point your browser at sodium/book/web/select-kefir.html.

6.3.3 And now…Flapjax

Here's the same example in Flapjax (see listing 6.7). Flapjax is based more on "classic" FRP, so it's a little closer to Sodium than to RxJS.

Flapjax uses the old-school names `Event` (for stream) and `Behavior` (for cell); hence the `E` and `B` suffixes of its primitives. `mapE` corresponds to Sodium's `map` on streams, and `liftB` corresponds to Sodium's `map` on cells.

These two double as listen functionality for feeding outputs to I/O handling. We're not so keen on this idea because we think it's better to keep these concepts separate in people's minds: "This is `mapE`, and it's for referentially transparent logic. This is `listen`, and it's for I/O."

`startsWith` corresponds to Sodium's `hold`—not to RxJS's `startWith()`. And `snapshotE` is exactly `snapshot`.

> **NOTE** We maintain that FRP is FRP is FRP—that despite some surface differences, all FRP systems are substantially based on the same small set of simple concepts.

Listing 6.7 select-flapjax.js: Select application again this time in Flapjax

```
function init() {
    var canvas = document.getElementById("myCanvas");
    var getXY = function(e) { return { x : e.pageX - canvas.offsetLeft,
                                       y : e.pageY - canvas.offsetTop }; };
    var mouseDown = extractEventE(canvas,'mousedown').mapE(getXY);
    var selected = mouseDown.mapE(function(pos) {
        for (var i = 0; i < shapes.length; i++)
            if (insidePolygon(pos, shapes[i]))
                return shapes[i].id;
        return null;
```

```
    }).startsWith("cat");
    var okButton = document.getElementById('ok');
    var ok = clicksE(okButton);
    snapshotE(ok, selected, function(ok, sel) { return sel; })
        .mapE(function(sel) {
            alert('You selected '+sel);
        });
    ...
```

To run this example, point your browser at sodium/book/web/select-flapjax.html.

6.4 *The latest of two observables with combineLatest*

Now we'll return to RxJS. The final state-keeping method we need to cover is combineLatest, which allows you to combine the current values of two Cell-like input observables. It works as expected when its inputs are BehaviorSubjects. When used like this, it corresponds to lift in Sodium.

Figure 6.4 shows the trivial but classic use case of FRP lift: adding two numbers represented as cells. Listings 6.8 and 6.9 give the code. Some browsers will retain the content of the text fields if you reload. You'll see that everything works in a properly cell-like manner, so the sum starts off correct.

$$\boxed{61} + \boxed{99} = 160$$

Figure 6.4   Adding two numbers together

Listing 6.8   add.html: Adding two numbers together

```html
<html><head>
    <title>Add two numbers</title>
    <style>
      #a { width: 80px; }
      #b { width: 80px; }
    </style>
    <script src="rx.all.min.js"></script>
    <script src="add.js"></script>
</head>
<body onload="init()">
    <input id="a" type="text"/> +
    <input id="b" type="text"/> =
    <span id="c"/>
</body>
</html>
```

Listing 6.9   add.js

```
function currentTextOf(input) {
    var sKeyPresses = Rx.Observable.fromEvent(input, 'keyup'),
        text = new Rx.BehaviorSubject(input.value);
    sKeyPresses.map(function (e) { return input.value; }).subscribe(text);
    return text;
}
function init() {
    var a = currentTextOf(document.getElementById('a'))
            .map(function(text) { return parseInt(text); }),
```

BehaviorSubject of the current text of an input field

```
        b = currentTextOf(document.getElementById('b'))
            .map(function(text) { return parseInt(text); }),
        cSpan = document.getElementById('c');
    var c = a.combineLatest(b, function(aa, bb) { return aa + bb; });
    c.subscribe(function(cc) { cSpan.innerHTML = cc; });
}
```

To run this example, point your browser at sodium/book/web/add.html.

6.4.1   Glitches in combineLatest

We said in chapter 1 that because Rx isn't based on denotational semantics, it isn't truly compositional, and this is one of the requirements of FRP. One way in which this manifests is the area of glitches. A true FRP system should be glitch-free.

A *glitch* is defined as a visible output that isn't consistent with the relationships defined by the FRP code. To demonstrate a glitch, you need simultaneous events. Recall that two simultaneous events must originate in a single stream. This is the sort of thing that doesn't come up in simple programs but starts to become a problem as they get more complex.

The quickest way to illustrate is with a contrived example. Suppose you have two simultaneous events—ones and hundreds. You'll feed the numbers 1 and 2 into ones. hundreds is ones multiplied by 100, and sum is the sum of ones and hundreds. In a perfect, glitch-free world, figure 6.5 shows what you would like to see visible in sum.

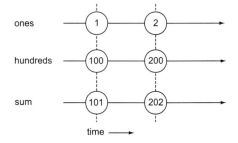

Figure 6.5   The sum of simultaneous events ones and hundreds

If you code this in RxJS (see listing 6.10) and then load it in the browser, you get these alerts:

- 101
- 102
- 202

The number 102 is referred to as a glitch because ones has the value of 2 at this point, so to be consistent, hundreds should be 200. 102 isn't consistent with the relationships described in the code. In an FRP system, no inconsistent state should be observable.

Listing 6.10   How RxJS handles simultaneous events

```
<html><head>
    <title>Glitch</title>
    <script src="rx.all.min.js"></script>
</head>
<body>
    <script type="text/javascript">
        var ones = Rx.Observable.range(1, 2);
        var hundreds = ones.map(function(x) { return x * 100; });
```

```
            var sum = ones.combineLatest(hundreds, function(o, h) {
            return o + h; });
            sum.subscribe(function(s) { alert(s); });
    </script>
</body>
```

To run this example, point your browser at sodium/book/web/glitch.html.

Listing 6.11 gives the Sodium equivalent. Sodium doesn't give glitches, so its output is as you'd like:

```
101
202
```

Listing 6.11 How Sodium handles simultaneous events

```
import nz.sodium.*;

public class glitch {
    public static void main(String[] args) {
        CellSink<Integer> ones = new CellSink<>(1);
        Cell<Integer> hundreds = ones.map(o -> o * 100);
        Cell<Integer> sum = ones.lift(hundreds, (o, h) -> o + h);
        Listener l = sum.listen(s -> System.out.println(s));
        ones.send(2);
        l.unlisten();
    }
}
```

When evaluating a system, you need to understand how it deals with simultaneous events and decide how important that is to your project. Once you've invested in a system for your project, you're stuck with its glitch behavior. It can't be fixed later.

What plagues does RxJS banish? See table 6.1.

Table 6.1 What plagues does RxJS banish?

Plague	Banished?
Unpredictable order	No
Missed first event	Yes
Messy state	Yes
Threading issues	Partially (see the following notes)
Leaking callbacks	Yes
Accidental recursion	No (see the following notes)

Notes:

- *Threading issues*—JavaScript doesn't have threads, so there are obviously no threading issues. The Rx system in other languages has imperfect ways of dealing with threading issues, but they're an improvement over traditional ways of doing things. This isn't as good as things could be. FRP systems can eliminate threading issues altogether, as Sodium demonstrates.

- *Accidental recursion*—Rx allows a subscriber's handler code to push events into an observable, which can lead to accidental recursion. Having said that, if you have the self-control not to do this, you should avoid this problem. Sodium strictly enforces a ban on doing this, as we'll explain in chapter 8. This is why it can completely eliminate this plague.

6.4.2   merge isn't compositional

A second, similar problem that RxJS and some other system have is that `merge` doesn't deal consistently with simultaneous events. This is exactly the same issue we described in section 5.3. This lack of compositionality creates more and more practical difficulties as program size increases, and as we've explained, these will eventually compound. You need to consider these issues when selecting an FRP system for your project.

> **Standardization of "streams" systems—an opportunity lost?**
>
> Rx-like systems are gaining wide acceptance and even becoming standards in some cases. We're concerned about the adoption of systems that lack compositional properties. It wouldn't take much additional effort to get things right. We think that when a broken form of FRP is adopted as standard, an important opportunity to improve the quality of software in the industry has been lost.

6.5   Creating your own hot observable

For the purposes of I/O handling, it's possible to create your own hot observables. We'll explain how here and give a concrete example in the next section. This is the skeleton:

```
var sOutput = Rx.Observable.create(function (observer) {
        ... asynchronous I/O stuff ...
        observer.onNext(outputValue);
        ...
    }).publish();
sOutput.connect();
```

There are four parts:

- You construct the observable, passing it a function that does the real work of supplying values to observers when they subscribe.
- Your asynchronous I/O code would then listen to some event source. When your code receives a callback and you want to push an event to subscribed observers, you call `onNext()` on the observer.
- Without `publish()`, if there were multiple subscribers, then the function you supplied would be executed more than once, creating one instance for each

subscriber. What `publish()` does is broadcast a single output stream: only one actual instance is created, and multiple subscribers each receive a copy of the same event.

- `publish()` doesn't start the single instance for which it broadcasts the output. You need to call `connect()` explicitly to make this happen.

6.5.1 Don't use this to implement logic

Creating your own hot observables is the right approach for pushing events from the I/O parts of your program into the FRP logic. But don't be tempted to use it to write stateful logic or implement your own primitives. To make this clear:

- You may want to write some code that receives events from an observable, keeps its own state, and outputs events based on that state.
- If it only does this, then you should use existing primitives instead. They were designed to guarantee compositionality with no effort on your part. If you can always assume compositionality, then there are large categories of potential bugs you don't even need to think about.
- If it does I/O as well, then it's probably best to do it with `subscribe()` by creating your own observables. The important thing is that you see it as being "outside the world of FRP."

The point of all this is so you can say, "*This* code is FRP, so I know it's compositional. *This* code is I/O, so I have to take care."

6.6 Example: autocomplete the FRP way

The examples we've given so far have been trivial ones to introduce individual primitives. Now let's put them all together in a more realistic example: the autocomplete functionality you commonly find on websites—done the FRP way (see figure 6.6). When the user selects a city, the example looks up and displays some information about the city (see figure 6.7).

Figure 6.6   Auto-complete implemented with FRP

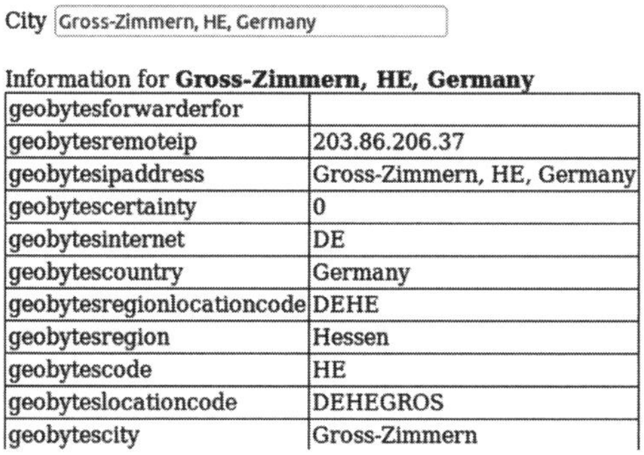

Information for **Gross-Zimmern, HE, Germany**

geobytesforwarderfor	
geobytesremoteip	203.86.206.37
geobytesipaddress	Gross-Zimmern, HE, Germany
geobytescertainty	0
geobytesinternet	DE
geobytescountry	Germany
geobytesregionlocationcode	DEHE
geobytesregion	Hessen
geobytescode	HE
geobyteslocationcode	DEHEGROS
geobytescity	Gross-Zimmern

Figure 6.7   You look up and display city info once the user selects it.

Look at listings 6.12 and 6.13. debounce() is an RxJS method giving you exactly what you need: it fires if there are no events for the specified time. You use this to tell you when the user has stopped typing for 100 ms before you look up the entered text on the server.

Listing 6.12   autocomplete.html: text field auto-complete, FRP style

```html
<html>
<head>
    <title>Autocomplete - Rx.JS</title>
    <style>
        #info { padding-top: 20px; }
        #city { width: 300px; }
        table { border-collapse: collapse; }
        table td { padding: 2px; border: 1px solid black; }
    </style>
    <script src="rx.all.min.js"></script>
    <script src="autocomplete.js"></script>
</head>
<body onload="init()">
    <div>
        <label for="city">City</label>
        <input id="city" type="text" />
    </div>
    <div id="info"></div>
</body>
</html>
```

Listing 6.13   autocomplete.js

```javascript
var jsonpCallbacks = {
    cntr: 0
};

function lookup(url, sRequest) {
    var sResponse = Rx.Observable.create(function (observer) {
        return sRequest.subscribe(function(req) {
            var fnName = "fn" + jsonpCallbacks.cntr++,
                script = document.createElement("script");
            script.type = "text/javascript";
            script.src = url+encodeURIComponent(req) +
                                "&callback=jsonpCallbacks." + fnName;
            jsonpCallbacks[fnName] = function(resp) {
                delete jsonpCallbacks[fnName];
                document.body.removeChild(script);
                observer.onNext([req, resp]);
            };
            document.body.appendChild(script);
        });
    }).publish();
    sResponse.connect();
    return sResponse;
}
```

Annotations:
- Looks up the city name on the server → `function lookup(url, sRequest) {`
- Constructs a hot observable to FRPify the I/O → `var sResponse = Rx.Observable.create(function (observer) {`
- I/O, so you're allowed to be stateful → `var fnName = "fn" + jsonpCallbacks.cntr++,`

```
function escapeHTML(text) {
    return text.replace(/&/g, '&amp;')
              .replace(/"/g, '&quot;')
                      .replace(/'/g, '&#39;')
                      .replace(/</g, '&lt;')
                      .replace(/>/g, '&gt;');
}

function calm(s) {
    return s.scan([null, null], function(prev_out, thiz) {
        return [thiz, thiz != prev_out[0] ? thiz : null];
    }).map(function(tpl) {
        return tpl[1];
    }).filter(function(a) {
        return a !== null;
    });
}

function currentTextOf(input) {
    var sKeyPresses = Rx.Observable.fromEvent(input, 'keyup'),
        text = new Rx.BehaviorSubject(input.value);
    sKeyPresses.map(function (e) { return input.value; }).subscribe(text);
    return text;
}

function autocomplete(textEdit) {
    var popup = document.createElement('select');
    popup.size = 15;
    popup.style.position = 'absolute';
    popup.style.zIndex = 100;
    popup.style.display = 'none';
    popup.style.width = textEdit.offsetWidth;
    popup.setAttribute('id', 'popup');
    document.body.appendChild(popup);
    var sClicked = Rx.Observable.fromEvent(popup, 'change')
                                .map(function (e) {
        return popup.value;
    });
    sClicked.subscribe(function (text) {
        return textEdit.value = text;
    });
    var editText = currentTextOf(textEdit),
        sKeyPresses = Rx.Observable.fromEvent(textEdit, 'keyup'),
        sDebounced = sKeyPresses.startWith(null).debounce(100),
        sTextUpdate = calm(sDebounced.withLatestFrom(editText,
            function (key, text) { return text; }));
    var sTabKey = sKeyPresses.filter(function(k) {
            return k.keyCode == 9; }),
        sEscapeKey = sKeyPresses.filter(function(k) {
            return k.keyCode == 27; }),
        sEnterKey = sKeyPresses.filter(function(k) {
            return k.keyCode == 13; });
    var sClearPopUp = sEscapeKey.merge(sEnterKey)
                                .merge(sClicked).map(null);
        lookedUp = lookup("http://gd.geobytes.com/AutoCompleteCity?q=",
```

Common FRP idiom: suppresses updates that are the same as previous values

From the add example: BehaviorSubject gives the current text of an input field.

City names selected from the pop-up

Pokes those into the text field

Fires if key presses are idle for 100 ms

Clears the pop-up if Esc or Enter is pressed or the user selects from the pop-up

Looks up on key presses idle or the Tab key

```
            sTextUpdate.merge(sTabKey.withLatestFrom(editText,
                function (key, text) {
                    return text;
                }
            ))
        ).map(function (req_resp) {
            var req = req_resp[0],
                resp = req_resp[1];
            return resp.length == 1 && (resp[0] == "%s"
                    || resp[0] == "" || resp[0] == req) ? null : resp;
        }).merge(sClearPopUp).startWith(null);
    lookedUp.subscribe(function(items) {
        if (items !== null) {
            var html = '';
            for (var i = 0; i < items.length; i++) {
                html += '<option>' + escapeHTML(items[i]) + '</option>';
            }
            popup.innerHTML = html;
            if (popup.style.display != 'block') {
                popup.style.left = textEdit.offsetLeft;
                popup.style.top = textEdit.offsetTop +
                                        textEdit.offsetHeight;
                popup.style.display = 'block';
            }
        }
        else {
            popup.style.display = 'none';
        }
    });
    return sEnterKey.withLatestFrom(editText, function (key, text) {
        return text;
    }).merge(sClicked);
}

function init() {
    var cityInput = document.getElementById("city"),
        infoDiv = document.getElementById("info"),
        sEntered = autocomplete(cityInput);
    lookup("http://getcitydetails.geobytes.com/GetCityDetails?fqcn=",
        sEntered).subscribe(function (city_info) {
        var city = city_info[0],
            info = city_info[1];
        var html = 'Information for <b>' + escapeHTML(city) +
                    '</b>' + '<table>';
        for (var key in info) {
            html += '<tr><td>' + escapeHTML(key) + '</td><td>' +
                    escapeHTML(info[key]) + '</td></tr>';
        }
        html += '</table>';
        infoDiv.innerHTML = html;
    });
}
```

Handles empty response cases from the server

Shows or doesn't show the pop-up based on lookedUp

Looks up city info

To run this example, point your browser at sodium/book/web/autocomplete.html.

6.7 RxJS/Sodium cheat sheet

RxJS includes the same concepts as Sodium, but with different names. Table 6.2 is a cheat sheet to get those concepts clear in your mind. See appendix C for comparison charts for many different FRP systems.

A reminder: our advice is that it's important to stick to FRP ways and avoid writing your own primitives. FRP is a powerful enough paradigm that you don't need to. The benefit is compositionality—or as near to compositionality as the particular system allows, if it isn't full FRP. This translates into fewer bugs in the real world.

Table 6.2 Equivalence between Sodium and RxJS

Sodium	RxJS
`Stream`	`Rx.Observable`
`new Stream()` (never fires)	`Rx.Observable.of()`
`s1.merge(s2)`	`s1.merge(s2)`
`s.map(f)`	`s.map(f)`
`s.filter(f)`	`s.filter(f)`
`s.snapshot(c, f)`	`s.withLatestFrom(c, f)`
`s.accum(i, f)`	`s.scan(i, f)`
`s.listen(handler)`	`s.subscribe(handler)`
`s.hold(i)`	`var c = new Rx.BehaviorSubject(i);` `s.subscribe(c);`
`Cell`	`Rx.BehaviorSubject`
`new Cell(constant)`	`Rx.Observable.of(constant)`
`c.map(f)`	`c.map(f)`
`c1.lift(c2, f)`	`c1.combineLatest(c2, f)`

`CellLoop.loop()`	`var c = new Rx.BehaviorSubject(i);`
	… code …
	`s.subscribe(c);`

`StreamLoop.loop()`	`var s0 = new Rx.Subject();`
	… code …
	`s.subscribe(s0);`

NOTE We'll cover `Stream.listen()` formally in chapter 8.

Functional Programming in JavaScript

FRP puts event-based code into a form that allows you to use the power of functional programming. You might want to check out *Functional Programming in JavaScript* by Luis Atencio (Manning, 2016) for a thorough treatment of the ways you can use this power.

6.8   *Static typing preferred*

When we think of web development, we usually think of JavaScript, which is a dynamically typed language. FRP does a lot of things to help prevent bugs, and a major part to this is the way it uses the power of static typing. Using a dynamically typed language, you miss out on some of the advantages that FRP provides.

Today, most languages can compile to JavaScript. If you're starting a new web project, we hope you'll consider a statically typed language, rather than assuming you have to use JavaScript. Languages with good type inference are better because you get type safety without the extra bashing away at the keyboard.

If you have an existing project, Microsoft's Typescript is a popular type-safe superset of JavaScript. Being a superset of JavaScript means you can easily port existing JavaScript applications to it. Typescript is just one example; there are plenty more to choose from.

6.9   *Summary*

- The RxJS observable is the same as the FRP concept of a stream of events.
- Instead of a `Cell`-equivalent type, three methods and one class are used to manage state: `scan()`, `withLatestFrom()`, `combineLatest()`, and `Behavior-Subject`.
- Observables can be cold—producing output immediately on subscription, or hot, producing output later as events happen. `BehaviorSubject` starts cold, outputting the current value once on initial subscription, and then becomes hot.
- `startWith()` is a shortcut for `BehaviorSubject`, but it's not exactly equivalent.
- RxJS doesn't prevent glitches and doesn't handle simultaneous events consistently, which means it doesn't have compositionality. This means it's not strictly a true FRP system.

Switch

FRP code describes data flow in a directed graph structure, and until now those graphs have been static. Cells for storing state are constructed using the `hold` primitive, and the total number of them hasn't been able to change as the program runs. `switch` allows you to change this structure dynamically. `sample` allows you to sample the value of a cell.

7.1   The sample primitive: getting a cell's value

What you're about to read may surprise you, coming from people as puritanical about compositionality as we are. Remember that in chapter 1 we talked about how people new to FRP will ask us, "How do you get the value?" We waved our hands around and gave some evasive answer. We wanted you to be thinking the right way before we told you that we can just say (for example)

```
Cell<Scene> scene = ...;
Scene sc = scene.sample();
```

and fetch the current value of a cell directly. Oh, the hypocrisy!

Now that you've calmed down and picked the book back up, a common case where `sample` is useful is in the `paint()` method of an animation. A `listen` callback might trigger a `repaint()`. For those who don't know about Java, this doesn't paint directly but schedules a `paint()` method to be executed "later."

When you come to do the actual paint, you can paint whatever the latest value is—fetched by `sample`. You might miss a frame, but so what? Sometimes there isn't enough CPU time, and that's the right thing to do.

Like all primitives, `sample` starts a small transaction if you don't do so explicitly. If you're doing several `sample`s, you may want them to be taken from the same instant in time. Wrapping them all in an explicit transaction will do this for you. We discussed transactions before, but they get a more complete treatment in section 8.3. You'll use `sample` in the next few examples because it makes some things more succinct.

7.2   *switch*

As we said, the FRP logic can be thought of as a data flow graph. Until now, this graph has been static. `switch`, also known as `flatten` or `join`, is the primitive that allows FRP to construct FRP, so the structure of the data flow graph can be changed dynamically as the program runs. Here are some common use cases:

- Add or remove monsters in a running game.
- Make invalid states not exist so they can't cause bugs.
- Divide an application into screens. For example, a video game might have an intro screen, preferences, the game itself, and a "game over" screen. Only the currently active screen should consume resources.

7.2.1   *The concept of switch: a TV remote control*

When I (Stephen) was a child, there were two TV channels with programs on them and a mysterious third channel that showed staticky fuzz. It was better than the other two channels, although I didn't realize that at the time.

To give a conceptual understanding of `switch`, imagine you're implementing a digital version of my old TV (see figure 7.1). As you know, a *cell* is a value that changes over time, so it makes sense to model a video stream as `Cell<Image>`—an image that changes over time.

`selected` is of type `Cell<Cell<Image>>` and holds the video stream that was most recently chosen with the remote control. You can see it as *a video stream (`Cell<Image>`) that changes over time*. That is, it's *an image that changes over time that changes over time*.

That translates to the type `Cell<Cell<Image>>`. To put the result on the screen, you need to convert it into the video stream type: that is, *flatten* it to `Cell<Image>`. This primitive is also called `switch`, because it switches from one chunk of logic to another,

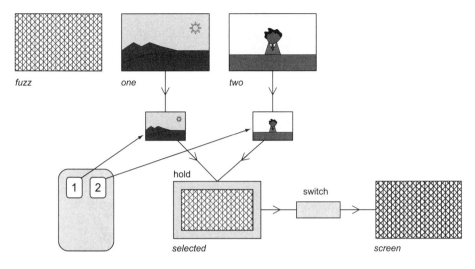

```
Cell<Image> fuzz = ...;
Cell<Image> one = ...;
Cell<Image> two = ...;
Stream<Unit> sButton1 = ...;
Stream<Unit> sButton2 = ...;
Cell<Cell<Image>> selected = sButton1.map(u -> one).orElse(
                                  sButton2.map(u -> two)).hold(fuzz);
Cell<Image> screen = Cell.switchC(selected);
```

Figure 7.1   Modeling a remote control that can switch between TV channels, showing the state before any button is pressed. The "fuzz" channel is selected by default.

or `join`, which is a term from functional programming. There's a stream variant and a cell variant of `switch`; we're using the cell variant here, called `switchC()` in Sodium.

7.3   *switch use case #1: zombies*

This section presents a video game example. We have two purposes in mind:

- FRP is great for video games because things are neatly encapsulated and composable. And it's especially good for monster AI. We want to show you how an FRP video game is normally structured.
- You may know that when a human is bitten by a zombie, they turn into a zombie themselves. We'll show how you can use `switch` to model this transformation.

With this in mind, we'll first introduce the video game character logic and later add `switch` functionality to implement the zombie bite transformation.

7.3.1 The end of the world

Figure 7.2 summarizes the strategies behind the human and zombie AI. Figure 7.3 shows the interaction between human and zombie AI in a running simulation: humans walk randomly, and zombies walk toward the nearest human.

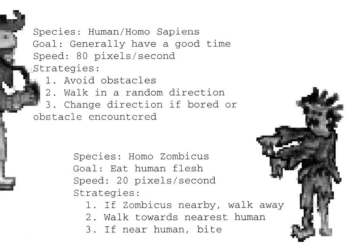

```
Species: Human/Homo Sapiens
Goal: Generally have a good time
Speed: 80 pixels/second
Strategies:
   1. Avoid obstacles
   2. Walk in a random direction
   3. Change direction if bored or
obstacle encountered

         Species: Homo Zombicus
         Goal: Eat human flesh
         Speed: 20 pixels/second
         Strategies:
            1. If Zombicus nearby, walk away
            2. Walk towards nearest human
            3. If near human, bite
```

Figure 7.2　Human and zombie strategies

Figure 7.3　A zombie apocalypse in progress

The layout of the scene is represented as a list of `Character` data structures, given in the following listing. It's used to draw the scene, but it's also used by zombies to decide what direction to walk in.

Listing 7.1 `Character`, describing an element of the scene

```
import java.awt.Point;

public class Character {
    public Character(int id, CharacterType type, Point pos,
                     Vector velocity) {
        this.id = id;
        this.type = type;
        this.pos = pos;
        this.velocity = velocity;
    }
    public final int id;                    ◁── Unique ID          Enum of SAPIENS
    public final CharacterType type;                           ◁──┘ or ZOMBICUS
    public final Point pos;
    public final Vector velocity;           ◁── Velocity
}
```

(x, y) position ──▷ (to `public final Point pos;`)

NOTE `Vector` is a class we wrote that does simple vector math. We won't list the code.

7.3.2   *A simple human*

Let's start with a simple human implementation in listing 7.2; then you'll animate it. The human is playing with a cellphone, rendering it oblivious to zombie predation. To simulate normal human motivation, it walks in a random direction; when it gets bored after 0.5 to 1.5 seconds, it picks a new direction.

Each character has a unique ID, which isn't needed yet. Later, you'll need it to identify who was bitten.

This code uses the newly introduced `sample` primitive in functions passed to `snapshot` three times. We'll explain this next.

Listing 7.2   A simple human character

```
import java.awt.Point;
import java.util.List;
import java.util.Optional;
import java.util.Random;
import nz.sodium.*;

public class SimpleHomoSapiens {
    public SimpleHomoSapiens(
        int self,                    ◁── Unique ID
        Point posInit,                                  ◁── Initial position
        Cell<Double> time,
        Stream<Unit> sTick)          ◁── Frame tick
    {
```

Animation time (seconds) ──▷ (to `Cell<Double> time,`)

```
                    final double speed = 80.0;
                    class Trajectory {
                        Trajectory(Random rng, double t0, Point orig) {
                            this.t0 = t0;
                            this.orig = orig;
                            this.period = rng.nextDouble() * 1 + 0.5;
                            double angle = rng.nextDouble() * Math.PI * 2;
                            velocity = new Vector(Math.sin(angle), Math.cos(angle))
                                         .mult(speed);
                        }
                        double t0;
                        Point orig;
                        double period;
                        Vector velocity;
                        Point positionAt(double t) {
                            return velocity.mult(t - t0).add(orig);
                        }
                    }
                    Random rng = new Random();
                    CellLoop<Trajectory> traj = new CellLoop<>();
                    Stream<Unit> sChange = Stream.filterOptional(
                        sTick.snapshot(traj, (u, traj_) ->
                            time.sample() - traj_.t0 >= traj_.period
                                ? Optional.of(Unit.UNIT)
                                : Optional.<Unit>empty()
                    ));
                    traj.loop(
                        sChange.snapshot(traj, (u, traj_) ->
                            new Trajectory(rng, time.sample(),
                                traj_.positionAt(time.sample())))
                        ).hold(new Trajectory(rng, time.sample(), posInit))
                    );
                    character = traj.lift(time, (traj_, t) ->
                        new Character(self, CharacterType.SAPIENS,
                            traj_.positionAt(t), traj_.velocity)
                    );
                }

            public final Cell<Character> character;
        }
```

Annotations:
- **Picks a random direction** → (points to `this.period` / `double angle` lines)
- **Position as a function of time** ← (points to `Point positionAt(double t)` line)
- **Accumulator for AI state** → (points to `CellLoop<Trajectory> traj` line)
- **Decides whether to change direction** ← (points to `Stream.filterOptional(` line)
- **Changes direction if "boredom" period expires** → (points to `sTick.snapshot` line)
- **New trajectory starts at current time and position** ← (points to `new Trajectory(rng, time.sample(),` line)
- **Output: representation in the scene** ← (points to `new Character(...)` line)

7.3.3   *Using sample in map or snapshot*

sample can be used in the function passed to map: this is equivalent to snapshot. The following code

```
Stream<Integer> sC = sA.snapshot(b, (a_, b_) -> a_ + b_);
```

can be written this way:

```
Stream<Integer> sC = sA.map(a_ -> a_ + b.sample());
```

These are equivalent.

> **NOTE**   Strictly speaking, snapshot isn't primitive because it can be written in terms of map and sample.

sample can also be used in snapshot as in the previous listing. Most FRP systems will allow you to snapshot more than one cell, but we're doing it this way to illustrate this use of sample.

Using sample in map or snapshot like this breaks the rule we gave in chapter 2: *functions passed to FRP primitives must be referentially transparent*. For a function to be referentially transparent, it must give the same answer for given inputs no matter when you run it. The output of sample depends on *when* it's called, so it doesn't comply.

We seem to be abusing the rules of FRP. We aren't, but in the light of both sample and switch, we need to modify the rule. sample is connected to the transactional context it runs in, so it can be used safely. If it runs in map or snapshot, then the value returned by sample is the value of the cell at the time of the event that triggered the passed function to be evaluated. Note that although sample is safe in such contexts, it wouldn't be safe to directly reference a normal mutable variable because the FRP system can't control when it's written.

This is the complete new rule:

- Functions passed to FRP primitives may contain code that's referentially transparent.
- Functions passed to FRP primitives that work with events (Stream.map, snapshot, filter, merge, Stream.accum) may use code that's connected to a transactional context. This includes sample and the construction of FRP logic using hold and other primitives.

NOTE sample isn't allowed in primitives that return cells, like lift and Cell.map, because the changes or steps in cell values shouldn't be treated as if they were events. We'll cover this in chapter 8.

To make switch useful, you need to allow the construction of FRP logic in event-based primitives. You'll see an example of this later when you construct new game characters while the game is running.

7.3.4 A game loop

Listing 7.3 gives a trivial game loop to animate a scene of several humans, even though nothing is looping yet. Animate contains the Java Swing code that does the actual drawing, and we won't list it here.

You lay out the humans across the screen and put their output character values into a list of type List<Cell<Character>>. But Animate wants a scene to draw, and that's a slightly different type: Cell<List<Character>>. You need to convert a list of cells of type A into a cell of a list of type A. It turns out there's a standard functional programming idiom to do this:

```
static <A> Cell<List<A>> sequence(Collection<Cell<A>> in)
```

Because this is such a general idea, we've borrowed its name from the Haskell programming language. An argument could be made to include this as a helper function in an FRP system.

It's important to understand that Animate—for which we don't list the code—invokes the FRP logic in three steps. Each step runs in a separate transaction:

1 Set time to the new time.

2 Push a UNIT value into sTick. This is the driver for all state updates.

3 Once the state updates are complete, read the scene out of the scene cell using sample, and draw it.

Remember that in Sodium, stream events cause cells to be updated, but the updates are delayed and aren't visible in the same transaction. You want the state changes triggered by sTick to see the new value of time, not the old one. Also, in step 3, you want to capture the new scene, not the old one. You achieve these things by performing each of these three steps in a transaction of its own.

We still haven't told you how to interface FRP logic to the rest of a program in Sodium, although we did for JavaScript in chapter 6. You've waited a long time, we know. It's coming in the next chapter.

NOTE   The three steps used to run this animation are similar to the technique for implementing continuous time. That's coming in chapter 9.

Listing 7.3   Animating several humans

```java
import java.awt.Dimension;
import java.awt.Point;
import java.util.ArrayList;
import java.util.Collection;
import java.util.List;
import nz.sodium.*;

public class simple {
    static <A> Cell<List<A>> sequence(Collection<Cell<A>> in) {        // The useful helper function
        Cell<List<A>> out = new Cell<>(new ArrayList<A>());
        for (Cell<A> c : in)
            out = out.lift(c,
                (list0, a) -> {
                    List<A> list = new ArrayList<A>(list0);
                    list.add(a);
                    return list;
                });
        return out;
    }
    public static void main(String[] args)
    {
        Animate.animate(
            "Zombicus simple",
            (Cell<Double> time, Stream<Unit> sTick,          // Passes a lambda to Animate to construct the scene
                                 Dimension windowSize) -> {
                List<Cell<Character>> chars = new ArrayList<>();
                int id = 0;
                for (int x = 100; x < windowSize.width; x += 100)
                    for (int y = 150; y < windowSize.height; y += 150) {
                        Point pos0 = new Point(x, y);
```

```
                    SimpleHomoSapiens h = new SimpleHomoSapiens(id,
                        pos0, time, sTick);
                    chars.add(h.character);
                    id++;
                }
                return sequence(chars);
            }
        );
    }
}
```

You can run it like this. Clone the git repository only if you haven't done so already:

```
git clone https://github.com/SodiumFRP/sodium
cd sodium/book/zombicus/java
mvn test -Psimple    or    ant simple
```

7.3.5   *An enhanced obstacle-avoiding human*

The humans are walking right off the screen. Listing 7.4 upgrades the human with obstacle-avoidance capabilities. The new human does two things:

- When picking a random direction for its trajectory, it retries up to 10 times if it gets a direction where there's an obstacle right in front of it.
- Hitting an obstacle is added as a new reason to pick a new trajectory.

In this simulation, the only obstacle is the edge of the screen.

You'll notice that there isn't a lot of complexity in the FRP bones of the logic. It's a simple state accumulator. Most of the complexity is in the details of the game itself. But this way of structuring a video game allows for any level of complexity you like in the game characters.

Listing 7.4   An obstacle-avoiding human

```
import java.awt.Point;
import java.util.List;
import java.util.Optional;
import java.util.Random;
import nz.sodium.*;

public class HomoSapiens {
    public HomoSapiens(
        World world,                          ⟵──┐ Contains obstacle
        int self,                                 │ information
        Point posInit,
        Cell<Double> time,
        Stream<Unit> sTick)
    {
        final double speed = 80.0;
        final double step = 0.02;
        class Trajectory {
            Trajectory(Random rng, double t0, Point orig) {
                this.t0 = t0;
                this.orig = orig;
```

```
                this.period = rng.nextDouble() * 1 + 0.5;
                for (int i = 0; i < 10; i++) {
                    double angle = rng.nextDouble() * Math.PI * 2;
                    velocity = new Vector(Math.sin(angle), Math.cos(angle))
                            .mult(speed);
                    if (!world.hitsObstacle(positionAt(t0 + step*2)))
                        break;
                }
            }
            double t0;
            Point orig;
            double period;
            Vector velocity;
            Point positionAt(double t) {
                return velocity.mult(t - t0).add(orig);
            }
        }

        Random rng = new Random();
        CellLoop<Trajectory> traj = new CellLoop<>();
        Stream<Unit> sChange = Stream.filterOptional(
            sTick.snapshot(traj,
                (u, traj_) -> {
                    double t = time.sample();
                    return world.hitsObstacle(traj_.positionAt(t + step))
                            || t - traj_.t0 >= traj_.period
                        ? Optional.of(Unit.UNIT)
                        : Optional.<Unit>empty();
                }));
        traj.loop(
            sChange.snapshot(traj, (u, traj_) ->
                new Trajectory(rng, time.sample(),
                    traj_.positionAt(time.sample())))
            ).hold(new Trajectory(rng, time.sample(), posInit))
        );
        character = traj.lift(time, (traj_, t) ->
            new Character(self, CharacterType.SAPIENS,
                traj_.positionAt(t), traj_.velocity)
        );
    }

    public final Cell<Character> character;
}
```

NOTE Our use of the Java random-number generator isn't strictly referentially transparent because it won't meet the requirement to always return the same output given the same input. In this case, the consequences aren't so bad, but if you want to do things properly, you might want to look into functional random-number generators.

We haven't listed the game loop code for this, but you can run it as follows. Clone the git repository only if you haven't done so already:

```
git clone https://github.com/SodiumFRP/sodium
cd sodium/book/zombicus/java
mvn test -Phumans     or     ant humans
```

7.3.6　*A flesh-eating zombie*

Listing 7.5 shows the Homo Zombicus logic. The zombie normally walks toward the nearest human, but if the nearest character is a zombie, and it's within 60 pixels, the first zombie will walk away from it. This is to prevent them from walking on top of each other so the scene looks better.

You update the zombie's direction every 0.2 seconds. You can't do it every frame, or you'll be viciously savaged by rounding errors because of the integer `Point` type you're using.

Notice that the initial `State` is constructed with an empty scene. The reason is that you don't have a value handy for the initial scene, so, you deal with this in the most expedient way: you stuff an empty scene into it the first time around. This means the zombies stand still for the first 0.2 second period.

Listing 7.5　Game logic for a zombie character

```java
import java.awt.Point;
import java.util.ArrayList;
import java.util.List;
import java.util.Optional;
import nz.sodium.*;

public class HomoZombicus {
    public HomoZombicus(
        int self,
        Point posInit,
        Cell<Double> time,
        Stream<Unit> sTick,
        Cell<List<Character>> scene)          ⟵── All characters currently
    {                                                 in the scene
        final double speed = 20.0;
        class State {
            State(double t0, Point orig, int self,
                                        List<Character> scene) {
                this.t0 = t0;
                this.orig = orig;
                double bestDist = 0.0;
                Optional<Character> oOther = nearest(self, scene);
                if (oOther.isPresent()) {
                    Character other = oOther.get();
                    this.velocity = Vector.subtract(other.pos, orig)
                                    .normalize().mult(
     Walks toward a  ⟶      other.type == CharacterType.SAPIENS
     human or away                  ? speed : -speed
       from a zombie            );
                }
                else
                    this.velocity = new Vector(0,0);
            }
            Optional<Character> nearest(int self, List<Character> scene) {
                double bestDist = 0.0;
                Optional<Character> best = Optional.empty();
```

```
                    for (Character ch : scene)
                        if (ch.id != self) {
                            double dist = Vector.distance(ch.pos, orig);
                            if (ch.type == CharacterType.ZOMBICUS && dist > 60)
                                ;
                            else
                            if (!best.isPresent() || dist < bestDist) {
                                bestDist = dist;
                                best = Optional.of(ch);
                            }
                        }
                    return best;
                }
                Optional<Character> nearestSapiens(int self,
                                                  List<Character> scene) {
                    List<Character> sapiens = new ArrayList<>();
                    for (Character ch : scene) {
                        if (ch.type == CharacterType.SAPIENS)
                            sapiens.add(ch);
                    }
                    return nearest(self, sapiens);
                }
                final double t0;
                final Point orig;
                final Vector velocity;
                Point positionAt(double t) {
                    return velocity.mult(t - t0).add(orig);
                }
            }

            CellLoop<State> state = new CellLoop<>();
            Stream<State> sChange = Stream.filterOptional(
                sTick.snapshot(state,
                    (u, st) -> {
                        double t = time.sample();
                        return t - st.t0 >= 0.2
                            ? Optional.of(new State(t, st.positionAt(t),
                                self, scene.sample()))
                            : Optional.<State>empty();
                    }
                ));
            List<Character> emptyScene = new ArrayList<Character>(0);
            state.loop(sChange.hold(
                new State(time.sample(), posInit, self, emptyScene)
            ));
            character = state.lift(time, (st, t) ->
                new Character(self, CharacterType.ZOMBICUS,
                    st.positionAt(time.sample()), st.velocity));
            sBite = Stream.filterOptional(
                sTick.snapshot(state,
                    (u, st) -> {
                        Optional<Character> oVictim = st.nearestSapiens(
                            self, scene.sample());
                        if (oVictim.isPresent()) {
```

Only cares about zombies that are nearby →

Position as a function of time →

Accumulator for AI state ←

Picks a new direction every 0.2 sec →

First time, decides based on an empty scene →

Output: representation in the scene ←

Bites if a human is within 10 pixels →

```
                        Character victim = oVictim.get();
                        Point myPos = st.positionAt(time.sample());
                        if (Vector.distance(victim.pos, myPos) < 10)
                            return Optional.<Integer>of(victim.id);
                    }
                    return Optional.<Integer>empty();
                }
            ));
    }

    public final Cell<Character> character;
    public final Stream<Integer> sBite;
}
```

7.3.7 Putting together the two characters

Now you'll put the human and zombie characters together into a simple animation that shows them moving. There is no transformation from human to zombie yet: you ignore the zombie's sBite output for now.

Figure 7.4 shows how it fits together. The inputs are simple: an animation clock cell and a tick stream for each frame. Why don't you combine time and sTick into one? Because time is conceptually continuous, so a cell is a suitable representation. Animation frames, on the other hand, are conceptually discrete, so a stream is sensible. We want to keep these ideas clear and separate. This code doesn't truly model continuous time. We'll show you how to do this properly in chapter 9.

Each character outputs a Character data structure describing its position and appearance. You gather them together into a list forming a scene, and this is what you draw. You also feed the scene into HomoZombicus

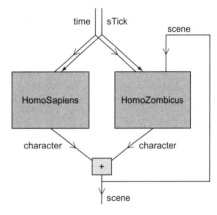

Figure 7.4   Putting the characters together in an animation: The code has multiple humans and zombies, but here we're showing one of each.

so that the zombies can see where the humans and other zombies are. We haven't shown you World, which is immutable.

We hope you'll agree that this is a simple and natural way to structure a game. The game characters maintain their own state internally, and you plumb everything as a data flow. Whenever you need data to go from point A to point B in the logic, you pass a cell or stream as necessary. FRP is a simple idea.

Listing 7.6 gives the code for the overall animation. The scene is constructed from the output of the characters. The outputs of the zombies depend on the scene, and this is a *cyclic dependency*. But because you use snapshot to sample the scene, and you know Sodium delays state updates, you're reading the scene from the previous frame and everything works well.

Listing 7.6 Putting the characters together

```
import java.awt.Dimension;
import java.awt.Point;
import java.util.ArrayList;
import java.util.Collection;
import java.util.List;
import nz.sodium.*;

public class characters {
    static <A> Cell<List<A>> sequence(Collection<Cell<A>> in) {
        Cell<List<A>> out = new Cell<>(new ArrayList<A>());
        for (Cell<A> c : in)
            out = out.lift(c,
                (list0, a) -> {
                    List<A> list = new ArrayList<A>(list0);
                    list.add(a);
                    return list;
                });
        return out;
    }
    static Cell<List<Character>> createCharacters(
            Cell<Double> time, Stream<Unit> sTick, World world,
            Cell<List<Character>> scene) {
        List<Cell<Character>> chars = new ArrayList<>();
        int id = 0;
        for (int x = 100; x < world.windowSize.width; x += 100)
            for (int y = 150; y < world.windowSize.height; y += 150) {
                Point pos0 = new Point(x, y);
                if (id != 3 && id != 6 && id != 7) {
                    HomoSapiens h = new HomoSapiens(world, id, pos0,
                        time, sTick);
                    chars.add(h.character);
                }
                else {
                    HomoZombicus z = new HomoZombicus(id, pos0,
                        time, sTick, scene);
                    chars.add(z.character);
                }
                id++;
            }
        return sequence(chars);
    }
    public static void main(String[] args)
    {
        Animate.animate(
            "Zombicus characters",
            (Cell<Double> time, Stream<Unit> sTick,
                                        Dimension windowSize) -> {
                World world = new World(windowSize);
                CellLoop<List<Character>> scene = new CellLoop<>();
                Cell<List<Character>> scene_ = createCharacters(
                    time, sTick, world, scene);
```

```
                scene.loop(scene_);
                return scene;
            }
        );
    }
}
```

You can run this with

```
git clone https://github.com/SodiumFRP/sodium
cd sodium/book/zombicus/java
mvn test -Pcharacters     or     ant characters
```

7.4 *Transforming the game character with switch*

HomoSapiens doesn't have any logic to handle a zombie bite. You'll make a new class called BitableHomoSapiens that starts off human and transforms itself into a zombie when it receives an sBite event.

In figure 7.5 we've attempted to draw what happens, but we can't depict it perfectly. The code in listing 7.7 fills in some details missing from the diagram. Effectively, when the bite event comes in, you replace a chunk of FRP logic with another, wiring things up as needed:

- The human is oblivious to its surroundings, so it doesn't use the scene input, but the zombie does.
- The human can't bite, so you start off outputting a never stream for sBite. The zombie outputs a real sBite stream.

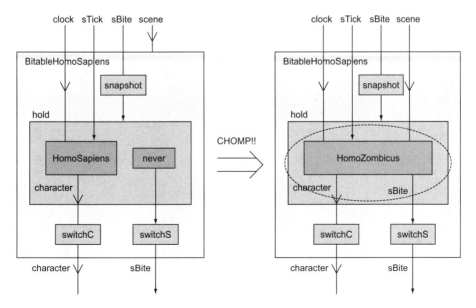

Figure 7.5 The logic in the hold is replaced when a human is bitten.

Note that the actual switch takes place on the output. There are two variants of switch: switchC to switch a cell, and switchS to switch a stream. You use these for character and sBite, respectively.

Listing 7.7   `BitableHomoSapiens` that transforms into a zombie when bitten

```
import java.awt.Point;
import java.util.List;
import java.util.Set;
import nz.sodium.*;

public class BitableHomoSapiens {
    public BitableHomoSapiens(
        World world,
        int self,
        Point posInit,
        Cell<Double> time,
        Stream<Unit> sTick,
        Stream<Set<Integer>> sBite,
        Cell<List<Character>> scene)
    {
        HomoSapiens h = new HomoSapiens(world, self, posInit,
            time, sTick);
        Stream<Set<Integer>> sBiteMe = sBite.filter(ids ->
            ids.contains(self));
        Stream<HomoZombicus> sBecome = sBiteMe.snapshot(
            h.character,
            (id, ch) -> new HomoZombicus(
                    self,
                    ch.pos,
                    time,
                    sTick, scene
            )
        );
        this.character = Cell.switchC(
            sBecome.map(z -> z.character).hold(h.character)
        );
        this.sBite = Cell.switchS(
            sBecome.map(z -> z.sBite).hold(new Stream<Integer>())
        );
    }
    public final Cell<Character> character;
    public final Stream<Integer> sBite;
}
```

Filters out a bite event if it isn't for this character → `Stream<Set<Integer>> sBiteMe = sBite.filter(ids -> ids.contains(self));`

`Stream<HomoZombicus> sBecome = sBiteMe.snapshot(` ← **Stream containing the new zombie**

Zombie starts at human's current position → `ch.pos,`

Starts as HomoSapiens, and then turns into the character from sBecome

Starts as a never, because humans don't bite, and then turns into the bite from sBecome → `this.sBite = Cell.switchS(`

To run this example, use the following:

```
git clone https://github.com/SodiumFRP/sodium
cd sodium/book/zombicus/java
mvn test -Pbite    or    ant bite
```

7.4.1   *If a tree falls...switch and memory management*

So far, we haven't talked much about memory management in this book. That's because FRP systems have, or should have, completely automated memory management, so you mostly don't even need to think about it. But it will be helpful to explain what's going on, and there are some subtleties worth noting.

IF A TREE FALLS IN THE FOREST...

You probably know this popular philosophical conundrum: "If a tree falls in the forest and no one is around to hear it, does it make a sound?" As this relates to the real world, we have no idea. But in FRP, the answer is, "No, it doesn't."

"If some FRP logic isn't observed by anyone, does it still execute?"

Because we require referential transparency, FRP can lock out all effects other than through cells and streams; in the absence of those, the only observable difference is the efficiency. While a bit of FRP logic is referenced by anything, it exists and consumes both memory and CPU resources. Once all references to it are dropped, it gets garbage-collected and vanishes.

In the example, you would like the memory used to store the human's state to be freed once it becomes a zombie. But the code won't clean it up because you haven't done it quite right. If you read the code carefully, you'll see that it's possible for the `BitableHomoSapiens` character to be bitten again even after it has become a zombie. In practice, this won't happen, because a zombie won't bite another zombie. But because of this possibility, the human logic is still referenced by the `snapshot` statement through this dependency chain: sBecome -> h.character. This will waste memory keeping the old human's logic alive even though it has no observable effect.

There are two ways to fix this:

- You can switch `sBecome` as you did with `character` and `sBite`, and then loop it back with a `StreamLoop`. It's a common idiom in FRP code for a fragment of logic to use `switch` to replace itself with a new implementation and so switch itself out of existence. You'll see an example of this shortly.
- You can use a method of `Stream` called `once()`—that we haven't mentioned before—in the definition of `sBiteMe`:

```
Stream<Integer> sBiteMe = sBite.filter(id -> id == self).once();
```

Most FRP systems have a `once`. What it does here is only ever let the `sBiteMe` event fire once. It should then free everything up.

In practice, it may not. It depends on the amount of cleverness in the implementation. Optimization in FRP systems will improve over time. In summary: apart from efficiency considerations, what isn't observed in FRP doesn't exist.

7.5 *switch use case #2: creation and destruction of game characters*

Each character in a game has its own logic and maintains its own state. As you know, FRP keeps state and logic together in neat modules. So far, you've created the characters at the start of the game and let them go, but games normally need to add and remove characters dynamically as they run. You can't do this without `switch`, because without `switch`, once FRP logic is constructed, its structure is static.

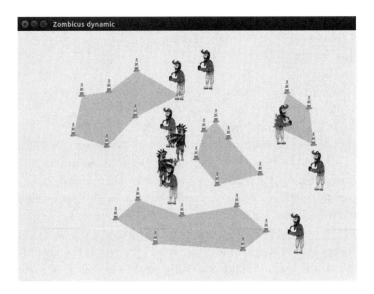

Figure 7.6   Creation and destruction: humans enter through a portal at the center, and zombies can fall down holes.

In this example, you'll have the humans enter the game every six seconds through an energetic portal at the center of the screen called Finsbury Park Tube Station. You'll also dig some holes in the road surrounded by traffic cones. Humans now have obstacle-avoidance logic, so they will be safe, but zombies can be destroyed by falling into the holes. See figure 7.6.

The code is shown in listing 7.8 on page 150. The key to the whole thing is that you maintain a State data structure with these fields:

```
int nextID;
Map<Integer, Cell<Character>> chars;
Map<Integer, Stream<Integer>> sBites;
Map<Integer, Stream<Integer>> sDestroys;
```

The Maps are indexed by a unique ID for each character. You could make a new data structure and put the values together into a single map, but it's slightly more convenient this way.

As usual, you accumulate the State data structure in a cell by looping snapshot and hold primitives, but State *contains* cells and stream, which you haven't done before. Note that sChange is a stream of functions that changes the state of the game by adding or removing characters:

```
CellLoop<State> state = new CellLoop<>();
...
Stream<Lambda1<State, State>> sChange = ...;
state.loop(sChange.snapshot(state, (f, st) -> f.apply(st))
                 .hold(initState));
```

You've seen the `character` cell and the `sBite` stream as the outputs of a character before, but now you add a new stream `sDestroy` that destroys the specified character. The mechanism is that each character can send a message that causes itself to be terminated by the top-level logic of the game loop. It's a common FRP idiom for a piece of logic to ask to be terminated in this way.

`state` is a `Cell<State>`, and `State` contains cells and streams within its structure. You want to extract three outputs from this so they can be used in the top-level game loop (`scene`, `sBite`, and `sDestroy`). This is done in two steps:

1. Merge the outputs of the characters. From `Cell<State>` state, you get values of type `Cell<Cell<...>>` and `Cell<Stream<...>>` using the map primitive.

2. You can't use these as they are, so you use `switch` to flatten them to `Cell<...>` and `Stream<...>`. Now they're usable.

For example, here's how you extract a single combined `sDestroy` stream from all the characters in the state:

```
Cell<Stream<Set<Integer>>> csDestroy = state.map(st ->
                        Helper.mergeToSet(st.sDestroys.values()));
this.sDestroy = Cell.switchS(csDestroy);
```

To merge streams, you use a helper, `mergeToSet()`, that collects simultaneous events into a set, because more than one character can be destroyed in the same transaction. The events of `sDestroy` give the set of all characters that are being destroyed in one frame tick. `mergeToSet()` would be less cumbersome with a proper immutable/functional implementation of `Set`. If immutable data structures become standard in Java, this could become a Sodium primitive. Here it is:

```
public static <A> Stream<Set<A>> mergeToSet(Iterable<Stream<A>> sa) {
    Vector<Stream<Set<A>>> asSets = new Vector<>();
    for (Stream<A> s : sa)
        asSets.add(s.map(a -> {
            TreeSet<A> set = new TreeSet<>();
            set.add(a);
            return set;
        }));
    return Stream.merge(asSets, (s1, s2) -> {
        TreeSet<A> out = new TreeSet<>(s1);
        out.addAll(s2);
        return out;
    });
}
```

To update the state, you have to process both the creations and the destructions of characters, and with many characters present in the game, creation and destruction events of different characters are likely to occur simultaneously. To combine them successfully, you'll first represent both `sAdd` and `sRemove` as streams of state transformations. Here's how you do it for `sRemove`:

```
Stream<Lambda1<State, State>> sRemove
            = sDestroy.map(ids -> st -> st.remove(ids));
```

Each state transformation is represented by a Lambda1<State, State>, which is a function that takes a State and returns a modified State.

The expression ids -> st -> st.remove(id) gives a function that takes a set of character ids and turns it into a Lambda1<State, State> state transformation. It may be clearer if you add parentheses and think of it as ids -> (st -> st.remove(id)). If you're new to functional programming, you may need a moment of contemplation. We'll pause the book.

Welcome back. Functional programmers call this *currying*, and you can read more about it online or in any book on functional programming.

Once the changes are represented as state transformations, you can then merge them with a combining function that chains two transformations together into a single lambda:

```
Stream<Lambda1<State, State>> sChange = sAdd.merge(sRemove,
    (f1, f2) -> a -> f1.apply(f2.apply(a)));
```

And finally, you apply the resulting single function to the state:

```
state.loop(sChange.snapshot(state, (f, st) -> f.apply(st))
                  .hold(initState));
```

Accumulating change functions like this is a common FRP idiom, so it's a candidate for a helper method in an FRP system.

Listing 7.8 Dynamically adding and removing characters

```
import java.awt.Dimension;
import java.awt.Point;
import java.awt.Polygon;
import java.util.ArrayList;
import java.util.Collection;
import java.util.HashMap;
import java.util.List;
import java.util.Map;
import java.util.Optional;
import java.util.Set;
import nz.sodium.*;

public class dynamic {
    static <A> Cell<List<A>> sequence(Collection<Cell<A>> in) {
        Cell<List<A>> out = new Cell<>(new ArrayList<A>());
        for (Cell<A> c : in)
            out = out.lift(c,
                (list0, a) -> {
                    List<A> list = new ArrayList<A>(list0);
                    list.add(a);
                    return list;
                });
        return out;
    }
    public static Stream<Unit> periodicTimer(          ⟵─┐ Fires at a regular
                                                          │ interval (see the
                                                          ┘ next section)
```

```
                    Cell<Double> time, Stream<Unit> sTick, double period) {
                CellLoop<Double> tAlarm = new CellLoop<>();
                Stream<Double> sAlarm = Stream.filterOptional(
                    sTick.snapshot(tAlarm,
                        (u, alarm) -> time.sample() >= alarm
                            ? Optional.of(time.sample() + period)
                            : Optional.<Double>empty())
                );
                double t0 = time.sample() + period;
                tAlarm.loop(sAlarm.hold(t0));
                return sAlarm.map(u -> Unit.UNIT);
            }
            static class State {
                State() {
                    this.nextID = 0;
                    this.chars = new HashMap<>();
                    this.sBites = new HashMap<>();
                    this.sDestroys = new HashMap<>();
                }
                State(int nextID, Map<Integer, Cell<Character>> chars,
                                Map<Integer, Stream<Integer>> sBites,
                                Map<Integer, Stream<Integer>> sDestroys) {
                    this.nextID = nextID;
                    this.chars = chars;
                    this.sBites = sBites;
                    this.sDestroys = sDestroys;
                }
                final int nextID;
                final Map<Integer, Cell<Character>> chars;
                final Map<Integer, Stream<Integer>> sBites;
                final Map<Integer, Stream<Integer>> sDestroys;

                State add(Cell<Character> chr, Stream<Integer> sBite,
                        Stream<Integer> sDestroy) {
                    Map<Integer, Cell<Character>> chars =
                                        new HashMap<>(this.chars);
                    Map<Integer, Stream<Integer>> sBites =
                                        new HashMap<>(this.sBites);
                    Map<Integer, Stream<Integer>> sDestroys =
                                        new HashMap<>(this.sDestroys);
                    chars.put(nextID, chr);
                    sBites.put(nextID, sBite);
                    sDestroys.put(nextID, sDestroy);
                    return new State(nextID+1, chars, sBites, sDestroys);
                }
                State remove(Set<Integer> ids) {
                    Map<Integer, Cell<Character>> chars =
                                        new HashMap<>(this.chars);
                    Map<Integer, Stream<Integer>> sBites =
                                        new HashMap<>(this.sBites);
                    Map<Integer, Stream<Integer>> sDestroys =
                                        new HashMap<>(this.sDestroys);
                    for (Integer id : ids) {
                        chars.remove(id);
                        sBites.remove(id);
```

Functional data structures would make this copying efficient.

```
                              sDestroys.remove(id);
                    }
                    return new State(nextID, chars, sBites, sDestroys);
             }
      }
      static Stream<Integer> fallDownHole(int self, Stream<Unit> sTick,
                              Cell<Character> character, World world) {
          return Stream.filterOptional(
              sTick.snapshot(character, (u, ch) ->
                  world.hitsHole(ch.pos) ? Optional.of(self)
                                         : Optional.<Integer>empty()
              ));
      }
      static class CreateCharacters {
          CreateCharacters(Cell<Double> time,
                  Stream<Unit> sTick, World world,
                  Cell<List<Character>> scene, Stream<Set<Integer>> sBite,
                  Stream<Set<Integer>> sDestroy) {
              State initState = new State();
              HomoZombicus z = new HomoZombicus(initState.nextID,
                  new Point(36,332), time, sTick, scene);
              initState = initState.add(z.character, z.sBite,
                  fallDownHole(initState.nextID, sTick, z.character, world));
              CellLoop<State> state = new CellLoop<>();
              Point center = new Point(world.windowSize.width / 2,
                                       world.windowSize.height / 2);
              Stream<Lambda1<State, State>> sAdd =
                  periodicTimer(time, sTick, 6.0)
                  .map(u ->
                      st -> {
                          BitableHomoSapiens h = new BitableHomoSapiens(
                              world, st.nextID, center, time, sTick,
                              sBite, scene);
                          return st.add(h.character, h.sBite,
                              fallDownHole(st.nextID, sTick, h.character,
                              world));
                      }
                  );
              Stream<Lambda1<State, State>> sRemove
                              = sDestroy.map(ids -> st -> st.remove(ids));
              Stream<Lambda1<State, State>> sChange = sAdd.merge(sRemove,
                  (f1, f2) -> a -> f1.apply(f2.apply(a)));
              state.loop(sChange.snapshot(state, (f, st) -> f.apply(st))
                              .hold(initState));
              Cell<Cell<List<Character>>> cchars = state.map(st ->
                                       sequence(st.chars.values()));
              this.scene = Cell.switchC(cchars);
              Cell<Stream<Set<Integer>>> csBite = state.map(st ->
                              Helper.mergeToSet(st.sBites.values()));
              this.sBite = Cell.switchS(csBite);
              Cell<Stream<Set<Integer>>> csDestroy = state.map(st ->
                              Helper.mergeToSet(st.sDestroys.values()));
              this.sDestroy = Cell.switchS(csDestroy);
          }
          final Cell<List<Character>> scene;
```

Annotations:
- **Starts with one zombie** → `HomoZombicus z = new HomoZombicus(initState.nextID,`
- **Creates a new human every six seconds** → `Stream<Lambda1<State, State>> sAdd =`
- **Function that returns a function** → the `.map` lambda block
- **Coalesces state changes into one** → `Stream<Lambda1<State, State>> sChange = sAdd.merge(sRemove,`
- **Applies the state change** → `state.loop(sChange.snapshot(state, (f, st) -> f.apply(st))`
- **Extracts outputs from the state** → `Cell<Cell<List<Character>>> cchars = state.map(st ->`, `Cell<Stream<Set<Integer>>> csBite = state.map(st ->`, `Cell<Stream<Set<Integer>>> csDestroy = state.map(st ->`

```
        final Stream<Set<Integer>> sBite;
        final Stream<Set<Integer>> sDestroy;
    }

    public static void main(String[] args)
    {
        ArrayList<Polygon> obstacles = new ArrayList<>();
        obstacles.add(...);                                        ←───┐  Numbers
        Animate.animate(                                                │  omitted
            "Zombicus dynamic",
            (Cell<Double> time, Stream<Unit> sTick,
                                      Dimension windowSize) -> {
                World world = new World(windowSize, obstacles);
                CellLoop<List<Character>> scene = new CellLoop<>();
                StreamLoop<Set<Integer>> sBite = new StreamLoop<>();
                StreamLoop<Set<Integer>> sDestroy = new StreamLoop<>();
                CreateCharacters cc = new CreateCharacters(
                    time, sTick, world, scene, sBite, sDestroy);
                scene.loop(cc.scene);
                sBite.loop(cc.sBite);
                sDestroy.loop(cc.sDestroy);
                return scene;
            },
            obstacles
        );
    }
}
```

To run this example, use the following:

```
git clone https://github.com/SodiumFRP/sodium
cd sodium/book/zombicus/java
mvn test -Pdynamic    or    ant dynamic
```

> **NOTE** In this example, we've achieved the FRP programmer's coveted "wall of code" effect. Mwahahaha!

7.5.1 *Not quite referentially transparent*

We said earlier that sample isn't referentially transparent: what value it returns depends on the context it runs in. We want to help cement this idea in your mind by directing your attention to a couple of examples from this code.

The previous listing had this function:

```
public static Stream<Unit> periodicTimer(
        Cell<Double> time, Stream<Unit> sTick, double period) {
    CellLoop<Double> tAlarm = new CellLoop<>();
    Stream<Double> sAlarm = Stream.filterOptional(
        sTick.snapshot(tAlarm,
            (u, alarm) -> time.sample() >= alarm
                ? Optional.of(time.sample() + period)        ←─── Next alarm
                : Optional.<Double>empty())
    );
    double t0 = time.sample() + period;                      ←─── Time of first alarm
```

Reached alarm time? (annotation pointing to `(u, alarm) -> time.sample() >= alarm`)

```
    tAlarm.loop(sAlarm.hold(t0));
    return sAlarm.map(u -> Unit.UNIT);
}
```

Update to a new alarm time
each time sAlarm fires

This is an example of `sample` giving different answers in different contexts, which means it isn't referentially transparent. In the `snapshot`, it gives you the time when `sTick` fired. In the body of `periodicTimer()`, it gives you the time when the `periodicTimer()` FRP logic is constructed.

Here's another example from that listing:

```
Stream<Lambda1<State, State>> sAdd =
    periodicTimer(time, sTick, 6.0)
    .map(u ->
        st -> {
            BitableHomoSapiens h = new BitableHomoSapiens(
                world, st.nextID, center, time, sTick,
                sBite, scene);
            return st.add(h.character, h.sBite,
                fallDownHole(st.nextID, sTick, h.character,
                    world));
        }
    );
```

The constructor of `BitableHomoSapiens` constructs `HomoSapiens`, and if you look back at this listing for `HomoSapiens`, you can see that it too invokes `time.sample()` at its top level (highlighted):

```
traj.loop(
    sChange.snapshot(traj, (u, traj_) ->
        new Trajectory(rng, time.sample(),
            traj_.positionAt(time.sample())))
    ).hold(new Trajectory(rng, time.sample(), posInit))
);
```

The time returned by this invocation is used in the initial trajectory of the human. Again, the value depends on the transactional context in which it's executed. In this case, it's the time of the `sAdd` when the human was constructed. The other two invocations of `time.sample()` are in a `snapshot`, so those happen later.

7.5.2   *Another "What are we doing this for?" moment*

FRP—like any other way you might choose to do things—has costs. It's more restrictive than other ways, and that leads to a certain level of bureaucracy. It's important to ask what you're getting in return.

FRP is restrictive?

The idea of FRP being "restrictive" is not necessarily so. It depends on your point of view.

It looks restrictive because you're not allowed to modify state directly. But what does this mean? It means you're not allowed to assume that the underlying machine is a von Neumann machine. It's only because you're so used to this assumption that you perceive not being able to make it as a "restriction." But is that a good assumption to make?

The way you've become accustomed to writing code is restrictive in ways that FRP isn't. For example you're restricted by having to specify things in a particular order. The difficulty comes in exchanging your old restriction and freedom for a new kind of restriction and freedom. FRP gives you what you need, not what you think you want.

We're telling you that FRP code is simple to reason about and close to the problem. But it would be helpful if we could illustrate this. As always, the problem is this: it would be good if we could show you some complex code and say, "Look how (relatively) simple this is." But doing so could make the book pretty unreadable.

Instead, we'll try this: imagine how you'd add transition animations to this code. Let's say that when a character is created, bitten, or destroyed, we show a nice animation and perhaps block certain input events while it's running. These are the sorts of complicating factors that make the difference between book examples and real-world code.

We hope you can see that everything is so nicely isolated and encapsulated that these changes would be easy to put into cleanly separated modules. You may also find that you can reuse a lot of code between the three situations.

FRP and static typing

FRP pushes the type system to its limit. In Java, you end up with a lot of very long types that you don't see in a dynamic language such as JavaScript. Static types don't do anything, and in Java all the type information in angle brackets (between < and >) evaporates when you compile your code. But static types do add more information to the source code, and they help you pick up type errors early.

Even with all the type information, the code is information-dense. It's simple, but it can be difficult to read because it does a lot of work in only a few lines. You can consider that the type information is a kind of white space. If may help to make the editor color for types lighter to give you a clearer view of the logic.

In a lot of cases, we've introduced intermediate variables to make the code easier to read. You may find it sufficient to inline some of the intermediate variables once your team is rocking FRP. This is especially true if you have a powerful IDE that shows the types of everything.

In chapter 15, we'll discuss *type inference* as a way to improve FRP. Type inference removes type clutter without a loss of type safety.

7.5.3   *An exercise for you*

Your challenge, if you like, is to turn this into a playable game by having the mouse cursor act as a little bird that awakens the human from its cellphone reverie, causing the human to walk toward the bird. The goal is to save the world by enticing the humans to stand in the right places so the zombies are lured to their demise in the roadwork holes.

7.6   *The efficiency of big merges*

Whenever a character is created or destroyed, the utility function `sequence()` and Sodium's collection variant of `Stream.merge()` are called to construct new outputs. These iterate over the entire list. Here's a naïve implementation of the collection variant of `merge()`:

```
static <A> Stream<A> merge(Collection<Stream<A>> in, Lambda2<A,A,A> f) {
    Stream<A> sOut = new Stream<>();
    for (Stream<A> c : in)
        sOut = sOut.merge(c, f);
    return sOut;
}
```

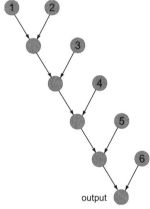

In figure 7.7, you can see that the resulting structure is in a long line, and if a node far from the end is updated, it has to go through *N*-1 nodes to reach the output. This clearly isn't scalable.

FRP and the requirement for referential transparency force us to do things this way, so we have to find a way to deal with this. We can easily improve the efficiency of the created data structure by constructing a balanced tree instead of a long line. Then the time to propagate a message is order log(*N*) instead of order *N*. A recursive version of `merge()` would look like this:

Figure 7.7   Merging six things into one the inefficient way

```
static <A> Stream<A> merge(Collection<Stream<A>> in, Lambda2<A,A,A> f) {
    if (in.isEmpty()) return new Stream<A>();
    if (in.size() == 1) return in.iterator().next();
    List<Stream<A>> l = new ArrayList<>();
    List<Stream<A>> h = new ArrayList<>();
    int i = 0;
    for (Stream<A> s : in) {
        if (i < in.size() / 2) l.add(s); else h.add(s);
        ++i;
    }
    return merge(l,f).merge(merge(h,f),f);
}
```

But if you're updating this tree frequently, it's inefficient to reconstruct the whole thing each time.

A proper solution would be to build switches into the tree so that each update only needs to reconstruct a local section. Note that this tree is a mutable data structure, not one of the immutable data structures we've described. Updates should then be order $\log(N)$. We'll discuss this and give a concrete example in section 8.6.

NOTE   Ryan Trinkle has done work on bettering these log factors in his *Reflex* FRP system at https://github.com/reflex-frp/reflex.

7.6.1   *Efficiency of this approach*

One of our reviewers said this about chapter 7:

Game characters change position every time, and this could lead to the creation of thousands of characters—for every tick in the game loop, all characters in the scene should be re-created. That's a lot of burden on the GC (garbage collector).

There are a number of things we would say about this:

- Functional languages execute code like this all the time and achieve some impressive speeds these days. They optimize the code, and their garbage collectors are efficient for short-lived objects. You can't assume memory allocation is happening, and if it's happening, you can't assume it's expensive.
- If you assume that modifying values in place is more efficient than copying them, then you're assuming your machine is a von Neumann machine. Although we don't know the exact performance characteristics, we hope we persuaded you in chapter 5 that these kinds of assumptions don't necessarily hold today and almost certainly won't in the future.
- FRP has potential for aggressive optimization, although at the time of writing this is still in the future.

We can't prove anything here, but our intuition is that FRP could be made extremely fast.

7.7   *Game characters and efficiency in RxJS*

Now we'll look at some of these efficiency considerations in an RxJS example that has the same basic structure as the zombie game. See figure 7.8: you're the groundskeeper for a golf course in Austria run by your uncle, a mad professor. To control the mole problem, he has issued you a large wooden mallet. You're sure this contravenes every animal welfare code since Charlemagne, but, having been caught evading import tax on Moroccan lanterns, you need to prove you're capable of honest work, or you'll lose your inheritance. Your "inheritance" is a golf course full of moles, but the penny hasn't dropped yet.

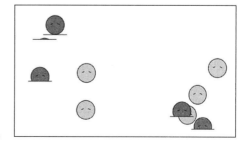

Figure 7.8   Video game "Whack That Mole!"

The first thing we'll look at is the mole itself, in listing 7.9. It's the same basic idea as the zombie and human characters in the previous example, except you don't need a view of the world because moles are blind. Here are the inputs:

- Unique ID for the mole.
- Constant x-y position.
- Animation clock. You're treating this as both a stream and a cell. This isn't in the spirit of FRP, but it allows you to represent the animation clock in a single variable, which is arguably an advantage.
- sClick stream to indicate that the user clicked the mole.

And here are the outputs:

- id—From the input
- drawable—Function that draws the mole character
- sDestroy—Stream allowing the mole to request its own destruction
- dispose—Described shortly

The mole has three states: *rising, up,* and *whacked.* The user can only whack the mole in the *rising* state. If it rises all the way without being whacked, its state changes to *up,* meaning it won; it will then laugh at you for 10 seconds. This is the first time we've done a game in JavaScript, but the FRP concepts used here are all the same.

You return a dispose function for this reason: the Rx.BehaviorSubject/ subscribe idiom in RxJS is like any use of subscribe, in returning a subscription object. When the logic is used in flatMapLatest(), which is RxJS's switch (as you'll do shortly), there will be a memory leak if you don't clean this up explicitly.

This is true at the time of writing, but the desirable situation is that this should be automatic, as it is in Sodium. If you used scan() instead of the Rx.BehaviorSubject/ subscribe idiom, this wouldn't be an issue. You could do it this way, but there are two advantages of using Rx.BehaviorSubject:

- You can rely on the cell-like semantics of the state value. The observable returned by scan() doesn't give you a current value on subscription. This might be important if you use withLatestFrom() on it later.
- You're combining sUp and sWhack, which originate from two different inputs. We think the Rx.BehaviorSubject/subscribe idiom expresses things a bit more naturally than scan() in this sort of case.

Listing 7.9 The mole's logic

```
function mkMole(id, x, y, clock, sClick)
{
    var tRise = 100,
        tWhack = 15,
        tUp = 500;
    function drawMole(ctx, x, y, up, fracVisible) {
```

Time to rise from hole

Time to descend when whacked

Time to hang around in the up state

```
          ...
    }
    var state = new Rx.BehaviorSubject({ phase : 'rising',
                                         t0 : clock.getValue() }),
        sUp = clock.withLatestFrom(state,
                function (t, state) {
                    return state.phase == 'rising' &&
                                t - state.t0 >= tRise
                        ? { phase : 'up', t0 : t }
                        : null;
                })
            .filter(function (state) { return state !== null; }),
        sWhack = sClick.withLatestFrom(clock, state,
                function (_, t, state) {
                    var dt = t - state.t0;
                    return state.phase == 'rising'
                        ? { phase : 'whacked',
                            t0 : t - (1 - dt / tRise) * tWhack }
                        : null;
                })
            .filter(function (state) { return state !== null; }),
        subscr1 = sUp.merge(sWhack).subscribe(state),
        drawable = clock.withLatestFrom(state, function (t, state) {
            return state.phase == 'rising' ? function (ctx) {
                    var dt = t - state.t0;
                    drawMole(ctx, x, y, false, dt / tRise); } :
                state.phase == 'up' ? function (ctx) {
                    drawMole(ctx, x, y, true, 1); } :
                function (ctx) {
                    var dt = t - state.t0;
                    if (dt < tWhack)
                        drawMole(ctx, x, y, false,
                            1 - dt / tWhack); };
        }),
        sDestroy = clock
            .withLatestFrom(state,
                function (t, st) {
                    var dur = t - st.t0;
                    return (st.phase == 'up' && dur >= tUp)
                        || (st.phase == 'whacked' && dur >= tWhack)
                            ? id : null;
                })
            .filter(function (id) { return id != null; });
    return {
        id : id,
        drawable : drawable,
        sDestroy : sDestroy,
        dispose  : function () { subscr1.dispose(); }
    };
}
```

Changes to the up state after tRise →

Changes to the whacked state if clicked while rising ←

Merges the two state transitions into state →

Function to draw the mole, updated every clock tick →

Graphics code omitted ←

Request to be terminated when the whacked or up state expires ←

Listing 7.10 gives a main program with everything written without caring too much about performance. As with the zombies, you extract a single `sDestroy` and `drawable` from the game state's current list of moles using RxJS's `switch` operation: `flatMapLatest()` is equivalent to a `map`, `hold`, and then `switch` in Sodium.

Note that when you destroy a mole, as mentioned earlier, you return a function to dispose it explicitly to avoid memory leaks. You call it using a `setTimeout` with a delay of `0` so you can guarantee it will be done safely after the current RxJS processing has completed.

As noted, the "restrictive" style of FRP that requires referential transparency does put a lot of work onto the garbage collector. The performance scalability of this code as presented is abysmal:

- The mole outputs a new `drawable` every frame and all of them are combined each frame.
- The combining of `drawables` has an algorithmic complexity of $O(N)$ for each mole update. Because each mole updates each frame, that's $O(N^2)$ per frame.
- Appending arrays by copying is inefficient if the arrays are long.

Next you'll see ways to improve these without going outside the FRP paradigm.

Listing 7.10   Main program for Whack That Mole!

```
function init() {
    var canvas = document.getElementById("myCanvas"),
        getXY = function(e) {
            return { x : e.pageX - canvas.offsetLeft,
                     y : e.pageY - canvas.offsetTop }; },
        sMouseDown = Rx.Observable.fromEvent(canvas, 'mousedown')
                                    .map(getXY),
        clock = new Rx.BehaviorSubject(0);
    Rx.Observable.interval(20).subscribe(clock);          ← 50 fps animation clock
    var state = new Rx.BehaviorSubject({ nextID : 0, moles : []}),
        sAddMole = clock                                  ← At random times ...
            .filter(function (_) { return Math.random() < 0.02; })
            .withLatestFrom(state, clock,
                function (_, state, t0) {                 ← ... creates a new mole
                    var x = 25+(canvas.width-50) * Math.random();
                    var y = 25+(canvas.height-50) * Math.random();
                    var sClick = sMouseDown.filter(function (pt) {   ← Clicks in the mole's area are passed to the mole.
                        return pt.x >= x - 20 && pt.x <= x + 20 &&
                               pt.y >= y - 20 && pt.y <= y + 30;
                    });
                    var newMoles = state.moles.slice();   ← Copies the list for referential transparency
                    newMoles.push(mkMole(state.nextID, x, y,
                                         clock, sClick));
                    state = { nextID : state.nextID+1,
                              moles : newMoles };
                    console.log("add mole "+state.nextID+
                        " ("+state.moles.length+")");
                    return state;
                }),
        sDestroy = state.flatMapLatest(                   ← Merges all moles' sDestroys into one
            function (state) {
                var sDestroy = Rx.Observable.of();
                for (var i = 0; i < state.moles.length; i++)
                    sDestroy = sDestroy.merge(state.moles[i].sDestroy);
```

```
                            return sDestroy;
                    });
```

Turns sDestroy into a state change

```
            sRemoveMole = sDestroy.withLatestFrom(state,
                function (id, state) {
                    var newMoles = [];
                    for (var i = 0; i < state.moles.length; i++)
                        if (state.moles[i].id != id)
                            newMoles.push(state.moles[i]);
                        else
                            setTimeout(state.moles[i].dispose, 0);
                    console.log("remove mole "+id+" ("+newMoles.length+")");
                    return { nextID : state.nextID, moles : newMoles };
                });
            sAddMole.merge(sRemoveMole).subscribe(state);
            var drawables = new Rx.BehaviorSubject([]);
            state.flatMapLatest(
                function (state) {
                    var drawables = new Rx.BehaviorSubject([]);
                    for (var i = 0; i < state.moles.length; i++) {
                        var thiz = state.moles[i].drawable.map(
                            function(draw) {
                                return [draw];
                            });
                        drawables = i == 0
                            ? thiz
                            : drawables.combineLatest(thiz,
                                function (d1, d2) { return d1.concat(d2); });
                    }
                    return drawables;
                }).subscribe(drawables);
            clock.subscribe(function(t) {
                var ctx = canvas.getContext("2d");
                ctx.fillStyle = '#00af00';
                ctx.fillRect(0, 0, canvas.width, canvas.height);
                var ds = drawables.getValue();
                for (var i = 0; i < ds.length; i++)
                    ds[i](ctx);
            });
        }
```

Copies non-destroyed moles (annotation pointing to `newMoles.push(state.moles[i]);`)

Explicitly disposes of deleted moles (annotation pointing to `setTimeout(state.moles[i].dispose, 0);`)

Merges state changes together into state (annotation pointing to `sAddMole.merge(sRemoveMole).subscribe(state);`)

Combines drawables into a single BehaviorSubject (annotation pointing to `state.flatMapLatest(`)

Redraws the screen every frame (annotation pointing to `clock.subscribe(function(t) {`)

To run this code, check it out if you haven't done so already, and point your browser at sodium/book/web/whack1.html. The code is in whack1.js.

Let's improve the performance. First, instead of updating the draw function every frame, you'll turn it into a function of time and update it only when the mole changes state. This change is trivial. Replace this section

```
var drawable = clock.withLatestFrom(state, function (t, state) {
        ...
```

with the following so the updating of drawables happens only on changes to the mole's state, not for every clock frame. t is now an argument of the returned function:

```
var drawable = state.map(function (state) {
        return state.phase == 'rising' ? function (ctx, t) {
```

```
                    var dt = t - state.t0;
                    drawMole(ctx, x, y, false, dt / tRise); } :
              state.phase == 'up' ? function (ctx, _) {
                    drawMole(ctx, x, y, true, 1); } :
              function (ctx, t) {
                    var dt = t - state.t0;
                    if (dt < tWhack)
                        drawMole(ctx, x, y, false,
                            1 - dt / tWhack); };
      });
```

Next, modify the main loop like this to pass the current time:

```
var ds = drawables.getValue();
for (var i = 0; i < ds.length; i++)
    ds[i](ctx, t);
```

The second improvement is to construct `drawables` in a binary tree structure instead of a flat structure, as described in section 7.6:

```
var drawables = new Rx.BehaviorSubject([]);
state.flatMapLatest(
    function (state) {
        var drawables = [];
        for (var i = 0; i < state.moles.length; i++)
            drawables.push(state.moles[i].drawable);
        return sequence(drawables);
    }).subscribe(drawables);
```

It uses a generalized `sequence()` function like the Java one you used earlier, but tuned up a bit. It converts a list of cells of values (the Java type would be `List<Cell<A>>`) to a cell of a list of values: `Cell<List<A>>`.

You split the list and work recursively so the number of `combineLatest` operations between any input cell and the cell you output is no more than $\log(N)$. Thus the algorithmic complexity of a single update is $O(\log N)$:

```
function sequence(xs)
{
    if (xs.length == 0)
        return new Rx.BehaviorSubject([]);
    else
    if (xs.length == 1)
        return xs[0].map(function(x) { return [x]; });
    else {
        var mid = Math.floor(xs.length/2),
            left = xs.slice(0, mid),
            right = xs.slice(mid);
        return sequence(left).combineLatest(sequence(right),
                function (x1, x2) { return x1.concat(x2); });
    }
}
```

Third, appending arrays by copying them is costly if the arrays are long. Recall that to ensure referential transparency, the values have to be immutable, so you must copy the arrays. It turns out you can get the best of both worlds: there's a data structure called a *2-3 finger tree* that is immutable, that behaves like an array, and for which appending has a complexity of $O(\log(\min(n1,n2)))$. There are JavaScript implementations of it.

We've done the first two modifications. To try the new version, point your browser at sodium/book/web/whack2.html. The code is in whack2.js.

7.8 Switch use case #3: removing invalid states

Let's extend one of the JavaScript examples from chapter 6 so you can drag around the cat and dog polygons. Three kinds of input mouse events are involved in a drag and drop: mouse down, mouse move, and mouse up (see figure 7.9).

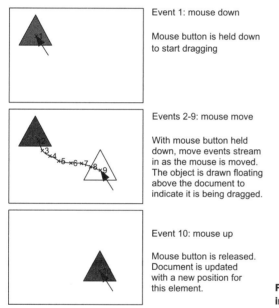

Event 1: mouse down

Mouse button is held down to start dragging

Events 2-9: mouse move

With mouse button held down, move events stream in as the mouse is moved. The object is drawn floating above the document to indicate it is being dragged.

Event 10: mouse up

Mouse button is released. Document is updated with a new position for this element.

Figure 7.9   Modeling the input mouse events in drag-and-drop logic

Listing 7.11 defines a `BehaviorSubject` for the `dragging` state, which is `null` when you aren't dragging. This works, but there's a risk of bugs, because the drag logic has to make sure dragging is non-`null` before it does its thing. This is what you'll improve shortly. Don't forget that the final `subscribe()` is the I/O part, which should be kept as far away from the logic as possible (in this case, the bottom of the file).

Listing 7.11   Dragging cat and dog polygons without `flatMapLatest`

```
function insidePolygon(pos, poly) {          ⟵── Code omitted
}
function find(doc, pos) {
```

```
      for (var i = 0; i < doc.length; i++)
        if (insidePolygon(pos, doc[i])) return doc[i];
      return null;
    }
    function insert(doc, shape) {
      doc = doc.slice();
      for (var i = 0; i < doc.length; i++)
        if (doc[i].id == shape.id) doc[i] = shape;
      return doc;
    }
    function shiftBy(shape, dx, dy) {
      var neu = { id: shape.id, coords : [] };
      for (var i = 0; i < shape.coords.length; i++) {
        var pt = shape.coords[i];
        neu.coords.push( { x : pt.x + dx, y : pt.y + dy } );
      }
      return neu;
    }

    function init() {
        var canvas = document.getElementById("myCanvas");
        var getXY = function(e) { return { x : e.pageX - canvas.offsetLeft,
                                           y : e.pageY - canvas.offsetTop }; };
        var sMouseDown = Rx.Observable.fromEvent(canvas, 'mousedown')
                                      .map(getXY);
        var sMouseMove = Rx.Observable.fromEvent(canvas, 'mousemove')
                                      .map(getXY);
        var sMouseUp = Rx.Observable.fromEvent(canvas, 'mouseup').map(getXY);
        var dragging = new Rx.BehaviorSubject(null);
        var doc = new Rx.BehaviorSubject([
            { id: "cat", coords: ... },                  ⟵─── Numbers omitted
            { id: "dog", coords: ... }
          ]);
        sMouseDown.withLatestFrom(doc, function(pos, doc) {
                var shape = find(doc, pos);
                if (shape === null) return null;
                else                      return { shape : shape, startPos : pos };
        }).merge(
            sMouseUp.map(function(pos) { return null; })
        ).subscribe(dragging);
        sMouseMove.withLatestFrom(dragging, doc, function(pos, dragging, doc) {
            if (dragging === null) return null;
            else {
                var dx = pos.x - dragging.startPos.x;
                var dy = pos.y - dragging.startPos.y;
                return insert(doc, shiftBy(dragging.shape, dx, dy));
            }
        }).filter(function(doc) { return doc !== null; })
          .subscribe(doc);
        doc.subscribe(function(doc) {
            var ctx=canvas.getContext("2d");
            ctx.clearRect(0, 0, canvas.width, canvas.height);
            for (var i = 0; i < doc.length; i++) {
                var coords = doc[i].coords;
                ctx.beginPath();
```

Sets the dragging state if mouseDown clicks a shape ⟶ (points to `sMouseDown.withLatestFrom...`)

Clears the dragging state on mouseUp ⟶ (points to `}).merge(`)

Careful! Make sure you're dragging! ⟶ (points to `if (dragging === null) return null;`)

The I/O part is separate from the logic part. ⟵─ (points to `doc.subscribe(function(doc) {`)

```
        ctx.moveTo(coords[0].x, coords[0].y);
        for (var j = 0; j < coords.length; j++)
            ctx.lineTo(coords[j].x, coords[j].y);
        ctx.closePath();
        ctx.fillStyle = '#D090ff';
        ctx.fill();
        }
    });
}
```

To run this example, check this out if necessary: git clone https://github.com/SodiumFRP/sodium. Then point your browser at sodium/book/web/drag1.html.

7.8.1   *And now, improved with flatMapLatest*

In functional programming, you strive to make it so invalid states aren't representable. What you want is for the dragging logic not to exist at all until you're dragging.

You can replace the code in bold from the previous listing with the code in listing 7.12. When you mouse-down on a valid shape, you output an observable that describes what to do from then on.

takeUntil() is an RxJS operation that terminates the observable when an event arrives on its argument, sMouseUp. It has no direct equivalent in Sodium, but you could write it. This does what you want: it instantiates the drag logic when you start the drag and destroys it when you stop. The drag logic can safely assume it's always dragging. The invalid state of mouse move when not dragging is eliminated, and so is any associated potential bug.

Listing 7.12   Dragging cat and dog polygons: improved with `flatMapLatest`

```
var dragging = ... ;
var doc = ... ;
sMouseDown.withLatestFrom(doc, function(pos, doc) {
    return { startPos : pos, shape : find(doc, pos) };
}).filter(function(x) { return x.shape !== null; })
  .flatMapLatest(function(x) {
      var startPos = x.startPos;
      var shape = x.shape;
      return sMouseMove.withLatestFrom(doc, function(pos, doc) {
          var dx = pos.x - startPos.x;
          var dy = pos.y - startPos.y;
          return insert(doc, shiftBy(shape, dx, dy));
      }).takeUntil(sMouseUp);
  }).subscribe(doc);
```

To run this example, check this out if necessary: git clone https://github.com/SodiumFRP/sodium. Then point your browser at sodium/book/web/drag2.html.

7.9   *Switch use case #4: switching between screens*

A real game has multiple screens (see figure 7.10). In video games, you usually want to redraw the entire scene every frame, so you'd typically model the scene—consisting of all the graphical elements to be drawn—as a single cell. Some infrastructures work well in this way (WebGL, OpenGL, and HTML5 Canvas), and some don't (DOM and SVG) but can be adapted.

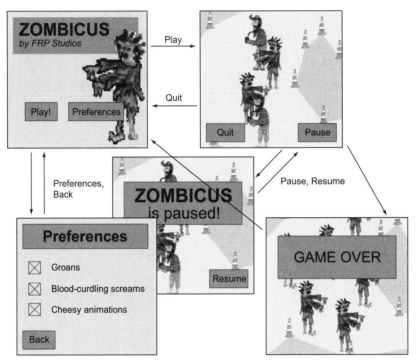

Figure 7.10   Example of the screens in a real game

Here's how you can implement this in FRP with `switch`. Each screen's logic outputs a `sChange` stream allowing it to fire with the screen you want to switch to; the main game loop handles the state transition. See figure 7.11.

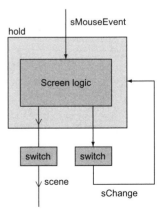

Figure 7.11   How a game switches screens

With this arrangement, it's easy to get clever and introduce transition animations between screens. The scene during a transition is a function of three things:

- The old screen's scene
- The new screen's scene
- The animation clock time

This can be expressed directly in FRP. To make it work neatly, you may also want to gate the mouse input so that only the new screen receives it, or neither screen receives it during the transition. Otherwise you'll get the strange situation where both screens are affected by the same mouse clicks during the transition.

Notice that sometimes you'll want screens to keep their state while they're not active, and sometimes you won't. For instance, when you start a new game, you want a completely new state. When you switch to the pause screen, you want a new pause screen, because it has no useful state to preserve. But when you switch back to the game, you want the game state to be preserved.

Achieving this is simpler than you may think. Do this:

- When you want a screen to have new state (new game or pause screen), execute FRP statements to construct new FRP logic.
- When you want to preserve the state of a screen—for instance, when you pause—pass the game screen's scene cell to the pause screen to hold onto. When it has finished pausing, it passes it out sChange. While the pause screen holds a reference to this cell, the game logic stays active in memory.

When all references to the scene of a screen are discarded, it's cleaned up. When you change to the Game Over screen, you throw away the game screen's scene. Because it's not being referenced any more, all the game state gets garbage-collected.

Note that for this to work properly, an additional mechanism is required: you need to gate the input events so only the active screen can see them. If you don't do this, then mouse clicks on the pause screen will be interpreted by the game screen as player input.

NOTE   While a game is paused, you don't want any state changes in the game logic. Typically there will be a game clock that causes monsters to walk around, and so on. To prevent this from happening during a pause, a recommended method is to give the pause screen a mechanism that lets it pause the game clock. For animations on the pause screen, you use a different clock.

To summarize, to implement screen-switching in a game, you might do it this way:

- Switch the output cells and streams of the screen logic.
- One of those outputs is a stream sChange for switching to a new screen, which is then held by the top-level game loop.
- If you need to retain the state for a screen, hold onto its outputs. To restore that screen, feed those outputs out as if they were a new screen through an event on sChange.

- Gate all the inputs so that screens that aren't visible also don't see any input events.
- Add transition animations to your heart's content.

7.10 Summary

- The `sample` primitive allows cells to be sampled directly. You can use it when constructing FRP logic or in functions passed to FRP primitives that work on events (`Stream.map`, `snapshot`, `filter`, `merge`, `Stream.accum`). Or it can be called any time from I/O code to sample a cell's current value.
- Without `switch`, the data-flow graph that implements the FRP logic is static.
- `switch` lets you use FRP to construct FRP, so you can change the FRP data-flow graph dynamically.
- Merging long lists of cells or streams has performance implications, but there are ways to make this scalable.
- Making invalid states not representable is desirable because it reduces the possibilities for bugs. `switch` can help with this.

Operational primitives

Cue some soft music as we reflect that you now have a good grounding in the 10 primitives that form the conceptual core of FRP: map, merge, hold, snapshot, filter, lift, never, constant, sample, and switch. Together they create a perfect world where everything is harmonious and wonderful.

Zzzzzzzzzzzzrrrrrrrrrppppppppppp! (That's the sound of ripping a record off a record player.) Certain issues dwell at the fringe of the FRP design space and don't quite fit. This chapter is about those and how to deal with them in Sodium. Each FRP system takes its own approach to these issues, so we introduce the *operational primitives*.

169

8.1   *Interfacing FRP code with the rest of your program*

For the entire book, you've been saying, "Just tell me already!" and we've been pretending to be Yoda from *Star Wars*, saying "Ready you are not! Hmmm?" Now we judge that your mind is sufficiently purified that you can learn how to send data into FRP logic and receive it out without your FRP programming being influenced by operational thinking. We're about to teach you something that is necessary but that you should do only when necessary.

> **NOTE**   What follows is how Sodium does it, which should be fairly typical, but there will be variations in different FRP systems. For information about how to do this in RxJS, see "Creating your own hot observable" in section 6.5.

8.1.1   *Sending and listening to streams*

Interfacing your FRP code to the rest of your program has two parts:

1 Push events into streams or cells.
2 Listen to the events from streams or cells.

Listing 8.1 shows both of these. You construct a `StreamSink`, which is a subclass of `Stream` that adds a method called `send()`, allowing you to push or send values into the stream.

> **NOTE**   With certain rules on listeners to be discussed shortly, it's absolutely thread-safe and safe in every other way to call `send()` from any context. The `send()` call will also never block on I/O.

When you export a `StreamSink` from a module for other parts of the program to consume the stream, you should upcast it to `Stream` before doing so, so the ability to push events into the stream isn't made public.

> **NOTE**   Your code can do all the I/O and state mutation it wants in between calls to `send()`. We're now in the Wild West where the strict rules of referential transparency don't apply.

To listen to a stream's events, you can register a listener on any `Stream` with the `listen()` method. It returns a `Listener` object that has an `unlisten()` method to deregister the listener when you've finished observing the values from the stream:

```
Listener l = ev.listen(value -> { ... do something ... ; });
...
l.unlisten();
```

You can also `append()` listeners together into one, so a common idiom to simplify unlistening is this:

```
Listener l = new Listener();
l = l.append(sX.listen(...));
l = l.append(sY.listen(...));
...                              Deregisters all
l.unlisten();                    callbacks
```

The following are Sodium-specific:

- The stuff that Sodium does behind the scenes is all automatic, but deregistering these explicit listeners is *not* automatic. If you forget to do so, the FRP logic is held in memory, and this could result in a memory leak. But FRP programs typically don't have many listeners to be concerned about, and often they exist for the life of the program anyway.
- When you listen to something with listen(), all the associated FRP logic is held in memory and isn't garbage-collected until you explicitly call unlisten(). There is a variant of listen() called listenWeak() that automatically deregisters the handler if the Listener object is garbage-collected.

Listing 8.1   Sending data into and listening to a stream

```
import nz.sodium.*;
public class stream {
    public static void main(String[] args) {
        StreamSink<Integer> sX = new StreamSink<>();
        Stream<Integer> sXPlus1 = sX.map(x -> x + 1);
        Listener l = sXPlus1.listen(x -> { System.out.println(x); });
        sX.send(1);
        sX.send(2);
        sX.send(3);
        l.unlisten();
    }
}
ant stream
stream:
     [java] 2
     [java] 3
     [java] 4
```

To run this, check it out if you haven't done so already, and then run it like this:

```
git clone https://github.com/SodiumFRP/sodium
cd sodium/book/operational/java
mvn test -Pstream     or     ant stream
```

8.1.2   *Multiple send()s in a single transaction*

NOTE   This section doesn't apply to Rx and other systems that lack a concept of transactions.

When you create an event by issuing a send(), it automatically starts a transaction within which all the state changes that result from it in your FRP logic take place. As we've mentioned before and will cover in more detail shortly, it's possible to start transactions explicitly. If you call send() on more than one StreamSink in a single transaction, the resulting events are simultaneous with each other.

But what if you send to the same StreamSink more than once? Sodium only allows one event per transaction on a given stream, so how does it deal with this situation? By default, it throws away the events from all but the last send().

If you want to do something different, you can use a variant of `StreamSink`'s constructor that takes a combining function. For example, if you're using the type `Stream-Sink<Integer>` and you want to add the numbers when combining, you can do this:

```
StreamSink<Integer> s = new StreamSink<>((a, b) -> a + b);
...
s.send(1);
Transaction.runVoid(() -> {           ⟵┐  Groups the two sends
    s.send(5);                           │  into a single transaction
    s.send(7);
});
s.send(100);
```

In this explicit transaction, the numbers are added together using the function specified giving a single event with the value 12. The events you'll see on s in this program are as follows:

```
1
12
100
```

8.1.3 *Sending and listening to cells*

Listing 8.2 constructs a `CellSink`. Because a cell must always have a value, it requires you to specify an initial value. `Cell.listen()` is the same as its stream counterpart, except that you're called back once on registration of the listener with the cell's current value. Note that the output shows the initial 0.

Listing 8.2 Sending data into and listening to a cell

```
import nz.sodium.*;
public class cell {
    public static void main(String[] args) {
        CellSink<Integer> x = new CellSink<>(0);
        Listener l = x.listen(x_ -> { System.out.println(x_); });
        x.send(10);
        x.send(20);
        x.send(30);
        l.unlisten();
    }
}
ant cell
cell:
     [java] 0
     [java] 10
     [java] 20
     [java] 30
```

To run this, check it out if you haven't done so already, and then run it like this:

```
cd sodium/book/operational/java
mvn test -Pcell      or      ant cell
```

8.1.4   *Threading model and callback requirements*

To make things work consistently, there are certain rules about what you can and can't do in a `listen()` callback. These rules should be considered a requirement in Sodium, but they're good advice in any FRP system.

Sodium currently works in the following way, but there's a good chance this could change in the future for performance reasons:

- In Sodium, you're called back on the thread that the `send()` that started the FRP processing was called on.

Other systems may behave differently. But no matter what FRP system you're using, you'll avoid many problems if you don't make assumptions about what thread you were called back on. The rules we give in this chapter are based on this idea.

Having said that, if you carefully inspect the implementation of the SWidgets library used in the examples, you'll see that we're using such assumptions to obtain specific behavior: we're trying to make Swing comply with some FRP-like assumptions about when state changes will occur. Sometimes this is the right thing to do. This will generally be when you're trying to wrap some non-FRP logic with an FRP interface, as in this case.

Without further ado, here are the rules you should use for `listen()` callbacks:

- You're not allowed to `send()` inside a callback. In Sodium, doing so throws an exception. There are two reasons. First, we don't encourage this style, and second, we can't maintain correct processing order. If you need to write your own primitive, this means we should improve Sodium. This may need to happen from time to time.
- You're not allowed to block inside a callback.
- Nonblocking I/O is acceptable.

The way to do blocking I/O is to delegate your processing to a worker thread. At the conclusion of the I/O, you can `send()` a result back into your FRP logic. Because the worker thread wouldn't be blocking the callback, this is valid.

The rules of interfacing with FRP in Sodium

We can summarize the rules of interfacing your I/O code with FRP like this:

- It's safe to call `send()` from any context except an FRP listener, and it never blocks.
- The functions passed to FRP logic can do anything that's referentially transparent, and functions that work with stream events may construct FRP logic and may use `sample`. I/O is forbidden.
- Listeners must not block or call `send()`, and they may do nonblocking I/O, including delegating work to other threads.

If these rules are followed, you'll never have threading issues. This is true in Sodium and may be true in other FRP systems.

8.2 Laziness solves loop craziness

This advice is Sodium-specific. Sometimes you write code that calls sample() during its construction. You saw an example of this in periodicTimer() from the previous chapter:

```
public static Stream<Unit> periodicTimer(
        Cell<Double> time, Stream<Unit> sTick, double period) {
    CellLoop<Double> tAlarm = new CellLoop<>();
    Stream<Double> sAlarm = Stream.filterOptional(
        sTick.snapshot(tAlarm,
            (u, alarm) -> time.sample() >= alarm
                ? Optional.of(time.sample() + period)
                : Optional.<Double>empty())
    );
    double t0 = time.sample() + period;
    tAlarm.loop(sAlarm.hold(t0));
    return sAlarm.map(u -> Unit.UNIT);
}
```

But what if the time passed in has been looped? Let's say it's called like this:

```
CellLoop<Double> time = new CellLoop<>();
Stream<Unit> eAlarm = periodicTimer(time, sTick, 2.0);
time.loop(...);
```

At the time when you call sample(), the time variable hasn't been looped yet. How can Java return the value when there's no way to know it yet? The previous code will throw an exception.

Sodium provides a way to solve this problem:

```
Lazy<double> t0 = time.sampleLazy().map(p -> p + period);
tAlarm.loop(sAlarm.holdLazy(t0));
```

sampleLazy() returns a proxy for the value that isn't available yet, and holdLazy() knows how to use it. There's a map() function to modify it, and it also has lift() functions for combining multiple lazy values.

> **NOTE** Haskell is the only language where this isn't a problem, because all values are lazily evaluated.

8.3 Transactions

listen brings us to the operational way of viewing things that we've been avoiding until now. Now we'll talk about transactions and what they are operationally.

> **NOTE** The Reactive Extensions (Rx) family of systems and many systems based on it don't have the concept of transactions.

In some FRP systems, a transaction is called a *moment,* and this is a better name because it's conceptual, not operational. Another good name would be an *instant.* We're sticking with *transaction* because it's the term people already know.

How do you initiate a transaction? First, in Sodium, if you don't create a transaction, one is created automatically. For instance, each send() here runs in a new transaction:

```
sSnk.send(5);          ◁── Transaction I
eSnk.send(6);                      ◁── Transaction 2
eSnk.send(7);                                  ◁── Transaction 3
```

Or you can create a transaction explicitly like this in Sodium:

```
Transaction.runVoid(() -> {
    ... transactional code ...
}
```

This uses the *loan pattern*, where you pass to runVoid() a lambda specifying the code you want it to execute in a transactional context.

The loan pattern

The loan pattern is a software design pattern in which a function that manages some resource is given a piece of code in the form of a lambda to run, and the function *loans* the resource to the passed code. The point of it is to reduce the chance of resource leaks by making it impossible for the caller to forget to close the resource.

The best-known use case for the loan pattern is opening and closing a file. Let's say you want to read the contents of a file into a byte array. Instead of opening and closing it yourself, you can imagine that there exists a loan pattern method called readFile() that does the work for you. Here's how you might invoke it:

```
byte[] text = readFile(filename, is -> {
    int size = is.available();
    byte[] text = new byte[size];
    h.read(text);
    return text;
});
```

readFile()'s job is to handle the opening and closing of the file for you so you can't get it wrong. It opens the requested file, passes the resulting InputStream is to the lambda function that the caller supplied, and ensures that all resources are cleaned up and exceptions are handled safely.

Sodium makes you use this pattern when you want to wrap the code in a transaction. Then there's no risk of accidentally leaving the transaction open.

If you want to return a value from a transactional block of code, there's a variant called run():

```
Stream<Integer> s = Transaction.run(() -> {
    ...
    Stream<Integer> s = ...;
    ...
    return s;
});
```

The transaction is tied to the thread that the code is running on, so there's no explicit transaction handle. Sodium knows how to retrieve the transactional context behind the scenes when it needs it.

Sodium executes a transaction in two steps:

1 Process all stream events simultaneously.
2 Update all cell values atomically.

During step 1, cells can't change their state, so event processing sees a single "moment" representing the state before the transaction started. As we explained in chapter 2, you can view all events processed in a single transaction as truly simultaneous with each other.

In step 2, you then apply the updates you queued up in step 1 atomically. Recall that *atomically* means it's impossible to observe a situation where some updates have been applied but not others.

8.3.1 *Constructing FRP logic under an explicit transaction*

We've mentioned this, but here we'll cover it formally:

- It's normal to construct FRP logic under an explicit transaction.
- It often makes sense for all the program initialization to be wrapped in a single, big FRP transaction. We'll come back to this in chapter 14.
- StreamLoop and CellLoop require an explicit transaction.

MIXING I/O WITH FRP CONSTRUCTION

A large program does a lot of initialization, and we recommend one big transaction wrapped around it. This implies, clearly, that there would normally be some I/O inside that transaction. Although you generally want a clear line between I/O and FRP, mixing I/O in with FRP construction during program startup isn't a problem in practice.

Bear in mind that if you spawn a thread during initialization, and that thread calls send() on StreamSink or CellSink, it could block until the initialization transaction closes on the initialization thread. This is probably what you want anyway, but we're making this clear. This could vary from one FRP system to another depending on how it's implemented.

LISTENING AND SENDING IN THE SAME TRANSACTION

In Sodium, if you send() and listen() to the same stream in the same transaction (as in listing 8.3), the sent value is guaranteed to be seen, no matter what order these two operations occur in. This property, combined with the "one big transaction" policy for program initialization, allows you to banish the *missed first event* plague described in detail in appendix B.

Listing 8.3 Sending and listening in the same transaction

```
import nz.sodium.*;

public class sametrans {
    public static void main(String[] args) {
```

```
            StreamSink<Integer> sX = new StreamSink<>();
            Stream<Integer> sXPlus1 = sX.map(x -> x + 1);
            Listener l = Transaction.run(() -> {
                sX.send(1);
                Listener l_ = sXPlus1.listen(x -> { System.out.println(x); });
                return l_;
            });
            sX.send(2);
            sX.send(3);
            l.unlisten();
        }
}
ant sametrans
sametrans:
        [java] 2
        [java] 3
        [java] 4
```

To run this example, check it out if you haven't done so already, and then run it like this:

```
git clone https://github.com/SodiumFRP/sodium
cd sodium/book/operational/java
mvn test -Psametrans    or    ant sametrans
```

8.4 Getting a stream from a cell with updates and value

There are two views of time in FRP systems:

- Discrete time
- Continuous time

This difference pertains to cells only. Streams are the same in both models. Sodium is mostly focused on discrete time, but you can express continuous time in it, and we'll cover this in detail in chapter 9.

In a discrete time system, state (cell) changes or steps happen in response to events, so the steps are discrete. A continuous time system allows this too, but it also has the ability for a cell's value to vary continuously over time. An obvious case where this would be useful would be in simulating physics, as you might do in a video game.

To protect the idea of a continuously varying cell, a true FRP system must ensure that changes in a cell's value aren't observable. The 10 core primitives we've listed are consistent with this because they give you no way to convert a cell into a stream. Note that listen() is an operational external interface thing and is not considered part of FRP.

We're about to introduce two primitives that break that nice property. They're sometimes needed for operational situations.

> **NOTE** In Rx, we recommend BehaviorSubject to do the job of an FRP cell, but BehaviorSubject is not a distinct data type in Rx. It can be treated directly as an Observable (the same as Stream in Sodium). Unfortunately this means there's no direct way to achieve the desirable property of concealing cell steps.

8.4.1   *Introducing updates and value*

The Sodium-specific primitives updates and value both take a cell and give you a stream. Here are two use cases for this. There aren't many (some others will come up in later chapters):

- You might want to send a cell over a network link. This would require deconstructing it into its current value and a stream of its updates, and holding the result on the other end of the wire.
- In chapter 12, we'll discuss a function called calm() that for performance reasons removes unnecessary steps from cells, where the value is a repeat of the previous firing. You need Operational.updates() to implement it, but it follows our rule and doesn't expose the steps to the caller.

We've given them the following deliberately cumbersome names because we want you always to be aware that by using them, you're breaking the non-detectability of cell steps:

- Operational.updates()
- Operational.value()

NOTE In Rx, as we mentioned, BehaviorSubject (cell) and Observable (stream) aren't distinct types. This means no equivalent of updates and value is needed to convert one to the other.

updates gives you the discrete updates to a cell. value differs from updates by firing once with the cell's current value in the transaction where it was invoked. updates is effectively the inverse of hold. To preserve the non-observability of cell steps, the general rule is this:

Functions that use Operational.updates() *shouldn't expose cell steps to the caller.*

NOTE Some systems use the term *changes* for updates, but it's important to note that they're not changes in the sense of being values that aren't equal. That is, Sodium doesn't filter out values that are equal to the previous value. If you want this functionality, you can write it yourself with FRP primitives.

EXAMPLE OF UPDATES

Listing 8.4 listens to the updates of a cell. The key thing to note is that this doesn't give you the current value in the first callback like when you called a cell's listen() method in an earlier example. In this example, the current value of x is 1 when you listen, but you don't see 1 in the output because updates only captures the updates that occur in the same transaction as or after you start listening.

> **Listing 8.4   Listening to the updates of a cell**

```
import nz.sodium.*;
public class updates {
    public static void main(String[] args) {
        CellSink<Integer> x = new CellSink<>(0);
```

```
            x.send(1);
            Listener l = Operational.updates(x).listen(x_ -> {
                System.out.println(x_);
            });
            x.send(2);
            x.send(3);
            l.unlisten();
        }
    }
    ant updates
    updates:
        [java] 2
        [java] 3
```

To run this, check it out if you haven't done so already, and then run it like this:

```
cd sodium/book/operational/java
mvn test -Pupdates     or     ant updates
```

EXAMPLE OF VALUE

Listing 8.5 doesn't give the effect you may expect. The reason is that it doesn't specify an explicit transaction. If a transaction doesn't already exist, Sodium primitives create a short-lived one automatically, so value() and listen() run in two separate transactions. By the time you listen, you've missed the current value that was output by value().

Listing 8.5   value not working as expected

```
import nz.sodium.*;
public class value1 {
    public static void main(String[] args) {
        CellSink<Integer> x = new CellSink<>(0);
        x.send(1);
        Listener l = Operational.value(x).listen(x_ -> {
            System.out.println(x_);
        });
        x.send(2);
        x.send(3);
        l.unlisten();
    }
}
ant value1                          What? Where's
value1:                        ◁─┘  the current value?
    [java] 2
    [java] 3
```

To run this, check it out if you haven't done so already, and then run it like this:

```
cd sodium/book/operational/java
mvn test -Pvalue1     or     ant value1
```

To solve this, you wrap this line in a transaction, which you'll find in the file value2.java:

```
x.send(1);
Listener l = Transaction.run(() -> {
    return Operational.value(x).listen(x_ -> {
        System.out.println(x_);
    });
});
x.send(2);
x.send(3);
```

Now you get the output you expect:

```
ant value2
value2:
     [java] 1
     [java] 2
     [java] 3
```

To run this, check it out if you haven't done so already, and then run it like this:

```
cd sodium/book/operational/java
mvn test -Pvalue2     or     ant value2
```

Note that Cell's listen() is equivalent to value().listen() in a transaction. It's a shorter way to do what you've done here. You can rewrite the earlier line as

```
Listener l = x.listen(x_ -> { System.out.println(x_); });
```

8.5   *Spawning new transactional contexts with the split primitive*

NOTE   Because Rx doesn't have transactions, this section doesn't apply to it.

Let's say you have data packets, each of which contains several commands, and you want to feed them into the FRP logic (see figure 8.1). Each packet is processed in a separate transaction, so in this diagram there are two transactions.

To write this, the logic would need to deal throughout with lists of commands. That would be a bit clunky. What you'd really like to do is split these commands out and process each one in its own transaction, as in figure 8.2.

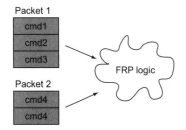

Figure 8.1   Packets come into the system, each containing a list of commands.

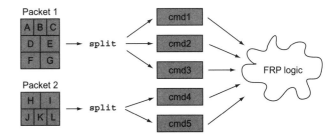

Figure 8.2   Let's split the packets into individual commands.

On the input side you have two transactions, but `split` lets you to turn that into five transactions. The original transactions are still there, so you get these seven transactions:

1 Packet 1
2 cmd1
3 cmd2
4 cmd3
5 Packet 2
6 cmd4
7 cmd5

The following listing shows some code that demonstrates this. Instead of executing commands, it adds numbers together.

NOTE   Recall that `accum()` is a helper that gives you an accumulator. It's shorthand for a simple `hold-snapshot` loop.

Listing 8.6   Splitting list elements into their own transactions

```
import nz.sodium.*;
import java.util.List;
import java.util.Arrays;

public class split {
    public static void main(String[] args) {
        StreamSink<List<Integer>> as = new StreamSink<>();
        Listener l = Operational.updates(
                Operational.split(as)
                        .<Integer>accum(0, (a, b) -> a + b)
            ).listen(total -> { System.out.println(total); });
        as.send(Arrays.asList(100, 15, 60));
        as.send(Arrays.asList(1, 5));
        l.unlisten();
    }
}
ant split
split:
     [java] 100
     [java] 115
     [java] 175
     [java] 176
     [java] 181
```

To run this, check it out if you haven't done so already, and then run it like this:

```
git clone https://github.com/SodiumFRP/sodium
cd sodium/book/operational/java
mvn test -Psplit     or     ant split
```

You can nest `split`, too. If you have a list of a list and `split` it twice, then each sub-element ends up in its own transaction; see figure 8.3.

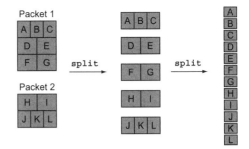

Figure 8.3   Split twice to flatten a list of lists.

8.5.1   *Deferring a single event to a new transaction*

If you want to put a single event into a new transaction, this is called *deferring* the event. It's implemented as a variant of `split` that works on a single event instead of a list. The `Operational.defer()` method provides that in the Java version of Sodium. This primitive gives you a way to read the new version of a cell's state.

Here's a use case for `defer`. Imagine you're writing the logic for a communication protocol, and you receive some sort of timeout event. You want to turn that into a retry event. Let's say the timeout sets an `idle` flag to `true`, indicating that a message is allowed to be sent. When the retry happens, you want it to see the `idle` flag *after* it's been set. `defer` allows you to do this.

Here's a sketch of the code. We briefly mentioned `gate()` in chapter 4—it's a helper based on `snapshot` and `filter` that lets events through when the `Boolean` cell you pass it is true:

```
Cell<Message> msg = ...;
Stream<Unit> sInitiate = ...;
StreamLoop<Unit> sRetry = new StreamLoop<>();
CellLoop<Boolean> idle = new CellLoop<>();
Stream<Message> sSend = sInitiate.merge(sRetry).snapshot(msg)
                                 .gate(idle);
Stream<Unit> sTimeout = ...;
idle.loop(sSend.map(u -> false).merge(
        sTimeout.map(u -> true)).hold(true));
sRetry.loop(Operational.defer(sTimeout));
```

Blocks send if not idle (annotation pointing to `.gate(idle)` / `Stream<Unit> sTimeout` line)

Defers the retry event so idle is true and the gate doesn't block the retry (annotation pointing to `sRetry.loop(Operational.defer(sTimeout));`)

It's a bit unrealistic as it is, but it's loosely based on a real-world case where this issue came up.

> **Sodium has an implicit delay**
>
> The problem in this example is a by-product of the fact that Sodium delays state updates until after the transaction has completed. In chapter 2, we said that you could alternatively view this `delay` as a separate primitive. Seen this way, Sodium implicitly adds `delay` to `hold`. Some systems (such as Yampa) do indeed have a separate delay primitive (`dHold` being equivalent to `hold` followed by the delay primitive `iPre`). In a strange way, therefore, `defer` could be seen as something that reverses `delay`.

The previous snippet also serves to illustrate why FRP feels like wooden teeth when you try to express sequences in it. You can write this in FRP, but a threaded style is more natural, like in this rough pseudo-code:

```
while (retryCount < 3) {
    send(msg);
    reply = timeout(1000, recv());
    if (reply != TIMEOUT)
        break;
    retryCount++;
}
```

FRP is a great hammer, but not every problem is a nail.

8.5.2 *Ending up in the same transaction*

When `defer` or `split` is used in more than one place in the program, the output events can end up in the same transaction:

```
StreamSink<String> in = new StreamSink<>();
Stream<String> lower = in.map(x -> x.toLowerCase());
Stream<String> both = Operational.defer(in)
                    .orElse(Operational.defer(lower));
List<String> out = new ArrayList();
both.listen(x -> out.add(x));
sink.send("A");
sink.send("B");
sink.send("C");
System.out.println(out);
```

This code outputs [A, B, C] because two `defer`s put the events into the same new transaction and `orElse()` gives precedence to `in` (the capital letters). Why didn't we just make Sodium put them into different new transactions? The denotational semantics make you do it this way because there's no compositional way to decide what order they should be in.

This is why we put `defer()` and `split()` into the `Operational` sin bin. They're potentially useful, but be aware that using `defer()` more than once in a program can generate simultaneous events.

8.6 *Scalable addressing*

In the Zombicus example in chapter 7, you routed zombie bites to their victims using a unique ID. You merged the bits together, and then each `BitableHomoSapiens` ignored the bites that weren't for it:

```
Stream<Set<Integer>> sBiteMe = sBite.filter(ids ->
    ids.contains(self));
```

This is great, except it doesn't scale. Each time you send a bite, if you have N humans, you have to do N comparisons. The algorithmic complexity is $O(N^2)$ for N humans and *N* bites. Imagine if a mail carrier had to deliver *N* letters to *N* houses and visited every house in town for each letter (see figure 8.4).

NOTE   In the 1970s, the New Zealand Post Office actually worked this way.

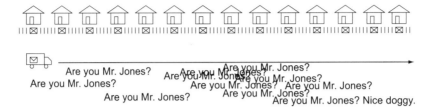

Figure 8.4   Delivering mail badly: asking each householder for each letter is O(*N*²).

NOTE   On some imaginary massively parallel machine, this scalability issue would be less of a problem. If you think about it, this issue is a product of both the FRP paradigm you're using and the machine.

If we hadn't been so fussy in Sodium and had allowed you to put `send()` in a `listen()` handler, then you could do it that way. In Rx, this sort of approach would be sensible, because Rx is designed to allow this. But it's easy to break compositionality if you're not careful.

At any rate, it would be nice to solve this problem in a way that guarantees compositionality. You could write a custom primitive for this, and that isn't a bad idea.

Another approach is to combine it with the solution we talked about in section 7.6. The idea is to make a special tree with switches built into it so you only need to update a portion of the tree each time you add or remove a game character. You can add addressing to this design so there are O(log*N*) comparisons per message instead of O(*N*).

This is one of those "You know you're a functional programmer when …" moments. What you're doing here is going to great lengths to do things functionally. It's the kind of thing functional programmers do because they know how powerful the paradigm is. Of course, there are cases when it isn't worthwhile. But don't forget—this problem only needs to be solved once, and it's been solved in general.

To demonstrate that this is possible, we've implemented a third version of the Whack That Mole! JavaScript example from chapter 7 that uses this approach. You can run it by pointing your browser at sodium/book/web/whack3.html in the Sodium project. The game logic is in whack3.js, and it uses a complex tree structure that you'll find in addressing.js.

The addressing function takes these three streams:

```
var sCreated = addressing(sAdd, sRemove, sIn);
```

sAdd is a stream that causes a new destination keyed on an ID to be registered, and sRemove causes one to be deregistered. To address a message to a particular address, the events that are received sIn must be paired with an ID. In response to sAdd, the output stream sCreated fires, containing an inner stream called sAddressee that outputs events that were addressed to that ID through sIn.

It's based on a simple binary tree, so the algorithmic complexity is nominally $O(\log N)$. But the tree isn't balanced. To do this properly, you would want to implement a self-balancing algorithm such as a red-black tree or 2-3 tree.

We're doing this to show that it's possible to solve this problem efficiently with the FRP semantics we've presented. If you can implement something without breaking FRP semantics, you get a mathematical proof of compositionality for free. If you then implement a new primitive with the same interface, you can achieve better-than-$O(\log N)$ complexity and know that the new primitive is compositional.

8.7 Summary

- listen() and send() are the interface between FRP and the outside world.
- The Operational.updates() and Operational.value() primitives convert a cell to a stream representing the state changes. They have deliberately cumbersome names to remind you to only use them for operational reasons because they break an important property of FRP where the steps in a cell's value shouldn't be detectable.
- split/defer primitives let you spawn new transactions.

Continuous time

9

The video games we've shown so far use a frame—of 1/60th of a second or whatever—as a basic unit of time. We'll show you how continuous time lets you remove the concept of a frame, and model the animation in a clean, natural, declarative way that's closer to the underlying concept. If it's a physics simulation, the model can more or less directly express the physics.

9.1 Rasterizing time

The difference between a discrete (or frame-based) and continuous representation of time is analogous to the representation of space in images. There are two basic models of images:

- *Raster graphics*—The image is represented as a bitmap where a pixel is the basic unit of space. The resolution of the image is baked into the image data, and changing the resolution usually results in a loss of quality. JPEG and PNG image formats work this way.

- *Vector graphics*—The image is described using lines and curves independently of any display resolution. Space is treated as continuous. VRML, X3D, and PDF use this representation.

A vector image can be *rasterized*, where it's converted to a raster image of a given resolution. The quality is limited only by the output resolution.

In an analogous way, FRP lets you define a continuous animation and then sample it at any frame rate you like. This is like rasterization, but in the time domain instead of space.

9.2 *Position as a function of time*

First we'll introduce the simple animation framework. You'll use the coordinate system shown in figure 9.1.

You'll represent an animated scene with the interface in listing 9.1. Timer-System is a class that comes with Sodium that enables you to handle time. We'll go into more detail soon. Point is a simple container class for an (X, Y) position with basic point/vector math (add, subtract, and multiply). We'll show Drawable next. To construct the animation, the anima-

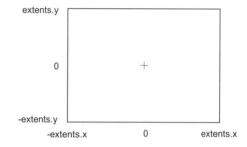

Figure 9.1 extents gives the extents of the coordinate system. The origin is at the center.

tion engine passes it a timer system and the extents of the coordinate space, and it returns a Cell<Drawable> representing the animated scene.

Listing 9.1 Representation of an animation

```
import nz.sodium.*;
import nz.sodium.time.*;

public interface Animation {
    public Cell<Drawable> create(TimerSystem<Double> sys, Point extents);
}
```

Listing 9.2 shows how you represent a drawable scene. This takes you right back to object-oriented programming books of the 1990s: you have an object with a polymorphic draw() method that does the work.

Now, we know what you're thinking. FRP is only allowed to deal with things that obey the rules of referential transparency, but Drawable represents I/O. This is OK, because a Drawable object represents I/O but doesn't perform it. It's not until the final drawable makes its way to the animation engine that you call the draw() method and any I/O is done. As long as this distinction is kept clear—as long as the manipulation of drawable objects is referentially transparent, you're fine. append() combines two Drawables into one, giving you the ability to construct an entire scene represented as one Drawable.

```
import java.awt.Graphics;

public class Drawable {
    public void draw(Graphics g, Point orig, double scale) {}
    public final Drawable append(Drawable second) {          ◁─┐ Combines two
        Drawable first = this;                                  │ Drawables into one
        return new Drawable() {
            public void draw(Graphics g, Point orig, double scale) {
                first.draw(g, orig, scale);
                second.draw(g, orig, scale);
            }
        };
    }
}
```

Listing 9.3 gives the building blocks for constructing scenes. You can do four things:

- Create a circle of radius 1.0 at the origin.
- Scale a drawable.
- Translate a drawable.
- Overlay one drawable on top of another.

You'll redraw the entire scene each frame. This is all you need to make multiple circles move around the scene. This is the bare bones of a system of composable animations, done in a functional programming style.

If you haven't seen this kind of thing before, we encourage you to play with the code. It's a great way to experience the power of functional programming. This sort of graphics code is easier to follow if the graphics back end can handle translating, scaling, and rotating the coordinate system. OpenGL is good, but Java's Graphics doesn't work this way, so you have to simulate it by passing numbers through the draw() methods.

```
import java.awt.Color;
import java.awt.Graphics;
import nz.sodium.*;

public class Shapes {
    public static Cell<Drawable> circle(Color color) {
        return new Cell<Drawable>(new Drawable() {
            public void draw(Graphics g, int ht, Point offset, double sc) {
                int rad = (int)sc;
                int x = (int)offset.x;
                int y = (int)offset.y;
```

```
                g.setColor(color);
                g.fillOval(x-rad, (ht-1-y)-rad, rad*2, rad*2);
                g.setColor(Color.black);
                g.drawOval(x-rad, (ht-1-y)-rad, rad*2, rad*2);
            }
        });
    }

    public static Cell<Drawable> scale(Cell<Drawable> drawable,
                                       Cell<Double> scale) {
        return drawable.lift(scale, (dr, newSc) -> new Drawable() {
            public void draw(Graphics g, int ht, Point offset, double sc) {
                dr.draw(g, ht, offset, sc * newSc);
            }
        });
    }

    public static Cell<Drawable> translate(Cell<Drawable> drawable,
                                           Cell<Point> offset) {
        return drawable.lift(offset, (dr, o) -> new Drawable() {
            public void draw(Graphics g, int ht, Point offset, double sc) {
                dr.draw(g, ht, offset.add(o.multiply(sc)), sc);
            }
        });
    }

    public static Cell<Drawable> over(Cell<Drawable> a, Cell<Drawable> b) {
        return a.lift(b, (dra, drb) -> new Drawable() {
            public void draw(Graphics g, int ht, Point offset, double sc) {
                drb.draw(g, ht, offset, sc);
                dra.draw(g, ht, offset, sc);
            }
        });
    }
}
```

Figure 9.2 shows a simple animation called *fwoomph*. It constructs a circle and changes its radius over time so it fwoomphs in and out like some kind of funky speaker thing.

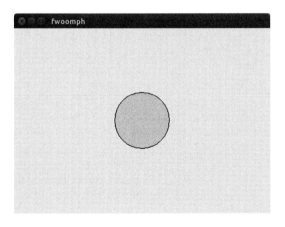

Figure 9.2   A circle that changes its radius over time

The code for this is shown in listing 9.4. Conceptually, `time` is a continuous number of seconds, and you scale the circle according to the fraction of the second of the current time. We'll show you a second example, and then we'll talk about the mechanics of how it works.

Listing 9.4   Fwoomph example: a circle with a changing radius

```java
import java.awt.Color;
import nz.sodium.*;

public class fwoomph extends Shapes {                          ⟵  Imports static methods
    public static void main(String[] args) {                      from the Shapes class
        Animate.animate("fwoomph", (sys, extents) -> {
            Cell<Double> time = sys.time;
            double maxSize = 200.0;
            return scale(
                circle(Color.green),
                time.map(t -> {
                    double frac = t - Math.floor(t);
                    return (frac < 0.5 ? frac : 1.0 - frac) * maxSize;
                })
            );
        });
    }
}
```

To run this, check it out if you haven't done so already, and then run it like this:

```
cd sodium/book/continuous-time/java
mvn test -Pfwoomph     or     ant fwoomph
```

Figure 9.3 shows a more complex example with two circles. They stay the same size, but one moves left and right, and the other moves up and down. They cross at the center.

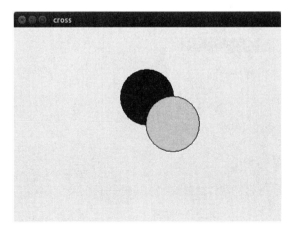

Figure 9.3   Cross example: the circles cross over each other.

The next listing gives the code. This is the same basic idea but with more elements combined. Instead of the radius, you're now varying the position continuously.

Listing 9.5   Cross example: circles crossing back and forth

```java
import java.awt.Color;
import nz.sodium.*;

public class cross extends Shapes {
    public static void main(String[] args) {
        Animate.animate("cross", (sys, extents) -> {
            Cell<Double> time = sys.time;
            double maxSize = 120;
            Cell<Double> offset = time.map(t -> {
                double frac = t - Math.floor(t);
                return (frac < 0.5 ? frac - 0.25 : 0.75 - frac)
                    * 4.0 * maxSize;
            });
            Cell<Double> fifty = new Cell<>(50.0);
            Cell<Drawable> greenBall = translate(
                scale(circle(Color.green), fifty),
                offset.map(x -> new Point(x, 0.0)));
            Cell<Drawable> blueBall = translate(
                scale(circle(Color.blue), fifty),
                offset.map(y -> new Point(0.0, y)));
            return over(greenBall, blueBall);
        });
    }
}
```

To run this, check it out if you haven't done so already, and then run it like this:

```
cd sodium/book/continuous-time/java
mvn test -Pcross    or    ant cross
```

9.3   *The animation loop*

The examples you've seen take a conceptually continuous time and use the map and lift primitives to produce a conceptually continuous animation. But because you're running this on a computer, and computers are inherently discrete, it can't really be continuous. What you're doing here is describing a continuous world in such a way that you can write an animation loop that can sample it at discrete times. You're "rasterizing time."

Listing 9.6 shows the animation loop. There's not that much to it, but a small amount of magic needs to be explained. When the class SecondsTimerSystem is constructed, it hooks itself into Sodium's transaction system so that whenever a transaction is initiated, it first writes the current time into sys.time. The transaction you initiate does nothing itself: it just causes the timer system's "set a new time" hook to be executed. The overall result is that the animation is moved forward to a new time. You then trigger a JPanel repaint, and the paint method samples the latest drawable and asks it to draw itself.

Do you see what's happening here? You have two worlds: a description of a continuous animation, and an animation loop that can wind that animation forward as far as it likes and then sample it. The continuous animation is completely unaware of the concept of a frame, just as a vector graphics image is represented with no awareness of the pixels it will ultimately be rendered into.

Listing 9.6   Animation loop that renders a continuous animation into frames

```java
import java.awt.Color;
import java.awt.Dimension;
import java.awt.Graphics;
import java.awt.Toolkit;
import javax.swing.JFrame;
import javax.swing.JPanel;
import nz.sodium.*;
import nz.sodium.time.*;

public class Animate extends JPanel {
    public Animate(Animation anim, Dimension windowSize) {
        Point extents = new Point(windowSize.width/2, windowSize.height/2);
        this.drawable = Transaction.run(() ->
            Shapes.translate(
                anim.create(new SecondsTimerSystem(), extents),
                new Cell<>(extents)));
        this.windowSize = windowSize;
    }
    private final Cell<Drawable> drawable;
    private final Dimension windowSize;

    public Dimension getPreferredSize() { return windowSize; }

    public void paintComponent(Graphics g) {
        super.paintComponent(g);
        drawable.sample()
                .draw(g, windowSize.height, new Point(0,0), 1.0);
        Toolkit.getDefaultToolkit().sync();
    }

    public static void animate(String title, Animation anim) {
        JFrame frame = new JFrame(title);
        frame.setDefaultCloseOperation(JFrame.EXIT_ON_CLOSE);
        CellSink<Double> clock = new CellSink<>(0.0);
        StreamSink<Unit> sAlarm = new StreamSink<>();
        JPanel view = new Animate(anim, new Dimension(500, 350));
        frame.setContentPane(view);
        frame.pack();
        frame.setVisible(true);
        long t0 = System.currentTimeMillis();
        long tLast = t0;
        while (true) {
            long t = System.currentTimeMillis();
            long tIdeal = tLast + 15;
            long toWait = tIdeal - t;
```

Translates so the origin is at the window's center ⟶ (points to `Shapes.translate(`)

Samples the drawable, and draws it ⟵ (points to `drawable.sample()`)

Some Java voodoo for smooth animation ⟵ (points to `Toolkit.getDefaultToolkit().sync();`)

Delays for one frame ⟵ (points to `long t = System.currentTimeMillis();`)

```
                    if (toWait > 0)
                        try { Thread.sleep(toWait); }
                        catch (InterruptedException e) {}
                    Transaction.runVoid(() -> {});
                    view.repaint(0);
                    tLast = tIdeal;
                }
            }
        }
```

Causes the JPanel to be repainted ⟶

Triggers the timer system's hook that updates sys.time. The drawable is then updated because the scene is defined in terms of sys.time.

9.4 Measuring time

The previous examples were animated in continuous time, but they weren't *reactive:* there were no state changes in response to events. Now let's model a bouncing ball, which reacts to hitting the walls and floor of an imaginary indoor squash court (see figure 9.4).

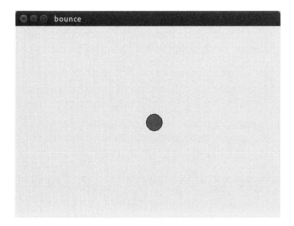

Figure 9.4 A bouncing ball

TimerSystem provides a Cell<T> time representing the current time. But to make full use of continuous time, you also need the ability to *measure time.* You do this with a second feature of TimerSystem: a method called at() that sets an alarm. It has this signature:

```
public Stream<T> at(Cell<Optional<T>> tAlarm);
```

If tAlarm's Optional has no value, then no alarm is set and the stream will never fire. Otherwise it fires at the specified time.

Listing 9.7 gives a simple example showing how at() works. An important rule of using at() is that the caller must arrange things so that when the returned Stream<T> fires, tAlarm must be updated. Otherwise the alarm stays set and the application will loop forever. You can see that this is exactly what periodic() does.

Note that at() timers fire at idealized times that exactly match the requested time, whereas main—being an event from an external source—is associated with a real time from the operating system. It orders things so as to guarantee that time is always non-decreasing.

NOTE   TimerSystem guarantees that values of time are non-decreasing.

Listing 9.7   Simple example of measuring time with at()

```
import nz.sodium.*;
import nz.sodium.time.*;
import java.util.Optional;

public class timers {
    static Stream<Long> periodic(TimerSystem sys, long period) {
        Cell<Long> time = sys.time;
        CellLoop<Optional<Long>> oAlarm = new CellLoop<>();
        Stream<Long> sAlarm = sys.at(oAlarm);
        oAlarm.loop(
            sAlarm.map(t -> Optional.of(t + period))
                .hold(Optional.<Long>of(time.sample() + period)));
        return sAlarm;
    }

    public static void main(String[] args) {
        TimerSystem sys = new MillisecondsTimerSystem();
        Cell<Long> time = sys.time;
        StreamSink<Unit> sMain = new StreamSink<Unit>();
        Listener l = Transaction.run(() -> {
            long t0 = time.sample();
            Listener l1 = periodic(sys, 1000).listen(t -> {
                System.out.println((t - t0)+" timer"); });
            Listener l2 = sMain.snapshot(time).listen(t -> {
                System.out.println((t - t0)+" main");
            });
            return l1.append(l2);
        });
        for (int i = 0; i < 5; i++) {
            sMain.send(Unit.UNIT);
            try { Thread.sleep(990); } catch (InterruptedException e) {}
        }
        l.unlisten();
    }
}

ant timers
timers:
     [java] 22 main
     [java] 1000 timer
     [java] 1013 main
     [java] 2000 timer
     [java] 2003 main
     [java] 2994 main
```

```
[java] 3000 timer
[java] 3984 main
[java] 4000 timer
```

To run this, check it out if you haven't done so already, and then run it like this:

```
cd sodium/book/continuous-time/java
mvn test -Ptimers     or     ant timers
```

9.4.1   *Newtonian physics primer*

Skip this section if you already know about Newtonian physics. The famous physicist Isaac Newton was sitting under a tree one day, minding his own business. Suddenly an apple fell on his head, causing him to see mathematical formulas. In an instant, calculus and the laws of physics were born.

He saw that the motion of a body could be expressed with three different quantities:

- *Position*
- *Velocity* (the rate of change of *position*)
- *Acceleration* (the rate of change of *velocity*)

He also realized that gravity is a constant acceleration downward. (To avoid emails from pedantic people, I'll add here that this is true on Earth but there might be planets where things fall upward.) You can represent the acceleration of gravity on Earth as a function of time, assuming positive numbers in the representation are up and negative ones are down:

$a(t) = -9.8 \text{ m/s}^2$

We're going to use a general form of equation called a *polynomial*. A polynomial has different *degrees*, which refers to the number of terms depending on *t*. *Terms* is mathematical jargon for things added together. We'll use these three polynomials:

- A *constant* (degree 0) doesn't change over time, so it ignores its *t* argument. It has a constant term only: $x(t) = c$.
- A *linear function* (degree 1) adds a *t* term: $x(t) = bt + c$.
- A *quadratic* (degree 2) adds a t^2 term: $x(t) = at^2 + bt + c$.

Mathematicians don't usually express the *t* argument as (*t*), but we're using functional programmer notation.

We said each quantity is the *rate of change* of the previous. An *integral* allows you to go in the other direction: *velocity* is the integral of *acceleration*, and *position* is the integral of *velocity*. There's a general formula for the integral of a polynomial, and this is what it looks like for a *linear function*:

$x(t) = bt + c$
integral of $x(t)$ with respect to $t = 0.5bt^2 + ct$

Newton's equations of motion pop straight out of this general formula. You don't need to understand why it works; all you need to understand is that an integral will convert an *acceleration* into a *velocity*, or a *velocity* into a *position*.

Note that the integral we've shown here doesn't have a constant term. When you convert a velocity to a position, for instance, you'll need to add an extra constant term to give the starting position as it is at time $t = 0$. In the code, you'll notice that the `integrate` function takes an `initial` argument for this purpose.

SOLVING A QUADRATIC

The formula for a quadratic tells you the value of $x(t)$ if you know t:

$$x(t) = at^2 + bt + c$$

There is a way to reverse this if you know $x(t)$ and want to find t. You'll use this to find out when the ball will hit the wall or floor. Let's say you want to know for what values of t the formula gives the value w representing the position of the wall. To solve this, you need to *solve* the equation, which means you need to rewrite

$$w = at^2 + bt + c$$

as

$$t = \dots \textit{something} \dots$$

There's a general formula for this, and it needs the equation to equal 0. You first rewrite the equation as

$$at^2 + bt + (c - w) = 0$$

and then apply the general formula for solving a quadratic. Because of the parabolic shape of the curve of a bouncing ball, there are two solutions to this, but you can fix it with a simple rule: take the earliest solution that isn't in the past.

9.4.2   *Signals for quadratic motion*

Let's write a class called `Signal` that you can use for all three quantities: position, velocity, and acceleration. It contains a quadratic describing the motion and a starting time `t0`. For a given time `t`, applying the quadratic to `t − t0` gives the value at that time.

You'll represent the Y position of the ball with a value of type `Cell<Signal>`. The `Signal` value represents the continuous motion of the ball between bounces. Each time a bounce occurs, a new signal is produced.

Figure 9.5 shows the Y position of the ball over time. t_0 is the time of the start of the animation, and $\{t_1, t_2, t_3, \dots\}$ are the bounce times. The position represented as a `Cell<Signal>` type starts with s_0, and then, when the bounce happens at t_1, it's updated to a new signal s_1, and so on.

Figure 9.5 represents the ball's position as a sequence of signals. Listing 9.8 gives the code for `Signal`. `t0` is the start time of the period described by the signal. There's no end time, so the signal is current until the containing cell is updated. You can do some tricks with this signal:

- `valueAt()` samples the signal's value at the specified time.

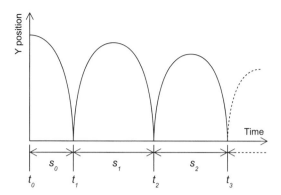

Figure 9.5 Y position of a bouncing ball plotted against time

- `when(double x)` solves the quadratic, returning the first time after `t0` when the signal gives a value of x or `Optional.empty()` if it never does.
- `integrate(double initial)` gives the mathematical integral of the signal, with a specified initial offset.
- The `static integrate()` method is for integrating a `Cell<Signal>`, allowing you to integrate the velocity of the bouncing ball to give its position.

Note that `integrate()` uses `Operational.updates()` to deconstruct the cell into its component signal steps. We've emphasized throughout the book that the non-observability of steps in a cell is an important property of FRP. This property is especially important with continuous time. In this case, `Operational.updates()` is permissible because `integrate()` doesn't expose cell steps to the caller.

Listing 9.8 `Signal`, representing a period of continuous motion

```
import nz.sodium.*;
import java.util.Optional;

public class Signal {
    public Signal(double t0, double a, double b, double c) {
        this.t0 = t0;
        this.a = a;
        this.b = b;
        this.c = c;
    }
    public final double t0, a, b, c;
    public double valueAt(double t) {                    ⟵ Samples signal at a
        double x = t - t0;                                  specified time
        return a*x*x + b*x + c;
    }
    public final static double quantum = 0.000001;
    public Optional<Double> when(double x) {             ⟵ Solves the time when the
        double c = this.c - x;                              signal's value reaches x
        if (a == 0) {
```

```
                    double t = (-c) / b;
                    return t >= quantum ? Optional.of(t + t0)
                                        : Optional.empty();
                }
                else {
                    double b24ac = Math.sqrt(b*b - 4*a*c);
                    double t1 = ((-b) + b24ac) / (2*a);
                    double t2 = ((-b) - b24ac) / (2*a);
                    return t1 >= quantum
                        ? t2 >= quantum ? Optional.of((t1 < t2 ? t1 : t2) + t0)
                                        : Optional.of(t1 + t0)
                        : t2 >= quantum ? Optional.of(t2 + t0)
                                        : Optional.empty();
                }
            }
```

| Integrates a signal step

```
            public Signal integrate(double initial) {      ←┘
                if (a != 0.0) throw new InternalError("Signal can't handle x^3");
```

Integrates a
sequence of
signal steps └─→

```
                return new Signal(t0, b/2, c, initial);
            }
            public static Cell<Signal> integrate(
                                        Cell<Signal> sig, double initial) {
                Stream<Signal> sSig = Operational.updates(sig);
                return sSig.accum(sig.sample().integrate(initial),
                    (neu, old) -> neu.integrate(old.valueAt(neu.t0)));
            }
        }
    }
```

9.4.3 *A natural representation of a bouncing ball*

And now you let the magic of FRP unfold. With the tools you've prepared, listing 9.9 is a natural representation of a bouncing ball. This description is *declarative*: you're saying what the ball *is*, not what it *does*. This is an FRP translation of the following English:

- The X component of the velocity is a sequence of bounces, with the initial signal of a constant value of 350 (positive numbers are to the right).
- Gravity is a constant value of -1,200 (negative numbers are down).
- The Y component of the velocity is a sequence of bounces, with an initial signal of the integral of gravity over time.
- The position X component is the integral of the velocity X component, starting at the left wall.
- The position Y component is the integral of the velocity Y component, starting at the roof.
- The bounces of the velocity X component are when you hit the left wall or right wall.
- The bounces of the velocity Y component are when you hit the floor.
- A bounce is the negation of the velocity component upon hitting a specified position, retaining the acceleration component. You also multiply the velocity by a coefficient of restitution to represent a loss of energy, so the ball will reach a lower height each time it bounces.

FRP keeps everything up-to-date in response to the constraints specified by the FRP logic. When a bounce happens, the next bounce is automatically calculated because of the cyclic dependency between the bounce event and the ball's position.

Listing 9.9 Modeling the bouncing ball

```java
import java.awt.Color;
import nz.sodium.*;
import nz.sodium.time.*;

public class bounce extends Shapes {
    public static void main(String[] args) {
        Animate.animate("bounce", (sys, extents) -> {
            Cell<Double> time = sys.time;
            double t0 = time.sample();
            double ballRadius = 15;
            double leftWall = -extents.x + ballRadius;
            double rightWall = extents.x - ballRadius;
            double floor = -extents.y + ballRadius;
            double roof = extents.y - ballRadius;
            Signal gravity = new Signal(t0, 0, 0, -1200);
            StreamLoop<Signal> sBounceX = new StreamLoop<>();
            StreamLoop<Signal> sBounceY = new StreamLoop<>();
            Cell<Signal> velx =
                    sBounceX.hold(new Signal(t0, 0, 0, 350));    // X has constant velocity.
            Cell<Signal> vely =
                    sBounceY.hold(gravity.integrate(0));          // Y is the integral of gravity.
            Cell<Signal> posx = Signal.integrate(velx, leftWall);
            Cell<Signal> posy = Signal.integrate(vely, roof);
            sBounceX.loop(bounceAt(sys, velx, posx, leftWall)
                            .orElse(bounceAt(sys, velx, posx, rightWall)));
            sBounceY.loop(bounceAt(sys, vely, posy, floor));
            return translate(
                scale(circle(Color.red), new Cell<Double>(ballRadius)),
                time.lift(posx, posy, (t, x, y) ->
                        new Point(x.valueAt(t), y.valueAt(t)))
            );
        });
    }
    static double restitution = 0.95;
    public static Stream<Signal> bounceAt(TimerSystem<Double> sys,
                    Cell<Signal> vel, Cell<Signal> pos, double target) {
        return sys.at(pos.map(p -> p.when(target)))       // Sets an alarm for when you hit the target
                .snapshot(vel, (t, v) ->
                    new Signal(t, v.a, v.b,
                            -v.valueAt(t)*restitution));
    }
}
```

Y is the integral of gravity.

X has constant velocity.

On bounce, negates the velocity's value but retains acceleration component

Sets an alarm for when you hit the target

To run this, check it out if you haven't done so already, and then run it like this:

```
cd sodium/book/continuous-time/java
mvn test -Pbounce      or      ant bounce
```

9.5   *Summary*

- We liken continuous-time FRP to vector graphics and animation frames to raster graphics, but in the domain of time instead of space.

- The mechanism of continuous time is to update a cell representing time before passing external events into the FRP system. Externally, you're saying, "Please sample the model at time t," but within the model, you can think of `time` as varying continuously. Different systems abstract these mechanics away in different ways.

- If you `lift` or `map` something against a continuously varying `time` variable, then the resulting value is continuous.

- Continuous time requires that you can measure time. Sodium provides `Timer-System.at()` to do this.

- With continuous-time FRP, you can simulate physics in a natural way.

Battle of the paradigms

This chapter covers

- One example (drag-and-drop) in three paradigms
- Comparing the merits of classic static machine vs. FRP vs. actor model
- Adding a feature to see how each approach copes

As you may have gathered, FRP is awesome. But for some tasks, the level of awesome is more limited, and other paradigms do a better job.

Drag-and-drop is a common task that fits FRP pretty well, but two other paradigms—classic state machine and the actor model—also do a nice job of it, for different reasons. We want you to understand why this is so you can make the right choices in your code.

10.1 Classic state machine vs. FRP vs. actor model

Figure 10.1 presents the same simple drag-and-drop example written in three different paradigms: *classic state machine*, *FRP*, and *actor model*. FRP and actor both require immutable data structures, but even when those aren't required, they're always a good idea. The polygons are called `Elements`, and you contain them in a `Document`.

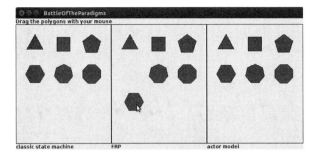

Figure 10.1   The same logic in three paradigms. Betraying an affectation of nonchalant elegance, you drag a hexagon with FRP.

Listing 10.1 shows the external interface for Document. We won't give the implementation, but you can find it in sodium/book/battle/java/battle/. getByPoint() allows you to find an element given an (x, y) mouse position. A string id identifies the elements in the document: if you insert an element with an id that already exists, the original element is replaced. insert() works immutably, returning a copy of the document with the element replaced.

Listing 10.1   External interface for a Document of polygons

```
class Entry {
    public final String id;
    public final Element element;
}
class Document {
    public Optional<Entry> getByPoint(Point pt);
    public Document insert(String id, Element polygon);
    public void draw(Graphics g);
}
```

The next listing gives the interface for Element. You can test whether a given point is inside the polygon with contains(). You can translate() it—again, immutably—according to a mouse drag from orig to pt. Finally, both Document and Element can be draw()n.

Listing 10.2   Element representing a polygon

```
class Element {
    public boolean contains(Point pt);
    public Element translate(Point orig, Point pt);
    public void draw(Graphics g);
}
```

Listing 10.3 gives the Paradigm interface that the implementation for each paradigm must conform to. Each paradigm implementation receives input events through a mouseEvent() method and outputs updated documents using the observer pattern. We used Java vernacular rather than FRP for the common interface here.

Listing 10.3　Interface for each of the three paradigms

```
interface Paradigm {
    interface DocumentListener {
        void documentUpdated(Document doc);
    }
    interface Factory {
        Paradigm create(Document initDoc, DocumentListener dl);
    }
    void mouseEvent(MouseEvt me);
    void dispose();
}
```

And now for the implementations. Ladies and gentlemen, start your engines!

10.1.1　*Classic state machine*

Listing 10.4 is the classic state-machine implementation. The external interface is the same classic/observer paradigm, so there's no impedance mismatch to bridge. This makes the code simpler, but even so, the FRP code is two lines shorter than the classic version.

Note that when handling MOVE, you have to explicitly check whether you're dragging. It's possible to make a mistake and forget to check. You can eliminate this potential source of bugs in both FRP and actor.

Listing 10.4　Drag-and-drop: classic state-machine version

```
class Classic implements Paradigm {
    public Classic(Document initDoc, DocumentListener dl) {
        this.doc = initDoc;
        this.dl = dl;
    }
    private final DocumentListener dl;

    private static class Dragging {
        Dragging(MouseEvt me1, Entry ent) {
            this.me1 = me1;
            this.ent = ent;
        }
        final MouseEvt me1;
        final Entry ent;
    }
    private Document doc;                                         Internal state is
    private Optional<Dragging> oDragging = Optional.empty();      kept in fields.

    public void mouseEvent(MouseEvt me) {
        switch (me.type) {
        case DOWN:
            Optional<Entry> oe = doc.getByPoint(me.pt);          If the user clicked
            if (oe.isPresent()) {                                an element …
                System.out.println("classic dragging " + oe.get().id);
        ...starts   oDragging = Optional.of(new Dragging(me, oe.get()));
        dragging.    }
            break;
```

```
                    case MOVE:                                    Potential source of bugs:
                        if (oDragging.isPresent()) {      ◁───┘  explicit state check
                            Dragging dr = oDragging.get();
  Updates the  ┌───▷      doc = doc.insert(dr.ent.id,
  internal state │            dr.ent.element.translate(dr.me1.pt, me.pt));
                            dl.documentUpdated(doc);
                        }
                        break;
                    case UP:
                        oDragging = Optional.empty();      ◁───┐  Stops
                        break;                                  │  dragging
                    }
                }
            public void dispose() {}
        }
```

10.1.2 FRP

The following listing gives the same logic in FRP. This code does the same thing as the
RxJS drag-and-drop code from section 7.8.1.

Listing 10.5   Drag-and-drop: FRP version

```
class FRP implements Paradigm {
    public FRP(Document initDoc, DocumentListener dl) {
        l = Transaction.run(() -> {
            CellLoop<Document> doc = new CellLoop<>();
            Stream<Stream<Document>> sStartDrag =
                                          Stream.filterOptional(
                sMouse.snapshot(doc, (me1, doc1) -> {
                    if (me1.type == Type.DOWN) {
                        Optional<Entry> oe = doc1.getByPoint(me1.pt);
                        if (oe.isPresent()) {
                            String id = oe.get().id;
                            Element elt = oe.get().element;
                            System.out.println("FRP dragging " + id);
                            Stream<Document> sMoves =
                                sMouse.filter(me -> me.type == Type.MOVE)
                                    .snapshot(doc, (me2, doc2) ->
                                    doc2.insert(id,
                                        elt.translate(me1.pt, me2.pt)));
                            return Optional.of(sMoves);
                        }
                    }
                    return Optional.empty();
                }));
            Stream<Document> sIdle = new Stream<>();
            Stream<Stream<Document>> sEndDrag =
                sMouse.filter(me -> me.type == Type.UP)
                    .map(me -> sIdle);
            Stream<Document> sDocUpdate = Cell.switchS(
                sStartDrag.orElse(sEndDrag).hold(sIdle)
            );
            doc.loop(sDocUpdate.hold(initDoc));
```

Annotations (left margin):
- Optionally switches to a new document stream
- If the user clicked an element ...
- Stream that updates the document on MOVE events
- Switches to the dragging state
- Outputs nothing
- Switches the document stream to "never"

Annotations (right margin):
- "Not dragging" state
- The actual switch

```
                    return sDocUpdate.listen(doc_ -> dl.documentUpdated(doc_));
        });
    }
    private final Listener l;
    private final StreamSink<MouseEvt> sMouse = new StreamSink<>();
    public void mouseEvent(MouseEvt me) { sMouse.send(me); }
    public void dispose() { l.unlisten(); }
}
```

Interface to the outside world

Even with your new familiarity with FRP, this code will be less obvious than the classic code. The key to understanding it is that you're switching between streams of document updates of type `Stream<Document>`. When you get a mouse `DOWN` on an element from the document, you enter the dragging state by switching to a stream that outputs updates in response to `MOVE` events. When you get a mouse `UP` event, you enter the "not dragging" state by switching to a `never` stream: don't output any document updates.

Recall what we said in chapter 7: `switch` lets you eliminate invalid states. The state of "what you are dragging" is invalid when you aren't dragging. Classic combined those two states using an `Optional` type, and that's the best you can do in that paradigm. But the handling of `MOVE` demands an explicit check to see whether you're dragging. With FRP and `switch`, you can achieve the ideal: the logic exists only when the state exists.

> **NOTE** Murphy's law says, "If anything can go wrong, it will." Invalid states are something that can go wrong, and this makes them a potential source of bugs. The philosophy of functional programming and of FRP is to eliminate things that can go wrong as much as possible.

10.1.3 Actor model

Listing 10.6 gives the *actor model* implementation. Of the three, this is the most natural. We argue that this is because actor is the best fit for this particular problem.

What is the actor model?

Actors often marry models, as you can see in the figure, but we'll leave our analysis of the entertainment industry for another time.

Actors are a model of concurrency first developed in the 1970s. The programming language Erlang and, more recently, reactive frameworks like Akka make extensive use of it. It's especially suited for distributed computing because of its ability to tolerate runtime failures and to hot-swap components. It's been proven in large-scale commercial applications.

An actor is a process whose job is to handle incoming messages from a single asynchronous input queue. Each actor has a public address, and other actors that

The actor model

(continued)

know the address can send the actor messages. Actors commonly use a reply mechanism that sends a message to the originator of an input message. Actors can spawn new actors, and they can send the address of an actor to another actor over a message.

Actors as they're commonly implemented have a thread-like flow of control. We think there's a lot of potential for FRP and actors to work together. You could, for example, implement the logic of an actor within an established actor-based framework using FRP.

Listing 10.6   Drag-and-drop: actor model version

```
class Actor implements Paradigm {
    public Actor(Document initDoc, DocumentListener dl) {
        ArrayBlockingQueue<Document> out = new ArrayBlockingQueue<>(1);
        t1 = new Thread(() -> {
            try {
                Document doc = initDoc;
                while (true) {
                    MouseEvt me1 = null;
                    Entry ent = null;
                    while (true) {
                        MouseEvt me = in.take();
                        if (me.type == Type.DOWN) {
                            Optional<Entry> oe = doc.getByPoint(me.pt);
                            if (oe.isPresent()) {
                                me1 = me;
                                ent = oe.get();
                                break;
                            }
                        }
                    }
                    System.out.println("actor dragging " + ent.id);
                    while (true) {
                        MouseEvt me = in.take();
                        if (me.type == Type.MOVE) {
                            doc = doc.insert(ent.id,
                                    ent.element.translate(me1.pt, me.pt));
                            out.put(doc);
                        }
                        else
                        if (me.type == Type.UP)
                            break;
                    }
                }
            } catch (InterruptedException e) {}
        });
        t1.start();
        t2 = new Thread(() -> {
            try {
```

Message queue ⟶ `ArrayBlockingQueue<Document> out = new ArrayBlockingQueue<>(1);`

What you're dragging ▷ `MouseEvt me1 = null;` `Entry ent = null;`

This loop corresponds to the non-dragging state. ◁ `while (true) {`

Blocks on an input message ▷ `MouseEvt me = in.take();`

Switches to the dragging state ◁ `break;`

This loop corresponds to the dragging state. ▷ `while (true) {`

Outputs an updated document ▷ `out.put(doc);`

Exits the dragging state on an UP event ◁ `break;`

Bridges the paradigms: drains the out queue into an external observer interface ◁ `t2 = new Thread(() -> {`

```
            while (true)
                dl.documentUpdated(out.take());
        } catch (InterruptedException e) {}
    });
    t2.start();
}
private final Thread t1, t2;
private final ArrayBlockingQueue<MouseEvt> in =
                                new ArrayBlockingQueue<>(1);
public void mouseEvent(MouseEvt me) {
    try {
        in.put(me);
    } catch (InterruptedException e) {}
}
public void dispose() { t1.interrupt(); t2.interrupt(); }
}
```

To run this, check it out if you haven't done so already, and then run it like this:

```
git clone https://github.com/SodiumFRP/sodium
cd sodium/book/battle/java
mvn test -Pbattle    or    ant battle
```

Actors have a *flow of control*, which is something that classic and FRP can't replicate. The state for this problem consists of two variables:

- Current document
- Whether you're dragging and, if you're dragging, what you're dragging

In classic, these are represented directly as variables (stored in object fields). In FRP, they directly map to cells.

A great advantage of actor is that it allows for *implicit state machines*, as they're called: you can make variable 2 (dragging) *implicit* in the flow of control. This gives the same advantage that FRP gave you of eliminating an invalid state. Like FRP, the logic exists only when the state exists.

10.1.4 And the winner is...

Actor won that round. It eliminated an invalid state, and it did so in a way that was natural and easy to understand.

But this is a book about FRP, so our egos demand that FRP can't be beaten. We've been arguing both from theory and anecdotally that FRP's advantage isn't that it's better than other paradigms in all situations, but that its solution complexity (or code complexity) increases more linearly with problem complexity. Our personal experience is shown roughly in figure 10.2.

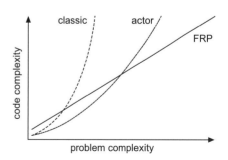

Figure 10.2 How we argue code complexity increases with problem complexity

The Agile software development methodology claims this same advantage, but FRP achieves it in a different way: by applying simple mathematical principles to your code. FRP may have some upper limit in its ability to deal with complexity, but we don't know where it is or how it manifests because we haven't hit it.

The advantage that actor has is that you can flatten the dragging state into a flow of control. The other state variable document can be neatly flattened into the same structure along with *dragging*.

10.2   *Let's add a feature: Shift key gives axis lock*

But what if you throw actor a curve ball? You're going to give it a second state variable that doesn't fit neatly with dragging:

- If you hold down the Shift key, the element's displacement is locked to the X or Y axis.

You should be familiar with this because most diagramming software has this feature.

Listing 10.7 gives the actor version with changes in bold. There are two problems:

- The code to change the axisLock state is duplicated. Of course, this can be put into a method, but it still has to be handled separately in both loops.
- In actor, it's common to use dynamic typing on input messages, so we've done that here. The disadvantage is that it's possible to accidentally send an object of a type that an actor doesn't know about, or forget to handle a type somewhere in your actor. For example, you could accidentally forget about Type (Shift key) messages in one of the two places.

Actor can flatten a state variable into a flow of control, and you've seen that this is a powerful technique. But it can only do this successfully with one state variable. We flattened dragging into the flow of control, and document worked nicely along with it. But axisLock doesn't fit this flow at all. Hence, the code is duplicated.

Listing 10.7   Drag-and-drop with axis lock: actor model version

```
class Actor implements Paradigm {
    public Actor(Document initDoc, DocumentListener dl) {
        ArrayBlockingQueue<Document> out = new ArrayBlockingQueue<>(1);
        t1 = new Thread(() -> {
            try {
                Document doc = initDoc;
                boolean axisLock = false;
                while (true) {
                    MouseEvt me1 = null;
                    Entry ent = null;
                    while (true) {
                        Object o = in.take();
                        if (o instanceof MouseEvt) {
                            MouseEvt me = (MouseEvt) o;
```

The input value is now dynamically typed.

```
                              if (me.type == Type.DOWN) {
                                  Optional<Entry> oe = doc.getByPoint(me.pt);
                                  if (oe.isPresent()) {
                                      me1 = me;
                                      ent = oe.get();
                                      break;
                                  }
                              }
                          }
                          if (o instanceof Type) {
                              Type t = (Type) o;
                              axisLock = t == Type.DOWN;
                          }
                      }
                      System.out.println("actor dragging " + ent.id);
                      while (true) {
                          Object o = in.take();
                          if (o instanceof MouseEvt) {
                              MouseEvt me = (MouseEvt) o;
                              if (me.type == Type.MOVE) {
                                  doc = doc.insert(ent.id,
                                      ent.element.translate(me1.pt, me.pt,
                                          axisLock));
                                  out.put(doc);
                              }
                              else
                              if (me.type == Type.UP)
                                  break;
                          }
                          if (o instanceof Type) {
                              Type t = (Type) o;
                              axisLock = t == Type.DOWN;
                          }
                      }
                  }
              } catch (InterruptedException e) {}
          });
          ...
      }
      private final Thread t1, t2;
      private final ArrayBlockingQueue<Object> in =
                                      new ArrayBlockingQueue<>(1);
      public void mouseEvent(MouseEvt me) {
          try {
              in.put(me);
          } catch (InterruptedException e) {}
      }
      public void shiftEvent(Type t) {
          try {
              in.put(t);
          } catch (InterruptedException e) {}
      }
      public void dispose() { t1.interrupt(); t2.interrupt(); }
  }
```

Shift key handling is duplicated.

Irrelevant code omitted

The next listing shows the same logic change in the FRP version. You can see that the change is fairly trivial.

Listing 10.8   Drag-and-drop with axis lock: FRP version

```
class FRP implements Paradigm {
    public FRP(Document initDoc, DocumentListener dl) {
        l = Transaction.run(() -> {
            CellLoop<Document> doc = new CellLoop<>();
            Cell<Boolean> axisLock = sShift.map(t -> t == Type.DOWN)
                                           .hold(false);
            Stream<Stream<Document>> sStartDrag = Stream.filterOptional(
                sMouse.snapshot(doc, (me1, doc1) -> {
                    if (me1.type == Type.DOWN) {
                        Optional<Entry> oe = doc1.getByPoint(me1.pt);
                        if (oe.isPresent()) {
                            String id = oe.get().id;
                            Element elt = oe.get().element;
                            System.out.println("FRP dragging " + id);
                            Stream<Document> sMoves = sMouse
                                .filter(me -> me.type == Type.MOVE)
                                .snapshot(doc, (me2, doc2) ->
                                    doc2.insert(id,
                                            elt.translate(me1.pt, me2.pt,
                                                axisLock.sample()))));
                            return Optional.of(sMoves);
                        }
                    }
                    return Optional.empty();
                }));
            Stream<Document> sIdle = new Stream<>();
            Stream<Stream<Document>> sEndDrag =
                sMouse.filter(me -> me.type == Type.UP)
                    .map(me -> sIdle);
            Stream<Document> sDocUpdate = Cell.switchS(
                sStartDrag.orElse(sEndDrag).hold(sIdle)
            );
            doc.loop(sDocUpdate.hold(initDoc));
            return sDocUpdate.listen(doc_ -> dl.documentUpdated(doc_));
        });
    }
    private final Listener l;
    private final StreamSink<MouseEvt> sMouse = new StreamSink<>();
    public void mouseEvent(MouseEvt me) { sMouse.send(me); }
    private final StreamSink<Type> sShift = new StreamSink<>();
    public void shiftEvent(Type t) { sShift.send(t); }
    public void dispose() { l.unlisten(); }
}
```

To run this, check it out if you haven't done so already, and then run it like this:

```
git clone https://github.com/SodiumFRP/sodium
cd sodium/book/battle/java
mvn test -Pshift     or     ant shift
```

The classic implementation, which we don't list here, is also a trivial change. We think FRP still beats classic because of the elimination of the invalid state. You'll find this code under sodium/book/battle/java/shift/.

10.3 *Improvement: Shift key updates the document*

In the previous Shift key/axis lock example, the change in the Shift key state doesn't cause the dragged element to be redrawn. You have to move the mouse infinitesimally to do it, and this feels wrong to the user. It'd be nice to fix each paradigm so shift-Event() also causes the element position to be updated.

We've implemented a third version of the code that does this. We'll give code snippets to illustrate the changes you need to make. You can read the full code at sodium/book/battle/java/shift2/.

To run this version, check it out if you haven't done so already, and then run it like this:

```
git clone https://github.com/SodiumFRP/sodium
cd sodium/book/battle/java
mvn test -Pshift2     or      ant shift2
```

10.3.1 *Changing this in the classic paradigm*

You need to add a new move field to remember the most recent move position, and you need to set it to an initial value in UP and then update it in MOVE. The output of the updated document is moved to a new updateMove() method:

```
private Point move;
...
    case DOWN:
        ...
        if (...) {
            move = me.pt;
        }
        break;
    case MOVE:
        move = me.pt;
        updateMove();
        break;
```

shiftEvent() is changed to call updateMove():

```
public void shiftEvent(Type t) {
    axisLock = t == Type.DOWN;
    updateMove();
}
```

The extra state variable move makes us a little uneasy. It belongs in the Dragging data structure. This would be cleaner, except that Optional isn't designed to be modified in place. We'll leave you to think about this.

10.3.2 *Changing this in FRP*

In FRP, you also need some new state to keep the most recent move position. The best way to do this is to model `move` and `axisLock` as cells instead of streams, because they're both stateful. You define `axisLock` like this at the top level:

```
Cell<Boolean> axisLock = sShift.map(t -> t == Type.DOWN)
                               .hold(false);
```

On the start of the drag state, you define `move`—the most recent mouse move position—like this:

```
Cell<Point> move =
    sMouse.filter(me -> me.type == Type.MOVE)
          .map(me -> me.pt)
          .hold(me1.pt);
```

> **NOTE** We've talked about this before: the fact that we're using `switch` means the transactional context in which the `holds` are executed is important. `axisLock` is in the transactional context of all the logic because it should be independent of when the drag starts and stops. But `move` must be defined in the transactional context of handling the mouse `DOWN` because it should exist during the dragging state only. Its initial value comes from the position of the `DOWN` event, which is only in scope within this transactional context.

Now it's simple to use `lift` to calculate where the dragged element should be:

```
Stream<Document> sMoves = Operational.updates(
        move.lift(axisLock, (mv, lck) ->
            elt.translate(me1.pt, mv, lck))
    )
    .snapshot(doc, (newElt, doc2) ->
        doc2.insert(id, newElt));
```

Finally, you break the rule of non-observability of cell steps (see section 8.4) and use `Operational.updates()` to turn that cell into a stream of the new element to be replaced in the document. This is a neat way to solve the problem, so we'll leave you to contemplate the philosophical issues yourself. Bear in mind that some FRP systems may not allow you to do this.

If you want to avoid this, it can be done in an equivalent but less neat way with two snapshots. For `move` and `axisLock`, you need both the stream and cell variants, so you need `move`, `sMove`, `axisLock`, and `sAxisLock`. When `sMove` fires, you want to capture the most recent `axisLock`, and vice versa with `sAxisLock` and `move`. So you merge an `sMove.snapshot(axisLock)` with an `sAxisLock.snapshot(move)`. Here it is, implemented in a second `Paradigm` implementation called `FRP2`:

```
class Pair {
    Pair(Point move, boolean lock) {
        this.move = move;
        this.lock = lock;
    }
```

```
    Point move;
    boolean lock;
}
Stream<Point> sMove =
    sMouse.filter(me -> me.type == Type.MOVE)
         .map(me -> me.pt);
Cell<Point> move = sMove.hold(me1.pt);
Stream<Pair> sPair = sMove.snapshot(axisLock,
        (m, l) -> new Pair(m, l))
    .orElse(sAxisLock.snapshot(move,
        (l, m) -> new Pair(m, l)));
Stream<Document> sMoves = sPair.snapshot(doc,
    (p, doc2) -> doc2.insert(id,
       elt.translate(me1.pt, p.move, p.lock)));
```

10.3.3 *Changing this in the actor model*

The change to the actor code is fairly straightforward. A document update can be triggered by two different events, so you use a temporary variable, toUpdate, for that:

```
Point move = me1.pt;
while (true) {
    Object o = in.take();
    boolean toUpdate = false;
    if (o instanceof MouseEvt) {
        MouseEvt me = (MouseEvt) o;
        if (me.type == Type.MOVE) {
            move = me.pt;
            toUpdate = true;
        }
        else
        if (me.type == Type.UP)
            break;
    }
    if (o instanceof Type) {
        Type t = (Type) o;
        axisLock = t == Type.DOWN;
        toUpdate = true;
    }
    if (toUpdate) {
        doc = doc.insert(ent.id,
            ent.element.translate(me1.pt, move,
                axisLock));
        out.put(doc);
    }
}
```

10.3.4 *How are the different paradigms doing?*

Let's reflect on how each paradigm is coping with what we've thrown at it:

- *Classic*—You've got to make sure you check whether you're in the dragging state, and it's also possible to inadvertently forget to call updateMove(). The classic paradigm often leads you to have one or more update() methods that bring things up to date and generate outputs. Forgetting to call `update()` is a common bug that can't occur in FRP.

- *FRP*—It coped well. It got verbose in one case when we tried to avoid the short-cut of using `Operational.updates()`, but it remained semantically tidy.
- *Actor*—The biggest problem was that we had to handle the `Type` (Shift key up/down) message twice and duplicate some logic, and there doesn't seem to be an easy way to solve this. Actor can also lead you into long methods with lots of local variables, and the example is getting there. Perhaps this can be split into two actors, but it isn't clear how to do this. The actor code also suffers a little from the same "update-itis" that classic has: it would be easy to inadvertently forget to set `toUpdate`. In FRP, the cell abstraction is effective at eliminating this problem.

10.3.5 *State machines with long sequences*

We'll reiterate something we've said before. FRP isn't ideal for things that naturally fall into a long linear sequence of state changes—that is, when a single state variable goes through a long, complex, branching and/or looping sequence. An example might be communicating with an SMTP server to send a list of emails and handling errors at each step. Actor/threads would be a more suitable abstraction for this kind of logic.

FRP is better for situations with multidimensional state transitions: a large number of state variables interacting in complex ways. We've given many examples where FRP is sensible.

So, even though FRP does well in the current example, there do exist nontrivial problems where actor would be more suitable than FRP. We like the idea of a combination of FRP and actors for some applications.

10.4 *Summary*

- The classic callback/listener style code often involves calling some kind of `update()` method. There are many opportunities to forget to do it or to call things in the wrong order.
- The actor model can flatten one state variable into a flow of control, often greatly simplifying the implementation. But it doesn't cope well when the problem demands more than one independent state variable.
- FRP copes well with multiple independent state variables. So does classic, but complexity is always threatening to creep in.
- Actor is best where the problem has a clear, linear flow of control.

Programming in the real world

Functional programming in general gives you an idealized programming model, allowing you to focus on the problem itself, and FRP does this too. In chapter 9, you bounced a ball in an ideal world of continuous time, as if in some Zen squash court from the movie *The Matrix*. Earlier, chapter 8 covered some of the uncharted, more operational areas of the FRP design space. But sooner or later, you'll have to deal with something even more terrifying: the real world.

I/O is notorious for presenting intractable difficulties and complexities. I/O and logic tend to mutually complicate each other, so the approach used in FRP—and in functional programming in general—is to keep them separate. FRP deals well with the complexities of logic, and I/O is simpler with the logic removed.

11.1   Dealing with I/O

A simple way to model I/O in FRP is as a function of this type:

```
Stream<B> myIO(Stream<A> sIn)
```

When the input stream fires, the I/O is initiated, and when the result of the I/O is ready, it appears on the output stream. The operation is asynchronous, so the output is in a different transactional context from the I/O initiation event.

The needs of Sodium in Java require you to write that type concretely as shown here, but of course, each language has its own way of representing function types:

```
Lambda1<Stream<A>, Stream<B>>
```

> **DEFINITION**   *I/O action*—The type `Stream<B> myIO(Stream<A> sIn)`, representing some I/O.

Once you have an I/O action in this form, it will play nicely with FRP. You'll use this to implement a dictionary lookup client; see figure 11.1.

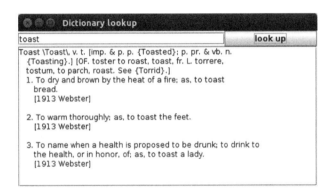

Figure 11.1   A dictionary lookup client: Click Look Up, and it fetches from the server a definition for the word you entered.

The I/O consists of connecting to a dictionary server to retrieve the definition, and it's written in the normal way. The skeleton for wrapping this up into the form you want is given in listing 11.1. In this example, the input is a `String` containing the word, and the output value is `Optional<String>` indicating either the definition retrieved from the server or an error if the value isn't present in the `Optional`.

> **NOTE**   The key idea is that viewed from the outside, an I/O action adheres to the strict rules of FRP, but on the inside it's free to roam the lawless lands of I/O.

Listing 11.1   Skeleton for an I/O action

```
public static final
Lambda1<Stream<String>, Stream<Optional<String>>> lookup = sWord -> {
    StreamSink<Optional<String>> sDefinition = new StreamSink<>();
```

```
    Listener l = sWord.listenWeak(wrd -> {
        new Thread() {                              ← Spawn a worker
            public void run() {                       thread.
                Optional<String> def = Optional.empty();
                try {
                    ...
                    def = Optional.of(...);
                }
                finally {
                    sDefinition.send(def);          ← I/O result handled in
                }                                     a new transaction
            }
        }.start();
    });
    return sDefinition.addCleanup(l);
};
```

We've omitted the I/O code here, but you'll find it in sodium/book/real-world/java/ lookup/Lookup.java. This listing introduces a new Sodium API method, `Stream.addCleanup()`, that takes a `Listener`. This causes that stream to keep the specified listener alive while it's alive. The Sodium API requires that you use `listen-Weak()` to obtain the listener that you pass to `addCleanup()`.

In this example, as long as the output stream `sDefinition` is referenced or used in some way, the listener stays registered, and it's automatically cleaned up when `sDefinition` is. This allows you to write your I/O in a fire-and-forget way.

Recall the rules of what you're allowed to do inside a listener from chapter 8:

- `send()` isn't allowed.
- Blocking I/O isn't allowed.
- Non-blocking I/O is acceptable.

Here you spawn a thread to ensure that the I/O doesn't block inside the handler you pass to `listen()`. Note that the `send()` doesn't break the first rule because it's running on a different thread.

11.1.1 Error-handling in FRP

In most languages, I/O errors are handled through the mechanism of *exceptions*. FRP can't cope with exceptions, and you must never throw them in normal FRP code. FRP only deals in values, so your I/O code needs to catch the exception and turn it into a value.

Rx and the systems based on it have error-handling capability built in. This isn't the same as a normal exception. Underneath, these errors are really just values, and Rx causes them to be propagated automatically in an exception-like way.

In systems without error-handling, such as Sodium, the way to model errors is through *optional* or *variant* types. Most languages have an equivalent of Java's `Optional`. If the value isn't present, then you treat it as an error.

NOTE   Rx automatically propagates errors through a chain of processing. In Sodium, you have to propagate the error state yourself by hand, but you can write helper code to make this easier.

A variant type allows your error value to be more meaningful. The value can be either an error message or a value. Functional programming languages typically make this easy, but it can be cumbersome in nonfunctional languages. Java has no direct equivalent of variant types, so you have to write one yourself. What you want is something like `Optional` but with a representation of the error (such as a string) instead of no value. In C++, you can use `boost::variant` from the Boost library. Part of the reason the designers of Rx built in error-handling may be to do with the fact that variant types aren't a common idiom in the most popular languages.

As we've said, exceptions aren't allowed, so the I/O code should always output some value, which might be a value representing an error. We used a `try` / `finally` block in listing 11.1 so it's guaranteed to output something. You should choose whatever style fits your error-handling needs.

11.1.2   *Executing an I/O action*

You can instantiate an I/O action like this:

```
Stream<Stream> sWord = ...;
Stream<Optional<String>> sOut = lookup.apply(sWord);
```

When the I/O runs, two FRP transactions are involved. The initiation of the I/O happens in one transaction, and the receiving of the result happens in a later transaction—see figure 11.2. Note that because you spawn a new thread to do the I/O, the `send()` method isn't explicitly inside a transactional context. But it will start a new transaction automatically.

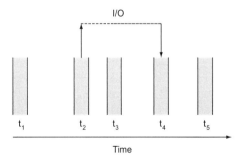

Figure 11.2   I/O is initiated in transaction 2, and the response comes back in transaction 4.

NOTE   It's sensible to add to the definition of an I/O action a requirement that the result should always arrive in a new transaction—not in the same transaction in which it was initiated. This permits you to always assume this is so when working with any I/O action.

Because the I/O action runs asynchronously, it's possible for a single I/O action instance to be executing more than once in parallel, as in figure 11.3. Note also that there's no guarantee that the responses will come back in the same order as the initiations of the I/O. You need to have some sort of policy to decide what you do about the possibility of overlapping I/O execution.

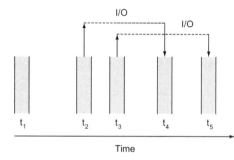

Figure 11.3 Multiple executions of I/O can overlap.

The current example will use a simple policy. You'll prevent overlapping I/O in the following way: you'll keep a busy state and allow I/O to be initiated only when busy is false. You can write a general utility class to help with this—see listing 11.2.

This utility instantiates the I/O action you pass to it by executing the action function. It outputs the stream containing the I/O action's output, along with a busy flag. It's the caller's responsibility to block input to the action based on busy.

Listing 11.2 General utility to track whether an I/O action is busy

```
class IsBusy<A,B> {
    public IsBusy(Lambda1<Stream<A>, Stream<B>> action, Stream<A> sIn) {
        sOut = action.apply(sIn);
        busy = sIn.map(i -> true)
                  .orElse(sOut.map(i -> false))
                  .hold(false);
    }
    public Stream<B> sOut;
    public Cell<Boolean> busy;
}
```

11.1.3 Putting the application together

Listing 11.3 puts together the Lookup application, with Java layout code omitted. The busy flag is used in three places:

- enabled is the logical NOT of busy. You pass that flag in to SButton so it's enabled only when the I/O isn't busy. This prevents initiation of I/O when it's already busy.
- You also pass enabled to the output text area, so it appears gray while the I/O request is in progress.

- When the I/O is busy, you show "Looking up…" in the output text area instead of the definition.

Listing 11.3   Dictionary lookup application

```
Transaction.runVoid(() -> {
    STextField word = new STextField("", 25);
    CellLoop<Boolean> enabled = new CellLoop<>();
    SButton button = new SButton("look up", enabled);
    Stream<String> sWord = button.sClicked.snapshot(word.text);
    IsBusy<String, Optional<String>> ib =
                          new IsBusy<>(lookup, sWord);
    Stream<String> sDefinition = ib.sOut
        .map(o -> o.isPresent() ? o.get() : "ERROR!");
    Cell<String> definition = sDefinition.hold("");
    Cell<String> output = definition.lift(ib.busy, (def, bsy) ->
        bsy ? "Looking up..." : def);
    enabled.loop(ib.busy.map(b -> !b));
    STextArea outputArea = new STextArea(output, enabled);
    view.add(word, c);
    view.add(button, c);
    view.add(new JScrollPane(outputArea), c);
});
```

As usual, check it out if you haven't done so already:

```
git clone https://github.com/SodiumFRP/sodium
```

Note that an extra step is required to run this if you're using Maven. You need to install the SWidgets library into your local Maven repository:

```
cd sodium/book/swidgets/java/swidgets
mvn install
cd ../../../../..
```

Then do this to run it:

```
cd sodium/book/real-world/java
mvn test -Plookup     or     ant lookup
```

11.2   *Promises/Futures*

The way you handled asynchronous I/O in the previous section works for simple cases, but sometimes you want to track some state with each outstanding I/O request. *Promises* are a popular abstraction these days, and they work well in FRP for this problem.

> **NOTE**   There are lots of opinions about the difference between the terms *promise* and *future*. We'll treat them as one and just talk about promises.

A promise models a value that's available either now or in the future. If it's not available now, you can be notified when it arrives. You can implement a promise as shown in listing 11.4.

NOTE In Sodium, listenOnce() is a variant of listen() that you haven't seen yet. It automatically deregisters and cleans up the listener after it has handled one event, so it will only fire once.

Listing 11.4 FRP-based implementation of Promise

```java
import nz.sodium.*;
import java.util.Optional;

public class Promise<A> {
    public Promise(Stream<A> sDeliver) {
        this.sDeliver = sDeliver.once();
        this.oValue = this.sDeliver.map(a -> Optional.of(a))
                                   .hold(Optional.empty());
    }
    public final Stream<A> sDeliver;
    public final Cell<Optional<A>> oValue;
    public final Stream<A> then() {
        return Stream.filterOptional(Operational.value(oValue))
            .orElse(sDeliver).once();
    }
    public final void thenDo(Handler<A> h) {
        Transaction.runVoid(() ->
            then().listenOnce(h)
        );
    }
}
```

Delivery of the value, which may have already occurred

Current value, which may or may not be present

Imperative interface to then()

Requests the value: returns a stream guaranteed to fire once with the value when it's available either now or in the future

The next listing tests this out.

Listing 11.5 Trying out Promise

```java
import nz.sodium.*;
import java.util.ArrayList;

public class promise1 {
    public static void main(String[] args) {
        System.out.println("*** test 1");
        {
            ArrayList<String> out = new ArrayList<>();
            StreamSink<String> s1 = new StreamSink<>();
            Promise<String> p1 = new Promise<>(s1);
            s1.send("Early");
            p1.thenDo(t -> System.out.println(t));
        }
        System.out.println("*** test 2");
        {
            ArrayList<String> out = new ArrayList<>();
            StreamSink<String> s1 = new StreamSink<>();
            Promise<String> p1 = new Promise<>(s1);
            p1.thenDo(t -> System.out.println(t));
            s1.send("Late");
        }
    }
}
```

```
}
------ Output ------
*** test 1
Early
*** test 2
Late
```

To run this example, check it out if you haven't done so already, and then run it like this:

```
git clone https://github.com/SodiumFRP/sodium
cd sodium/book/real-world/java
mvn test -Ppromise1    or    ant promise1
```

Listing 11.6 gives another useful feature you could add to `Promise`. You lift a function into promises like you do cells. The combined promise's value is delivered when both of its inputs are delivered. If you're prepared to use `Operational.updates()`, then lifting the cell will do everything you need. `Promise.lift()` can be implemented without `Operational.updates()`, but the code is longer. See the file PromiseWithout-Updates.java if you're interested.

Listing 11.6   Lifting a function into promises

```
private Promise(Cell<Optional<A>> oValue) {
    this.sDeliver = Stream.filterOptional(Operational.updates(oValue));
    this.oValue = oValue;
}

public <B,C> Promise<C> lift(Promise<B> pb,
                             final Lambda2<A, B, C> f) {
    return Transaction.run(() -> new Promise<C>(
        this.oValue.lift(pb.oValue,
            (oa, ob) ->
                oa.isPresent() && ob.isPresent()
                    ? Optional.of(f.apply(oa.get(), ob.get()))
                    : Optional.empty()
        )));
}
```

Let's test this as shown in the following listing.

Listing 11.7   Testing lifting functions into promises

```
import nz.sodium.*;
import java.util.ArrayList;

public class promise2 {
    public static void main(String[] args) {
        System.out.println("*** Simple test");
        {
            ArrayList<String> out = new ArrayList<>();
            StreamSink<String> sa = new StreamSink<>();
```

```
                    Promise<String> pa = new Promise<>(sa);
                    StreamSink<String> sb = new StreamSink<>();
                    Promise<String> pb = new Promise<>(sb);
                    Promise<String> p = pa.lift(pb, (a, b) -> a + " " + b);
                    sa.send("Hello");
                    p.thenDo(t -> System.out.println(t));
                    sb.send("World");
                }
                System.out.println("*** Simultaneous case");
                {
                    ArrayList<String> out = new ArrayList<>();
                    StreamSink<String> sa = new StreamSink<>();
                    Promise<String> pa = new Promise<>(sa);
                    StreamSink<String> sb = new StreamSink<>();
                    Promise<String> pb = new Promise<>(sb);
                    Promise<String> p = pa.lift(pb, (a, b) -> a + " " + b);
                    p.thenDo(t -> System.out.println(t));
                    Transaction.runVoid(() -> {
                        sa.send("Hello");
                        sb.send("World");
                    });
                }
            }
        }
------ Output ------
*** Simple test
Hello World
*** Simultaneous case
Hello World
```

To run this example, check it out if you haven't done so already, and then run it like this:

```
git clone https://github.com/SodiumFRP/sodium
cd sodium/book/real-world/java
mvn test -Ppromise2    or    ant promise2
```

11.2.1 *A map viewer example using Promise*

Let's say you're developing an application that draws maps fetched from a map server (see figure 11.4). As the user scrolls and zooms around the world, the map area changes. That's the area of the world that corresponds to the visible window. It's indicated with a black rectangle in the figure. The map area at any time is converted into a set of segments that need to be fetched and displayed to fill the window. In this example, there are six of them.

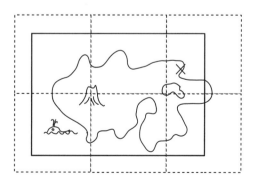

Figure 11.4 You need to fetch six segments from the server to fill the window.

The map viewer's state consists of a key/value mapping from segment coordinates to image promises. An image promise has the type Promise<Image>, so this mapping has this type:

```
Cell<Map<SegmentID, Promise<Image>>>
```

We've coded this example up in RxJS. Point your browser at sodium/book/web/ map.html in the Sodium project to run it. You can drag the map around, and you'll see it load map squares from a server as needed.

Here's the code to convert a URL into an image promise:

```
function imagePromise(url)
{
    var sLoaded = Rx.Observable.create(function (observer) {
        var img = new Image();
        img.onload = function() { observer.onNext(img); };
        img.src = url;
    }).publish();
    sLoaded.connect();
    var image = new Rx.BehaviorSubject(null),
        subscr1 = sLoaded.subscribe(image);
    return { image : image,
             dispose : function() { subscr1.dispose(); } };
}
```

You represent a promise as a BehaviorSubject that has a value of null initially and is replaced by the image once it has been loaded.

Listing 11.8 gives the body of the code. We've left out sequence(), which is defined in the Whack That Mole example in chapter 7; dragging(), which handles the moving of the scroll origin with mouse drag events; and draw(), which draws the scene.

Listing 11.8   Map viewer that loads map segments on demand

```
var baseURL = 'http://reactiveprogramming.org/~blackh/frp-map/',
    xTiles = 44, yTiles = 34,
    tileWidth = 200, tileHeight = 200,
    noOfTiles = xTiles * yTiles;
function tileX(tile) { return (tile % xTiles) * tileWidth; }
function tileY(tile) { return Math.floor(tile / xTiles) * tileHeight; }

function init() {
    var canvas = document.getElementById("myCanvas"),
        scrollOrigin = dragging(canvas),
        sTilesNeeded = scrollOrigin.map(function (so) {
            var tiles = [],
                x0 = Math.floor(so.x / tileWidth),
                y0 = Math.floor(so.y / tileHeight),
                wid = canvas.width,
                ht = canvas.height;
            for (var x = x0; ((x) * tileWidth - so.x <= wid); x++)
                for (var y = y0; ((y) * tileHeight - so.y <= ht); y++) {
                    var tile = x + y * xTiles;
```

For a given scroll origin, works out what tiles you need to draw

```
                                  if (tile >= 0 && tile < noOfTiles)
                                      tiles.push(tile);
                          }
                          return tiles;
                      }),
                      tilePromises = new Rx.BehaviorSubject([]);
                  sTilesNeeded.withLatestFrom(tilePromises,
                      function (needed, promises) {
                          var newPromises = [],
                              promises = promises.slice();
                          for (var i = 0; i < needed.length; i++) {
                              var tile = needed[i];
                              var found = false;
                              for (var j = 0; j < promises.length; j++) {
                                  if (promises[j].tile == tile) {
                                      newPromises.push(promises.splice(j, 1)[0]);
                                      found = true;
                                      break;
                                  }
                              }
                              if (!found)
                                  newPromises.push({
                                      tile : tile,
                                      promise : imagePromise(
                                          baseURL+"tile_"+tile+".png")
                                  });
                          }
                          for (var j = 0; j < promises.length; j++)
                              setTimeout(promises[j].promise.dispose, 0);
                          return newPromises;
                      }).subscribe(tilePromises);
                  var scene = tilePromises.flatMapLatest(function (promises) {
                      var outImages = [];
                      for (var i = 0; i < promises.length; i++) {
                          outImages.push(function (tile, image) {
                                  return image.map(
                                      function (img) {
                                          return { tile : tile, image : img };
                                      });
                              } (promises[i].tile, promises[i].promise.image));
                      }
                      return sequence(outImages);
                  });
                  var sTileLoaded = tilePromises.flatMapLatest(function (promises) {
                      var sLoaded = Rx.Observable.of();
                      for (var i = 0; i < promises.length; i++)
                          sLoaded = sLoaded.merge(
                              promises[i].promise.image.filter(function (img) {
                                  return img !== null; }));
                      return sLoaded;
                  });

                  function draw(toDraw) {
                      var so = toDraw.so;
                      var scene = toDraw.scene;
                      ...
                  }
```

Annotations:

— Instantiates and destroys promises as needed, given list of needed tiles

— Disposes of promises that are no longer needed

— Flattens the promised images into a single scene

— sequence() helper defined in chapter 7

— Stream that fires when any tile is loaded

```
        sTileLoaded.withLatestFrom(scrollOrigin, scene,
            function (_, so, scene) {
                return { so : so, scene : scene };
            }
        ).subscribe(draw);
        scrollOrigin.withLatestFrom(scene,
            function (so, scene) {
                return { so : so, scene : scene };
            }
        ).subscribe(draw);
}
```

← Redraws if the scroll origin changes

← Redraws when a tile is loaded

11.2.2 Initiating I/O with the spark idiom

The map example works fine in RxJS, but we took a semantic shortcut: image-Promise() performs I/O and so isn't referentially transparent. It shouldn't be used in the function you passed to withLatestFrom(). Yet what you've done feels OK.

   The rules of FRP exist to prevent bugs, so let's see how you can implement this within the rules. What's the correct way to initiate I/O in this situation? Let's switch to Sodium—which is clearer about such rules—to look at this question.

   Say you already have an I/O action defined for fetching a map tile in the same style you used in the dictionary lookup example from the beginning of this chapter. Its type would be

```
Stream<Image> fetchTile(Stream<TileID> tileID)
```

which is represented as Java/Sodium lambda in this way:

```
Lambda1<Stream<TileID>,Stream<Image>> fetchTile
```

For simplicity, we'll pretend that errors can't happen.

   Given an I/O action lambda, you can write a general promisize() function to convert an I/O action into something that produces promises. We'll give the code for promisize() shortly. promisize() lets you write a Java/Sodium version of the map application in this way:

```
Stream<Set<TileID>> sTilesNeeded = Operational.value(scrollOrigin).map(
    ... );
CellLoop<Map<TileID, Promise<Image>> tilePromises;
tilePromises.loop(sTilesNeeded.snapshot(tilePromises, (needed, prs) -> {
    ...
    for (TileID tileID : needed) {
        ...
        if (!found) {
            Promise<Image> img = promisize(fetchTile, tileID);
            ...
        }
    }
    ...
})).hold(new HashMap<TileID, Promise<Image>()));
```

CONVERTING A CONSTANT TO A STREAM

How do you write `promisize()`? `fetchTile` wants a `Stream<TileID>`, but all you have is a `TileID`. How do you construct this required stream? How can a constant initiate an I/O operation?

In this code, you're constructing FRP logic in a lambda you've passed to `snapshot`. You know that this code runs in response to a stream event. To get the stream that `fetchTile` requires as input, you could use the same stream that was passed to `snapshot` because you can deduce that it fired in the same transaction in which you want the I/O to be initiated.

`sTilesNeeded` is the stream in question, but you only want to initiate I/O once for each tile. The stream to initiate the I/O could be constructed like this:

```
Stream<TileID> sInitiateIO = sTilesNeeded.once().map(tn -> tileID);
```

Then you'd pass `sInitiateIO` explicitly as a new third argument to `promisize()`, which would work fine:

```
tilePromises.loop(sTilesNeeded.snapshot(tilePromises, (needed, prs) -> {
    ...
    for (TileID tileID : needed) {
        ...
        if (!found) {
            Stream<TileID> sInitiateIO = sTilesNeeded.once()
                                                .map(tn -> tileID);
            Promise<Image> img = promisize(fetchTile, tileID, sInitiateIO);
            ...
        }
    }
    ...
}).hold(new HashMap<TileID, Promise<Image>>()));
```

THE SPARK IDIOM

But there's a more convenient way. It's possible to convert a constant a of type `A` into a `Stream<A>` using the following idiom:

```
Operational.value(new Cell<A>(a))
```

Recall that the stream returned by `Operational.value()` always fires once with the current value of the cell you gave it. If you hand it a constant cell, it will fire once with any value you want. Effectively, you're creating a stream event out of thin air. We refer to this as a *spark*.

This *spark* idiom gives you a more convenient way of initiating the I/O. Because you're processing a `snapshot`, you know an event must exist. You've inferred the existence of an event, and, on the strength of that, you reconstruct it (without its payload, which you can't infer).

We're getting into the deep semantics of FRP, but the questions aren't that difficult. Recall that with the introduction of `switch` and `sample`, we had to revise the rules of what was permitted in functions passed to FRP primitives (see section 7.3.3). We said this:

- Functions passed to FRP primitives that work with events (`Stream.map`, `snapshot`, `filter`, `merge`, and `Stream.accum`) may use code that's connected to a transactional context. This includes `sample` and construction of FRP logic using `hold` and other primitives. Note that `sample` isn't allowed in primitives that return cells, like `lift` and `Cell.map`.

The reasoning is the same for `Operational.value()` because it's also connected to a transactional context. Within the context of FRP primitives that work with events, you can infer the existence of a stream event. That implied event is the reason that within such a context, `sample` is semantically equivalent to `snapshot`. Now we're saying it's legitimate to reconstruct that event (without its payload) in a new stream, and that's what the spark idiom does. The code for `promisize()` is given in the next listing.

> **Listing 11.9   Using a promise to represent the output of an I/O action**

```
<A,B> Promise<B> promisize(Lambda1<Stream<A>, Stream<B>> action,
                           A a) {
    Stream<A> sSpark = Operational.value(new Cell<A>(a));
    return new Promise<>(action.apply(sSpark));
}
```

11.3   *Distributed processing*

FRP can be useful for implementing distributed systems. But FRP is basic infrastructure and doesn't provide a turnkey solution by itself. Distributed systems are a complex topic, and we'll only sketch out a few basic ideas here.

We've shown you a way of modeling I/O in FRP. This can be useful in distributed systems. For instance, it would work well if you wanted to model some sort of a remote procedure call (RPC). But distributed systems don't always work this way. We need to take a step back.

11.3.1   *Sacrificing consistency*

Distributed systems are subject to Eric Brewer's *CAP theorem*. The initials pertain to three desired properties of a system:

- *Consistency*—A read anywhere in the system sees the results of all previously completed writes.
- *Availability*—Reads and writes always succeed.
- *Partition tolerance*—The system operates in spite of communication problems between nodes.

The theorem essentially says that during a network partition, a distributed system must choose either *consistency* or *availability*. Partitions are a fact of distributed systems and can't be avoided. *Availability* is usually—but not always—the more important of these two goals. Therefore, to achieve availability, distributed systems must sacrifice consistency.

11.3.2 A stream that goes over a network connection

FRP gives you a strong consistency guarantee by default. It's easy to take a stream of some serializable value, pass the values over a network connection, and have them appear as a stream on a remote node. But FRP transactions and the consistency they provide can only work locally. There's no way to make any guarantees about the arrival times of messages or even whether the messages will arrive at all. Many issues will arise, and they're the same as the ones you'd get in an actor-based distributed system.

You must use logic to deal with these issues, and FRP is ideal for this sort of complex logic. We think FRP would make a great basis for distributed systems, and we'd like to see FRP-based distributed frameworks.

But don't expect a magic-bullet solution that gives FRP-like consistency across a distributed system. The CAP theorem tells us this is impossible.

11.4 Unit testing

The real world throws quality requirements at you. Unit testing can be a powerful way to ensure that you meet them. FRP has some interesting properties with regard to unit testing.

11.4.1 Unit testing FRP code

Let's say you want to unit test the `Keypad` class from chapter 4. The external interface looks like this:

```
public class Keypad {
    public final Cell<Integer> value;
    public final Stream<Unit> sBeep;
    public Keypad(Stream<Key> sKeypad, Stream<Unit> sClear) {
    }
}
```

FRP doesn't allow any implicit state to exist, so all code is automatically testable. Here's what a test case for this code might look like:

```
StreamSink<Key> sKeypad = new StreamSink<>();
StreamSink<Unit> sClear = new StreamSink<>();
Keypad keypad = new Keypad(sKeypad, sClear);
sKeypad.send(Key.ONE);
sKeypad.send(Key.SEVEN);
assertEquals(17, keypad.value.sample());
```

Testing the value of a cell is simple with `sample()`. But to check that stream events such as beeps occurred, we recommend using `hold()` or `accum()` to stuff the stream event into a cell. Or you can attach a listener using `listen()`. Here's one way:

```
{
    Cell<Optional<Unit>> beeped = keypad.sBeep.map(u -> Optional.of(u))
                                       .hold(Optional<Unit>());
```

```
        sKeypad.send(Key.ONE);
        assertEquals(Optional.of(Unit.UNIT), beeped.sample());
    }
    {

        Cell<Optional<Unit>> beeped = keypad.sBeep.map(u -> Optional.of(u))
                                         .hold(Optional<Unit>());
        sKeypad.send(Key.SEVEN);
        assertEquals(Optional.of(Unit.UNIT), beeped.sample());
    }
```

A helper method would shorten this code.

11.4.2 *We don't recommend test-driven development (TDD)*

There are two ways to apply unit testing in your project. The first way is to write your code and then selectively write tests where you think there is benefit in doing so.

The second way is *test-driven development (TDD)*, which is a radically different way of writing code. In TDD, you add to your code one feature at a time. For each feature, you follow a three-step process:

- *Red*—Write a test to test whether the feature works. Because the code hasn't been written yet, the test will fail, so the test harness will show red.
- *Green*—Write the minimum code required to make the test pass. The test harness will show green.
- *Refactor*—Tidy up the code, and factor out any repeated code. Refactoring is safe because the existing tests will make breakage almost impossible.

You can take TDD even further with *pair programming*. Two programmers share a single computer. One writes the tests, and the other writes the code. An *evil coder* does only the minimum coding to make the test pass, so the tester is forced to write tests for every aspect of the code.

We can see the point of all this, but we generally don't recommend TDD for FRP. We give our reasons next.

11.4.3 *FRP is type-driven development*

With FRP code in a statically typed language, you get a lot of checking for free. Several major classes of bugs are automatically eliminated.

The benefits of static typing are greater in FRP than you get with normal or imperative code. You may have noticed that in this book we talk a lot about the data types we're using. FRP—and functional programming in general—can be said to be *type-driven development*. In FRP, the data types constrain the problem and prevent you from making mistakes in a way similar to the way tests do in TDD, but with less effort.

To some extent, TDD exists to compensate for the lack of checking that's inherent in imperative programming. In dynamically typed languages there is even less checking, so TDD becomes even more important.

11.4.4 *FRP code is safe to refactor*

A major purpose of TDD is to lock down the code so it can be refactored safely. This advantage doesn't apply to FRP in a statically typed language because it's already safe to refactor. We'll go into this in more depth in chapter 13.

11.4.5 *FRP code is inherently testable*

An advantage of TDD is that it makes your code testable. Because a given piece of code has to interface both to the rest of the program and to the tests, it pushes you into a desirably modular, loosely coupled style that's flexible and easy to refactor. FRP forces you to write your code loosely coupled anyway, so TDD doesn't add much.

11.4.6 *Testing your logic*

As we've argued, FRP gives you most of the advantages of TDD automatically. If you use TDD to write FRP code, you'll be duplicating a lot of work that FRP gives you for free. We think this isn't productive in the common case, but if your project has a high assurance requirement, then TDD may be justified.

But there's one advantage of TDD that FRP doesn't give you: FRP doesn't protect you from mistakes in your logic. We generally recommend that you write your FRP code, and write tests either beforehand or afterward that test to be sure the logic is correct.

11.5 *Summary*

- In FRP, you can model an I/O action as a function from `Stream<A>` to `Stream<B>`.
- We've given an implementation of promises based on FRP.
- If you want to associate state with the execution of I/O, it can be useful to use `switch` and model the I/O result as a promise.
- It's good to write unit tests to verify the correctness of your logic, but we don't generally recommend test-driven development for FRP.

Helpers and patterns

This chapter covers

- Removing duplicate values
- Pausing a game
- Junction or client registry
- Writable remote values
- Persistence
- Unique ID generation
- An FRP-based GUI system

The highly abstracted nature of FRP means solutions can be very general. This opens us up to uncharted oceans of new ways of dealing with programming problems. We (the authors) have only just gotten our feet wet, compared with what the community will discover in time.

This chapter covers some solutions we've found to common problems. Some of these examples are complex and will take some unraveling. They're best treated as reference material for how to solve specific problems, or tests to see how good you are at FRP comprehension. But we hope this chapter will give you a glimpse of what sorts of things are possible.

12.1 Calming: removing duplicate values

We'll start with a simple one. Sometimes we have a situation where there are unnecessary updates and this adversely affects performance. For example, a particular operation may double the amount of processing, and it may be structured so that this happens several times. The good news is that these cases are generally easy to reason about, but the bad news is that things can get inefficient. We discussed some of these implications in section 7.6. A common way to deal with this is to "calm" a stream or cell by removing values that are repeats of the previous value.

We've said that `Operational.updates()` should be used for operational situations where the steps in cells aren't exposed. The cell variant of `calm` complies: it uses `Operational.updates()` but doesn't expose any of this to the caller. As long as you respect this principle consistently, `calm` has performance implications only, but no semantic ones.

Why not calm cells automatically?

We've been asked why we don't just make all cells automatically calmed in Sodium. There are two reasons.

First, we can't assume that a concept of equality exists for all values. A cell can legitimately contain a function, for example, and there's no general way to test equality for functions.

Second, auto-calming would require doing equality tests for each update. For some data types, such as large key/value `Maps`, this would be prohibitively expensive in terms of CPU time.

Listing 12.1 gives the code for stream and cell variants of `calm()`. This example illustrates some things we've touched on before. First, we've talked about `sampleLazy()` and `holdLazy()`. These are variants of `sample()` and `hold()` that work correctly with `CellLoops`. In any generalized code, this is important. Plain `sample()` will throw an exception if it's used before `CellLoop.loop()` is called, because the actual value doesn't exist yet. `sampleLazy()` gives a representation of the value as it will be after `loop()` is called later. This is a sort of promise.

Second, until now, when you've implemented any sort of state accumulator, you've used a `hold-snapshot`. Sodium provides a helper method, `collect()`, to make this more concise, letting you write a state accumulator based on an update lambda. This is a basic state machine or *Mealy machine*. It takes the new input value and the current state value, and it outputs a tuple of (output value, new state). Sodium provides a tuple type `Tuple2` that's used for this. `collectLazy()` is a variant of `collect()` that accepts a lazy initial value.

Listing 12.1 Removing duplicate values: stream and cell variants of `calm`

```
import nz.sodium.*;
import java.util.Optional;

public class calm {
    public static <A> Stream<A> calm(Stream<A> sA,
                                     Lazy<Optional<A>> oInit) {
        return Stream.filterOptional(
            sA.<Optional<A>,Optional<A>>collectLazy(
                oInit,
                (A a, Optional<A> oLastA) -> {
                    Optional<A> oa = Optional.of(a);
                    return oa.equals(oLastA)
                        ? new Tuple2<Optional<A>,Optional<A>>(
                            Optional.empty(), oLastA)
                        : new Tuple2<Optional<A>,Optional<A>>(oa, oa);
                }
            ));
    }

    public static <A> Stream<A> calm(Stream<A> sA) {
        return calm(sA, new Lazy<Optional<A>>(Optional.empty()));
    }

    public static <A> Cell<A> calm(Cell<A> a) {
        Lazy<A> initA = a.sampleLazy();
        Lazy<Optional<A>> oInitA = initA.map(a_ -> Optional.of(a_));
        return calm(Operational.updates(a), oInitA).holdLazy(initA);
    }

    public static void main(String[] args) {
        CellSink<Integer> sa = new CellSink<>(1);
        Listener l = calm(sa).listen(i -> System.out.println(i));
        sa.send(1);
        sa.send(2);
        sa.send(2);
        sa.send(4);
        sa.send(4);
        sa.send(1);
        l.unlisten();
    }
}

ant calm
calm:
     [java] 1
     [java] 2
     [java] 4
     [java] 1
```

Annotations:
- Filters out duplicates → `return Stream.filterOptional(`
- Initial state → `oInit,`
- Determines what's a duplicate → `sA.<Optional<A>,Optional<A>>collectLazy(`
- Is the new value the same as the last? → `return oa.equals(oLastA)`
- Yes: output nothing, and don't change the state. → `? new Tuple2<Optional<A>,Optional<A>>( Optional.empty(), oLastA)`
- No: output the new value and set the state to it. → `: new Tuple2<Optional<A>,Optional<A>>(oa, oa);`
- Common stream case where there's no initial value → `public static <A> Stream<A> calm(Stream<A> sA) {`
- Cell case: deal with the initial value. → `public static <A> Cell<A> calm(Cell<A> a) {`

To run this, check it out if you haven't done so already, and then run it like this:

```
git clone https://github.com/SodiumFRP/sodium
cd sodium/book/patterns/java
mvn test -Pcalm    or    ant calm
```

12.2 Pausing a game

A game often has a clock of this type:

```
Cell<Double> time
```

When you pause the game, it can be useful to stop the game clock. Listing 12.2 gives a little code fragment that does this.

You might want animation in your user interface that still works when the game is paused. How do you achieve that? Simple! Use `mainClock` for the user interface and `gameClock` for the game itself. You can't accidentally use the wrong clock in your game logic because you don't pass `mainClock` to it, so it can't be in scope.

We think this is elegant. It illustrates the power you have in FRP to give a strong isolation guarantee by limiting scope. This isn't exclusive to FRP, but it's natural to the functional programming concepts that underlie FRP.

Listing 12.2 Pausing a game clock

```java
import nz.sodium.*;
import java.util.Optional;

public class pause {
    public static Cell<Double> pausableClock(Stream<Unit> sPause,
            Stream<Unit> sResume, Cell<Double> clock) {
        Cell<Optional<Double>> pauseTime =
            sPause.snapshot(clock, (u, t) -> Optional.<Double>of(t))
                .orElse(sResume.map(u -> Optional.<Double>empty()))
                .hold(Optional.<Double>empty());
        Cell<Double> lostTime = sResume.<Double>accum(
            0.0,
            (u, total) -> {
                double tPause = pauseTime.sample().get();
                double now    = clock.sample();
                return total + (now - tPause);
            });
        return pauseTime.lift(clock, lostTime,
            (otPause, tClk, tLost) ->
                (otPause.isPresent() ? otPause.get()
                                     : tClk)
                - tLost);
    }

    public static void main(String[] args) {
        CellSink<Double> mainClock = new CellSink<>(0.0);
        StreamSink<Unit> sPause = new StreamSink<>();
        StreamSink<Unit> sResume = new StreamSink<>();
        Cell<Double> gameClock = pausableClock(sPause, sResume, mainClock);
        Listener l = mainClock.lift(gameClock,
                            (m, g) -> "main="+m+" game="+g)
                        .listen(txt -> System.out.println(txt));
        mainClock.send(1.0);
        mainClock.send(2.0);
        mainClock.send(3.0);
```

Annotations:
- On pause start, captures the clock time
- On unpause, accumulates the total lost time
- When paused, takes the pause time
- When not paused, takes the clock
- Subtracts the total lost time

```
        sPause.send(Unit.UNIT);
        mainClock.send(4.0);
        mainClock.send(5.0);
        mainClock.send(6.0);
        sResume.send(Unit.UNIT);
        mainClock.send(7.0);
        l.unlisten();
    }
}
```

```
ant pause
pause:
     [java] main=0.0 game=0.0
     [java] main=1.0 game=1.0
     [java] main=2.0 game=2.0
     [java] main=3.0 game=3.0
     [java] main=3.0 game=3.0
     [java] main=4.0 game=3.0
     [java] main=5.0 game=3.0
     [java] main=6.0 game=3.0
     [java] main=6.0 game=3.0
     [java] main=7.0 game=4.0
```

To run this, check it out if you haven't done so already, and then run it like this:

```
git clone https://github.com/SodiumFRP/sodium
cd sodium/book/patterns/java
mvn test -Ppause     or     ant pause
```

12.3   *Junction or client registry*

Mobile phones have a notification area with notifications from different places. Mine says

- 1 update available
- Playing: One Day You Will Cry
- Message received: Raining! Bring in the washing.

I know that phones aren't normally designed as a single program. But if you imagine that you were designing the entire phone as a single FRP application, you'd have to say this:

```
UpdateManager umgr = new UpdateManager(...);
MediaPlayer mediaPlyr = new MediaPlayer(...);
Messenger messenger = new Messenger(...);
Cell<List<Message>> notifications = umgr.notifications.lift(
    mediaPlyr.notifications, messenger.notifications,
    (ms1, ms2, ms2) -> appendList(ms1, appendList(ms2, ms3))
);
NotificationArea notArea = new NotificationArea(notifications);
```

You have to decide what applications you want notifications for during initialization. This is a typically functional way to do things, and it's not extensible because you can't come along later and start an arbitrary new module/application that then registers itself with notArea.

In this design, you want more freedom to add and remove applications, and this may happen at different times as the program runs. You need an extensible way for an application to register itself as a new client of the notifications list, allowing it to push its own notifications.

What you'd like to do is this:

```
CellJunction<List<Message>> notifications = new CellJunction<>(
    new List<Message>(), appendList);
NotificationArea notArea = new NotificationArea(notifications.out);
UpdateManager umgr = new UpdateManager(notifications, ...);
MediaPlayer mediaPlyr = new MediaPlayer(notifications, ...);
Messenger messenger = new Messenger(notifications, ...);
```

⟵ **appendList: tells the CellJunction how to combine message list**

The construction of each application may not happen during initialization of the program, as you see here.

Note that this approach is imperative, not functional, because the process of registering a client causes a state change. You're exchanging the semantic tidiness of functional programming for extensibility. It's affected by the sequence in which registrations happen, and so on. This isn't a bad thing in itself; it's just that it's important to make that distinction in your mind.

We'll give the code for `CellJunction` and `StreamJunction` here, and the next section uses a junction in a concrete example. First you define `Junction`, which is a superclass for both stream and cell variants, as shown in the following listing.

Listing 12.3 Superclass for `CellJunction` and `StreamJunction`

```
import nz.sodium.*;
import java.util.Collection;
import java.util.HashMap;
import java.util.Map;

public abstract class Junction<ContainerA, A> {
    private int nextID;
    private StreamSink<Lambda1<Map<Integer, ContainerA>,
                                Map<Integer, ContainerA>> sUpdate
        = new StreamSink<>((f1, f2) -> a -> f1.apply(f2.apply(a)));
    protected Cell<Collection<ContainerA>> clients;
    public Junction() {
        clients = sUpdate
            .<Map<Integer, ContainerA>>accum(
                new HashMap<Integer, ContainerA>(),
                (f, m) -> f.apply(m))
            .map(m -> m.values());
    }
    public Listener add(ContainerA c) {
        int id;
        synchronized (this) {
            id = nextID++;
        }
```

Coalesces update functions into one if there's more than one in a transaction ⟶

Starts with a stream of change functions ⟵

Applies the update function ⟶

Accumulates updates to the client registry ⟵

Turns it into a list ⟵

Method to add a new client. ContainerA could be a stream or cell. ⟵

Allocates each client a unique ID ⟶

Fires an "add to registry" event

```
sUpade.send(m0 -> {
    java.util.HashMap<Integer, ContainerA> m = new HashMap(m0);
    m.put(id, c);
    return m;
});
return new Listener() {
    public void unlisten() {
        sUpade.send(m0 -> {
            java.util.HashMap<Integer, ContainerA> m
                                              = new HashMap(m0);
            m.remove(id);
            return m;
        });
    }
};
}
}
```

Returns a Listener, allowing the caller to deregister

Fires a "delete from registry" event

Copies the map so you're referentially transparent

This code uses an FRP idiom you encountered in the Zombicus game in chapter 7. You have a stream of state transformations represented as `Lambda1<X,X>`, and you accumulate that into a current state of the client registry.

You're using the variant of `StreamSink`'s constructor where you pass it a function to combine values if more than one is sent in a single transaction. This happens often in practice. This combining function combines two lambdas into a single lambda that applies the two of them in sequence.

The next listing gives the stream variant. The current list of clients is merged together to give an output stream.

Listing 12.4   `StreamJunction`

```
import nz.sodium.*;
import java.util.Collection;

public class StreamJunction<A> extends Junction<Stream<A>, A> {
    public StreamJunction(Lambda2<A,A,A> combine) {
        this.out = Cell.switchS(clients.map(cls ->
            Stream.merge(cls, combine)));
    }
    public Stream<A> out;
}
```

Function to combine in case of simultaneous events

Merges all events coming from currently registered/added clients

Listing 12.5 gives the cell variant. In the stream variant, the combining operation is `merge`. For cells, it's `lift`, but the caller needs to supply a `null` value to use in the case where no clients have registered yet.

In the notification area example, each module registers itself as a source of notification messages this way:

```
MediaPlayer(CellJunction<List<Message>> notifications, ...) {
    Cell<List<Message>> playingMsgs = ...;
```

```
            this.l = notifications.add(playingMsgs);
    }
    Listener l;
```
To be cleaned up when MediaPlayer ⊣ closes/wants to stop notifying

Listing 12.5 `CellJunction`

```
import nz.sodium.*;
import java.util.Collection;

public class CellJunction<A> extends Junction<Cell<A>, A> {
    static <A> Cell<A> combines(Collection<Cell<A>> in,
                                A nullValue, Lambda2<A,A,A> combine) {
        Cell<A> cOut = new Cell<>(nullValue);
        for (Cell<A> c : in)
            cOut = cOut.lift(c, combine);
        return cOut;
    }
    public CellJunction(A nullValue, Lambda2<A,A,A> combine) {
        this.out = Cell.switchC(
            clients.map(cls -> combines(cls, nullValue, combine)));
    }
    public Cell<A> out;
}
```

Initial/default value of the output. Function to combine values coming from registered/added clients.

Combination of the values from all registered/ added clients

To look at the source code, check it out if you haven't done so already:

```
git clone https://github.com/SodiumFRP/sodium
```

You'll find the files in sodium/book/writable-remote/java/.

12.4 *Writable remote values*

We'll reiterate one of the selling points of FRP: you can manipulate event-handling logic using code written in a functional style. This isn't possible with the observer pattern or with actors.

Here's why you can do this: the stream and cell values in FRP are immutable values with compositional properties. Because they're so well behaved, you can use functional programming techniques on them. This gives you a lot of power.

Here's a concrete example, based on the real five-year commercial project that ended up selling one of the authors on FRP. Let's say you have a remote data store, and you want to view and modify fields in it through a GUI form. It could be a server, a database, or perhaps a piece of networking equipment. You also have these requirements:

- You want to support multiple clients that are always kept up to date.
- You want the screen representation to be driven by the needs of the user, not the structure of the database, so you want to apply transformations to the database representation to make it suitable for the user.

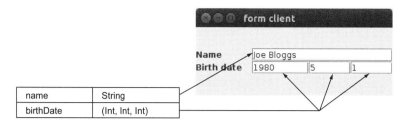

Figure 12.1   Transformation between database and user view: Split `birthDate` into three fields.

Figure 12.1 shows the example. You'll transform `birthDate` from a single field in the database into three fields for the user to edit.

Listing 12.6 shows the `Value` data type used to represents a writable value on the remote server. A `Value` can be instantiated by passing a stream to its `construct()` method. Events on that stream originate locally and are sent as updates to the remote database. `construct()` returns a pair of values in a `ValueOutput` structure:

- A `Cell<Optional<A>>` representing the current value of the `Value` in the remote store
- A `Listener` representing the cleanup that must be performed by the caller when it's finished with the value

Listing 12.6   Writable remote `Value` data type

```
import nz.sodium.*;
import java.util.Optional;

public abstract class Value<A> {
    public abstract ValueOutput<A> construct(Stream<A> sWrite);
}


import nz.sodium.*;
import java.util.Optional;

public class ValueOutput<A> {
    public ValueOutput(Cell<Optional<A>> value, Listener cleanup) {
        this.value = value;
        this.cleanup = cleanup;
    }
    public final Cell<Optional<A>> value;
    public final Listener cleanup;
}
```

Cleanup to be performed by the caller when finished ⟶

No value if you're waiting for it to be fetched

Listing 12.7 gives a simple test case showing how you can instantiate and use `Value`s. You're using delays here because `BackEnd` simulates some network delays. First you construct a value and start listening to it. You wait for it to give its value, and then you set it to 5 and wait some more so you can see it echoing that update back to you. `Back-End` outputs some diagnostic lines, too, starting with "`BackEnd:`".

Listing 12.7   Simple example of using a `Value`

```
import nz.sodium.*;
import java.util.Optional;

public class simple {
    public static void main(String[] args) {
        BackEnd be = new BackEnd();
        Value<Integer> vAge = be.allocate("age", 0);
        StreamSink<Integer> sAge = new StreamSink<>();
        ValueOutput<Integer> out = vAge.construct(sAge);
        Cell<Optional<Integer>> age = out.value;
        Listener l = age.listen(oa -> {
            System.out.println("age = "+(
                oa.isPresent() ? Integer.toString(oa.get())
                               : "<empty>"));
        });
        try { Thread.sleep(1000); } catch (InterruptedException e) {}
        System.out.println("SEND 5");
        sAge.send(5);
        try { Thread.sleep(1000); } catch (InterruptedException e) {}
        l.unlisten();
    }
}
```

See the next listing. → *(BackEnd be = new BackEnd();)*

Creates a new Value in the back end with the default value → *(Value<Integer> vAge = be.allocate("age", 0);)*

For sending updates to the database → *(StreamSink<Integer> sAge = new StreamSink<>();)*

Constructs it ← *(ValueOutput<Integer> out = vAge.construct(sAge);)*

Shows the current value on the console → *(Listener l = age.listen...)*

Waits for the initial value to be retrieved → *(try { Thread.sleep(1000); ...)*

Sends an update to the server → *(sAge.send(5);)*

Waits for the update to be echoed back → *(try { Thread.sleep(1000); ...)*

```
ant simple
simple:
     [java] age = <empty>
     [java] BackEnd: age -> 0
     [java] age = 0
     [java] SEND 5
     [java] BackEnd: age <- 5
     [java] BackEnd: age -> 5
     [java] age = 5
```

As usual, check it out if you haven't done so already:

```
git clone https://github.com/SodiumFRP/sodium
```

Note that an extra step is required to run the projects in this directory if you're using Maven. One of the examples depends on the SWidgets library, so you need to install it into your local Maven repository:

```
cd sodium/book/swidgets/java/swidgets
mvn install
cd ../../../../..
```

Then do this to run it:

```
cd sodium/book/writeable-remote/java
mvn test -Psimple     or     ant simple
```

The following listing gives the implementation of the simulated remote database back end. You use `StreamJunction` from the previous section to do a lot of the work. Look back a few pages for this code.

Listing 12.8   Simulated database back end

```
import nz.sodium.*;
import java.util.Optional;

public class BackEnd {
    public BackEnd() {}
    public final <A> Value<A> allocate(String name, A initA) {
        StreamJunction<A> j = new StreamJunction<>((l, r) -> l);
        StreamSink<A> s0 = new StreamSink<>();
        Listener l = j.out.listenWeak(a -> {
            new Thread(() -> {
                try { Thread.sleep(50); }
                    catch (InterruptedException e) {}
                System.out.println("BackEnd: "+name+" <- " +a);
                s0.send(a);
            }).start();
        });
        Cell<A> c = s0.addCleanup(l).hold(initA);
        return new Value<A>() {
            public ValueOutput<A> construct(Stream<A> sWrite) {
                CellSink<Optional<A>> recvd =
                            new CellSink<>(Optional.empty());
                Listener l =
                    j.add(sWrite)
                    .append(
                        c.listen(a -> {
                            new Thread(() -> {
                                try { Thread.sleep(50); }
                                    catch (InterruptedException e) {}
                                System.out.println("BackEnd: "
                                                +name+" -> " +a);
                                recvd.send(Optional.of(a));
                            }).start();
                        })
                    );
                return new ValueOutput<A>(recvd, l);
            }
        };
    }
}
```

Merges all clients's Writes → (points to `StreamJunction<A> j = ...`)

When a client writes to the value, simulates a network transfer … → (points to `Listener l = j.out.listenWeak(a -> {`)

… and then updates the state → (points to `s0.send(a);`)

Value's state on the "server" → (points to `Cell<A> c = s0.addCleanup(l).hold(initA);`)

Constructs a new client for this Value → (points to `public ValueOutput<A> construct(Stream<A> sWrite) {`)

Merges this client's sWrite → (points to `j.add(sWrite)`)

Combine two Listeners together → (points to `.append(`)

When the server state is updated, simulates a network transfer… → (points to `c.listen(a -> {`)

…and then feeds to the client → (points to `recvd.send(Optional.of(a));`)

Figure 12.2 shows the GUI example client again.

Listing 12.9 gives the important code snippets for implementing the client shown in figure 12.2. If you want to see the entire program, download and look at   sodium/book/writeable-remote/java/form.java and the related files in the same directory.

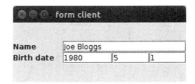

Figure 12.2   The GUI client example

This code uses three components, which we'll introduce next:

- A lens() method on Value that lets you split the date into fields using a getter and a setter function for each field.
- A map() method on Value that lets you transform a value, in this case converting Integer to String. Because you need to convert in both directions (client to server, server to client), the function you pass must be reversible. Bijection is a simple container class to represent a pair of a function and its inverse.
- A VTextField for each field. It handles the GUI side of things for you.

We're only demonstrating a couple of transformations of Values here. You can use your imagination to see what else could be done. We've also left out a lot of detail. For example, we aren't even attempting to get any consistency.

But we hope you can see that you're manipulating Values in a clean, high-level way. This approach utterly transformed the real project this example was based on: Maintainability was improved by an order of magnitude.

Listing 12.9 GUI client for remote server values

```
class Date {
    public Date(int year, int month, int day) {
        this.year = year; this.month = month; this.day = day; }
    public final int year, month, day;
    public final Date setYear(int year_) {
                           return new Date(year_, month,  day); }
    public final Date setMonth(int month_) {
                           return new Date(year,  month_, day); }
    public final Date setDay(int day_) {
                           return new Date(year,  month,  day_); }
    public String toString() { return year+"."+month+"."+day; }
}
...
                BackEnd be = new BackEnd();
                Value<String> vName     = be.allocate("name", "Joe Bloggs");
                Value<Date> vBirthDate = be.allocate("birthDate",
                    new Date(1980, 5, 1));

                Value<Integer> vYear = vBirthDate.lens(
                    d -> d.year,
                    (dt, y) -> dt.setYear(y)
                );
                Value<Integer> vMonth = vBirthDate.lens(
                    d -> d.month,
                    (dt, y) -> dt.setMonth(y)
                );
                Value<Integer> vDay = vBirthDate.lens(
                    d -> d.day,
                    (dt, y) -> dt.setDay(y)
                );
                Bijection<Integer,String> toString = new Bijection<>(
                        i -> Integer.toString(i),
```

Constructs the database fields

Uses lenses to split birthDate into year, month, and day

Forward function: formats the integer as a string

**Reverse function: parses
the string to an integer**

```
s -> {
    try { return Integer.parseInt(s); }
    catch (NumberFormatException e) {
        return 0;
    }
});
Value<String> vYearStr = vYear.map(toString);
Value<String> vMonthStr = vMonth.map(toString);
Value<String> vDayStr = vDay.map(toString);
```

**Converts to string
values for VtextField**

. . .

**Plunks them
on the screen**

```
client.add(new JLabel("Name"), c);
client.add(new VTextField(vName, 15), c);
client.add(new JLabel("Birth date"), c);
client.add(new VTextField(vYearStr, 4), c);
client.add(new VTextField(vMonthStr, 2), c);
client.add(new VTextField(vDayStr, 2), c);

client.setSize(300,100);
client.setVisible(true);
```

Now let's look at each of the components we used to construct the client. First, listing 12.10 gives VTextField. You have three constructors because this is a Java idiom for constructing things to pass to the superclass in such a way that you can reference them afterward.

This is just a thin wrapper around STextField, the FRP-enhanced widget you've been using throughout the book. Essentially, all you're doing is constructing the value and then connecting it to the STextField. You also take the cleanup returned from constructing the Value and execute it in the Java-specific removeNotify() method so everything is nicely cleaned up when the Java GUI element is disposed.

Note that sUserChanges is something exported by STextField that you haven't seen before. It gives you the changes instigated by the user, ignoring changes made to the widget externally. If you took all changes, then a change would loop around between the server and the widget forever.

Listing 12.10 VTextField: a widget that edits Values

```
class VTextField extends STextField {
    public VTextField(Value<String> v, int width) {
        this(new StreamLoop<String>(), v, width);
    }
    private VTextField(StreamLoop<String> sRemoteWrite, Value<String> v,
                                                            int width) {
        this(sRemoteWrite, v.construct(sRemoteWrite), width);
    }
    private VTextField(StreamLoop<String> sRemoteWrite,
                    ValueOutput<String> outRemote, int width) {
        super(
            Stream.filterOptional(outRemote.value.value()),
            "",
            width,
```

**Widget text
modified by the
Value output**

**Widget starts with
an empty string**

`width,`   ◁—— **Size of the widget on screen**

Feeds user edits to the remote value →

```
                outRemote.value.map(oV -> oV.isPresent())
        );
        sRemoteWrite.loop(sUserChanges);
        this.cleanup = outRemote.cleanup;
    }
    public void removeNotify() {
        cleanup.unlisten();
        super.removeNotify();
    }
    private Listener cleanup;
}
```

Makes the widget editable only when the remote Value is present (points to `outRemote.value.map(oV -> oV.isPresent())`)

Releases Value resources on widget dispose (points to `removeNotify()`)

The next listing shows the `Value.map()` method and also `Bijection`, which is a simple container for two functions (a function and its inverse).

Listing 12.11 Mapping a `Value` with a reversible function

```
public abstract class Value<A> {
    ...
    public final <B> Value<B> map(Bijection<A,B> bij) {
        Value<A> va = this;
        return new Value<B>() {
            public ValueOutput<B> construct(Stream<B> sWriteB) {
                ValueOutput<A> out = va.construct(sWriteB.map(bij.fInv));
                return new ValueOutput<B>(
                    out.value.map(oa ->
                        oa.isPresent() ? Optional.of(bij.f.apply(oa.get()))
                                       : Optional.empty()),
                    out.cleanup);
            }
        };
    }
}
...
import nz.sodium.Lambda1;

public class Bijection<A,B> {
    public Bijection(Lambda1<A,B> f, Lambda1<B,A> fInv) {
        this.f = f;
        this.fInv = fInv;
    }
    public final Lambda1<A,B> f;
    public final Lambda1<B,A> fInv;
}
```

Applies the reverse function on the client to server updates → (points to `ValueOutput<A> out = va.construct(sWriteB.map(bij.fInv));`)

Applies the forward function on the server to client notifications → (points to `out.value.map(oa ->`)

Passes the same cleanup through (points to `out.cleanup`)

Represents a reversible function (points to `public class Bijection<A,B> {`)

Forward function (points to `public final Lambda1<A,B> f;`)

Reverse function → (points to `public final Lambda1<B,A> fInv;`)

Listing 12.12 gives `Value.lens()`, which follows the same idea as `Value.map()` but is slightly more complicated. `lens()` allows you to take a date and zoom in on the year, for example. The `getter` extracts the year, and the `setter` changes it to a new value, leaving the rest of the date unchanged. Recall that this is how you used it:

```
Value<Integer> vYear = vBirthDate.lens(
        d -> d.year,
        (dt, y) -> dt.setYear(y)
    );
```

Getter function (points to `d -> d.year,`)

Setter function (points to `(dt, y) -> dt.setYear(y)`)

Listing 12.12 Lens: a Value to represent a field of another Value

```
public abstract class Value<A> {
    ...
    public final <B> Value<B> lens(
        Lambda1<A, B> getter,
        Lambda2<A, B, A> setter)
    {
        Value<A> va = this;
        return new Value<B>() {
            public ValueOutput<B> construct(Stream<B> sWriteB) {
                return Transaction.run(() -> {
                    StreamLoop<A> sWriteA = new StreamLoop<>();
                    ValueOutput<A> out = va.construct(sWriteA);
                    Cell<Optional<A>> oa = out.value;
                    sWriteA.loop(Stream.filterOptional(
                        sWriteB.snapshot(oa, (wb, oa_) ->
                            oa_.isPresent()
                                ? Optional.of(setter.apply(oa_.get(), wb))
                                : Optional.empty()
                        )
                    ));
                    return new ValueOutput<B>(
                        oa.map(oa_ ->
                            oa_.isPresent()
                                ? Optional.of(getter.apply(oa_.get()))
                                : Optional.empty()),
                        out.cleanup
                    );
                });
            }
        };
    }
}
```

Because you're using a loop, starts an explicit transaction for safety. ⟶ (points to `return Transaction.run((() -> {`)

Uses the setter to update the field ⟶ (points to `sWriteA.loop(Stream.filterOptional(`)

Uses the getter to retrieve the field ⟶ (points to `return new ValueOutput<B>(`)

To run the form example, check it out if you haven't done so already, and then run it like this:

```
git clone https://github.com/SodiumFRP/sodium
cd sodium/book/writeable-remote/java
mvn test -Pform    or    ant form
```

This code shows how you can invent a derived abstraction Value out of a stream going in one direction and a cell in the other, and how you can manipulate this abstraction in simple ways. Under the covers, lots of FRP gets constructed, and this happens once for each field at the end when construct() is finally called by the VTextField. This *reifies* the Value (as in section 1.17) into the actual code that does the job. It's a form of meta-programming.

This sort of approach is common in functional programming, and it can be powerful. What FRP adds to the picture is the ability to use this functional approach on event-based logic. This is something that actor, the observer, or even plain functional programming doesn't give you. Later, we'll give you an even more ambitious example of this principle: how to implement a GUI library in FRP.

12.5 *Persistence*

All FRP state is kept in cells. Sometimes you want to get the entire state of some complex logic and capture it so it can be stored on disk. The basic approach to persistence in FRP is this:

- You write a container class containing all the state you want to persist, and write the persistence functions for it. Let's call it `State`.
- You load the initial state of the system from disk before initializing your FRP logic. You then pass `State state0` (where the 0 means *initial*) or parts of it as needed to all code that constructs FRP logic. That logic then picks the right values and passes them to the `hold()` and `accum()` methods that construct the cells in which you keep your state.
- You also need to be able to snapshot the current state of the logic. You do this by using `lift` primitives to put together a `Cell<GlobalState> state` reflecting the entire persistent state of the system, and returning parts of this as needed from the code that constructs FRP logic. Generally, the `state0` going into a fragment of code and the `state` going out are of types `A` and `Cell<A>`, respectively.

Here's the general pattern:

```
public class SomeLogic {
    public static class State {
        public State(A a, B b, C c) {
            this.a = a;
            this.b = b;
            this.c = c;
        }
        public final A a;
        public final B b;
        public final C c;
    }
    public final Cell<State> state;
    public SomeLogic(State state0, ...) {
        Cell<A> a = <something>.hold(state0.a);
        Cell<B> b = <something>.hold(state0.b);
        Cell<C> c = <something>.hold(state0.c);
        state = a.lift(b, c, (a_, b_, c_) -> new State(a_, b_, c_));
    }
}
```

To snapshot the state and commit it to disk, you use `snapshot`, like this:

```
Stream<Unit> sSave = ...;
Listener l = sSave.snapshot(state).listen(st -> {
    ...write st to disk...
});
```

←⌐ **Initiates saving the state to disk**

This pattern is clean and easy to implement, and illustrates the power of the orderly state management that FRP gives you.

12.6 *Unique ID generation*

Functional programming—and FRP—requires everything to be referentially transparent. Sometimes you want to be able to generate IDs that you know are unique throughout the program. Listing 12.13 gives a special trick to do this in a referentially transparent way.

This code is imperative and stateful on the inside but referentially transparent on the outside. The evil has been contained in a neat little box! Zeus, Hermes, and Pandora will be pleased.

Listing 12.13 Generating unique IDs in a referentially transparent way

```java
package fridgets;

import java.util.Optional;

public class Supply {
    private static class Impl {
        private long nextID = 0;
        public final synchronized long alloc() { return ++nextID; }
    }
    public Supply() { this.impl = new Impl(); }
    private Supply(Impl impl) { this.impl = impl; }
    private final Impl impl;
    private Optional<Long> oID = Optional.empty();
    private Optional<Supply> oChild1 = Optional.empty();
    private Optional<Supply> oChild2 = Optional.empty();
    public final synchronized long get() {
        if (!oID.isPresent())
            oID = Optional.of(impl.alloc());
        return oID.get();
    }
    public final synchronized Supply child1() {
        if (!oChild1.isPresent())
            oChild1 = Optional.of(new Supply(impl));
        return oChild1.get();
    }
    public final synchronized Supply child2() {
        if (!oChild2.isPresent())
            oChild2 = Optional.of(new Supply(impl));
        return oChild2.get();
    }
}
```

A Supply represents a unique ID value that can be obtained with get(). It also has the ability to give birth to two children, imaginatively called child1() and child2(). The two children are guaranteed to yield different ID values from their parent and from each other. The referential transparency comes from guaranteeing that get(), `child1()`, and `child2()` always return the same value, no matter how many times they're called.

In this way, you can pass `Supply`s around far and wide, and, as long as you've been careful to call `child1()` and `child2()` in the right places, the IDs will be guaranteed unique throughout the program. Unfortunately, it's possible to make mistakes and pass the same supply to two different places, so take care.

> **NOTE** Random numbers can be generated functionally in a similar way, but we won't cover that.

You'll make extensive use of this class in the next section.

12.7 *An FRP-based GUI system*

The implementation of a graphical user interface (GUI) system was one of the early use cases of object-oriented programming. Today, pretty much every GUI system has the same basic design—to the point that people have trouble imagining any other way of doing things.

We think FRP is a superior paradigm for this particular problem, and we'll prove it. We would love to see a full GUI system implemented using FRP, so we introduce Fridgets, a tiny GUI system implemented entirely in FRP. It handles the drawing of widgets, input handling, focus, and form layout.

12.7.1 *Drawable*

Fridgets draws its own widgets using 2D graphics. Things to be drawn are represented by a `Drawable` class like the one used in chapter 9. In the following listing, you can see that it's a base class with a polymorphic `draw()` method. You can also append drawables together.

> **Listing 12.14 A thing that can be drawn**

```
package fridgets;

import java.awt.Graphics;

public class Drawable {
    public void draw(Graphics g) {}
    public final Drawable append(Drawable second) {
        Drawable first = this;
        return new Drawable() {
            public void draw(Graphics g) {
                first.draw(g);
                second.draw(g);
            }
        };
    }
}
```

12.7.2 *Fridget*

Fridget is short for "FRP widget," and `Fridget` is the base class for all fridgets. Figure 12.3 shows a fat `FrButton` fridget.

Figure 12.3   `FrButton` **fridget**

`Fridget` (listing 12.15) is a container for a function of five inputs and three outputs. The inputs are as follows:

- `Cell<Optional<Dimension>> size`—The actual size of the fridget after layout. This can be `Optional.empty()`, meaning the size isn't yet known.
- `Stream<MouseEvent> sMouse`—Mouse input events.
- `Stream<KeyEvent> sKey`—Keyboard input events.
- `Cell<Long> focus`—The ID of the fridget that currently has focus.
- `Supply idSupply`—A supply of unique IDs.

And these are the outputs:

- `Cell<Drawable> drawable`—How to draw the fridget.
- `Cell<Dimension> desiredSize`—The size the fridget wants to be, which is the input to the layout algorithm.
- `Stream<Long> sChangeFocus`—A request to change keyboard input focus to the fridget with the specified ID.

Listing 12.15   Fridget interface

```
package fridgets;

import java.awt.Dimension;
import java.awt.event.KeyEvent;
import java.awt.event.MouseEvent;
import java.util.Optional;
import nz.sodium.*;

public abstract class Fridget {
    public static class Output {
        public Output(
                Cell<Drawable> drawable,
                Cell<Dimension> desiredSize,
                Stream<Long> sChangeFocus) {
            this.drawable = drawable;
            this.desiredSize = desiredSize;
            this.sChangeFocus = sChangeFocus;
        }
        public Cell<Drawable> drawable;
        public Cell<Dimension> desiredSize;
        public Stream<Long> sChangeFocus;
    }
    public Fridget(Lambda5<
            Cell<Optional<Dimension>>, Stream<MouseEvent>,
            Stream<KeyEvent>, Cell<Long>, Supply, Output> reify_) {
        this.reify_ = reify_;
```

```
        }
        private final Lambda5<
                Cell<Optional<Dimension>>, Stream<MouseEvent>,
                Stream<KeyEvent>, Cell<Long>, Supply, Output> reify_;
        public final Output reify(
                Cell<Optional<Dimension>> size,
                Stream<MouseEvent> sMouse, Stream<KeyEvent> sKey,
                Cell<Long> focus, Supply idSupply) {
            return reify_.apply(size, sMouse, sKey, focus, idSupply);
        }
}
```

12.7.3 *Your first fridget: FrButton*

Listing 12.16 gives the code for the button fridget. It calculates its desired size based on measuring the label text but draws itself as it's told to by the input size. In addition to meeting the requirements of the Fridget interface, it also exports a stream, sClicked, that fires when the button is clicked. It draws itself differently when the mouse is held down.

Listing 12.16 `FrButton`, the button fridget

```
package fridgets;

import java.awt.*;
import java.awt.event.MouseEvent;
import java.util.Optional;
import nz.sodium.*;

public class FrButton extends Fridget {
    public FrButton(Cell<String> label) {
        this(label, new StreamLoop<Unit>());
    }
    private FrButton(Cell<String> label, StreamLoop<Unit> sClicked) {
        super((size, sMouse, sKey, focus, idSupply) -> {
            Stream<Unit> sPressed = Stream.filterOptional(
                sMouse.snapshot(size, (e, osz) ->
                    osz.isPresent() &&
                    e.getID() == MouseEvent.MOUSE_PRESSED
                        && e.getX() >= 2 && e.getX() < osz.get().width-2
                        && e.getY() >= 2 && e.getY() < osz.get().height-2
                    ? Optional.of(Unit.UNIT)
                    : Optional.empty()
                )
            );
            Stream<Unit> sReleased = Stream.filterOptional(
                sMouse.map(e -> e.getID() == MouseEvent.MOUSE_RELEASED
                    ? Optional.of(Unit.UNIT)
                    : Optional.empty()));
            Cell<Boolean> pressed =
                sPressed.map(u -> true)
                        .orElse(sReleased.map(u -> false))
                        .hold(false);
            sClicked.loop(sReleased.gate(pressed));
            Font font = new Font("Helvetica", Font.PLAIN, 13);
            Canvas c = new Canvas();
```

```
                    FontMetrics fm = c.getFontMetrics(font);
                    Cell<Dimension> desiredSize = label.map(label_ ->
                        new Dimension(
                            fm.stringWidth(label_) + 14,
                            fm.getHeight() + 10));
                    return new Output(
                        label.lift(size, pressed,
                            (label_, osz, pressed_) -> new Drawable() {
                                public void draw(Graphics g) {
                                    if (osz.isPresent()) {
                                        Dimension sz = osz.get();
                                        int w = fm.stringWidth(label_);
                                        g.setColor(pressed_ ? Color.darkGray
                                                            : Color.lightGray);
                                        g.fillRect(3, 3, sz.width-6, sz.height-6);
                                        g.setColor(Color.black);
                                        g.drawRect(2, 2, sz.width-5, sz.height-5);
                                        int centerX = sz.width / 2;
                                        g.setFont(font);
                                        g.drawString(label_,
                                            (sz.width - w)/2,
                                            (sz.height - fm.getHeight())/2
                                                    + fm.getAscent());
                                    }
                                } }
                        ),
                        desiredSize,
                        new Stream<Long>()
                    );
                });
            this.sClicked = sClicked;
        }
    public final Stream<Unit> sClicked;
}
```

Note that each fridget sees the world in such a way that its top left is at the origin (0,0). Mouse input events and drawables are adjusted to create this illusion. That way, the fridget doesn't need to care where it is in the window.

Listing 12.17 shows how you construct the widgets. The way you do this is similar to the SWidgets used in chapters 1 and 2. FrView converts a Fridget into a Swing component so you can attach it as the content of your application's Swing frame. You'll see the code for that shortly.

> **Listing 12.17   Button fridget example**

```
import fridgets.*;
import javax.swing.*;
import nz.sodium.*;

public class button {
    public static void main(String[] args) {
```

```
        JFrame frame = new JFrame("button");
        frame.setDefaultCloseOperation(JFrame.EXIT_ON_CLOSE);
        frame.setContentPane(Transaction.run(() -> {
            FrButton b = new FrButton(new Cell<>("OK"));
            Listener l = b.sClicked.listen(
                u -> System.out.println("clicked!"));
            return new FrView(frame, b) {
                public void removeNotify() {
                    super.removeNotify();
                    l.unlisten();
                }
            };
        }));
        frame.setSize(360,120);
        frame.setVisible(true);
    }
}
```

Javaism to stop listening when the component is disposed

To run this, check it out if you haven't done so already, and then run it like this:

```
git clone https://github.com/SodiumFRP/sodium
cd sodium/book/fridgets/java
mvn test -Pbutton      or      ant button
```

12.7.4 *Bringing a Fridget to life with FrView*

Listing 12.18 shows how you interface a `Fridget` to Java Swing. The code basically feeds in the mouse, keyboard, and window resize events and tells the `Fridget` to take up the entire window. You don't do any layout here.

Handling of current focus is trivially simple. You `hold()` what the fridget sets it to and feed that back in.

Listing 12.18 Viewing a `Fridget` as a Swing component

```
package fridgets;

import java.awt.event.ComponentAdapter;
import java.awt.event.ComponentEvent;
import java.awt.event.KeyAdapter;
import java.awt.event.KeyEvent;
import java.awt.event.MouseAdapter;
import java.awt.event.MouseMotionListener;
import java.awt.event.MouseEvent;
import java.awt.*;
import javax.swing.*;
import java.util.Optional;
import nz.sodium.*;

public class FrView extends JPanel {
    public FrView(JFrame frame, Fridget fr) {
        StreamSink<MouseEvent> sMouse = new StreamSink<>();
        StreamSink<KeyEvent> sKey = new StreamSink<>();
```

```
        addMouseListener(new MouseAdapter() {
            public void mousePressed(MouseEvent e) {
                sMouse.send(e);
            }
            public void mouseReleased(MouseEvent e) {
                sMouse.send(e);
            }
        });
        addMouseMotionListener(new MouseMotionListener() {
            public void mouseDragged(MouseEvent e) {
                sMouse.send(e);
            }
            public void mouseMoved(MouseEvent e) {
                sMouse.send(e);
            }
        });
        size = new CellSink<Optional<Dimension>>(Optional.empty());
        addComponentListener(new ComponentAdapter() {
            public void componentResized(ComponentEvent e) {
                if (e.getID() == ComponentEvent.COMPONENT_RESIZED)
                    size.send(Optional.of(getSize()));
            }
        });
        frame.addKeyListener(new KeyAdapter() {
            public void keyTyped(KeyEvent e) {
                sKey.send(e);
            }
        });
        CellLoop<Long> focus = new CellLoop<>();
        Fridget.Output fo = fr.reify(size, sMouse, sKey, focus,
            new Supply());
        focus.loop(fo.sChangeFocus.hold(-1l));
        this.drawable = fo.drawable;
        l = l.append(Operational.updates(drawable).listen(d -> {
            repaint();
        }));
    }

    private Listener l = new Listener();
    private final CellSink<Optional<Dimension>> size;
    private final Cell<Drawable> drawable;

    public void paintComponent(Graphics g) {
        super.paintComponent(g);
        drawable.sample().draw(g);
    }
    public void removeNotify() {
        l.unlisten();
        super.removeNotify();
    }
    public void handleKeys(JFrame frame) {
    }
}
```

12.7.5 Layout

Layout of widgets in the window is handled by a `FrFlow` fridget. It takes as input a direction, `HORIZONTAL` or `VERTICAL`, and a list of child fridgets to lay out. It lays them out one after another, horizontally or vertically according to each fridget's requested size. Figure 12.4 shows an example of `FrFlow`; the code is in the next listing.

Figure 12.4   Laying out two buttons horizontally with `FrFlow`

Listing 12.19   Widget layout with `FrFlow`

```java
package fridgets;

import java.awt.Dimension;
import java.util.Collection;
import java.util.Optional;
import nz.sodium.*;

public class FrFlow extends Fridget {
    public enum Direction { HORIZONTAL, VERTICAL };

    public FrFlow(Direction dir, Collection<Fridget> fridgets) {
        super((size, sMouse, sKey, focus, idSupply) -> {
            Cell<Dimension> desiredSize = new Cell<>(new Dimension(0,0));
            Cell<Drawable> drawable = new Cell<>(new Drawable());
            Stream<Long> sChangeFocus = new Stream<Long>();
            for (Fridget fridget : fridgets) {
                CellLoop<Optional<Dimension>> childSz = new CellLoop<>();
                Fridget.Output fo = new FrTranslate(fridget,
                    dir == Direction.HORIZONTAL
                        ? desiredSize.map(dsz -> new Dimension(dsz.width, 0))
                        : desiredSize.map(dsz -> new Dimension(0, dsz.height)))
                    .reify(childSz, sMouse, sKey, focus,
                        idSupply.child1());
                idSupply = idSupply.child2();
                childSz.loop(
                    size.lift(fo.desiredSize, (osz, foDsz) ->
                        osz.isPresent()
                            ? Optional.of(dir == Direction.HORIZONTAL
                                ? new Dimension(foDsz.width,
                                                osz.get().height)
                                : new Dimension(osz.get().width,
                                                foDsz.height))
                            : Optional.empty()
                    )
                );
                desiredSize = desiredSize.lift(fo.desiredSize,
                    dir == Direction.HORIZONTAL
                        ? (dsz, foDsz) -> new Dimension(
                            dsz.width + foDsz.width,
```

Translates the child's coordinate space(see listing 12.20)

Peels off a unique ID for the child widget

The width is the child's desired width.

The height of the child is your height.

Desired width: sum of children

Desired height:
maximum of children

```
                          dsz.height > foDsz.height ? dsz.height
                                                    : foDsz.height)
              : (dsz, foDsz) -> new Dimension(
                  dsz.width > foDsz.width ? dsz.width
                                          : foDsz.width,
                  dsz.height + foDsz.height));
```
Combines
drawables
```
              drawable = drawable.lift(fo.drawable,
                  (drA, drB) -> drA.append(drB));
```
Combines focus
requests
```
              sChangeFocus = sChangeFocus.orElse(fo.sChangeFocus);
          }
          return new Fridget.Output(drawable, desiredSize, sChangeFocus);
        });
    }
}
```

NOTE FrFlow takes a static collection of fridgets to display, but you could enhance this code to make it dynamic by passing Cell<Collection<Fridget>> instead. There's an exercise for you if you'd like one.

Listing 12.19 used FrTranslate, which we give in the next listing. It intercepts incoming mouse events and outgoing drawables, translating their coordinate space according to a specified (x,y) offset.

Listing 12.20   FrTranslate: **translating a fridget's coordinate space**

```
package fridgets;

import java.awt.Dimension;
import java.awt.Graphics;
import java.awt.event.MouseEvent;
import nz.sodium.*;

public class FrTranslate extends Fridget {
    public FrTranslate(Fridget fr, Cell<Dimension> offset) {
        super((size, sMouse, sKey, focus, idSupply) -> {
            Stream<MouseEvent> sMouseNew =
                sMouse.snapshot(offset, (e, o) ->
                    new MouseEvent(e.getComponent(), e.getID(),
                        e.getWhen(), e.getModifiers(),
                        e.getX() - o.width, e.getY() - o.height,
                        e.getClickCount(), e.isPopupTrigger())));
            Fridget.Output fo = fr.reify(size, sMouseNew,
                sKey, focus, idSupply);
            Cell<Drawable> drawableNew = fo.drawable.lift(offset,
                (dr, o) -> new Drawable() {
                    public void draw(Graphics g) {
                        g.translate(o.width, o.height);
                        dr.draw(g);
                        g.translate(-o.width, -o.height);
                    } });
            return new Fridget.Output(drawableNew,
                fo.desiredSize, fo.sChangeFocus);
        });
    }
}
```

The next listing shows the main program `flow` that demonstrates the use of `FrFlow`.

Listing 12.21 `flow` example main program

```java
import fridgets.*;
import javax.swing.*;
import java.util.ArrayList;
import nz.sodium.*;

public class flow {
    public static void main(String[] args) {
        JFrame frame = new JFrame("flow");
        frame.setDefaultCloseOperation(JFrame.EXIT_ON_CLOSE);
        frame.setContentPane(Transaction.run(() -> {
            FrButton ok = new FrButton(new Cell<>("OK"));
            FrButton cancel = new FrButton(new Cell<>("Cancel"));
            ArrayList<Fridget> fridgets = new ArrayList<>();
            fridgets.add(ok);
            fridgets.add(cancel);
            Fridget dialog = new FrFlow(FrFlow.Direction.HORIZONTAL,
                fridgets);
            Listener l =
                ok.sClicked.listen(
                    u -> System.out.println("OK"))
                  .append(
                    cancel.sClicked.listen(
                        u -> System.out.println("Cancel")
                    )
                  );
            return new FrView(frame, dialog) {
                public void removeNotify() {
                    super.removeNotify();
                    l.unlisten();
                }
            };
        }));
        frame.setSize(360,120);
        frame.setVisible(true);
    }
}
```

To run this, check it out if you haven't done so already, and then run it like this:

```
git clone https://github.com/SodiumFRP/sodium
cd sodium/book/fridgets/java
mvn test -Pflow     or     ant flow
```

12.7.6 *A form with text fields*

Now let's look at a more complex example: a form with two text fields and two buttons. See figure 12.5.

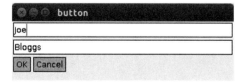

Figure 12.5   A complex example: two text fields and two buttons

The next listing shows `FrTextField`. It's a lot of code, but think about how much work it does. Yet it's not much more complicated than `FrButton`.

Listing 12.22   `FrTextField` fridget

```
package fridgets;

import java.awt.*;
import java.awt.event.MouseEvent;
import java.util.Optional;
import nz.sodium.*;

class TextUpdate {
    TextUpdate(String txt, int newX) {
        this.txt = txt;
        this.newX = newX;
    }
    String txt;
    int newX;
};

public class FrTextField extends Fridget {
    public FrTextField(String initText) {
        this(initText, new CellLoop<String>());
    }
    private FrTextField(String initText, CellLoop<String> text) {
        super((size, sMouse, sKey, focus, idSupply) -> {
            Stream<Integer> sPressed = Stream.filterOptional(
                sMouse.snapshot(size, (e, osz) ->
                    osz.isPresent() &&
                    e.getID() == MouseEvent.MOUSE_PRESSED
                        && e.getX() >= 2 && e.getX() < osz.get().width-2
                        && e.getY() >= 2 && e.getY() < osz.get().height-2
                    ? Optional.of(e.getX() - 2)
                    : Optional.empty()
                )
            );
            CellLoop<Integer> x = new CellLoop<>();
            long myId = idSupply.get();
            Cell<Boolean> haveFocus = focus.map(f_id -> f_id == myId);
            Font font = new Font("Helvetica", Font.PLAIN, 13);
            Canvas c = new Canvas();
            FontMetrics fm = c.getFontMetrics(font);
            Stream<TextUpdate> sTextUpdate = Stream.filterOptional(
                sKey.gate(haveFocus)
                    .snapshot(text, (key, txt) -> {
                        int x_ = x.sample();
                        if (key.getKeyChar() == (char)8) {
                            if (x_ > 0)
                                return Optional.of(new TextUpdate(
                                    txt.substring(0,x_-1)+
                                    txt.substring(x_),
                                    x_-1));
                            else
                                return Optional.empty();
```

Annotations:
- **X position in the text field where the mouse was clicked** → (points to `Stream<Integer> sPressed = Stream.filterOptional(`)
- **Do you have focus?** → (points to `Cell<Boolean> haveFocus = focus.map(f_id -> f_id == myId);`)
- **Updates the text contents according to keypress, current text, and cursor position** → (points to `.snapshot(text, (key, txt) -> {`)
- **Ignores keypresses if no focus** → (points to `sKey.gate(haveFocus)`)

```
                                      }
                                      else {
                                          char[] keyChs = new char[1];
                                          keyChs[0] = key.getKeyChar();
                                          return Optional.of(new TextUpdate(
                                              txt.substring(0, x_)+
                                              new String(keyChs)+
                                              txt.substring(x_),
                                              x_ + 1));
                                      }
                                  })
                          );
                          x.loop(sPressed.snapshot(text,
                              (xCoord, txt) -> {
                                  for (int x_ = 1; x_ <= txt.length(); x_++)
                                      if (xCoord < fm.stringWidth(txt.substring(0, x_)))
                                          return x_-1;
                                  return txt.length();
                              })
                              .orElse(sTextUpdate.map(tu -> tu.newX))
                              .hold(0));
                          text.loop(sTextUpdate.map(tu -> tu.txt).hold(initText));
                          Cell<Dimension> desiredSize = text.map(txt ->
                              new Dimension(
                                  fm.stringWidth(txt) + 14,
                                  fm.getHeight() + 10));
                          return new Output(
                              text.lift(x, haveFocus, size,
                                  (txt, x_, haveFocus_, osz) -> new Drawable() {
                                      public void draw(Graphics g) {
                                          if (osz.isPresent()) {
                                              Dimension sz = osz.get();
                                              g.setColor(Color.white);
                                              g.fillRect(3, 3, sz.width-6, sz.height-6);
                                              g.setColor(Color.black);
                                              g.drawRect(2, 2, sz.width-5, sz.height-5);
                                              int centerX = sz.width / 2;
                                              g.setFont(font);
                                              int cursorX = fm.stringWidth(
                                                  txt.substring(0, x_));
                                              g.drawString(txt,
                                                  4,
                                                  (sz.height - fm.getHeight())/2
                                                      + fm.getAscent());
                                              if (haveFocus_) {
                                                  g.setColor(Color.red);
                                                  g.drawLine(4 + cursorX, 4,
                                                      4 + cursorX, sz.height - 5);
                                              }
                                          }
                                      }
                                  }),
                              desiredSize,
                              sPressed.map(xCoord -> myId)
                          );
                      });
```

Moves the cursor on a mouse click ← (annotation pointing to `x.loop(sPressed.snapshot(text,`)

Moves the cursor after a keypress → (annotation pointing to `.orElse(sTextUpdate.map(tu -> tu.newX))`)

Holds text changes → (annotation pointing to `text.loop(sTextUpdate.map(tu -> tu.txt).hold(initText));`)

Draws the cursor only if you have focus → (annotation pointing to `if (haveFocus_) {`)

```
            this.text = text;
        }
        public final Cell<String> text;
    }
```

Following is the main program for `textfield`.

Listing 12.23   `textfield` example main program

```
import fridgets.*;
import javax.swing.*;
import java.util.ArrayList;
import nz.sodium.*;

public class textfield {
    public static void main(String[] args) {
        JFrame frame = new JFrame("button");
        frame.setDefaultCloseOperation(JFrame.EXIT_ON_CLOSE);
        frame.setContentPane(Transaction.run(() -> {
            FrTextField firstName = new FrTextField("Joe");
            FrTextField lastName = new FrTextField("Bloggs");
            FrButton ok = new FrButton(new Cell<>("OK"));
            FrButton cancel = new FrButton(new Cell<>("Cancel"));
            ArrayList<Fridget> fridgets = new ArrayList<>();
            fridgets.add(ok);
            fridgets.add(cancel);
            Fridget buttons = new FrFlow(FrFlow.Direction.HORIZONTAL,
                fridgets);
            fridgets = new ArrayList<>();
            fridgets.add(firstName);
            fridgets.add(lastName);
            fridgets.add(buttons);
            Fridget dialog =
                new FrFlow(FrFlow.Direction.VERTICAL, fridgets);
            Listener l =
                ok.sClicked
                    .map(u -> firstName.text.sample()+" "+
                            lastName.text.sample())
                    .listen(name -> System.out.println("OK: "+name))
                  .append(
                    cancel.sClicked.listen(
                        u -> System.out.println("Cancel")
                    )
                );
            return new FrView(frame, dialog) {
                public void removeNotify() {
                    super.removeNotify();
                    l.unlisten();
                }
            };
        }));
        frame.setSize(360,120);
        frame.setVisible(true);
    }
}
```

To run this, check it out if you haven't done so already, and then run it like this:

```
git clone https://github.com/SodiumFRP/sodium
cd sodium/book/fridgets/java
mvn test -Ptextfield    or     ant textfield
```

12.8 Summary

- It can be useful to remove duplicate values from cells with a `calm()` method.
- `Junction` is an imperative idea, but it allows you to instantiate modules extensibly that can push their own data into a preexisting stream or cell.
- Writable remote values are a way to deal neatly with impedance mismatches between a data back end and a GUI interface.
- The orderliness of state management in FRP means snapshotting the current state of something complex for persistent storage is easy to achieve.
- *Supply* is a technique from functional programming to generate unique IDs in a way that's referentially transparent to the caller.
- A graphical user interface (GUI) library can be implemented nicely in FRP—and the code is arguably much better than the common object-oriented approach.

Refactoring

This chapter covers

- A drag-and-drop example
- Adding some features
- Contrasting refactoring between OOP and FRP code

In your job as a programmer, you'll often add a feature or fix a bug by adding extra code to a class or method. As the code gets longer, it can get messier. In this chapter, we'll illustrate that process by example.

As the Agile software development methodology emphasizes, when you start to smell that "code smell" of untidy code, it's usually a good idea to refactor the code by breaking the class or method into smaller pieces. This is important because messy code is complex code, and we've argued that complexity can compound. We've also argued that this should be less of an issue in FRP due to its compositionality, but refactoring is still important. Fortunately, refactoring with FRP is as easy as falling off a log.

13.1 To refactor or not to refactor?

If you add extra state and logic to an existing class, this is the question you must ask yourself. Latent problems in code usually manifest when you make modifications.

Often, deep in your heart, you'll hear a little voice calling, "Refactor me!" But do you always listen?

The complexity you added gives you an uneasy feeling. That's because you know at some point you'll need to split things up. "It's only a few small changes," you reply to yourself. But the longer you put off refactoring, the more work it will eventually be, as you can see in figure 13.1.

Sometimes it's difficult to see a neat way to do it. Sometimes you don't want to incur hours of testing and be blamed for refactoring breakage in someone else's code; adding an extra variable and a couple of lines of logic seems infinitely preferable. Yes, sometimes short-term considerations win out. This is exactly the process by which Frankenstein created his famous monster.

Figure 13.1 Dale regrets having put off refactoring.

13.2 A drag-and-drop example

To show FRP refactoring in action, we'll use a variation on the drag-and-drop examples developed in chapters 7 and 10. Recall from chapter 7 that there are three types of mouse event, each associated with an (x, y) position in the window:

- *Mouse down*—The mouse button is pressed down.
- *Mouse move*—The mouse position changes, but there is no change to the buttons.
- *Mouse up*—The mouse button is released.

This implementation doesn't use `switch` because we'll be drawing diagrams and we haven't figured out a way to diagram the dynamic changes of a `switch`.

13.2.1 *Coding it the traditional way*

Let's first look at how you write this in a traditional object-oriented / listener / state machine style. You typically write a class called `DragAndDrop` that does the following:

- Registers listeners on the input events
- Has fields for the state

To keep things tidy, you'll use two container classes. `Dragging` holds the state you need to keep while dragging. Instead of updating the diagram for each mouse move, you'll draw the element separately as it's dragged and update the document only at the end. You add a helper method to give a representation of this in a second class, `Floating-Element`. This information is used in the `paint` method to draw the floating element:

Omitting boilerplate

Original mouse position of the drag

```
class Dragging {
    Dragging(Element elt, Point origMousePos) { ... }
    Element elt;
    Point origMousePos;

    FloatingElement floatingElement(Point curMousePos) {
        Vector moveBy = curMousePos.subtract(origMousePos);

        return new FloatingElement(elt.getPosition().add(moveBy), elt);
    }
}

class FloatingElement {
    FloatingElement(Point position, Element elt) { ... }
    Point position;
    Element elt;
}
```

Container class for the drag state used during drag

Element you're dragging

Helper method that returns a representation of the floating element

New position = original position + distance traveled

Selected element and the position to draw it at while floating

Before we get to the rest of the code, we'll sketch out the logic in a simplified version of the diagram style used in chapter 2. It uses

- Round corners for things that output *streams*
- *Square* corners for state (cells)

We'll keep it simple and leave out the `mouseMove` event handling, so for now the floating element won't be drawn as you drag.

In figure 13.2, the top rounded-corner box (logic) is activated when a `mouseDown` event comes in. It snapshots from the `document` (note the arrow from `document`) and asks if an element exists at the mouse position. If it does, it updates `dragging` with a value of `new Dragging(elt, pos)`. You're now dragging `elt`.

The rounded-corner box at left is activated by the `mouseUp` event. If you're dragging (that is, the `dragging` variable has a non-null value), you'll end the drag. You produce an event labeled `drop`, and if you follow the arrows, you can see that it causes three things to happen:

1 `null` is written into the `dragging` variable, which puts you back in the idle state (not dragging).

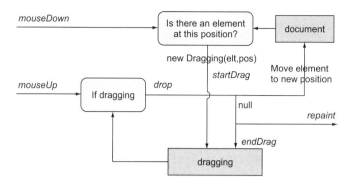

Figure 13.2 Minimal drag-and-drop logic

2 You update the document with the new position for the element.

3 You repaint the window.

The Java pseudocode is shown in the following listing. Shortly we'll contrast it against the equivalent FRP.

Listing 13.1 Pseudo Java for drag-and-drop logic, traditional object-oriented style

```
class Dragging {                                          ◁—— Container class for the drag
    Dragging(Element elt, Point origMousePos) { ... }         state used during drag
    Element elt;                               ◁—— Element you're
    Point origMousePos;                             dragging

    FloatingElement floatingElement(Point curMousePos) {   ◁—— Helper method that
        Vector moveBy = curMousePos.subtract(origMousePos);      returns a representation
                                                                 of the floating element
        return new FloatingElement(elt.getPosition().add(moveBy), elt); ◁——
    }                                            New position = original
}                                                position + distance traveled

class FloatingElement {                          ◁——
    FloatingElement(Point position, Element elt) { ... }
    Point position;                              Selected element and
    Element elt;                                 the position to draw
}                                                it at while floating

class DragAndDrop implements MouseListener
{
    Document doc;
    Window window;
    Dragging dragging = null;

    DragAndDrop(Document doc, Window window) {
        ...                                      Asks the window to call you
        window.addMouseListener(this);      ◁—— back with mouse events
    }
```

Omitting boilerplate

Original mouse position of the drag

```
void mouseDown(Point mousePos) {                                    Starts dragging if you
    Element elt = doc.lookupByPosition(mousePos);                   press down on a
    if (elt != null)                                               document element
        dragging = new Dragging(elt, mousePos);
}
void mouseMove(Point mousePos) {
}
void mouseUp(Point mousePos) {
    if (dragging != null) {
        FloatingElement flt = dragging.floatingElement(mousePos);
        doc.moveTo(flt.elt, flt.position);
        dragging = null;
        window.repaint();
    }
}
}
```

If you're dragging…

…moves the document element to its floating position

Repaint: assumes the paint() method reads from the document directly

13.2.2 *The FRP way: diagrams to code*

As we said at the beginning of the book, FRP code directly reflects a box-and-arrows diagram. Let's translate our diagram into code.

In figure 13.3, we put the diagram side-by-side with the equivalent FRP pseudocode. The structure of FRP code is fundamentally the same as the structure of the diagram.

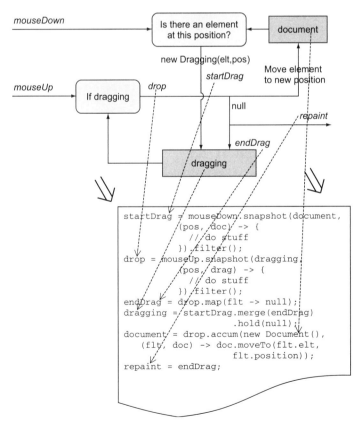

Figure 13.3 The structure of FRP code corresponds closely to a "boxes and arrows" diagram.

Observe the following:

- For brevity, we've left out the types in the variable assignments.
- Each variable (rectangular box) and each italicized label we've added to an arrow corresponds to a statement in the FRP code. These statements are written as assignments to named variables.
- Whenever a statement references a variable declared elsewhere, there's a corresponding arrow in the diagram.

13.3 Adding a feature: drawing the floating element

As it is, the user doesn't get any visual feedback when they drag an element. You'd like to draw the element floating as the user drags it. The traditional way would be to make the `mouseMove()` method cause a repaint if you're dragging. The `Window` instance's `paint()` method, which does the real work, will use `document` directly to draw the document, and it will call the `Dragging` class's `floatingElement()` method to find out where and how to draw the floating element (we won't show the code for `paint()`):

```
FloatingElement floatElt = null;

void mouseMove(Point mousePos) {
    if (dragging != null)                              Records floating
        floatElt = dragging.floatingElement(mousePos); element information
    else
        floatElt = null;             Requests the window
    window.repaint();                to be repainted      Window's paint() calls this
}                                                         to ask about the floating
FloatingElement floatingElement() {                       element and its position.
    return floatElt;
}
```

Now let's add this `mouseMove` handling to the diagram. The additions are shown in bold; see figure 13.4.

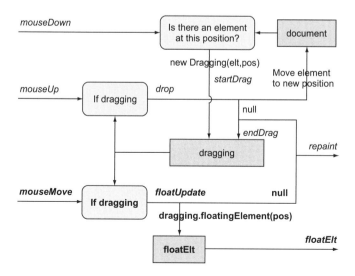

Figure 13.4 Add repaint on `mouseMove` so you see the element floating as you drag it. Additions are in bold.

13.4 *Fixing a bug: clicks are being treated as drags*

This code has an undocumented feature that annoys the user: clicks are being misinterpreted as drags, so when the user clicks an object, it often gets moved slightly. Let's fix that by having two phases:

- *Pending*—The mouse button has been pressed down, but you haven't started moving yet.
- *Dragging*—You've detected mouse motion while in the pending phase, so the element is now really being dragged.

You'll detect mouse motion if the mouse has moved five pixels or more from the point where the mouse button was pressed. See figure 13.5: it's not until you get outside a five-pixel radius of the drag origin that the drag starts, at event 3.

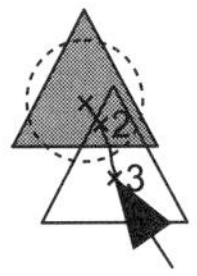

Figure 13.5 Start the drag only when you move outside a five-pixel radius of the drag origin.

The next listing shows the changed lines in bold to add the extra pending phase. Note that you have to be careful to use the right state variable in the right place.

Listing 13.2 Code changes to add a pending phase before drag, traditional-style

```
class DragAndDrop implements MouseListener
{
    Document doc;
    Window window;
    Dragging pending = null;
    Dragging dragging = null;
    FloatingElement floatElt = null;

    DragAndDrop(Document doc, Window window) {
        ...
        window.addMouseListener(this);
    }
    void mouseDown(Point mousePos) {
        Element elt = doc.lookupByPosition(mousePos);
        if (elt != null)
            pending = new Dragging(elt, mousePos);
    }
    void mouseMove(Point mousePos) {
        if (pending != null &&
                mousePos.distance(pending.origMousePos) >= 5)
            dragging = pending;
        if (dragging != null)
            floatElt = dragging.floatingElement(mousePos);
        else
            floatElt = null;
        window.repaint();
    }
    FloatingElement floatingElement() {
        return floatElt;
    }
```

```
void mouseUp(Point mousePos) {
    if (dragging != null) {
        FloatingElement flt = dragging.floatingElement(mousePos);
        doc.moveTo(flt.elt, flt.position);
        dragging = null;
        window.repaint();
    }
    pending = null;
}
}
```

Figure 13.6 adds this logic to the previous FRP diagram (which was figure 1.7). Additions are again in bold.

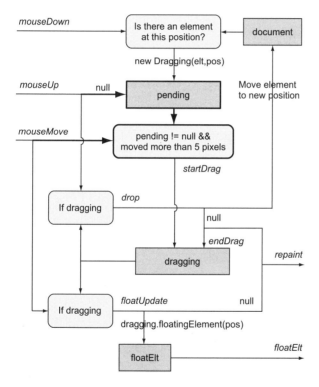

Figure 13.6 Add a pending phase before the drag starts. Additions are in bold.

13.5 *FRP: refactoring is a breeze*

The code in the previous example has a problem: it's getting messy. In the traditional-style code presented, it would be easy to make a mistake and mix up `pending` and `dragging`.

You can improve this by refactoring each variable into a separate class to limit the scope so one part of the logic sees only `pending` and the other sees only `dragging`, and the interface between the classes is clearly delineated. You'll separate this logic into three classes:

- DragPending—Manages pending state
- Dragging—Manages dragging state
- DrawFloating—Manages floatElt state

Figure 13.7 shows a typical refactoring in the traditional programming style. You move the bits of code relating to each state into classes of their own. After that, you'd neaten up the interfaces between them; for example, DragPending would call a new start-Drag() method on Dragging to set its dragging state.

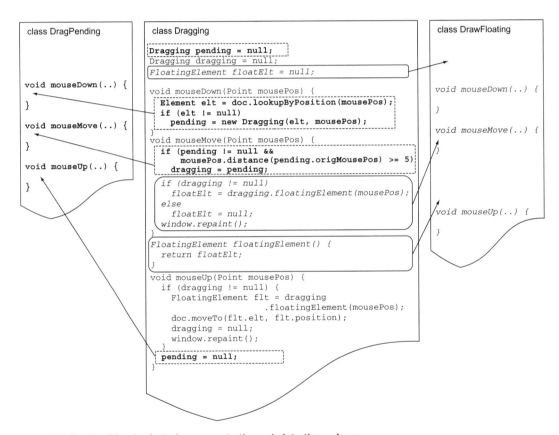

Figure 13.7   Traditional refactoring: separate the code into three classes.

Figure 13.8 shows how you refactor in FRP. In practice, you'd do this directly with code, but we're using a diagram to get the concept across.

We've "drawn" circles around groups of boxes that are conceptually related, so that the number of incoming and outgoing arrows is small, and we've given the circles

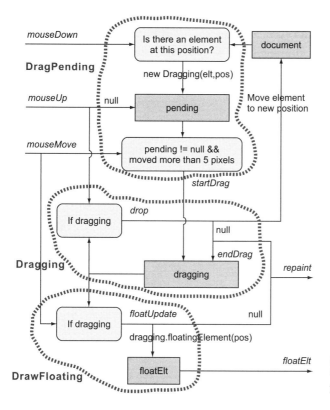

Figure 13.8 FRP refactoring: just "draw" circles around the modules you want, and label them.

names. Each box corresponds to a statement in the FRP code. You just move those statements into new classes and fix up the variable references.

You'd create a structure like the following. We arrived at this by going round the edge of the lines in the diagram. Each incoming arrow becomes a constructor argument, and each outgoing arrow becomes a field. In practice, you'd look at each statement and its dependencies:

```
class DragPending {
    DragPending(Stream<MouseEvent> sMouseDown, Stream<MouseEvent> sMouseUp,
                Stream<MouseEvent> sMouseMove, Cell<Document> document) {}
    Stream<Unit> sStartDrag;
}
class Dragging {
    Dragging(Stream<Unit> sStartDrag, Stream<MouseEvent> sMouseUp) {}
    Cell<Dragging> dragging;
    Stream<DocumentUpdate> sDrop;
    Stream<Unit> sRepaint;
}
class DrawFloating {
    DrawFloating(Stream<MouseEvent> sMouseMove, Cell<Dragging> dragging) {}
    Stream<Unit> sRepaint;
    Cell<Optional<FloatingElement>> floatElt;
}
```

Then you paste the existing FRP statements into the new constructors. Done.

You don't have to tease the code apart as you did with the traditional code. Furthermore, the compiler will do a good job of making sure you don't make mistakes: if something is out of scope or you paste a statement into the wrong constructor, the code won't compile. If you get the order of arguments wrong, the compiler is likely (but not certain) to complain about a type mismatch.

We'll repeat what we said in section 11.4: unit tests are normally used to protect against code breakage. FRP has so much built-in checking that it generally isn't necessary to use tests to protect the code against refactoring breakage. But of course, tests can never hurt. As a result of all this, FRP programmers don't experience the same "Should I? Shouldn't I?" refactoring dilemma.

13.6   *Summary*

- Sometimes the difficulty and risk of refactoring lead us to favor short-term considerations. Refactoring gets put off, and code gets messy.
- FRP code doesn't get messy as easily due to its compositionality.
- FRP code is automatically safe and easy to refactor.
- FRP protects against refactoring breakage so well that unit tests aren't necessary for this purpose.
- The dilemma of short-term versus long-term considerations largely disappears with FRP.

Adding FRP to existing projects

This chapter covers

- Changing over to immutable data structures
- Replacing callbacks with streams and cells
- Program-initialization techniques
- Combining information sources extensibly with `Junctions`

Cast your mind back to the beginning of the book where we told the sad tale of a project hitting the *complexity wall*. The authors have both lived through this. It's actually the underlying motivation for our interest in FRP.

We think software quality and the costs of achieving it are a serious issue for industry. Software is being called on to solve more and more complex problems. There are many reasons for this, but parallelism will be an increasingly important factor. Existing methods are coming under strain. We need stronger techniques to deal with this greater complexity, and that's why industry is looking to what functional programming can offer. FRP is part of that. We think that for certain types of projects—anywhere there's a lot of event handling—FRP can help turn intractable code into maintainable code so you can navigate the *complexity wall* barrier.

14.1 Where can FRP help?

Here are some situations where you might consider adding FRP to an existing project:

- Your project has brittle parts that are FRP-like problems. Perhaps they resemble some of the examples in this book.
- Your project is getting the sorts of bugs we described as the *six plagues* in appendix B, and there have been repeated attempts to fix them.
- Parts of the code are becoming intractable, or you can see them heading in that direction.

FRP isn't an all-or-nothing deal. You can try FRP in limited areas, see how it goes, and continue if it's successful. Now we'll discuss some tips and tricks to make it a smooth process.

14.2 Changing to immutable data structures

As we said in section 5.5.1, FRP requires the values it works with to be immutable. *Immutability* means if a piece of code or FRP logic holds a reference to some data, you're absolutely assured that data can't be changed by some other part of the program. The data must not be able to be modified in place.

We suggest that once you've identified part of the code where FRP might be useful, as a first step you should change over to using *immutable* data structures, also known as *functional* or *persistent* data structures. This last term has an unfortunate double meaning: we aren't talking about writing data structures to persistent storage.

> **NOTE**   Changing over to immutable data structures is a good idea. By itself it will give you the benefits of thread safety and compositionality. This is the essence of functional programming.

Some data types, such as `String` in Java, are already immutable. But it's common for people to use mutable dictionary data types: maps, sets, queues, and arrays. These all have immutable equivalents that are as efficient or nearly as efficient.

For example, if you wanted to catalog the tracks in the media library of a media player by song title, a mutable implementation might look like this:

```
class MediaLibrary {
    public MediaLibrary() {}
    private Map<Title, Track> tracks = new HashMap<>();
    public void addTrack(Track t) { tracks.put(t.getTitle(), t); }
}
```

Before you can introduce FRP, you need to make this immutable. You first need to find an implementation of an immutable dictionary. If you assume one called `Immutable-Map`, then here's an idea of the code:

```
class MediaLibrary {
    public MediaLibrary() { this(new ImmutableMap<Title, Track>()); }
    private MediaLibrary(ImmutableMap<Title, Track> tracks) {
        this.tracks = tracks;
```

```
    }
    private final ImmutableMap<Title, Track> tracks;
    public MediaLibrary addTrack(Track t) {
        return new MediaLibrary(tracks.insert(t.getTitle(), t));
    }
}
```

You also need to change the place from which addTrack() is called so it overwrites its own state with the returned MediaLibrary.

Once these changes are complete, it becomes possible to keep the media library state in an FRP cell, like this:

```
Stream<Track> sAddTrack = ...;
Cell<MediaLibrary> mediaLibrary = sAddTrack.accum(initialTracks,
    (track, library) -> library.addTrack(track));
```

Make sure you understand why using the mutable implementation of MediaLibrary shown here would be forbidden by the rules of FRP.

14.3 *Stream as a drop-in replacement for callbacks*

In many cases, a stream in Sodium can be treated as a drop-in replacement for a listener/callback/observer pattern mechanism. Here's an example of making this replacement.

Let's say you're writing a Player component for your media player that handles the I/O for the playback. It publishes three things:

- Whether it's paused
- Where you're up to in the track (seconds)
- When the track has finished playing

This is shown in the following listing.

Listing 14.1 Media player component with observer interface

```
public class Player {
    public interface Listener {
        public void paused(boolean isPaused);
        public void seconds(int seconds);
        public void ended();
    }
    private List<Listener> listeners = new ArrayList<>();
    public void addListener(Listener l) {
        listeners.add(l);
    }
    public void removeListener(Listener l) {
        listeners.remove(l);
    }
    public void play(Track t) { ... }
    public void pause() { ... }
    public void resume() { ... }
    public boolean isPaused() { ... }
```

```
    public int getSeconds() { ... }
    private void notifyPaused(boolean p) {
        for (l : listeners) l.paused(p); }
    private void notifySeconds(int s) {
        for (l : listeners) l.seconds(s); }
    private void notifyEnded() {
        for (l : listeners) l.ended(); }
}
```

You can replace seconds and paused with cells and ended with a stream, as in the next
listing. Note that you keep the sink sides of the cells and streams private, and you
export them as a Cell or Stream subclass. These classes don't have a send() method,
so the consumer of the exported cells and streams won't be able to write to them.

Listing 14.2   Media player component, FRPized

```
public class Player {
    public void play(Track t) { ... }
    public void pause() { ... }
    public void resume() { ... }
    private final CellSink<Boolean> pausedSnk = new CellSink<>(false);
    public final Cell<Boolean> paused = pausedSnk;
    private final CellSink<Integer> secondsSnk = new CellSink<>(0);
    public final Cell<Integer> seconds = secondsSnk;
    private final StreamSink<Unit> sEndedSnk = new StreamSink<Unit>();
    public final Stream<Unit> sEnded = sEndedSnk;
    private void notifyPaused(boolean p) { pausedSnk.send(p); }
    private void notifySeconds(int s) { secondsSnk.send(s); }
    private void notifyEnded() { endedSnk.send(Unit.UNIT); }
}
```

You might define a controller that plays the next track when a track ends, as shown in
the next listing.

Listing 14.3   Controller to play the next song using the observer interface

```
public class Controller implements Player.Listener {
    public Controller(Player player) {
        this.player = player;
        player.addListener(this);
        playNext();
    }
    private Player player;
    public void ended() {
        playNext();
    }
    public void playNext() { ... }
}
```

The following listing rewrites this based on the FRP version of Player.

Listing 14.4   Controller to play the next song, FRPized

```java
public class Controller {
    public Controller(Player player) {
        this.player = player;
        player.sEnded.listen(() -> playNext());
        playNext();
    }
    private Player player;
    public void playNext() { ... }
}
```

14.3.1 *Caveat: you can't send() inside a listener*

These changes are easy to make, but there's an important caveat. Sodium has a restriction: it doesn't allow `StreamSink.send()` or `CellSink.send()` to be called from inside a listener. It will throw an exception at runtime if you do this. This is the case for two reasons:

- To ensure that messages are propagated in strict dependency order. If you use `send()` directly, then Sodium can't track the dependency, so we don't allow it.
- To discourage writing "FRP code" in an imperative style.

Other FRP systems may not have this restriction, but they tend not to have strict *denotational semantics* and therefore aren't "true FRP." We discussed the importance of this issue in section 1.2.1 and talked about how RxJS doesn't comply in chapter 6.

In the FRPized `Controller` in the previous example, it's likely that `playNext()`, which is called from this handler

```java
player.sEnded.listen(() -> playNext());
```

could call `send()`. Then `playNext()` would probably call `Player.play()`, which would in turn do this:

```java
secondsSnk.send(0);
```

This wouldn't be allowed because it breaks the restriction. There are two ways to deal with this. Which one you choose depends on how much of your program you want to refactor.

THE CONSERVATIVE WAY: DELEGATING TO ANOTHER THREAD

Instead of doing this

```java
player.sEnded.listen(() -> playNext());
```

you can dump the processing onto a new thread:

```java
player.sEnded.listen(() -> new Thread() {
    void run() { Player.this.playNext(); }
}.start());
```

> **NOTE** In Sodium, a `listen()` handler isn't allowed to make any assumptions about what thread it's running on. Each FRP system has different rules for this.

Spawning a thread like this requires that `Player` is thread-safe. A better way may be to use an asynchronous message queue and have `Player` run its own thread to process the requests. This is an *actor model*-like approach, and it neatly solves the concurrency issues. When dealing with I/O, we generally recommend this approach.

Doing things this way, you're treating `play()` more as I/O than as a state update. This means your state updates won't be as "tight." To state this more precisely, the state transition from ending one track to starting the next isn't *atomic*. Depending on how the rest of the program works, it may be possible to observe a state between tracks when nothing is being played. This could be problematic, for example, if you wanted to detect when the player was idle. It might falsely come to that conclusion between songs. A full FRP approach eliminates this issue.

THE RADICAL WAY: TRANSFORMING PLAY() INTO A STREAM

Instead of this

```
Player() { ... }
void play(Track t) {
    secondsSnk.send(0);
    ... Initiate I/O ...
}
```

you can write

```
Player(Stream<Track> sPlay) {
    sPlay.listen(t -> { ... Initiate I/O ... });
    seconds = sPlay.map(t -> 0).merge( ... other stuff ... ).hold(0);
}
```

where `... other stuff ...` is a placeholder for whatever mechanism makes the seconds tick. For this to work properly, you also need to change `Controller` to manage all of its state using FRP. Now the code is turning completely into FRP. You're bringing discipline to the state management and making the whole thing thread-safe. That's the good news.

But if your program is large, taking this sort of approach consistently may force you to make too many changes at once. The best approach is to transform code into the world of FRP in stages, always maintaining a bridge between the imperative and FRP parts. It's important to do this in small chunks so you can test as you go.

14.3.2 *Choosing the right chunk size*

As we said, converting a project to use FRP should be done in small chunks so you can keep the code tested and running. It's best to find self-contained modules where you can initially keep the same interface on the outside. You need to ask these questions:

- How much of the state is still mutable, and how much work is involved in changing to immutable data structures?
- What are the implications for threading when I try to maintain the same external interface?

Then do the work and retest before moving on to the next chunk.

14.4 *Program initialization with one big transaction*

A lot of programs are structured at the top level a bit like the following code. There are many dependencies, so sometimes, something akin to `c.setD(d);` is required, although this may be in the constructor of d rather than at the top level:

```
public class Main {
    public static void main(String[] args) {
        ModuleA a = new ModuleA();
        ModuleB b = new ModuleB(a);
        ModuleC c = new ModuleC(a);
        ModuleD d = new ModuleD(b, c);
        c.setD(d);
        while (true) {
            ... main loop ...
        }
    }
}
```

In large applications, this construction can be pages long and get complex, messy, and brittle. When the relationships between modules have to be changed, things can break.

The major source of grief is that a lot of this initialization code is order-dependent. An example is that things like `c.setD(d);` imply that c's reference to d is initially a `null` reference. If c tries to access d before `setD()` is called, then you get a `NullPointer-Exception`. In a complex program, it's difficult to guarantee that this won't happen.

FRP tends to eliminate these problems completely because FRP code can be rearranged into any order and always has the same meaning. FRP references can never be `null`. Instead, cyclic dependencies are expressed with `StreamLoop` and `CellLoop`, and these can be safely referenced before the loop is resolved.

As a first step to FRP-ing your code, you typically put a big transaction around the construction of the modules. Then you can start adding Sodium bit by bit to tidy up the initialization. The transaction does two things:

- It allows `CellLoop` and `StreamLoop` to be used between modules, because in Sodium, they have a requirement that their `loop()` method is called in the same transaction as their construction.
- It ensures that if one module calls `StreamSink.send()` during initialization on a stream that it's exporting, other modules are guaranteed to receive the sent value, regardless of initialization order. In our six plagues, we call this the plague of *missed first event*.

There's a minor issue here that pertains only to Sodium. Because Sodium uses the loan pattern for explicit transactions, it's not straightforward to keep the variables a, b, c, and d in scope during the main loop to keep them alive, but you can solve this by putting the construction of your application into a class. You could make a new class, but this example writes a constructor for Main because you're not using it for anything else:

```
public class Main {
    Main() {
        a = new ModuleA();
```

```
        b = new ModuleB(a);
        c = new ModuleC(a);
        d = new ModuleD(b, c);
        c.setD(d);
    }
    final ModuleA a;
    final ModuleB b;
    final ModuleC c;
    final ModuleD d;
    public static void main(String[] args) {
        Main m = Transaction.run(() -> new Main());
        while (true) {
            ... main loop ...
        }
    }
}
```

The cyclic dependency between c and d is now better expressed this way:

```
StreamLoop<Something> sOutputD = new StreamLoop<>();
c = new ModuleC(a, sOutputD);
d = new ModuleD(b, c);
sOutputD.loop(d.sOutputD);
```

If you forget to call sOutputD.loop(), you'll get a runtime exception telling you so, but this will happen consistently and nothing is dependent on execution order.

14.5   *Module extensibility with junction/client registry*

At the beginning of this chapter, we suggested that you could replace Player's play() method with a stream, using this constructor:

```
Player(Stream<Track> sPlay)
```

Using this pattern, the program initialization for the media player might look like this:

```
StreamLoop<Track> sPlay = new StreamLoop<>();
Player p = new Player(sPlay);
Controller c = new Controller(p);
sPlay.loop(c.sPlay);
```

But what if multiple controllers in the program wanted to be able to start songs playing? Each would export an sPlay, and you would need to merge them together. You could of course do this:

```
sPlay.loop(c.sPlay.orElse(c2.sPlay)
                .orElse(c3.sPlay)
                .orElse(c4.sPlay));
```

There's a risk you might forget one of them. In addition, this approach isn't very extensible.

StreamJunction and CellJunction from section 12.3 can be used for these problems. Let's return to the example from that chapter. Imagine a mobile phone with a notification area at the top of the screen. Different applications can publish notifications there. You did this on an imaginary cellphone operating system in which everything runs in one process. The code worked like this:

```
CellJunction<List<Message>> notifications = new CellJunction<>(
    new List<Message>(), appendList);
NotificationArea notArea = new NotificationArea(notifications.out);
UpdateManager umgr = new UpdateManager(notifications, ...);
MediaPlayer mediaPlyr = new MediaPlayer(notifications, ...);
Messenger messenger = new Messenger(notifications, ...);
```

Each constructor registers its own source of notifications with the junction:

```
Cell<List<Message>> myNotifications = ...;
Listener l = notifications.add(myNotifications);
```

`notifications.out` is then a concatenation of all the different notification sources.

This is a useful construct when you're adding FRP to an existing program. You may want to look over that section again.

14.6 *Cells can replace mutable variables*

Let's say your application has a `Mailbox` class with a "number of messages available" value that can be read, but no notification infrastructure:

```
class Mailbox {
    private int noOfMessages;
    public final getNoOfMessages() { return noOfMessage; }
}
```

You can use a cell as a drop-in replacement for this, as in the media player example. You write into it with `noOfMessageSnk.send()` and read out of it with `noOf-Messages.sample()`:

```
class Mailbox {
    private final CellSink<Integer> noOfMessageSnk
                                       = new CellSink<Integer>(0);
    public final Cell<Integer> noOfMessages = noOfMessagesSnk;
}
```

Suddenly, this variable is thread-safe, and it has the extra features that cell gives you, such as the ability to listen for changes. It also plays nicely with all your FRP code. The usual rule applies, though, that the value contained in the cell must be an immutable data type.

14.7 *Summary*

- Streams and cells can be used as drop-in replacements for listeners and mutable variables, respectively.
- FRP requires values to be immutable, so it can be a good policy to refactor your code to use immutable variables first. This is a good idea in any case.

- When refactoring with FRP, you should do it in small chunks where you can keep the external interface so existing code can use it.
- We recommend that you put one big transaction around your program initialization.
- The Junction class described in section 12.3 can be a useful helper when you need extensibility.

Future directions 15

At the time of writing, given what is possible, it's still early days for FRP. Like characters from a Hayao Miyazaki movie, we'll now let our hair cascade in the wind, the sun glinting in our goggles as we squint uncomprehendingly at the horizon. In this chapter, we'll talk about some of the directions we'd like to see FRP go in.

15.1 Performance

An FRP system knows its data dependencies and can measure its usage patterns at runtime. There is enormous scope for just-in-time (JIT) compilation and live optimization based on performance characteristics measured at runtime. We think FRP could be made to run very quickly indeed.

We should also look at nontraditional computing architectures. FRP abstracts the machine away, and there may be machines that are well suited for FRP.

15.2 Precompiled FRP for performance or embedded systems

Precompiling FRP would be one way to improve performance, but it would also be useful for resource-constrained environments. Without `switch`, it should be easy to statically compile FRP code into C or for deployment on field programmable gate arrays (FPGAs). This would be useful on embedded systems, which are often used for control applications—an application domain that fits FRP well. Implementing `switch` would be more of a challenge but should be eminently possible.

15.3 Parallelism

It should be possible to automatically parallelize FRP code to run on multicore systems. We have to be careful here because implementing automated parallelism tends to look a lot easier than it really is.

We have a good starting point. An FRP engine knows all the dependencies and data flows in the FRP logic, so it can be guaranteed to give the right answer in all cases, but with total flexibility in how it arranges for the answer to be calculated.

The simplest approach to parallelism would be to use software transactional memory (STM) to implement cells. This approach to parallelism works beautifully in Haskell but runs into problems in other languages because only languages like Haskell can lock things down sufficiently to ensure that you can't break some important rules. FRP achieves a similar level of lockdown due to its highly restricted computational model, so STM should work well in an FRP engine even in more liberal languages.

The STM approach would work like this:

- Two FRP transactions run in parallel, and initially their logical order relative to each other isn't decided.
- If they try to lock the same state, a decision is made as to which transaction is logically first; the other is rolled back and automatically restarted. This is similar to what happens in many relational database systems. The efficiency of this approach would depend on making sure this is a relatively rare occurrence.
- If they don't access the same state, the decision about which is logically first never needs to be made, and the transactions will run in parallel.

A more complicated way to implement parallelism would be to use the techniques of a JIT compiler to measure processing times and execution patterns at runtime so intelligent decisions could be made about scheduling on multiple processors.

As for implementing FRP on GPUs, this probably doesn't make much sense. GPUs suit a different kind of parallelism called *data parallelism* where the same operation is performed many times on large data sets.

15.4 Syntax improvements

The syntax of FRP is clunky in most languages and could be improved hugely with some kind of preprocessing. There are several things we can do.

15.4.1 *Auto-lifting*

One key concept is auto-lifting. It should be possible to write this

```
Cell<Integer> c = a.lift(b, (a_, b_) -> a_ + b_);
```

in the following way:

```
c <- a + b
```

The language would know that a and b are cells and would "auto-lift" the + operator. The Flapjax FRP system authors did some work in this area.

15.4.2 *Implicit forward references*

In the Java version of Sodium, you need to use *loop* classes to allow forward references for accumulators and such:

```
CellLoop<Integer> count;
count.loop(sCount.snapshot(count, (u, total) -> total + 1))
            .hold(0));
```

We'd like forward references to be automatic, so we could just write this:

```
count <- sCount.snapshot(count, (u, total) -> total + 1)
            .hold(0)
```

In the Haskell programming language, this exists already. It's enabled by the RecursiveDo language extension and the rec keyword.

15.4.3 *Infix operators*

The Reactive Banana FRP system uses the infix operators <@> and <@ for snapshot. In our imaginary syntax, this code

```
count <- sCount.snapshot(count, (u, total) -> total + 1)
            .hold(0)
```

might become

```
count <- ((count + 1) <@ sCount).hold(0)
```

This sort of thing is great for making the syntax more succinct, at the risk of scaring away people new to FRP.

15.4.4 *Type inference*

Most languages require many types to be written out explicitly. Java's lambda syntax is excellent in this respect:

```
Stream<Integer> sTotal = eExtra.snapshot(total, (ex, to) -> ex + to);
```

But C++11 is pretty bad because lambda arguments require type signatures:

```
stream<int> sTotal = sExtra.snapshot<int,int>(total,
    [] (int ex, int to) { return ex + to; });
```

We'd like to write it like this:

```
sTotal <- sExtra.snapshot(total, (ex, to) -> ex + to);
```

In FRP, most types can be inferred. This may seem like a small thing, but it can make a huge difference to the readability of FRP code. This is most pronounced when you have complex types like Maps and tuples.

The Haskell programming language already does this. It's statically typed, but the bureaucracy of the type checking is mostly hidden so it doesn't impair code readability.

15.5   Standardization and code reuse

We think FRP should be basic infrastructure, like threading and networking. Standardization will, of course, require wide agreement about how things should be done. FRP is a powerful infrastructure for developing reusable components. A profusion of different FRP systems that all do the same job to varying degrees of quality isn't helpful for innovation in this area.

We think the major problems have been solved, but we don't want standardization too early, either—we're keen to ensure that we don't stifle innovation of FRP systems. One of the aims of this book is to take us toward standardization. We do *not* wish to propose a standard directly, but we want to establish a common reference point for concepts and terminology. We want to describe something people can use in real applications so they learn the intricacies and pitfalls. We hope this lays some groundwork out of which a standard can emerge.

It's imperative that this standard be based on denotational semantics. There is currently a serious risk of broken forms of FRP becoming standardized. This would be a terrible shame. Compositionality is both within our reach and vitally important in this age of increasing software complexity. We hope the theory we laid down in chapter 5 has helped you understand how important it is. Why throw it away? It's unnecessary.

15.5.1   Code reuse and FRP abstractions

We've talked a lot about how to make the FRP engine better. But what about the possibilities of innovation in FRP logic? There are undreamed vistas of libraries, abstractions, and paradigms we could build on top of an FRP infrastructure.

A lack of standardization is a serious hindrance to this. For example, many FRP systems have their own animation libraries and GUI widget libraries. If we can agree on what the FRP looks like, we can avoid this replication of effort.

15.5.2   FRP engine performance

Standardization would decouple FRP engine innovation from innovation in FRP-based abstractions. As things stand, we're at serious risk of wasting our efforts with these kinds of fragmentation:

- Innovative designs in FRP abstractions built on badly supported FRP engines
- The same engine optimizations replicated in different FRP engines

15.5.3 *Common syntax between languages*

The fact that we have many programming languages to deal with makes the fragmentation even worse. A common syntax that works across languages would hugely improve this situation.

15.6 *FRP database applications*

The models of persistence we've described in this book have been very basic: snapshot the state and write the resulting data structure to disk. But we think it's possible to implement an FRP system where each cell is automatically associated with a database key and the values are automatically persistent. An FRP transaction would correspond to a transaction in the database.

A web application would be modeled like this:

```
Stream<Response> application(Stream<Request> sReq);
```

If a new user comes along, then a `switch` would allow new cells to be created dynamically to retain that user's state.

15.7 *Visualization and debugging tools*

Visualization and debugging tools could provide a graphical representation of FRP state over time. They would allow us to debug FRP logic without stepping into the FRP engine implementation. It would also be easy to implement replay debugging, in which it's possible to step through the processing both forward and backward in time.

15.8 *Visual programming*

We think FRP lends itself to visual programming, where the code is manipulated in a graphical instead of textual form. If you want to see an example of this, Matter-Machine.com is a private company that uses a web-based FRP-like form of visual programming to specify constraints for manufacturing.

15.9 *Refactoring tools*

Refactoring is already easy in FRP, but it could be automated. You should be able to drag-and-drop the lines of code you want to factor out into a new module, and have the variable references fixed up automatically.

15.10 *Summary*

- Standardization is highly desirable.
- FRP syntax tends to be clunky and could be greatly improved.
- We think FRP has the potential to go very fast.
- FRP is currently constructed at runtime, making it suitable for just-in-time compilers and runtime optimization. But we think it could also be compiled statically for embedded systems.

- We think FRP could be developed to express database applications, such as those found commonly on the web.
- We think FRP could be well suited to visual programming, visual debugging tools, and automatic refactoring.

That's it! We hope you've enjoyed the book and that we've opened some new possibilities for you.

appendix A
Sodium API

A.1 Package nz.sodium

Table A.1   Interfaces

`Handler<A>`	An interface for event handlers
`Lambda0<A>`	An interface for zero-argument lambda functions
`Lambda1<A,B>`	An interface for one-argument lambda functions
`Lambda2<A,B,C>`	An interface for two-argument lambda functions
`Lambda3<A,B,C,D>`	An interface for three-argument lambda functions
`Lambda4<A,B,C,D,E>`	An interface for four-argument lambda functions
`Lambda5<A,B,C,D,E,F>`	An interface for five-argument lambda functions
`Lambda6<A,B,C,D,E,F,G>`	An interface for six-argument lambda functions

Table A.2   Classes

`Cell<A>`	Represents a value of type A that changes over time
`CellLoop<A>`	A forward reference for a Cell equivalent to the Cell that is referenced
`CellSink<A>`	A cell that allows values to be pushed into it, acting as an interface between the world of I/O and the world of FRP
`Lazy<A>`	A representation for a value that may not be available until the current transaction is closed
`Listener`	A handle for a listener that was registered with `Cell.listen(Handler)` or `Stream.listen(Handler)`
`Operational`	Operational primitives that must be used with care because they break non-detectability of cell steps/updates

Table A.2   Classes *(continued)*

`Stream<A>`	Represents a stream of discrete events/firings containing values of type A
`StreamLoop<A>`	A forward reference for a Stream equivalent to the Stream that is referenced
`StreamSink<A>`	A Stream that allows values to be pushed into it, acting as an interface between the world of I/O and the world of FRP
`Transaction`	Functions for controlling transactions
`Tuple2<A,B>`	A generalized 2-tuple

A.1.1   Interface Handler<A>

An interface for event handlers:

```
void run(A a)
```

A.1.2   Interface Lambda0<A>

An interface for zero-argument lambda functions:

```
A apply()
```

A.1.3   Interface Lambda1<A,B>

An interface for one-argument lambda functions:

```
B apply(A a)
```

A.1.4   Interface Lambda2<A,B,C>

An interface for two-argument lambda functions:

```
C apply(A a, B b)
```

A.1.5   Interface Lambda3<A,B,C,D>

An interface for three-argument lambda functions:

```
D apply(A a, B b, C c)
```

A.1.6   Interface Lambda4<A,B,C,D,E>

An interface for four-argument lambda functions:

```
E apply(A a, B b, C c, D d)
```

A.1.7   Interface Lambda5<A,B,C,D,E,F>

An interface for five-argument lambda functions:

```
F apply(A a, B b, C c, D d, E e)
```

A.1.8   Interface Lambda6<A,B,C,D,E,F,G>

An interface for six-argument lambda functions:

```
G apply(A a, B b, C c, D d, E e, F f)
```

A.1.9 Class Cell<A>

Represents a value of type A that changes over time.

A cell with a constant value:

```
Cell(A value)
```

Apply a value in a cell to a function in a cell. This is the primitive for all function lifting:

```
static <A,B> Cell<B> apply(Cell<Lambda1<A,B>> bf, Cell<A> ba)
```

Lift a binary function into cells so the returned `Cell` always reflects the specified function applied to the input cells' values:

```
<B,C> Cell<C> lift(Cell<B> b, Lambda2<A,B,C> fn)
```

Parameter: f, function to apply. It must be referentially transparent.

Lift a ternary function into cells so the returned `Cell` always reflects the specified function applied to the input cells' values:

```
<B,C,D> Cell<D> lift(Cell<B> b, Cell<C> c, Lambda3<A,B,C,D> fn)
```

Parameter: f, function to apply. It must be referentially transparent.

Lift a quaternary function into cells so the returned `Cell` always reflects the specified function applied to the input cells' values:

```
<B,C,D,E> Cell<E> lift(Cell<B> b, Cell<C> c, Cell<D> d,
    Lambda4<A,B,C,D,E> fn)
```

Parameter: f, function to apply. It must be referentially transparent.

Lift a five-argument function into cells so the returned `Cell` always reflects the specified function applied to the input cells' values:

```
<B,C,D,E,F> Cell<F> lift(Cell<B> b, Cell<C> c, Cell<D> d, Cell<E> e,
    Lambda5<A,B,C,D,E,F> fn)
```

Parameter: fn, function to apply. It must be referentially transparent.

Lift a six-argument function into cells so the returned `Cell` always reflects the specified function applied to the input cells' values:

```
<B,C,D,E,F,G> Cell<G> lift(Cell<B> b, Cell<C> c, Cell<D> d, Cell<E> e,
    Cell<F> f, Lambda6<A,B,C,D,E,F,G> fn)
```

Parameter: f, function to apply. It must be referentially transparent.

Listen for updates to the value of this cell:

```
Listener listen(Handler<A> action)
```

This is the observer pattern. The returned listener has a `Listener.unlisten()` method to cause the listener to be removed. This is an operational mechanism for interfacing between the world of I/O and FRP.

Parameter: `action`, the handler to execute when there's a new value. You should make no assumptions about what thread you're called on, and the handler shouldn't block. You aren't allowed to use `CellSink.send()` or `StreamSink.send()` in the handler. An exception will be thrown because you aren't meant to use this to create your own primitives.

Transform the cell's value according to the supplied function so the returned `Cell` always reflects the value of the function applied to the input `Cell`'s value:

```
<B> Cell<B> map(Lambda1<A,B> f)
```

Parameter: `f`, function to apply to convert the values. It must be referentially transparent.

Sample the cell's current value:

```
A sample()
```

It may be used in the functions passed to primitives that apply them to `Stream`s, including `Stream.map()`, in which case it's equivalent to snapshotting the cell, `Stream.snapshot()`, `Stream.filter()`, and `Stream.merge()`. It should generally be avoided in favor of `listen()` so you don't miss any updates, but in many circumstances it makes sense.

A variant of `sample()` that works with `CellLoop`s when they haven't been looped yet:

```
Lazy<A> sampleLazy()
```

It should be used in any code that's general enough that it could be passed a `Cell-Loop`. See also: `Stream.holdLazy()`.

Unwrap a cell in another cell to give a time-varying cell implementation:

```
static <A> Cell<A> switchC(Cell<Cell<A>> bba)
```

Unwrap a stream in a cell to give a time-varying stream implementation:

```
static <A> Stream<A> switchS(Cell<Stream<A>> bea)
```

A.1.10 Class CellLoop<A> extends Cell<A>

A forward reference for a `Cell` equivalent to the `Cell` that is referenced.

Constructor:

```
CellLoop()
```

Resolve the loop to specify what the `CellLoop` was a forward reference to:

```
void loop(Cell<A> a_out)
```

It must be invoked in the same transaction as the place where the `CellLoop` is used. This requires you to create an explicit transaction with `Transaction.run()` or `Transaction.runVoid()`.

A.1.11 Class CellSink<A> extends Cell<A>

A cell that allows values to be pushed into it, acting as an interface between the world of I/O and the world of FRP. Code that exports `CellSink`s for read-only use should downcast to `Cell`.

Construct a writable cell with the specified initial value. If multiple values are sent in the same transaction, the last one is used:

```
CellSink(A initValue)
```

Construct a writable cell with the specified initial value. If multiple values are sent in the same transaction, the specified function is used to combine them:

```
CellSink(A initValue, Lambda2<A,A,A> f)
```

Send a value, modifying the value of the cell:

```
void send(A a)
```

send() may not be used in handlers registered with Stream.listen() variants or Cell.listen(). An exception will be thrown because CellSink is for interfacing I/O to FRP only. You aren't meant to use this to define your own primitives.

Parameter: a, value to push into the cell.

A.1.12 *Class Lazy<A>*

A representation for a value that may not be available until the current transaction is closed.

Constructors:

```
Lazy(Lambda0<A> f)
Lazy(A a)
A get()
```

Get the value if available, or throw an exception if not:

`A get()`

In the general case, this should only be used in transactions after the Lazy was obtained.

Map the lazy value according to the specified function so the returned Lazy reflects the value of the function applied to the input Lazy's value:

```
<B> Lazy<B> map(Lambda1<A,B> f)
```

Parameter: f, function to apply to the contained value. It must be referentially transparent.

Lift a binary function into lazy values so the returned Lazy reflects the value of the function applied to the input Lazy's values:

```
<B,C> Lazy<C> lift(Lazy<B> b, Lambda2<A,B,C> f)
```

Lift a ternary function into lazy values so the returned Lazy reflects the value of the function applied to the input Lazy's values:

```
<B,C,D> Lazy<D> lift(Lazy<B> b, Lazy<C> c, Lambda3<A,B,C,D> f)
```

Lift a quaternary function into lazy values so the returned Lazy reflects the value of the function applied to the input Lazy's values:

```
<B,C,D,E> Lazy<E> lift(Lazy<B> b, Lazy<C> c, Lazy<D> d,
    Lambda4<A,B,C,D,E> f)
```

A.1.13 *Class Listener*

A handle for a listener that was registered with `Cell.listen()` or `Stream.listen()` variants. Deregister the listener that was registered so it will no longer be called back, allowing associated resources to be garbage-collected:

```
void unlisten()
```

Combine listeners into one so that invoking `unlisten()` on the returned listener will unlisten both the inputs:

```
Listener append(Listener two)
```

A.1.14 *Class Operational*

Operational primitives that must be used with care.

Push each event onto a new transaction guaranteed to come before the next externally initiated transaction. Same as `split(Stream)`, but it works on a single value:

```
static <A> Stream<A> defer(Stream<A> s)
```

Push each event in the list onto a newly created transaction guaranteed to come before the next externally initiated transaction:

```
static <A,C extends java.lang.Iterable<A>> Stream<A> split(Stream<C> s)
```

Note that the semantics are such that two different invocations of `split()` can put events into the same new transaction, so the resulting stream's events could be simultaneous with events output by `split()` or `defer(Stream)` invoked elsewhere in the code.

A stream that gives the updates/steps for a `Cell`:

```
static <A> Stream<A> updates(Cell<A> c)
```

This is an operational primitive, which isn't part of the main Sodium API. It breaks the property of non-detectability of cell steps/updates. The rule with this primitive is that you should only use it in functions that don't allow the caller to detect the cell updates.

A stream that's guaranteed to fire once in the transaction where `value()` is invoked, giving the current value of the cell, and thereafter behaves like `updates()`, firing for each update/step of the cell's value:

```
static <A> Stream<A> value(Cell<A> c)
```

This is an operational primitive, which isn't part of the main Sodium API. It breaks the property of non-detectability of cell steps/updates. The rule with this primitive is that you should only use it in functions that don't allow the caller to detect the cell updates.

A.1.15 *Class Stream<A>*

Represents a stream of discrete events/firings containing values of type A.

A stream that never fires:

```
Stream()
```

Accumulate on an input event, outputting the new state each time:

```
<S> Cell<S> accum(S initState, Lambda2<A,S,S> f)
```

Parameter: f, function to apply to update the state. It may construct FRP logic or use Cell.sample(), in which case it's equivalent to snapshot()ing the cell. In addition, the function must be referentially transparent.

A variant of accum() that takes an initial state returned by Cell.sampleLazy():

```
<S> Cell<S> accumLazy(Lazy<S> initState, Lambda2<A,S,S> f)
```

Attach a listener to this stream so that its Listener.unlisten()is invoked when this stream is garbage-collected. Useful for functions that initiate I/O, returning the result of it through a stream:

```
Stream<A> addCleanup(Listener cleanup)
```

You must use this only with listeners returned by listenWeak(Handler) so that things aren't kept alive when they shouldn't be.

Transform an event with a generalized state loop (a Mealy machine). The function is passed the input and the old state and returns the new state and output value:

```
<B,S> Stream<B> collect(S initState, Lambda2<A,S,Tuple2<B,S>> f)
```

Parameter: f, function to apply to update the state. It may construct FRP logic or use Cell.sample(), in which case it's equivalent to snapshot()ing the cell. In addition, the function must be referentially transparent.

A variant of collect() that takes an initial state returned by Cell.sampleLazy():

```
<B,S> Stream<B> collectLazy(Lazy<S> initState, Lambda2<A,S,Tuple2<B,S>> f)
```

Return a stream that only outputs events for which the predicate returns true:

```
Stream<A> filter(Lambda1<A,java.lang.Boolean> predicate)
```

Return a stream that only outputs events that have present values, removing the Optional wrapper and discarding empty values:

```
static <A> Stream<A> filterOptional(Stream<java.util.Optional<A>> ev)
```

Return a stream that only outputs events from the input stream when the specified Cell's value is true:

```
Stream<A> gate(Cell<java.lang.Boolean> c)
```

Create a Cell with the specified initial value, which is updated by this stream's event values:

```
Cell<A> hold(A initValue)
```

There's an implicit delay: state updates caused by event firings don't become visible as the cell's current value as viewed by snapshot() until the following transaction. To put this another way, snapshot() always sees the value of a cell as it was before any state changes from the current transaction.

A variant of hold() with an initial value captured by Cell.sampleLazy():

```
Cell<A> holdLazy(Lazy<A> initValue)
```

Listen for events/firings on this stream:

```
Listener listen(Handler<A> handler)
```

This is the observer pattern. The returned Listener has a Listener.unlisten() method to cause the listener to be removed. This is an operational mechanism for interfacing between the world of I/O and FRP.

Parameter: handler, the handler to execute when there's a new value. You should make no assumptions about what thread you're called on, and the handler shouldn't block. You aren't allowed to use CellSink.send() or StreamSink.send() in the handler. An exception will be thrown, because you aren't meant to use this to create your own primitives.

A variant of listen(Handler) that handles the first event and then automatically deregisters itself:

```
Listener listenOnce(Handler<A> handler)
```

This is useful for implementing things that work like promises.

A variant of listen(Handler) that will deregister the listener automatically if the listener is garbage-collected:

```
Listener listenWeak(Handler<A> action)
```

With listen(Handler), the listener is only deregistered if Listener.unlisten() is called explicitly. This method should be used for listeners that are to be passed to addCleanup(Listener) to ensure that things aren't kept alive when they shouldn't be.

Transform the stream's event values according to the supplied function so the returned Stream's event values reflect the value of the function applied to the input Stream's event values:

```
<B> Stream<B> map(Lambda1<A,B> f)
```

Parameter: f, function to apply to convert the values. It may construct FRP logic or use Cell.sample(), in which case it's equivalent to snapshot()ing the cell. In addition, the function must be referentially transparent.

Transform the stream's event values into the specified constant value:

```
<B> Stream<B> mapTo(final B b)
```

Parameter: b, constant value.

Merge two streams of the same type into one, so that events on either input appear on the returned stream:

```
Stream<A> merge(Stream<A> s, Lambda2<A,A,A> f)
```

If the events are simultaneous (that is, one event from this and one from s occur in the same transaction), combine them into one using the specified combining function so that the returned stream is guaranteed only ever to have one event per transaction. The event from this will appear at the left input of the combining function, and the event from s will appear at the right.

Parameter: f, function to combine the values. It may construct FRP logic or use Cell.sample(). In addition, the function must be referentially transparent.

Variant of merge(Stream,Lambda2) that merges a collection of streams:

```
static <A> Stream<A> merge(java.lang.Iterable<Stream<A>> ss, Lambda2<A,A,A> f)
```

Return a stream that outputs only one value, which is the next event of the input stream, starting from the transaction in which once() was invoked:

```
Stream<A> once()
```

Variant of merge(Stream, Lambda2) that merges two streams and drops an event in the simultaneous case:

```
Stream<A> orElse(Stream<A> s)
```

In the case where two events are simultaneous (both in the same transaction), the event from this takes precedence, and the event from s is dropped. If you want to specify your own combining function, use merge(Stream, Lambda2). s1.orElse(s2) is equivalent to s1.merge(s2, (l, r) -> l). The name orElse() is used instead of merge() to make it clear that care should be taken because events can be dropped.

Variant of orElse(Stream) that merges a collection of streams:

```
public static <A> Stream<A> orElse(java.lang.Iterable<Stream<A>> ss)
```

Variant of snapshot() that captures the cell's value at the time of the event firing, ignoring the stream's value:

```
<B> Stream<B> snapshot(Cell<B> c)
```

Return a stream whose events are the result of the combination using the specified function of the input stream's event value and the value of the cell at that time:

```
<B,C> Stream<C> snapshot(Cell<B> c, Lambda2<A,B,C> f)
```

There's an implicit delay: state updates caused by event firings being held with hold() don't become visible as the cell's current value until the following transaction. To put this another way, snapshot() always sees the value of a cell as it was before any state changes from the current transaction.

Variant of snapshot() that captures the values of two cells:

```
<B,C,D> Stream<D> snapshot(Cell<B> cb, Cell<C> cc, Lambda3<A,B,C,D> fn)
```

Variant of snapshot() that captures the values of three cells:

```
<B,C,D,E> Stream<E> snapshot(Cell<B> cb, Cell<C> cc, Cell<D> cd,
    Lambda4<A,B,C,D,E> fn)
```

Variant of snapshot() that captures the values of four cells:

```
<B,C,D,E,F> Stream<F> snapshot(Cell<B> cb, Cell<C> cc, Cell<D> cd,
    Cell<E> ce, Lambda5<A,B,C,D,E,F> fn)
```

Variant of snapshot() that captures the values of five cells:

```
<B,C,D,E,F,G> Stream<G> snapshot(Cell<B> cb, Cell<C> cc, Cell<D> cd,
    Cell<E> ce, Cell<F> cf, Lambda6<A,B,C,D,E,F,G> fn)
```

A.1.16   Class StreamLoop<A> extends Stream<A>

A forward reference for a Stream equivalent to the Stream that is referenced.
   Constructor:

```
StreamLoop()
```

Resolve the loop to specify what the StreamLoop was a forward reference to:

```
void loop(Stream<A> ea_out)
```

It must be invoked in the same transaction as the place where the StreamLoop is used.
This requires you to create an explicit transaction with Transaction.run() or
Transaction.runVoid().

A.1.17   Class StreamSink<A> extends Stream<A>

A stream that allows values to be pushed into it, acting as an interface between the
world of I/O and the world of FRP. Code that exports StreamSinks for read-only use
should downcast to Stream.
   Construct a StreamSink that allows send() to be called once on it per transaction:

```
StreamSink()
```

If you call send() more than once, it will throw an exception. If you need to do this,
then use StreamSink(Lambda).
   If you send more than one event in a transaction, they're combined into a single
event using the specified function. The combining function should be *associative.*

```
StreamSink(Lambda2<A,A,A> f)
```

Parameter: f, function to combine the values. It may construct FRP logic or use
Cell.sample(). In addition, the function must be referentially transparent.
   Send a value to be made available to consumers of the stream:

```
void send(A a)
```

send() may not be used in handlers registered with Stream.listen() variants or
Cell.listen(). An exception will be thrown because StreamSink is for interfacing
I/O to FRP only. You aren't meant to use this to define your own primitives.
   Parameter: a, value to push into the cell.

A.1.18 Class Transaction

Functions for controlling transactions.

Run the specified code in a single transaction, with the contained code returning a value of the parameter type A:

```
static <A> A run(Lambda0<A> code)
```

In most cases this isn't needed because the primitives always create their own transaction automatically, but it's required in some circumstances.

Run the specified code in a single transaction:

```
static void runVoid(java.lang.Runnable code)
```

In most cases this isn't needed because the primitives always create their own transaction automatically, but it's required in some circumstances.

Add a runnable that will be executed whenever a transaction is started:

```
public static void onStart(java.lang.Runnable r)
```

That runnable may start transactions itself, which won't cause the hooks to be run recursively. The main use case for this is the implementation of a time/alarm system.

Execute the specified code after the current transaction is closed, or immediately if there is no current transaction:

```
public static void post(java.lang.Runnable action)
```

A.1.19 Class Tuple2<A,B>

A generalized 2-tuple.

Constructor:

```
Tuple2(A a, B b)
```

First value:

```
A a
```

Second value:

```
B b
```

A.2 Package nz.sodium.time

A.2.1 Interface Timer

A handle for a pending timer:

```
void cancel()
```

A.2.2 Interface TimerSystemImpl<T>

An interface for implementations of FRP timer systems.

Return the current clock time:

```
T now()
```

Run all pending timers scheduled for up to and including the specified time:

```
void runTimersTo(T t)
```

Set a timer that will execute the specified callback at the specified time:

```
Timer setTimer(T t, java.lang.Runnable callback)
```

Returns a handle that can be used to cancel the timer.

A.2.3   Class MillisecondsTimerSystem extends TimerSystem<java.lang.Long>

A timer system implementation using Java's `System.currentTimeMillis()` clock:

```
MillisecondsTimerSystem()
```

A.2.4   Class SecondsTimerSystem extends TimerSystem<java.lang.Double>

A timer system implementation where the clock is a floating-point number of seconds since program start:

```
SecondsTimerSystem()
```

A.2.5   Class TimerSystem<T extends java.lang.Comparable>

A system for time and timers.
Constructor:

```
TimerSystem(TimerSystemImpl<T> impl)
```

A cell giving the current clock time:

```
Cell<T extends java.lang.Comparable> time
```

A timer that fires at the specified time:

```
Stream<T> at(Cell<java.util.Optional<T>> tAlarm)
```

appendix B
The six plagues of event handling

We've identified six sources of bugs in the observer pattern. FRP banishes all of them. Here we'll describe each problem in detail, with a short explanation of how FRP fixes it.

B.1 Plague 1: unpredictable order

Let's say you're developing a program for drawing diagrams, in which graphical elements can be selected or deselected. The rules are these:

- If you click an item, it's selected.
- If an item is selected and you click elsewhere, it gets deselected.
- When nothing is selected, you see a crosshair cursor.
- When any element is selected, the cursor is an arrow.

Figure B.1 shows three steps performed with the diagram program:

1. At first nothing is selected, and you're ready to click the triangle.
2. When you've clicked the triangle, it's highlighted, and you see an arrow cursor.
3. You get ready to click the octagon.

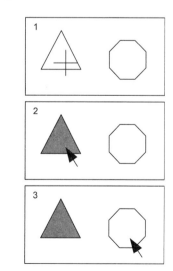

Figure B.1 Three steps in using the diagram program

At this point, a single mouse click will cause two events to be generated:

- Deselecting the triangle.
- Selecting the octagon.

The following listing shows the code to set the shape of the cursor depending on how many items are selected.

Listing B.1   Setting the mouse cursor according to the number of items selected

```
public interface SelectionListener {
    void selected(Item i);
    void deselected(Item I);
}

public class CursorMonitor implements SelectionListener {
    private HashSet<Item> selectedItems = new HashSet();
    public void selected(Item i) {
        selectedItems.add(i);
        updateCursor();
    }
    public void deselected(Item i) {
        selectedItems.remove(i);
        updateCursor();
    }
    private void updateCursor() {
        if (selectedElts.isEmpty()) crosshairCursor(); else
                                    arrowCursor();
    }
}
```

Now, what if the customer wants the cursor to stay solidly as an arrow in this case, without any brief flicker?

To achieve this, you need to either guarantee to process the selection before the deselection or wrap the whole thing in some sort of transaction and update the cursor at the end of it. The first option is difficult because the order of event arrival is unpredictable; it depends on the order in which the listeners were registered, and this is out of your control in this part of the code. The second option is possible but could complicate the code significantly. FRP is transactional, so it deals with these sorts of issues very neatly.

B.2   *Plague 2: missed first event*

Let's say you have a class that establishes a connection to a server when it's demanded:

```
Connector conn = new Connector();
conn.requestConnect(true);
```

You can also register listeners to do whatever is needed to communicate with the server once the session has been established. The public interface for this class is shown next.

Listing B.2 `Connector class`

```
public class Connector {
    public interface Listener {
        public void online(Session s);
        public void offline(Session s);
    }
    public void addListener(Listener l);
    public void removeListener(Listener l);
    public void requestConnect(boolean toConnect);
    ...
}
```

During program initialization you have these lines:

```
Connector conn = new Connector();
Demander dem = new Demander(conn);
Talker tkr = new Talker(conn);
```

The job of `Demander` is to decide when you want a session to be started, and `Talker` performs the job of communicating with the server. In the `Talker` constructor, it registers itself as a listener using `conn.addListener()`.

The program works great, but then someone makes this change:

- Make `Demander` persist its `requestConnect()` state to disk so it can be `true` as soon as the program starts.

This continues to work great because the establishment of a connection to the server is asynchronous, so `Talker` gets a chance to be initialized before the connection is established in practice.

All is well until the customer decides to use some sort of proxy running on the local machine. They configure the program to talk to a server on localhost. The socket code just happens to be written in such a way that the socket connection completes immediately in this case, and this happens before `Talker` is constructed. `Talker` has now missed the first `online()` event, so the program connects, but it doesn't actually talk to the server.

Many problems of this sort have their origin in issues of initialization order and processing order. FRP solves these problems by all but eliminating processing order as a consideration in your code.

B.3 *Plague 3: messy state*

State machine is a term used to describe any piece of program logic that has a set of internal states and a set of transitions between those states, triggered by asynchronous external events. A state machine can be represented as a diagram of circles (representing states) with arrows between them (representing state transitions caused by events).

The observer pattern tends to push you toward a classic state-machine style. When a class is listening to multiple event sources, this can get messy.

For example, let's say you take `Connector` from the previous example and add this functionality:

- Cooperatively tear down a session: When `Connector` receives `requestConnect(false)`, it will send a `tearDown()` request to a number of active sessions, passing a callback they must use to notify `Connector` when they have completed their tear-down sequence.

The new interface is shown in the next listing.

Listing B.3 Modified `Connector.Listener`

```
public interface Listener {
    public void online(Session s);
    public void offline(Session s);
    public interface TearDownCallBack {
        public void tornDown();
    }
    public void tearDown(Session s, TearDownCallBack cb);
}
```

Connector now has four possible states:

- `OFFLINE`
- `CONNECTING`
- `ONLINE`
- `TEARING_DOWN` (waiting for one or more sessions to tear down)

Following are the events you'll receive. You have to make sure each event is handled correctly in each state:

- `requestConnect()` transitions to `true`.
- Network connection is established.
- Network connection failed.
- `requestConnect()` transitions to `false`.
- Client acknowledges tear-down.

Four states multiplied by 5 input events gives 20 combinations, many of which are invalid. But you have to think carefully to make sure these invalid states won't occur.

There are also some edge cases:

- Network connection succeeds or fails synchronously. That is, the callback happens before the method to initiate the connection returns.
- Zero clients, in which case you skip the `TEARING_DOWN` state.
- Client calls back synchronously (before the call to `tearDown()` returns).

We won't sketch out the code, but hopefully you can imagine that the implementation of `Connector` might be bad, but not awful. But throw in a few more complicating factors, and it could get that way. Networking is a great source of complication.

In this style of coding, it's easy to make mistakes and difficult to debug them. For example, what if one of your "talkers" has an intermittent bug and never calls back `tornDown()`? Can you find this bug when all you have to work with is an event log? FRP brings a considerable amount of order to this chaos.

B.4 *Plague 4: threading issues*

Was that last example complex enough for you? Let's make it thread-safe.

The five input events could now come in on different threads. In addition, `addListener()` and `removeListener()` calls could come in on any thread, and you need to guarantee that once `removeListener()` has returned to its caller, no more callbacks can happen.

If you do nothing, race conditions will make the program collapse in on itself in a smoldering ruin. You could use the `synchronized` keyword, which tells Java to lock a mutex attached to the class instance—in this case, `Connector`. This mostly works. The following listing shows one way to make `notifyOnline()` thread-safe, but it's a bit dangerous.

Listing B.4 Dangerous thread-safe `notify`

```
protected synchronized void notifyOnline(Session s)
{
    for (l : listeners) l.online(s);
}
```

It's dangerous because you don't know what the listener's handler might do. It might lock something, too. Its listener might lock something. It might work perfectly a thousand times. It might work perfectly a million times. But the specter of the deadlock walks close behind, shadowing your footsteps.

If this doesn't send cold fingers of dread creeping up your spinal column, then welcome to your new career as a programmer—you're young and inexperienced. If the *wehi*—the fear—doesn't keep you awake at night, then vats of coffee will, while you take phone calls every half hour from your customer, reassuring them it will be fixed by morning…as your heart sinks with doubt about whether it really will be.

NOTE Now you know what led us to FRP and to writing this book. There had to be a better way.

To sidestep this horror, you typically take a thread-safe copy of the `listeners` list so you can notify listeners outside the `synchronized` block, as shown in the next listing.

Listing B.5 Much better thread-safe `notify`

```
protected void notifyOnline(Session s) {
    List<Listener> ls;
    synchronized (this) {
        ls = listeners.clone();
```

```
    }
    for (l : ls) l.online(s);
}
```

Problem solved.

Oh you think so, do you? The following listing is an attempt to implement a thread-safe `removeListener()`.

Listing B.6   Thread-safely removing a listener—or does it?

```
public synchronized void removeListener(Listener l) {
    listeners.remove(l);
}
```

Now look back at `notifyOnline()` in listing B.5. How do you guarantee that there will be no more callbacks after `removeListener()` has returned to its caller? This isn't at all straightforward.

FRP makes all these threading problems vanish into thin air, in a Harry Potter sort of way. (Yes, you really did buy this book from the nonfiction section.)

Threads (wrongly?) considered harmful

Many have argued that we should stop reaching for a thread when we need concurrency, including John Ousterhout in his short 1995 presentation, "Why Threads Are a Bad Idea (for Most Purposes)" (https://web.stanford.edu/~ouster/cgi-bin/papers/threads.pdf). They're "very hard to program," he says. "Unless we need true CPU concurrency, events are better."

Ah, yes, things were so simple in 1995. Fast-forward to the multicore age, and threads are no longer optional.

Threads are defined as multiple independent execution streams, shared mutable state, preemptive scheduling, synchronization. But wait a minute! What if there's no shared state? Then there's no synchronization, either. Threads don't look so bad after all. Is shared state so deeply rooted in our belief system that we blame threads, when shared mutable state is the real culprit? We think so.

Are the synchronization problems in this section really a problem with threads, or with shared mutable state?

B.5   *Plague 5: leaking callbacks*

Let's say you registered a listener with some event source, but when you were finished with it, you inadvertently forget to call `removeListener()`. Your listener is still referenced by that event source's `listeners` list, so your listener is kept alive and chews up memory even though you don't need it to. Not only that, it wastes CPU time every time it's called back. What happened to the safety that garbage collection was supposed to give you?

As we said in chapter 1, the main point of the observer pattern is that it inverts the natural dependency so the producer doesn't depend on the consumer. But the producer still keeps the consumer alive. Ideally, we would like this reversed also. FRP does exactly this.

B.6 Plague 6: accidental recursion

Returning to the connector example, the following code fragment is how you might implement cooperative tear-down of sessions, with some bugs added to shake things up.

Listing B.7 Cooperative tear-down of a session, with bugs

```
public class Connector {
    public interface Listener {
        public void online(Session s);
        public void offline(Session s);
        public interface TearDownCallBack {
            public void tornDown();
        }
        public void tearDown(Session s, TearDownCallBack cb);
    }
    private boolean shouldBeOnline;
    private Map<Session, Listener> activeSessions = new HashMap<>();
    ...

    public void requestConnect(boolean req) {
        this.shouldBeOnline = req;
        update();
    }

    private void notifyTearDown() {
        for (Map.Entry<Session, Listener> e : activeSessions.entrySet()) {
            final Session s = e.getKey();
            final Listener l = e.getValue();
            Listener.TearDownCallBack cb =
                        new Listener.TearDownCallBack() {
                            void tornDown() {
                                activeSessions.remove(s);
                                update();
                            }
                        };
            e.getKey().tearDown(s, cb);
        }
    }

    private void update() {
        switch (state) {
            ...
            case State.ONLINE:
                if (!shouldBeOnline) {
                    notifyTearDown();
                    state = State.TEARING_DOWN;        ←──────┐
                }                                              ❶ Bug 1
```

```
            break;
        case State.TEARING_DOWN:
            if (activeSessions.isEmpty()) {
                notifyOffline();
                state = State.OFFLINE;
            }
            else
                break;
        ...
    }
}
...
}
```

❷ Bug 2

During the call to `notifyTearDown()` ❶, one of the handlers notifies `tornDown()` immediately if it has no work to do. This doesn't work properly, because you haven't changed state to `TEARING_DOWN` yet. The `isEmpty()` check will never be performed. This is easily fixed by reversing the order of the two lines, like this:

```
state = State.TEARING_DOWN;
notifyTearDown();
```

The same problem exists ❷ when you notify that the session is offline, if the offline handler calls you back for some reason (perhaps to go back online again).

As we said, this is easily fixed. But you need to think carefully to make sure you don't make mistakes like this. Wouldn't it be nice if these sorts of errors were impossible? In FRP, they are.

Did you spot the other bug we slipped in there—the case where there are zero sessions isn't handled correctly? You need to put the break inside an `else` so you drop through and handle the `State.TEARING_DOWN` case once after the call to `notifyTear-Down()`. Here's the corrected code:

```
case State.ONLINE:
    if (!shouldBeOnline) {
        state = State.TEARING_DOWN;
        notifyTearDown();
    }
    else
        break;
```

This style of coding is just bad. We hope this book contributes to reducing the amount of it in the world, although FRP doesn't have a monopoly on solving these problems.

appendix C
Comparison of FRP systems

The tables in this appendix relate the primitives named in this book to each system's API. They're not necessarily directly equivalent, but you will be able to tell where in that system's API to start looking. If a field is blank, there is no equivalent.

Variable names give clues, mainly these:

- s—Stream
- c—Cell
- i—Initial value
- h—Handler
- a—Value

Table C.1 Cheat sheet for Sodium, RxJS, and Bacon.JS

Primitive	Sodium (Java)	RxJS (JS)	Bacon.JS (JS)
Stream	Stream	Rx.Observable	EventStream
Cell	Cell	Rx.BehaviorSubject	Property
never	new Stream()	Rx.Observable.of()	Bacon.never()
constant	new Cell(i)	Rx.Observable.of(i)	Bacon.constant(i)
map (S)	s.map(f)	s.map(f)	e.map(f)
map (C)	c.map(f)	c.map(f)	p.map(f)
merge	s1.orElse(s2) s1.merge(s2)	s1.merge(s2)	s1.merge(s2)
hold	s.hold(i)	var c = new Rx.BehaviorSubject(i); s.subscribe(c);	s.toProperty(i)

Table C.1   Cheat sheet for Sodium, RxJS, and Bacon.JS *(continued)*

Primitive	Sodium (Java)	RxJS (JS)	Bacon.JS (JS)
snapshot	`s.snapshot(c, f)`	`s.withLatestFrom(c, f)`	`c.sampledBy(s, f)`
filter	`s.filter(f)`	`s.filter(f)`	`s.filter(f)`
lift	`c1.lift(c2, f)`	`c1.combineLatest(c2, f)`	`c1.combine(c2, f)`
sample	`c.sample()`		
switch	`Cell.switchS()` `Cell.switchC()`	`s.flatMapLatest(f)`	`s.flatMapLatest(f)`
accum	`s.accum(i, f)`	`s.scan(i, f)`	`s.scan(i, f)`
listen	`s.listen(h)` `c.listen(h)`	`s.subscribe(h)`	`s.listen(h)` `p.listen(h)`
send	`StreamSink / ss.send(a) CellSink / cs.send(a)`	`Rx.Observable.create(f)`	`new Bacon.EventStream(f)`

Table C.2   Cheat sheet for Kefir.js, Flapjax, and Reactive Banana

Primitive	Kefir.js (JS)	Flapjax (JS)	Reactive Banana (Haskell)
Stream	`Stream`	`EventStream`	`Event`
Cell	`Property`	`Behavior`	`Behavior`
never	`Kefir.never()`	`zeroE()`	`never`
constant	`Kefir.constant(i)`	`constantB(i)`	`pure i`
map (S)	`s.map(f)`	`mapE(f, s)`	`fmap f s`
map (C)	`p.map(f)`	`liftB(f, c)`	`fmap f c`
merge	`s1.merge(s2)`	`mergeE(s1, s2)`	`union`
hold	`s.toProperty(function () { return k; })`	`startsWith(s, i)`	`stepper i s`
snapshot	`p.sampledBy(s, f)`	`snapshotE(s, c)`	`c <@ s` `fmap f c <@> s`
filter	`s.filter(f)`	`filterE(s, f)`	`filterE f s`
lift	`p1.combine(p2, f)`	`liftB(f, c1, c2)`	`liftA2 f c1 c2`
sample		`valueNow(c)`	`valueB`
switch	`s.flatMapLatest(f)`	`switchE(s)` `switchB(c)`	`switchE s` `switchB c`

Table C.2   Cheat sheet for Kefir.js, Flapjax, and Reactive Banana

Primitive	Kefir.js (JS)	Flapjax (JS)	Reactive Banana (Haskell)
accum	`s.scan(f, i)`	`collectE(s, i, f)`	`accumE s`
listen	`s.onValue(h)`	`mapE(h)`	Done differently
send	`Kefir.stream(f)`	`ReceiverE() / sendEvent(a, s)`	Done differently

Table C.3   Cheat sheet for ReactFX and ReactiveCocoa

Primitive	ReactFX (Java)	ReactiveCocoa (Objective-C)
Stream	`EventStream`	`RACSignal`
Cell	`Val`	`RACBehaviorSubject`
never	`new EventStreamBase()`	`[RACSignal never]`
constant	`Val.constant(i)`	`[RACSignal return:i]`
map (S)	`s.map(f)`	`[s map:f]`
map (C)	`c.map(f)`	`[c map:f]`
merge	`EventStreams.merge(s1, s2)`	`[RACSignal merge:@[s1, s2]]`
hold	`Val.wrap(s.toBinding(i))`	`c = [RACBehaviorSubject behaviorSubjectWithDefaultValue:i]` `[c subscribe:s]`
snapshot	`c.emitOn(s)`	`[c sample:s]`
filter	`s.filter(f)`	`[s filter:f]`
lift	`Val.combine(c1, c2, f)`	`[combineLatest:@[c1,c2] reduce:f]`
sample	`c.get()`	
switch	`s.flatMap(f)`	`[s flatten:1]`
accum	`s.accumulate(i, f)`	`[s scanWithStart:i reduce:f]`
listen	`s.subscribe(h)`	`[s subscribeNext:h]`
send	`new EventSource<>() / s.push(a)`	`RACSubject* s = [RACSubject subject]` `[s sendNext:a]`

appendix D
A section for managers

D.1 Doing what you said you'd do

As a manager, you need to be able to set reasonable expectations and deliver on them. The Agile movement has traded a short-term benefit of showing progress early for an ability to predict on an ongoing basis. Agile delivers on that promise, but the project's success or failure still relies on the quality of the code you write.

Whether you've got an Agile team or not, it's important for you to get consistent results. It doesn't matter whether your organization values consistency or efficiency. They go hand in hand, and if you have buggy software, you end up with neither. Having a comprehensive test suite helps you find bugs, but it's still better not to have the bugs in the first place.

Let's write a definition of what *ideal* looks like for the engineering manager of an e-commerce site. The business people ask for a new feature. You deliver a working prototype within a few hours. You get their feedback, which involves a number of changes. You make the functional changes in a few days and leave the aesthetic ones on a prioritized backlog. From very early in the project, you have something that works, and you spend most of your time counting pixels to make sure it looks just right. You meet your business deadline according to your estimate. It isn't perfect, but it does a pretty good job.

Two things aren't ideal. The first is the cost of redoing things because you don't always understand what the business people want up front. The second is the ongoing cost of real bugs. *Real bugs* are where the code does something different from what you intended. You wouldn't believe us if we told you that FRP code always does what it looks like it does. It doesn't, and we wouldn't make such a claim. But we'll ask you to look for the six plagues in your recent bug reports and imagine how life would be if those bugs had never happened. We're saying that a certain subset of the problems that you have is preventable, even though they've plagued the industry for decades.

There's always a new snake oil; a new buzzword; some product, language, or scheme that promises to fix all your woes. We're sure you've seen it all before. Some of these things help a little, and many of them are blind alleys. Often they're just new terms for things you're already doing. It puts us in a difficult position when it comes to making claims. This is why we're very specific about the kinds of problems we claim to solve. You need to be able to run your own numbers.

We've always had success making some level of investment in the team's worst paper cuts. If you find your team is working around the same problem time and time again, then making time to fix it usually pays off. If our six plagues are showing up in your bug reports, then FRP can probably help. This will depend on what type of code your project consists of. If there's a lot of event handling, then FRP may be worth trying out.

D.2 What is the investment?

We hope your lead developer has read this book and is already excited. If not, you need to find someone who is motivated to do things differently and give them this book to read. You should be able to find a FRP library for the programming language you're using. Otherwise you'll need to port an existing FRP system, but this isn't difficult. You'll also need to spend some time adding FRP bindings to existing widgets, devices, or whatever the I/O parts of your system are.

Once you have the basic building blocks, you can start the clock and compare writing a new feature using FRP. We're sure you'll pay attention to the time it takes to write the code. You should pay special attention to the number of bugs you find and especially whether you see any of the six plagues. If the six plagues are banished, then FRP does what it says on the box.

Depending on the size of the codebase, you'll see an ongoing cost for converting your old code into FRP code. Usually this works out to be quicker and easier than fixing bugs in the old code, but it's definitely something you need to be active about managing. These costs will be offset by a reduced number of bugs in new features.

D.3 Can I hire people with FRP experience?

Maybe, although more than likely FRP programmers are happy in their current jobs. But people interested in general functional programming will be lining up to come work for you. Our experience in hiring people is that it takes three to six months to become a true FRP expert. Hiring graduates is a good proposition because you don't have to pay for the more conventional experience that you're not going to use. You should still make sure you have experienced programmers on your team.

D.4 Who else is using FRP?

People's perception of technology seems to be heavily swayed by the high-profile companies that have made a success out of using it. Today, the biggest company we can point to that uses FRP is Netflix, which uses Rx.Java for its server-side systems.

This question is often asked because it's risky to invest in technology, especially languages that don't see much mainstream use. This is mostly due to fear of the technology going into end of life. The risk is low for FRP because its popularity is expanding, and you can use your existing language. All that's needed is a small FRP library. This means it can be trialed on a small scale, and you'll quickly find out whether it works in your project. FRP isn't difficult, as such, but it's radically different, so the main cost of such a trial will be the learning curve for the team member concerned. But once they understand it, they can teach the others relatively quickly.

FRP is based on the ideas of functional programming, and functional programming is rapidly becoming popular. Functional programming ideas can benefit any project. But the size of the leap required to gain these benefits has always been an obstacle. This problem is slowly disappearing as functional programming ideas seep into more and more areas of computing. FRP contains the most important of these ideas in a concentrated form, if you will, without the esoteric stuff or the overhead of learning a new programming language. In this way, it serves as an efficient training ground for functional programming. Even if you don't ultimately use FRP, it will still make whoever comes in contact with it a better programmer.

Productivity is less important to a huge established business than it is to a smaller company with a smaller cash flow. If you have a small company with one developer and no testers, then you need to do everything you can to eliminate bugs and reduce costs.

D.5   *The burden of success*

We'll give you some advice you won't believe you need. Feel free to skip over it and come back to it when your team has too much time on their hands.

With FRP, you'll need a lot fewer people to do the same amount of work. The hardest hit will be the testers, who will have increasing difficulty finding interesting bugs. Once you get into the swing of things, you'll need to get better at finding work for your team. If your testers are interested, you can retrain them to do software development. They should get some enjoyment out of rewriting existing code so that they can fix the bugs that have been bugging them for the longest time.

You'll still need a strong development lead, but you won't need as many strong developers, so you can diversify by hiring people with a broader mix of skills: people who are good at data visualization or communicating with other teams. You'll also need to increase your team's portfolio so they can do more things.

appendix E
Denotational semantics
of Sodium

Revision 1.1—26 Apr 2016

E.1 Introduction

This document is the formal specification of the semantics of Sodium, an FRP system based on the concepts from Conal Elliott's paper "Push-Pull FRP." The code in this document is in Haskell, and a basic knowledge of Haskell is required to understand it. Most readers won't need this information, but people interested in FRP semantics and developers of FRP systems will find it useful. Note that this has nothing to do with the Haskell implementation of Sodium. The executable version of this specification can be found at https://github.com/SodiumFRP/sodium/blob/master/denotational/.

E.2 Revision history

- 1.0 (19 May 2015)—First version
- 1.1 (24 July 2015)—The times for streams changed to increasing instead of nondecreasing so that multiple events per time are no longer representable
- 1.1 (8 Oct 2015, 26 Apr 2016)—Minor corrections; no semantic change

E.3 Data types

Sodium has two data types:

- `Stream a`—A sequence of events, equivalent to Conal's `Event`
- `Cell a`—A value that changes over time, equivalent to Conal's `Behavior`

We replace Conal's term *event occurrence* with *event*.

E.4   *Primitives*

We define a type T representing time that is a total order. For the Split primitive, we need to extend that definition to be hierarchical so that for any time t we can add children numbered with natural numbers that are all greater than t but smaller than any greater sibling of t. In the executable version, we have used the type

```
type T = [Int]
```

with comparison defined so that early list elements have precedence over later ones.

Sodium has 16 primitives. Primitives marked with * are non-primitive because they can be defined in terms of other primitives:

- Never :: Stream a
- MapS :: (a → b) → Stream a → Stream b
- Snapshot* :: (a → b → c) → Stream a → Cell b → Stream c
- Merge :: Stream a → Stream a → (a → a → a) → Stream a
- Filter :: (a → Bool) → Stream a → Stream a
- SwitchS :: Cell (Stream a) → Stream a
- Execute :: Stream (Reactive a) → Stream a
- Updates :: Cell a → Stream a
- Value :: Cell a → T → Stream a
- Split :: Stream [a] → Stream a
- Constant* :: a → Cell a
- Hold :: a → Stream a → T → Cell a
- MapC :: (a → b) → Cell a → Cell b
- Apply :: Cell (a → b) → Cell a → Cell b
- SwitchC :: Cell (Cell a) → T → Cell a
- Sample :: Cell a → T → a

Reactive is a helper monad that's equivalent to Reader T. It represents a computation that's executed at a particular instant in time. Its declaration is as follows:

```
data Reactive a = Reactive { run :: T → a }
```

Execute works with this monad. In the Haskell implementation, Reactive is part of the public interface of Sodium used to construct the four primitives that take a T argument representing the time when that primitive was constructed: Value, Hold, SwitchC, and Sample. Most languages don't support monads, so they instead use a concept of transactions, but the meaning is the same. The output values of those four primitives can never be sampled before the time t they were constructed, for these reasons:

- The public interface only allows Value, Hold, SwitchC, and Sample to be constructed through Reactive.
- The time at which the simulation is sampled is always increasing.
- The public interface only allows Reactive to be resolved once the simulation has reached time t.
- The public interface only allows streams and cells to be sampled at the current simulation time.

We define semantic domains `S a` and `C a` for streams and cells:

- `type S a = [(T, a)]` for increasing T values
- `type C a = (a, [(T, a)])` for increasing T values

`S a` represents a list of time/value pairs describing the events of the stream. `C a` represents (initial value, steps) for the cell: the initial value pertains to all times before the first step, and the time/value pairs give the discrete steps in the cell's value.

We define these semantic functions to transform streams and cells to their semantic domains:

```
occs :: Stream a → S a
steps :: Cell a → C a
```

`C a` is different than Conal Elliott's semantic domain for `behavior`, which was

```
type B a = T → a
```

The reason for this choice is that it makes `Updates` and `Value` possible, and it allows the cell variant of switch to take `Cell (Cell a)` as its argument instead of `Cell a →` `Stream (Cell a)`, effectively decoupling it from stepper/hold functionality. Something roughly equivalent to Conal's `switcher` can be defined as follows, if we posit that `[0]` is the smallest possible value of `T`:

```
switcher :: Cell a → Stream (Cell a) → Cell a
switcher c s = SwitchC (Hold c s [0]) [0]
```

We can derive Conal's `B a` from `C a` with an at function:

```
at :: C a → T → a
at (a, sts) t = last (a : map snd (filter (\(tt, a) → tt < t) sts))
```

E.5 *Test cases*

Now we'll give the definitions of the semantic functions `occs` and `steps` for each primitive, with test cases to show things are working as expected. `MkStream` is the inverse of `occs`, constructing a `Stream a` from an `S a`. We use it to feed input into our test cases.

E.5.1 *Never*

```
Never :: Stream a
```

A stream that never fires:

```
occs Never = []
```

TEST CASES

See figure E.1:

```
let s = Never
```

Figure E.1 `Never` test

E.5.2 *MapS*

```
MapS :: (a → b) → Stream a → Stream b
```

Map a function over a stream:

```
occs (MapS f s) = map (\(t, a) → (t, f a)) (occs s)
```

TEST CASES

See figure E.2:

```
let s1 = MkStream [([0], 5), ([1], 10), ([2], 12)]
let s2 = MapS (1+) s1
```

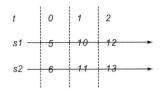

Figure E.2 MapS test

E.5.3 *Snapshot*

```
Snapshot :: (a → b → c) → Stream a → Cell b → Stream c
```

Capture the cell's observable value at the time when the stream fires:

```
occs (Snapshot f s c) = map (\(t, a) → (t, f a (at stsb t))) (occs s)
  where stsb = steps c
```

NOTE Snapshot is non-primitive. It can be defined in terms of MapS, Sample, and Execute:

```
snapshot2 f s c = Execute (MapS (\a → f a <$> sample c) s)
```

NOTE To make it easier to see the underlying meaning, we're diagramming cells in their "cooked" form with the observable values it would give us and vertical lines to indicate the steps, not directly in their B a representation of initial value and steps.

TEST CASES

See figure E.3:

```
let c = Hold 3 (MkStream [([1], 4), ([5], 7)]) [0]
let s1 = MkStream [([0], 'a'), ([3], 'b'), ([5], 'c')]
let s2 = Snapshot (flip const) s1 c
```

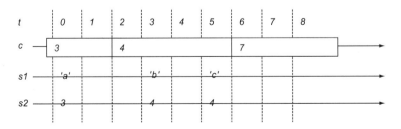

Figure E.3 Snapshot test

E.5.4 *Merge*

```
Merge :: Stream a → Stream a → (a → a → a) → Stream a
```

Merge the events from two streams into one. A stream can have simultaneous events, meaning two or more events with the same value t, which have an order. s3 in the following diagram gives an example. Merge is left-biased, meaning for time t, events originating in the left input event are output before ones from the right:

```
occs (Merge sa sb) = coalesce f (knit (occs sa) (occs sb))
   where knit ((ta, a):as) bs@((tb, _):_) | ta <= tb = (ta, a) : knit as bs
         knit as@((ta, _):_) ((tb, b):bs) = (tb, b) : knit as bs
         knit as bs = as ++ bs
coalesce :: (a → a → a) → S a → S a
coalesce f ((t1, a1):(t2, a2):as) | t1 == t2 = coalesce f ((t1, f a1 a2):as)
coalesce f (ta:as) = ta : coalesce f as
coalesce f [] = []
```

TEST CASES

See figure E.4:

```
let s1 = MkStream [([0], 0), ([2], 2)]
let s2 = MkStream [([1], 10), ([2], 20), ([3], 30)]
let s3 = Merge s1 s2 (+)
```

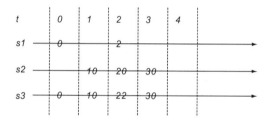

Figure E.4 Merge **test**

E.5.5 *Filter*

```
Filter :: (a → Bool) → Stream a → Stream a
```

Filter events by a predicate:

```
occs (Filter pred s) = filter (\(t, a) → pred a) (occs s)
```

TEST CASES

See figure E.5:

```
let s1 = MkStream [([0], 5), ([1], 6), ([2], 7)]
let s2 = Filter odd s1
```

Figure E.5 Filter **test**

E.5.6 SwitchS

```
SwitchS  :: Cell (Stream a) → Stream a
```

Act like the stream that is the current value of the cell:

```
occs (SwitchS c) = scan Nothing a sts
  where (a, sts) = steps c
        scan mt0 a0 ((t1, a1):as) =
            filter (\(t, a) → maybe True (t >) mt0 && t <= t1) (occs a0)
            ++ scan (Just t1) a1 as
        scan mt0 a0 [] =
            filter (\(t, a) → maybe True (t >) mt0) (occs a0)
```

TEST CASES

See figure E.6:

```
let s1 = MkStream [([0], 'a'), ([1], 'b'), ([2], 'c'), ([3], 'd')]
let s2 = MkStream [([0], 'W'), ([1], 'X'), ([2], 'Y'), ([3], 'Z')]
let c = Hold s1 (MkStream [([1], s2)]) [0]
let s3 = SwitchS c
```

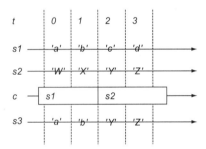

Figure E.6 SwitchS **test**

E.5.7 Execute

```
Execute  :: Stream (Reactive a) → Stream a
```

Unwrap the Reactive helper monad value of the occurrences, passing it the time of the occurrence. This is commonly used when we want to construct new logic to activate with SwitchC or SwitchS:

```
occs (Execute s) = map (\(t, ma) → (t, run ma t)) (occs s)
```

TEST CASES

See figure E.7:

```
let s1 = MkStream [([0], return 'a')]
let s2 = Execute s1
```

t	0
s1	*return 'a'*
s2	*'a'*

Figure E.7 Execute **test**

E.5.8 Updates

```
Updates :: Cell a → Stream a
```

A stream representing the steps in a cell, which breaks the principle of non-detectability of cell steps. Updates must therefore be treated as operational primitives, for use only in defining functions that don't expose cell steps to the caller. If the cell had been the Hold of stream s, it would be equivalent to Coalesce (flip const) s.

```
occs (Updates c) = sts
  where (_, sts) = steps c
```

TEST CASES

See figure E.8:

```
let c = Hold 'a' (MkStream [([1], 'b'), ([3], 'c')]) [0]
```

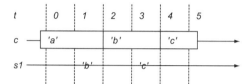

Figure E.8 Updates test

E.5.9 *Value*

```
Value :: Cell a → T → Stream a
```

This is like Updates, except it also fires once with the current cell value at the time t0 when it's constructed. Also like Updates, Value breaks the non-detectability of cell steps and so is treated as an operational primitive:

```
occs (Value c t0) = coalesce (flip const) ((t0, a) : sts)
  where (a, sts) = chopFront (steps c) t0
chopFront :: C a → T → C a
chopFront (i, sts) t0 = (at (i, sts) t0, filter (\(t, a) → t >= t0) sts)
```

Note that Value has the property that it can create an event occurrence out of nothing. It's possible to argue that it's reconstructing an event occurrence that we can prove exists—the one that drives the Execute that must have executed this instance of Value. It's the same event occurrence that Sample implies the existence of, if it's seen as being based on Snapshot.

TEST CASES

See figure E.9:

```
let c = Hold 'a' (MkStream [([1], 'b'), ([3], 'c')]) [0]
let s = Value c [0]
```

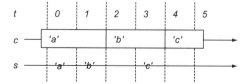

Figure E.9 Value test 1

See figure E.10:

```
let c = Hold 'a' (MkStream [([0], 'b'), ([1], 'c'), ([3], 'd')]) [0]
let s = Value c [0]
```

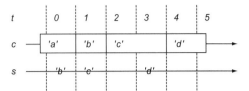

Figure E.10   Value **test 2**

E.5.10 *Split*

```
Split :: Stream [a] → Stream a
```

Put the values into newly created child time steps:

```
occs (Split s) = concatMap split (coalesce (++) (occs s))
  where split (t, as) = zipWith (\n a → (t++[n], a)) [0..] as
```

TEST CASES

See figure E.11:

```
let s1 = MkStream [([0], ['a', 'b']), ([1],['c'])]
let s2 = Split s1
```

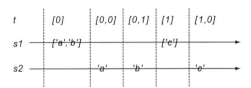

Figure E.11   Split **test**

E.5.11 *Constant*

```
Constant :: a → Cell a
```

A cell with an initial value but no steps:

```
steps (Constant a) = (a, [])
```

Note that Constant is non-primitive. It can be defined in terms of Hold and Never.

TEST CASES

See figure E.12:

```
let c = Constant 'a'
```

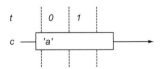

Figure E.12   Constant **test**

E.5.12 *Hold*

```
Hold :: a → Stream a → T → Cell a
```

A cell with an initial value of a and the specified steps, ignoring any steps before specified t0:

```
steps (Hold a s t0) = (a, coalesce (flip const)
    (filter (\(t, a) → t >= t0) (occs s)))
```

We coalesce to maintain the invariant that step times in `C a` are increasing. Where input events are simultaneous, the last is taken. Events before t0 are discarded.

TEST CASES

See figure E.13:

```
let c = Hold 'a' (MkStream [([1], 'b'), ([3], 'c')]) [0]
```

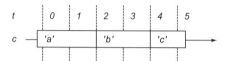

Figure E.13 `Hold` **test**

E.5.13 *MapC*

```
MapC :: (a → b) → Cell a → Cell b
```

Map a function over a cell:

```
steps (MapC f c) = (f a, map (\(t, a) → (t, f a)) sts)
    where (a, sts) = steps c
```

TEST CASES

See figure E.14:

```
let c1 = Hold 0 (MkStream [([2], 3), ([3], 5)]) [0]
let c2 = MapC (1+) c1
```

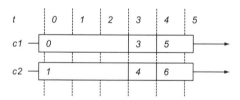

Figure E.14 `MapC` **test**

E.5.14 *Apply*

```
Apply :: Cell (a → b) → Cell a → Cell b
```

Applicative "apply" operation, as the basis for function lifting:

```
steps (Apply cf ca) = (f a, knit f fsts a asts)
    where (f, fsts) = steps cf
          (a, asts) = steps ca
          knit _ ((tf, f):fs) a as@((ta, _):_)
```

```
                             | tf < ta = (tf, f a) : knit f fs a as
             knit f fs@((tf, _):_) _ ((ta, a):as)
                             | tf > ta = (ta, f a) : knit f fs a as
             knit _ ((tf, f):fs) _ ((ta, a):as)
                             | tf == ta = (tf, f a) : knit f fs a as
             knit _ ((tf, f):fs) a [] = (tf, f a) : knit f fs a []
             knit f [] _ ((ta, a):as) = (ta, f a) : knit f [] a as
             knit _ [] _ [] = []
```

Note the "no glitch" rule: where both cells are updated in the same time t, we output only one output step.

TEST CASES

See figure E.15:

```
let cf = Hold (0+) (MkStream [([1], (5+)), ([3], (6+))]) [0]
let ca = Hold (100 :: Int) (MkStream [([1], 200), ([2], 300),
                                       ([4], 400)]) [0]

let cb = Apply cf ca
```

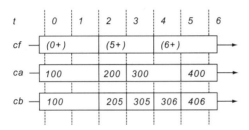

Figure E.15   `Apply` **test**

E.5.15 *SwitchC*

```
SwitchC :: Cell (Cell a) → T → Cell a
```

Act like the current cell that's contained in the cell:

```
steps (SwitchC c t0) = (at (steps (at (steps c) t0)) t0,
        coalesce (flip const) (scan t0 a sts))
    where (a, sts) = steps c
        scan t0 a0 ((t1, a1):as) =
            let (b, stsb) = normalize (chopBack
                                       (chopFront (steps a0) t0) t1)
            in  ((t0, b) : stsb) ++ scan t1 a1 as
        scan t0 a0 [] =
            let (b, stsb) = normalize (chopFront (steps a0) t0)
            in  ((t0, b) : stsb)
        normalize :: C a → C a
        normalize (_, (t1, a) : as) | t1 == t0 = (a, as)
        normalize as = as
        chopBack :: C a → T → C a
        chopBack (i, sts) tEnd = (i, filter (\(t, a) → t < tEnd) sts)
```

The purpose of `normalize` is to get rid of simultaneousness returned by `chopFront`, where the first step occurs at the chop point t0. It discards the initial value and replaces that with the first step value. This is different than how Value uses chopFront: in that case, we keep the simultaneous events.

TEST CASES

See figure E.16:

```
let c1 = Hold 'a' (MkStream [([0], 'b'), ([1], 'c'),
                            ([2], 'd'), ([3], 'e')]) [0]
let c2 = Hold 'V' (MkStream [([0], 'W'), ([1], 'X'),
                            ([2], 'Y'), ([3], 'Z')]) [0]
let c3 = Hold c1 (MkStream [([1], c2)]) [0]
let c4 = SwitchC c3 [0]
```

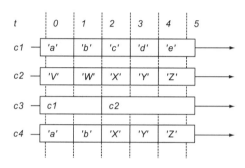

Figure E.16 SwitchC **test 1**

See figure E.17:

```
let c1 = Hold 'a' (MkStream [([0], 'b'), ([1], 'c'), ([2], 'd'),
                            ([3], 'e')]) [0]
let c2 = Hold 'W' (MkStream [([1], 'X'), ([2], 'Y'), ([3], 'Z')]) [0]
let c3 = Hold c1 (MkStream [([1], c2)]) [0]
let c4 = SwitchC c3 [0]
```

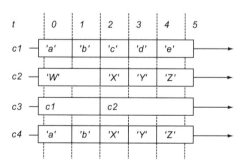

Figure E.17 SwitchC **test 2**

See figure E.18:

```
let c1 = Hold 'a' (MkStream [([0], 'b'), ([1], 'c'),
                            ([2], 'd'), ([3], 'e')]) [0]
let c2 = Hold 'X' (MkStream [([2], 'Y'), ([3], 'Z')]) [0]
```

```
let c3 = Hold c1 (MkStream [([1], c2)]) [0]
let c4 = SwitchC c3 [0]
```

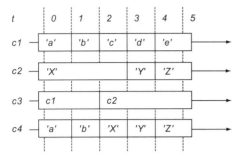

Figure E.18   `SwitchC` **test 3**

See figure E.19:

```
let c1 = Hold 'a' (MkStream [([0], 'b'), ([1], 'c'),
                             ([2], 'd'), ([3], 'e')]) [0]
let c2 = Hold 'V' (MkStream [([0], 'W'), ([1], 'X'),
                             ([2], 'Y'), ([3], 'Z')]) [0]
let c3 = Hold '1' (MkStream [([0], '2'), ([1], '3'),
                             ([2], '4'), ([3], '5')]) [0]
let c4 = Hold c1 (MkStream [([1], c2), ([3], c3)]) [0]
let c5 = SwitchC c4 [0]
```

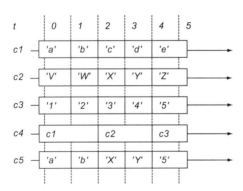

Figure E.19   `SwitchC` **test 4**

E.5.16 *Sample*

```
Sample :: Cell a → T → a
```

Extract the observable value of the cell at time t:

```
sample :: Cell a → Reactive a
sample c = Reactive (at (steps c))
```

TEST CASES

See figure E.20:

```
let c = Hold 'a' (MkStream [([1], 'b')]) [0]
let a1 = run (sample c) [1]
let a2 = run (sample c) [2]
```

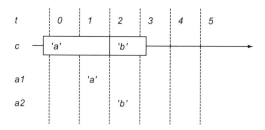

Figure E.20 Sample test

index

MORE TITLES FROM MANNING

Functional Programming in JavaScript
by Luis Atencio

ISBN: 9781617292828
272 pages
$44.99
June 2016

Functional Programming in Java
How to improve your Java programs using
functional techniques

by Pierre-Yves Saumont

ISBN: 9781617292736
300 pages
$49.99
December 2016

Functional Programming in Scala
by Paul Chiusano and Rúnar Bjarnason

ISBN: 9781617290657
320 pages
$44.99
September 2014